D1446902

STAGG VS. YOST

STAGG VS. YOST

THE BIRTH OF CUTTHROAT FOOTBALL

John Kryk

ROWMAN & LITTLEFIELD
Lanham • Boulder • New York • London

Published by Rowman & Littlefield
A wholly owned subsidiary of The Rowman & Littlefield Publishing Group,
Inc.
4501 Forbes Boulevard, Suite 200, Lanham, Maryland 20706
www.rowman.com

Unit A, Whitacre Mews, 26-34 Stannary Street, London SE11 4AB

British Library Cataloguing in Publication Information Available

Library of Congress Cataloging-in-Publication Data

Kryk, John.
Stagg vs. Yost : the birth of cutthroat football / John Kryk.
pages cm
Includes bibliographical references and index.
ISBN 978-1-4422-4825-0 (hardcover : alk. paper) — ISBN 978-1-4422-4826-7 (ebook)
1. Stagg, Amos Alonzo, 1862–1965. 2. University of Chicago—Football—History. 3. Yost, Fielding
Harris, 1871–1946. 4. University of Michigan—Football—History. 5. Football coaches—United
States—Biography. 6. Football—United States—History. 7. Football—Corrupt practices—United
States. 8. College sports—United States. I. Title.
GV939.S7K79 2015
796.332'630977311—dc23
2015005157

∞™ The paper used in this publication meets the minimum requirements of
American National Standard for Information Sciences Permanence of Paper
for Printed Library Materials, ANSI/NISO Z39.48-1992.

Printed in the United States of America

CONTENTS

INTRODUCTION

U.S. President John F. Kennedy in 1963 said of Amos Alonzo Stagg, on his one hundredth birthday, "Few men in history have set so persuasive and shining an example as teacher, coach and citizen."[1]

Stagg lived for such tributes. As a young man, however, his burning desire to win eclipsed even his maniacal mission to be seen as America's most incorruptible sportsman.

This is the untold story of how early in his iconic college football career, Stagg covertly punted many of the principles he espoused while nearly working himself to death—all to dismantle one of the most powerful machines the game has known: Fielding H. Yost's "Point-a-Minute" Michigan Wolverines. With cutthroat flair, Yost's teams from 1901 to 1905 bewildered foes and ran up enormous scores in debuting football's first "hurry-up" attack. "Eat everybody up," said Yost, a supreme braggart. "Big or little, send 'em all the same way."[2] It drove Stagg to desperation to see his Chicago Maroons annually sent that way. The cutthroat extent to which Stagg schemed to wipe that perpetual victory smile from Yost's face and the depths to which he buried his constantly publicized ideals are revealed here.

This is not the book I set out to write. Rather, as a Michigan football historian and lifelong follower of the Wolverines, I had always wondered why and how Yost's point-a-minute teams could so dominate the opposition. It was as inconceivable then as now that any head coach of a major college football program could start out 55–0–1 over his first five seasons, as Yost did at Michigan. It wasn't so much that Yost's UM teams avoided defeat for so long; rather, it's that his Wolverines out-scored the opposition 2,821 to 40 in the fifty-six games before experi-encing defeat, with fifty of the wins coming by shutout. How could those teams have been so dominant? That's what I set out to answer, starting in 2009.

Soon after I began poring through the athletic and personal papers of the contemporaneous UM principals at that university's Bentley His-torical Library, the scope of this project necessarily had to expand. I did not yet know about Robin Lester's groundbreaking 1995 book *Stagg's University*, so I believed what I'd read for decades in football history books spanning the twentieth century: that Stagg had no equal in the all-American, paragon-of-virtue coaching fraternity. The full century's worth of Stagg hagiography is so voluminous, so emphatic, and so con-vincing as to cause any researcher to doubt his discordant finds or to question the conclusions that must inescapably be reached.

These new findings on Stagg underscore the landmark claims first made in 1995 by Lester, who unpeeled the man's myth-fired armor. Lester's sources were impeccable. As the University of Chicago scholar tasked with organizing and logging the contents of hundreds of boxes containing Stagg's lifelong personal and professional papers, Lester re-vealed so many of Stagg's fiercely guarded actions behind the scenes. Lester published his exposé rather quietly in a University of Illinois Press book. It did not get its due.

New research here reveals many more surprising examples of, and insight into, Stagg's early-career hypocrisy. My primary sources are the never-before-published internal correspondence of Stagg's archrival athletic leaders at the UM, found at the Bentley Library; Stagg's own surviving correspondence with superiors, subordinates, potential re-cruits, and other universities' athletic leaders, stored in the Special Col-lections Research Centre within the University of Chicago's Joseph L. Regenstein Library; and reports in newspapers and periodicals of the day, so many of which were conveniently and scrupulously scrapbooked for posterity either by or for Stagg.

The core story here is timeless and familiar to all football fans, in-deed to all sports fans: one man's obsession to end the pain of a long losing streak to a hated rival.

Football fans captivated by Xs and Os will marvel at how Yost creat-ed a virtually perfect football machine, featuring the game's first hurry-up offensive attack. No college football historian has previously explained how Yost came to conceive it and achieve it. The Michigan coach was the first to enjoy the many advantages of an extreme up-tempo attack, to which modern fans can relate more than ever.

Football followers who despise the NCAA—and who see that governing body's 46,000 words of recruiting rules as ridiculous, unnecessarily burdensome, bureaucracy flecked, and unfair—might soften their stances after reading this book. *Stagg vs. Yost* reveals some of the deplorable depths to which coaches, recruiters, and alumni will sink when uninhibited.

To properly tell this story, we must first explain how the two principals—Stagg and Yost—came into their positions by 1901 from entirely different directions. And we must set up the state of college football in 1901: how barbaric and strategically stale it had become on the field and how sly recruiting had become off it, with little more than peer pressure and the naïve presumption of honesty to curb abuse.

Part I

Before 1901

I

THE PRAYING PITCHER

Amos Alonzo Stagg

This is how Michigan found out.

It was autumn 1894, and distrust soaked football relations between Wolverine athletic leaders and their counterparts at Oberlin College of Ohio. An officiating disagreement at the end of their 1892 game had led to each team claiming victory.[1] Now, reps from the two wary sides haggled over the selection of officials for their coming November 17 game in Ann Arbor.

Football fever in the early 1890s had swept so fast across the "West" (what we now call the Midwest) that the game's organizers could not keep pace. Matters such as arranging officials proved vexing. It was hard enough for teams west of the Appalachians to find a coach (or "coacher") who knew what he was doing. It was even more difficult to find a nearby, impartial football expert both willing and able to come officiate. The use of incompetents, or co-referees named by each team, often led to these nasty disputes.

To break this stalemate, Oberlin's new football manager, Alvan W. Sherrill, suggested in a letter to his Michigan counterpart, Charles Baird, that they "leave it to Mr. Stagg to settle the affair of umpire." Namely, Amos Alonzo Stagg. In year three of his storied forty-year tenure as the University of Chicago's athletic director and coach-of-everything, the thirty-two-year-old Stagg already enjoyed a gleaming reputation as one of America's most incorruptible sportsmen. "I believe

Figure 1.1.   Amos Alonzo Stagg, age thirty-two, in 1894. *Source:* Amos Alonzo
Stagg Papers, Special Collections Research Centre, University of Chicago Library.

him to be a perfectly honest man," Sherrill wrote Baird, "and so far as I
know, neutral." Baird ultimately agreed to Sherrill's proposition. So did
Stagg.[2]

Michigan had been the first school to take up football in the West in 1879, and the Wolverines remained a perennial contender for regional honors. This year's team proved particularly powerful and knocked off Oberlin 14–6, a result closer than expected. As umpire, Stagg observed play amid the thick of the action. A week later, Stagg saw Michigan play again. He and two of his best University of Chicago players watched from the stands in Detroit as Michigan scored a landmark victory for a Western football team—12–4 over Cornell, one of the upper-tier Eastern squads.

Five days after that, on November 28, Stagg's Maroons played host to the Wolverines in their now annual Thanksgiving Day season closer in Chicago. The vastly undermanned Maroons gave the "Champions of the West" a surprisingly tight fight that day. Beyond the fact that the Wolverines' wounds from their clash with Cornell were still fresh, Michigan's offensive plays barely worked. Eventually, the Wolverines figured out why.

Chicago knew their signals.

The Wolverines released a statement after the game to the *Chicago Inter Ocean* daily in which UM athletic director Baird claimed that when his younger brother, wily Wolverine quarterback Jimmy Baird, barked out plays, "the Chicago captain would call out where to mass to meet the play, and this was done repeatedly." Later, the *Michigan Alumnus* magazine cut to the crux: "Stagg had secured our signals and made use of the knowledge, hoping to win the game by any means, however questionable." Resorting to subterfuge such as lip-reading might be commonplace in twenty-first-century sport, but securing an opponent's signals by any means in the nineteenth century amounted to scandalous, despicable form. The *Michigan Daily* student newspaper offered more proof: "Chicago claims she did not know the signals. . . . It seems strange, then, that when the [Michigan] ends were called back and a signal given for a center play, Chicago massed her men on the center and paid no attention to the ends, where the position of the men would indicate that the play would go. Once, captain Baird purposely changed the signals three times, and each time Chicago massed to meet them."[3]

The Wolverines won 6–4 only when Jimmy Baird came up with this foxy antidote late in the game, near the Chicago goal line: he called an off-tackle play to the right for all to hear, but whispered to halfback

Gustave Ferbert to take the ball around the left end. That he did, for the winning touchdown—without any blocking and, according to the *Michigan Daily*, "without opposition," as the Maroons had massed on the opposite side to stop the called off-tackle play.

Michigan people of that generation never forgot the incident, even if history eventually did until now.[4] In the years surrounding the turn of the twentieth century, Stagg might have routinely fooled the public, the sporting press, and most of his fellow academics who ran what would become known as the Big Ten Conference. But because of incidents such as this, Stagg's Midwestern athletic contemporaries were on to him practically from the start. Observed the *Michigan Daily* after the stolen-signals caper: "[Stagg] came out here to purify western athletics [but] has gotten Chicago into trouble with almost every institution she has met in contests."

It was not enough for Stagg to be regarded as "a" paragon of sportsmanship and virtue even in these formative years. He viewed himself as unrivalled in this regard; he coveted the "the." Stagg's celebrated mission at the fledgling University of Chicago starting in 1892 was to tame college sports' morally wild West, on the athletic fields and off. Through the end of the nineteenth century and into the twentieth, Stagg labored as tirelessly as any coach in college sports history to propagate that mission, and thus to further gloss his image.

The press and public ate it up. Dissenting voices eventually gave up. From the 1920s onward, Stagg's admirers and hagiographers always spit-polished this gem from his autobiography, which practically became synonymous with the coach himself: "I hate a man, a team, a school or a people who cheat. I should prefer to lose every game than win one unfairly."[5]

The historical record begs to differ, at least from 1892 to 1906—the scope of research for this book. In the prime of his life, when Stagg's youthful competitive passions still raged, he in fact was as ruthless, as desperate, as conniving a victory seeker—and as shameless and creative a clandestine manipulator—as intercollegiate athletics has known. Stacking the deck became Stagg's modus operandi. The advantages he continually sought could be broad and systemic or subtle and minute— but always clever, seldom without plausible deniability, and sometimes even entirely legal. In a word, *slick*. Such as in the following incident from 1897, again involving the UC's archrival, Michigan.

For the second consecutive year, Stagg had arranged for his Maroons to play the Wolverines indoors at the Chicago Coliseum. Apparently, it did not concern either Stagg or Michigan authorities that the size of the crowd would be limited to ten thousand, that the field would be misshapen, or that it broke a charter rule of the fledgling Big Seven Conference even to play at the Coliseum, for its grounds were not owned or under direct control of either school. But the teams and the crowd would be sheltered from the typically harsh late-November elements near the shore of Lake Michigan, and no one would complain about that.

Stagg's Maroons had upset the Wolverines on the Coliseum's sand-and-dirt playing surface the year before, 7–6, on a safety and a (then five-point) forty-yard dropkick field goal booted by their great kicker, Clarence Herschberger. Herschberger's accurate, booming punts had been a decisive factor, too.[6]

Seven weeks before the 1897 Thanksgiving Day rematch, Michigan received a handwritten tip that Herschberger had now become an expert at placekicking field goals rather than dropkicking them, the latter being the near-universal method at the time. Herschberger was consistently making placekicks in practice from forty and fifty yards out, the tipster wrote, and Stagg set about "building their team up around Herschberger & his kicking." What's more, the UM informant said he had "good reason to believe that Herschberger has been instructed to fail in his kicking goals in the public games—in order to lull us into a false feeling of security."[7]

Alarmed, Michigan authorities concluded that playing indoors would be an immense benefit to the Maroons, as booting placement field goals for any kicker, let alone Herschberger, could be done a lot easier indoors in calm conditions and on dry dirt, rather than outdoors potentially in the wind, or on wet or snowy grass—or mud. With the goalposts situated on the goal line back then, every time Chicago advanced the ball to the Wolverine forty-yard line, they'd be a threat to score.

Michigan tried to move the game outdoors. Stagg would not budge. A Michigan alumnus rep in Chicago reported back to Ann Arbor that even though Stagg "admits freely the great advantage he has indoors," he denied that it had "any weight with him" in keeping the game at the Coliseum. Indeed, Stagg told the UM alum he had "an absolute indif-

ference" to the advantage, "saying the game will not be won" by a
Herschberger field goal from placement.[8]

Stagg was right. The game was won by three Herschberger field
goals from placement—one of which he booted from forty-five yards
out and at a severe angle. For the second straight year, Michigan scored
more touchdowns than Chicago (2–1) but lost, this time 21–12. In those
days, the team that scored more touchdowns almost always won.

The next year, Michigan insisted the game against Chicago be held
outdoors, and the Wolverines vanquished Herschberger and the Maroons on their UC field 12–11 to cap an undefeated season for the
Wolverines and their first conference championship.

Stagg's 1890s run-ins with Michigan were but an appetizer compared to the feast that lay ahead right after the turn of the century.
Fielding H. Yost's arrival in Ann Arbor in 1901 as the new Wolverine
head coach would jar Stagg as few events in his life ever did.

* * *

Amos Alonzo "Lon" or "Lonnie" Stagg was born on August 16, 1862, in
West Orange, New Jersey—the fifth of eight children to Amos Lindsley
Stagg and his wife, Eunice. The Stagg family roots burrow deep into
New Jersey's colonial past, to the early 1600s—seven generations'
worth. Amos Alonzo's great-great-great-great-grandfather, Thomas
Stagg, was born in the Garden State's Bergen County in 1645, according to one researcher's perusal of online ancestry records. Other Stagg
family surname branches—Pierson, Tompkins, Condit, Durie, Ro-
meyn, Williams, and Dodd—similarly reach back to America's early
pioneer days. His grandfather, Jacob Stagg, married the granddaughter
of David Condit—a Revolutionary War hero.[9]

Probably it was at the foot of his father that Lonnie learned so
successfully to wage his off-field athletic battles. His dad may have been
only a shoemaker and general laborer whose large family, Stagg always
claimed, was "at close grips with poverty,"[10] but Amos Stagg the elder
wasn't nearly as simple and humble as his son wanted everyone to
believe and as has been written until now.

According to an 1898 genealogical history of Essex County, New
Jersey, Amos Lindsley Stagg escaped his disadvantaged youth as a
motherless, indentured shoemaker's apprentice to become a man "of

natural abilities and superior ambition" who "spent much of his time" reading and, significantly, took "an active part in the public affairs of his home city" as a staunch Republican.[11] Maybe it was in those intense political settings that the young Amos developed a love of intrigue, an uncommon acumen for analyzing the political factors of—and fallout from—a complex problem, and the cunning necessary to emerge victorious more times than not.

Stagg maintained in his autobiography that his father was "superbly honest and just"—and that if he himself were "lazy or cowardly or dishonest, the blame is not my father's or mother's." Stagg also recalled a youthful fascination with the local saloons of West Orange. There the neighborhood adults—a mix of deep-rooted Americans and Irish immigrants—provided all the entertainment and streetwise enlightenment a youth on the Jersey side of the New York City metropolis could ever hope to acquire in those booming post–Civil War years. Stagg wrote in 1927:

> These saloons were our substitutes for the movies, the theater, the motor car, the radio, the seashore, reading and all. In bad luck, men drowned theirs sorrows at the bar; in good luck, they celebrated it there. When too warm, they drank; when too cold, they drank. In high spirits, they let off steam at the saloon; when bored, they bought high spirits from the bartender. If we had no movies, we did not miss them. We got our drama at first hand and in the raw form from the saloon, and the show was continuous. . . . Carrying pails of beer from the saloon was as routine a chore for most of the boys I knew as carrying in coal or cordwood. When it flowed freely, the family wash was aired on the front fence, so to speak.[12]

Those experiences might have compelled Stagg to become a lifelong teetotaler; he also abstained from caffeine and tobacco. Stagg's colorful neighborhood appears to have provided him with a deep understanding of the human psyche.

His rigorous upbringing included assisting his father for eight summers in cutting hay on the mosquito-infested salt meadows of Newark Bay. "By inheritance I had a stocky, sturdy body, and work and play developed it," Stagg recalled. That and natural athleticism carried him to Phillips Exeter Academy, one of the East Coast's most prestigious prep schools. There, he starred in baseball.[13]

Stagg next chose to attend Yale University, over Dartmouth, because Yale had a theological seminary; he always would claim that his original career ambition was to become a minister. Stagg confounded batters at Yale for six years, from 1885 to 1890. This was before any hard rule limited playing eligibility. Stagg was so proficient a pitcher he became a household name, known coast to coast. "The greatest man in America today undoubtedly is Pitcher Stagg," one newspaper touted. [14]

He earned the nickname the "Praying Pitcher" because, the *Chicago Tribune* asserted years later, "of his strict adherence to his ideals and his Christian principles."[15] In truth, Stagg earned the nickname after admitting during a much-publicized YMCA speech in New York City that he prayed before every starting assignment. "My prayer has not been for victory," he once said. "It has simply been, 'Let me do my best.'"[16]

Stagg excelled as a pitcher thanks to his impressive arsenal of curveballs and also because of his cool head, no matter how much trouble he might find himself in on the mound. Naturally, the pros were soon hot after him. At a time when Stagg was subsisting at Yale on a "starvation diet" and earning only fifty cents a week sweeping out a chapel to barely cover his room, board, and other incidentals, a Boston team offered him a three-thousand-dollar salary to turn pro.[17] The average American salary at the time was less than five hundred dollars. Stagg refused, preferring to remain an amateur. Boston raised the offer to $5,000. Stagg still declined.

Six National League teams eventually offered him contracts. He turned them all down, as well as the small-town pro teams offering him twenty-five dollars per game in the summer. Instead, in the first summer in which he was a hot commodity, 1886, Stagg said he "went home to cut hay on the Newark salt meadows five days a week and to pitch every Saturday for the Orange Athletic Club, an amateur team." In his autobiography, Stagg cited two reasons for his famous turndowns:

> The first was loyalty to Yale, inasmuch as I should be lost to the team if I played professionally. The second was the character of professional baseball. . . . The professionals of [the] day were a hard-bitten lot, about whom grouped hangers-on, men and women, who were worse. There was a bar in every ball park, and the whole tone of the game was smelly. I had a great deal of confidence in my ability to say a loud and ringing no, but not quite enough to dare it that far. I had pride, too, in my financial independence and integrity.

These actions earned Stagg gushing press from coast to coast. The nation concluded he must be as honest as he was incorruptible.[18]

It wasn't until his final two years at Yale that Stagg, as a postgraduate in theological studies, starred in football, too. He was fast, if squat (at 5'6"), and played end. He made Caspar Whitney's first All-American team in 1888.

In the spring of 1890, Stagg switched career tacks. Frustrated at struggling as a public speaker, he decided he wasn't cut out as a man of the cloth. "I could influence others to Christian ideals more effectively on the field than in the pulpit," he recalled. With that, Stagg devoted his life to athletics.[19]

His first stop was Springfield College in Massachusetts, then known as the International YMCA training school. There he both enrolled as a student and joined the faculty as instructor in the theory and practice of training. He also coached his first football team. He did so again in 1891, but by then he had accepted an unprecedented offer. Former Yale professor William Rainey Harper was to become president of the new University of Chicago, set to open in 1892. Harper contracted Stagg to serve on the faculty as a department head at the new university, to run intercollegiate and intramural athletics. Stagg also would coach intercollegiate football, baseball, and track and field. In 1904, Harper recalled:

> I first became acquainted with Mr. Stagg when he was at the height of his student athletic career at Yale. For three years he was a student in my [Semitic languages and biblical literature] classes. An attachment was formed between us. . . . I remember distinctly the interviews in which we discussed the question of his coming to Chicago and taking charge of the [D]epartment of [P]hysical [C]ulture and [A]thletics. It was evident he had certain ideals of athletic work and of athletic policy, and his coming to Chicago was dependent wholly upon his having every opportunity to work out these ideals. He came; he was given the opportunity he desired, and as a result it is not too much to say that western university athletics have been altogether transformed. . . .
>
> Mr. Stagg has contributed to this transformation more than all other agencies combined. His intense love for pure sport, his incorruptible spirit, his indefatigable effort, his broad minded zeal and his absolute fairness of mind and honesty of heart have exerted an influ-

ence upon western university and college athletics that has been felt far and wide, and produced results of which we may all be reasonably proud.[20]

2

JUDICIOUS EXPENDITURES OF MONEY

Amos Alonzo Stagg was hardly the first hypocrite in college football. Indeed, the sport was already grimy when Americans started falling in love with it in the 1880s. In the 130-odd years since, college football's leaders haven't looked very hard for a soap that works.

College-athletics dirt even predates football. The first intercollegiate athletic contest of any kind took place in 1852, in New Hampshire—a rowing race between Harvard and Yale. It was the brainchild of a capitalist who wanted to develop the Lake Winnepesaukee area, and he figured an Oxbridge-style regatta would attract publicity for his planned resort. What's more, according to college sports historian Murray Sperber,

> a number of members of both crews were not registered students at the school; probably they were professional rowers who hired themselves out to gentlemen's clubs in Boston and New York. On this day they were ringers hired to help their employers (Yale or Harvard) win the race. Thus, in the very first college sports contest in American history, even before the starting gun went off or an oar hit the water, two elements were at play: the event was totally commercial, and the participants were cheating. The history of intercollegiate athletics has gone downhill from there.[1]

It hasn't mattered whether the rulebook of the day was nonexistent (1852), one page long (1896), pamphlet size (1925), or a few inches thick (2012)—cheating has always taken place in college athletics.[2] Not by everyone, mind you. But every NCAA rule exists because some coach, or athletic director, or player, or alumnus, or booster, was over-doing that described action in a manipulative attempt to gain a competi-tive advantage. When outraged rivals raised hell, that action eventually was barred. The schemers merely moved on to the next loophole, ex-ploited it, hell rose again, the rule book thickened, and so on.

Football's first eligibility disputes in the 1880s involved all of the "Big Three"—Yale, Princeton, and Harvard—plus other Eastern schools. Arguments centered on these issues: (1) whether all members of a team were legitimately enrolled students making normal progress toward a degree, (2) whether graduate or professional-school students should be allowed to join undergraduates on a team, (3) whether a limit of four playing years should be implemented, and (4) whether players stained by the brush of professionalism should be allowed to compete.[3]

These issues perplexed all sides. On the fourth issue, the famed British ideal of amateurism had immigrated to America in the late nine-teenth century. A man was supposed to play a sport for the sport's sake, not for any pecuniary gain. This attitude was especially embraced by elitist Yale, Harvard, and Princeton. Ivy League football historian Mark F. Bernstein elaborates:

> Not playing for money, being above things material, became a sign that distinguished the wealthy not just from the working class (many of them immigrants), but from the entrepreneurial middle class, as well. American apostles of amateurism, such as Walter Camp, in-voked the British ideal of Oxford and Cambridge—hardly democrat-ic institutions—at which the line between amateur and professional was plainly based on class. Gentlemen did not have to earn their living by playing for money, and shunned those who did.[4]

Except they didn't shun them; they became them. On the sly, many "gentlemen" from Yale, Harvard, and Princeton were paid outright, or were assisted through school by alumni in other covert ways. Lesser football schools across the East did likewise.

The first eligibility crisis in college football illuminates the lengths to which students and football-friendly alumni were prepared to go to field the best team possible, and how they'd react when accused of going too far. At a fall 1889 summit of the Big Three, Yale's Camp charged Princeton and Harvard "not only with playing athletes who had received money for participating and for recruiting athletes from prep schools, offering them inducements by paying tuition, board, and other costs, but also with bringing back older players who had graduated, entering them in professional schools and allowing them to continue competing." Then came a seminal moment in the history of American sport. Walter Camp, college sports' lawgiver, proposed a pair of high-minded fixes in the name of purification. These sacred scrolls passed into law in the East. But, in reality, they were so laughably, impossibly unattainable as to ignobly serve these past thirteen decades as the bedrock on which every college-sports crackdown, every scandal, every under-the-table payment, every probationary penalty, every academic sham rested, that even the very existence of the NCAA itself—all of it—has been stacked.

That is, Camp proposed that only students who were (1) purely amateurs and (2) keeping up in their studies ought to be eligible to play college football.

These two rules passed—and proved an immediate failure. Within months Yale charged that football archrival Princeton had acquired three more bought-and-paid-for players. Princeton attempted to dodge the accusatory finger-points with a tactic that would become another of college football's most enduring traditions: deny and deflect. That is, to avoid punishment, first, by denying to the death all charges, and then by deflecting the witch hunt to another target—in Princeton's case, by counterproposing that all graduate and professional-school students be barred from playing. It just so happened that Harvard relied heavily on professional schools for both its student body and its football talent. And on it went.[5]

Through the turn of the twentieth century, however, the Big Three largely avoided major scandals. It's not because the American sporting press was in its infancy at the time; what sports writers there were had no qualms about raking muck. A large factor was that arguably the most prominent and influential sports writer of the bunch, Caspar Whitney, could not have been more of an apologist for the East if he'd been hired as chief publicist.

Whitney wrote in the 1890s for the nationally popular *Harper's Monthly* magazine and *Harper's Weekly Review*, and in the first decade of the twentieth century for his own sports magazine, *Outing*. Football was one of Whitney's favorite sports, and because of his position at

Harper's he was viewed as one of the game's foremost authorities. (It was Whitney's brainchild in 1889 to name the first mythical All-American college football team.) No matter which competitive sport he wrote about, Whitney's hobbyhorse was rooting out the evils of professionalism. A zealous, outspoken advocate of amateurism, he used his national pulpit to rail against the impure. But Whitney, a Boston native and New York City resident, repeatedly gave Eastern college football a clean bill of health—writing that there were only "isolated cases" of professionalism in the East. Instead, he absolutely skewered conditions in the West time and again. It didn't help his credibility among Westernites that, in the 1890s and well into the first decade of the twentieth century, he also continually disparaged the standard of football played in the West compared to that in his beloved East.

Why did Whitney protect the East? Perhaps because athletic leaders there had convinced him that their football was clean, and he gullibly bought it; or maybe it was because he was so stained by his Eastern bias that he was in on the con; or it's possible he just turned a blind eye because so many of his friends were Ivy League alums. Lending credence to the latter theory is that in 1900 he and a group of ten well-heeled grads from Yale, Harvard, Princeton, and Penn (some of them former varsity athletes) purchased *Outing*, and they anointed Whitney as editor. Walter Camp was among the ten.[6]

Whatever his reasons, Whitney's first impactful broadside aimed at the West appeared in *Harper's Weekly* in November 1895. That article kicked off a series of events over the next ten months—some known, some long-since forgotten, others revealed here for the first time—that affixed college football to the trajectory it would take right through the twentieth century and, indeed, up to today. Not one man in a thousand on the Atlantic coast, Whitney charged,

> has any conception of the rottenness of the whole structure through the middle and far West. Men are bought and sold like cattle to play this autumn on "strictly amateur" college elevens. Men offer and sell themselves for an afternoon for from $25 to $250, and apparently there is something like a scale of prices just as there is for horses and cows and grain. A list of a few cases here and there . . . show a state of affairs as disgraceful to the honor of gentlemen as it is destructive to the health—even to the life—of amateur sport in this country, and it

is high time that a direct statement of facts, a list of names and prices paid, should be presented to all men.

Whitney proceeded to do just that, rattling off a list of deplorable examples at the Universities of Michigan, Chicago, Minnesota, and Illinois and at Northwestern University.[7]

Western footballists went ballistic, issuing hot denials. Whether Whitney's allegations were accurate in substance (and most probably were), he left himself wide open to criticism because his reporting was both sloppy and lazy—to the extent that "his whole article was generally discredited in the West," the *Chicago Tribune* said, "and his employers became deluged with affidavits, protests, and contradictions, until it became necessary to send the author of the trouble to Chicago to investigate the charges."[8]

Once in the Windy City, Whitney interviewed college sports leaders as well as several star Western football players. His follow-up article in *Harper's* hit the streets in December 1895. He not only defended what he had written in November, but leveled additional charges, both of which only further infuriated the West. "Chicago football players characterize [Whitney's follow-up] as being fully as inaccurate as the first," the *Tribune* reported. What's more, some eight to ten of these star Western players threatened to write affidavits "stating specifically offers of money made to them to go to Eastern colleges to play football," because "Mr. Whitney has no hesitation in saying the East has long since purified itself from the taint of professionalism which he discovers in the West."[9]

Supporting that contention was former star Cornell quarterback Morris Hatcher, who earlier in 1895 had been puzzled by the growing misconception that the East was purer. "It is no uncommon thing down East," Hatcher told the *Chicago Tribune* in rebuttal, "to take good care of an athletic student and see that his expenses cost him nothing. The Western colleges are hardly up to that point yet, and their students are bona fide."[10]

All these years later it can be stated that Whitney was, in essence, as correct about his depiction of conditions in the West as he was wrong about those in the East. The West was indeed wild, but, as in the East, concerned faculty had already begun modest yet sincere attempts to clean up their years-old messes.

The significant difference, which Whitney seized upon, was that unlike the new rule barring professionalism in the East, few in the West cared whether athletes had, or were, earning money on the side, either as football coaches or as athletes in other sports such as summer baseball. Here's why: the nation was still in the throes of its worst economic slide yet. The Depression of 1893 would be superseded only by the Great Depression of the 1930s. One estimate pegged national unemployment in 1896 at 14.5 percent. Farmers—most of them not well-to-do to begin with—were particularly hard hit because crop prices plummeted, and some 43 percent of Midwestern workers were employed in agriculture as of 1890, compared to only 15 percent in the Northeast. Midwestern cities were harder hit as well.[11] Thus, the majority of Midwestern college-age men could not rely on their parents to help them through school. Added one Midwestern academic at the time:

> It is argued with some show of plausibility . . . that the Eastern colleges contain more well-to-do men, who are not obliged to pay their own way. Therefore, it is urged, men who by playing ball for money in minor [baseball] leagues, or by coaching, can earn enough in the summer and early fall to pay a large part of their college expenses, ought to be allowed to do so without thereby disqualifying themselves as college athletes. Mr. Whitney's standard, they say, makes of athletics an aristocratic institution, and is therefore not in harmony with the democratic spirit of the West.[12]

Worse, suiting up ringers was commonplace and an accepted part of college football in the West through at least 1892. Conditions got so bad under the pressure to win that seven of the Wolverines who embarked on a trip to Purdue in 1892 were nonstudent ringers. And ringers didn't play for free. Another such season of long road trips and questionable rosters prompted Michigan authorities in December 1893 to create a faculty-run Board in Control of Athletics, whose duty it was to crack down on these abuses. It failed miserably in only its second season, 1895, when it was discovered afterward that two Wolverine players "were not bona fide students, and that they had been compensated for playing by some over-zealous students and alumni," the faculty chairman of the Board in Control reported.[13]

Similar faculty takeovers of athletics occurred, or were about to occur, at Wisconsin, Minnesota, Purdue, Illinois, Northwestern, and the new University of Chicago. In January 1895, presidents of these six universities gathered in Chicago with the intention of barring professional athletes (Michigan's president was invited but unable to attend). The presidents proposed ten rules for adoption by their respective faculties. Rule 5 would ban any player who had ever received compensation for coaching or competing in any sport. That rule proved most contentious. Northwestern, for one, would lose its star players for the coming '95 season and refused to adopt it. By autumn, this attempt to unite the big seven universities of the West had failed.[14]

Whitney's exposés hit newsstands in late 1895, which reignited serious introspection among academics across the West. As a direct result of Whitney's charges, the University of Michigan's monthly student magazine, *The Inlander*, devoted a section of its January 1896 edition to this topic, titling it "A Symposium on Professionalism in Western Athletics." Short, cogent essays were written by the UM faculty, students, and alumni most closely associated with Wolverine athletic policy. This symposium remains one of the most insightful, honest, warts-and-all self-examinations ever conducted in public by a football-playing American university.

Whitney had closed his first article by suggesting that the "most direct way" the whole "calamity" in the West could be corrected was "for all these college faculties to act promptly to root out the evil their very indifference has permitted to exist." It was a call to action that was not ignored. Michigan's symposium gave the movement added momentum.

Although Whitney is given zero credit for it today, his diatribes likely proved the primary catalyst for the arrangement of a second, and this time successful, attempt—in February 1896—to form America's first lasting, prominent college athletics league, or conference, eventually known as the Big Ten. Indeed, the chief reason professors formed the conference was not to create a regional super-college sports league, but rather to unite in purpose the similarly vexed faculties of these nearby schools in an attempt to cage their football beasts.

This time each of the seven presidents dispatched to Chicago the chairman of his school's faculty board in control of athletics. The rules adopted at this convention, and later ratified by the Big Seven faculties, were nearly identical to the first set proposed thirteen months earlier.[15]

New rules were all well and good, but then there was the matter of enforcement. No one was naive enough to believe professionalism had just been eliminated in the West with the strokes of seven pens; one just had to look east for proof of that.

The students and alumni who still ran the day-to-day operations of most conference football teams now faced one hell of a crossroads. What to do? Observe the new rules to the letter of the law, which likely would severely hamstring their talent-retaining and collecting abilities, or figure out new, covert means to keep the money yet flowing? Over the next few years, the press would publish enough concrete examples of rules bending and outright cheating to indicate there was still a long way to go for everybody. But were these isolated cases, or was such commerce still systemic? The press and public could only speculate.

The definitive answer, at least for Michigan, comes from the UM's archives, in the papers of Charles Baird stored at the Bentley Historical Library. Baird did not officially become Michigan's first athletic director until 1898, but he had effectively been in that job since 1893—except for two years. As fate would have it, those two years were 1896 and 1897. During that time Baird tried to make a go of a law career in Chicago, but his opinion on matters such as UM football scheduling and player procurement still mattered greatly, so he was continually being consulted back in Ann Arbor by his graduate-manager successors and leading football players. If Baird had remained at Michigan, he would have just held these discussions in person and likely there never would have been any record of them. As it was, these discussions were conducted in letters, handwritten by dip pens—including during the crucial months that immediately followed the introduction of the charter conference rules in February 1896. Even better for our purposes today, the communication strings are unbroken because Baird insisted that his outgoing letters on these sensitive matters always be returned to him along with the recipient's reply. For whatever reason, Baird never destroyed any of them. It wasn't until nine years after he died in 1944 that these letters were included among the two banker boxes full of Baird's personal papers, circa 1892 to 1933, that his survivors donated to UM.[16]

The author evidently was the first college football researcher to discover the existence of this remarkable, unobstructed window into what was happening behind the scenes in 1896, which was this:

- Up to the formation of the conference, Michigan students and alumni had indeed been quietly paying star players outright, with money either from the UM Athletic Association coffers run by students or from alumni. For example, star backfield man and future Michigan head coach Gustave Ferbert, as of February 1896, "was hard up," Baird wrote football manager "Buck" Richards, "and is working you for what he can get. He is a valuable man and we should bid what he is worth to us and if he demands more, let him go. Unless it is necessary to settle at once, hold him off until spring. We will then decide what he is worth to us and if I tell him that we will give no more, he will believe it."[17] What's more, by the start of the second semester, star left guard Bert Carr had evidently used up all the money that was to have lasted him the entire 1895–1896 school year. "I think it will still pay to keep him if he will promise to settle down to business [i.e., hit the books]," Baird wrote captain-elect "Mort" Senter. "I would not pay him more than $25 a month and only in monthly payments. Keep the whole matter as quiet as possible and please return this letter to me the next time you write me."[18] Come May, Carr—who evidently liked to binge drink—needed an additional $25 to make ends meet.[19]

- Baird, the football players, and student managers all deeply resented not having had a say in the passing of the new rules. "American men nor boys do not obey laws or rules made for them unless they have a hand in making the same," Baird wrote.[20]

- Upon his return to Michigan as athletic director in 1898, Baird would work closely with, and under the wing of, Professor Albert H. Pattengill, the leading member of UM's faculty Board in Control. But in March 1896, Baird begrudged Pattengill's decision to interview some of the scrub football players, apparently in an attempt to find out if any of the stars were still being paid. Clearly, Pattengill and the faculty knew nothing for sure about such payments, as Baird and select student managers and alumni were trying to do it all behind their backs. "It was just like Old Pat [Pattengill]," Baird wrote Carr. "He is always doing some little trick like that. Those [new] rules are not bothering me much. . . . As to 'taking the pledge,' I think we can fix that all right. We can beat the Devil at his own game. If anybody goes to questioning you about the past just tell them that you consider they have no right to question [you] on such matters, and that as a matter of principle you decline to answer."[21] Football manager Richards, though, informed Baird in April that faculty members of the board "feel as though you got around them last year and they are going to put a stop to it."[22]

- As more proof of what was still happening back East at universities large and small, the captain of the Washington & Jefferson College football team in Pennsylvania, T. Wintrode Frye, wrote his Michigan counterpart asking if Michigan could match the sweet offers he had received from both Dickinson College in Pennsylvania and Cornell of New York—namely, that his full year's tuition, room, and board would be covered if he played football in the fall and baseball in the spring. Frye never came to Michigan.[23]

- Baird and company proceeded to promise money again to many star Michigan players from the 1895 Western championship team who were set to return in 1896. In June 1896, left tackle Giovanni "The Count" Villa was "a little sore" at manager Baird "because we had not offered him more," so Baird advised Richards that Villa's offer be raised to $200.[24] Villa returned to the team come September. But it probably wasn't a $200 cash handout.

- Of all the revelations in the Baird papers, the most intriguing and historically important is how left guard Carr and other players were fixed up for the 1896 season. Baird and other prominent Chicago alumni must have been racking their brains to figure out a way around the new rules. Someone came up with this gem of an idea, which became the key recruitment tool at Michigan, and soon perhaps everywhere in the conference, for years to come— and it's never been known publicly until now. Baird's letter to guard Bert Carr dated June 8, 1896, doubled as a contract, and explains it all:

> Dear Friend Bert:
> In accordance with our conversation of last Sunday I have been trying to see what can be done towards keeping you in college next year.
>   Of course the Athletic Association can render no assistance as that is strictly forbidden by the rules. However some friends

of the U of M desiring to assist a deserving student and also help the football team have expressed a willingness to make you a loan on the following terms.

The friend whom I mentioned to you last Sunday will guarantee you three hundred dollars absolutely in any event, and will advance one hundred more if he can raise the money in any way.

This money shall be used exclusively for your actual college expenses for the entire college year of 1896–97. The payments shall be made thus:

1—At the opening of college there shall be paid you the amount of your tuition and book and laboratory expenses for the first semester. Feb 15th you shall be paid your book and laboratory expenses for the second semester.

2—The estimated cost of your tuition and book and laboratory expenses for the year shall be deducted from $300 and the balance paid you in nine (9) equal installations, payable on the first of each and every month.

3—Payment on the amount in excess of $300 shall begin Feb 1st 1897, and be made in five equal monthly installments.

In consideration of this loan you agree to attend college regularly for the entire year, keep your work up to the ordinary standard, and conduct yourself in a moral manner.

You also agree to play football on the U of M team during the fall of 1896 unless in the judgment of the trainer you are physically unable to do so, and to help coach, and do all in your power to get a winning team, both by example in training and otherwise.

This loan shall bear no interest and shall be paid back through me when you are able.

All payments shall be made through me or someone designated by me.

If this agreement is satisfactory, sign your name below mine and it will then be binding on both parties. I guarantee the payment of the above.

Yours truly,

Charles Baird [signed]

Bert M. Carr [signed][25]

- Come September, Baird offered halfback Ferbert a similar loan from "a friend of the U of M," this one for $400. Baird underscored that there would be no more cash handouts; this was a loan that had to be paid back, through Baird, to the "friend." Baird furthermore warned Ferbert,

> Besides us three, there must be absolute secrecy about this matter. We must take no chance of evidence leaking out. You will be questioned as I will be but we must keep a stiff upper lip and it will be all right. There can be no perjury for that is a violation of a legal oath and if anyone should presume to ask you to make a sworn affidavit just say that they have no right to ask it. . . . You will be asked by the Board of Control to sign a certificate that you have received no money to play football. You can easily do that because you have been paid nothing. If a friend chooses to loan money to you that is no business of anyone else. There is just one thing to do and that is for everybody to make absolute denial in all seriousness on all occasions, and keep our mouths shut.[26]

The revelation of this loan scheme raises myriad issues, not least of which was Baird's concern about perjury. He was a lawyer. Perjury was not something he—nor any other lawyers among UM's football-boosting Chicago alumni—could afford to be found guilty of. Indeed, their law careers and reputations were at stake.

The amount of these loans might seem high, given that the average American salary in 1900 was $438.[27] But the costs to attend Michigan were significantly higher than at other state universities in the West. A four-year education at Michigan (between annual fees, matriculation fee, diploma fee, and tuition) totaled $190, compared to $142 at Illinois (the next most expensive) and only $60 at Wisconsin, $25 at Minnesota, and $20 at Nebraska. After adding room, board, books, and incidentals, it cost a student an average of $375 each year to attend UM.[28] So the loan amounts being arranged by Baird were indeed intended merely to cover a player's expenses. A Michigan student's added financial burden undoubtedly was seen by football-boosting UM alumni as a recruiting disadvantage, unless of course something could be done to help offset their alma mater's higher cost.

Yet another issue was the morality of loaning money to a player, as opposed to merely paying him the money outright. Was it still cheating? Baird, a lawyer, seemed sure it was both legal and obeying the letter of the new conference rule, which stated merely that "no person shall be admitted to any intercollegiate contest who receives any gift, remuneration, or pay for his services on the college team."[29] Was a loan a form of gift, remuneration, or pay? Baird seemed sure it wasn't. Then again, as the above letters prove, he went to great lengths to keep the loan scheme vaulted.

Whether any other conference school's alumni similarly adopted a loan get-around scheme in 1896 is unknown. Perhaps many did. It might not have taken long for word of Michigan's loan policy to reach other schools' athletic men. But hiring players outright, on the sly, was far less complicated if costlier in the long-term—and that practice continued.

The events of 1895–1896 in the West set in motion the cat-and-mouse game that continues nationwide in college football to this day—between well-intentioned but slow-moving or naïve reformers and the formidable front comprising handout-seeking athletes, victory-obsessed alumni, and devious team leaders. Simply put, a school in the late 1890s could not remain competitive in football if it obeyed both the letter and spirit of the new college football laws, West or East.

This was lucidly pointed out by Roger Sherman, a leading football-boosting Michigan alumnus in Chicago who was outed by Whitney as a key UM talent-securing bagman. Sherman also happened to be Charles Baird's best friend.[30] Sherman wrote an essay for that 1896 UM symposium on professionalism. His frank comments sum up exactly why corner cutting wasn't ever going to go away in college football:

> The most successful teams in the country today have built up their reputations and their success by the judicious expenditure of money in securing the services of good players. That nearly all of them still cling to this practice is well known to those who are in the possession of the true state of facts. Practice makes perfect. In the East the system now runs with so little friction that its very existence is denied by as astute an observer as Caspar W. Whitney. In the West, success is no less than in the East the guiding star. . . .
>
> The ideal and the real are in bitter conflict. We all hope and look for the time when the ideal will prevail. While one eye is fixed on the future and the ideal, the other looks steadfastly at the present and on the real. If down in our hearts we could say that the true and only

end of all contest is the pleasure of honorably contending, then we would one and all declare for purity *instanter*.

But the majority of us are near sighted and anxious to win; we are practical and the present appeals strongly to us. Until we can put aside this sordid desire to succeed we will inevitably look for the surest and most practicable means of winning.[31]

3

THE CLEANEST TEAM ON EARTH

Starting an athletic program from scratch at a university starting from scratch proved as daunting as you might expect, no matter how much of a financial kick-start J. D. Rockefeller endowed. [1]

Short of quality football material in the University of Chicago Maroons' inaugural season, 1892, Stagg himself suited up. The Maroons won one of seven games. He retired from playing college athletics for good after that. The '93 UC team's 6–4–2 record included upset wins against Michigan and Northwestern.

Stagg's Maroons painstakingly inched toward formidability. The snail's pace could not be blamed on the disadvantage of untaintedness. Caspar Whitney recalled that in 1894 he had been shocked to learn that Stagg's Maroons were "in it with the rest of the schools. When I asked him what it all meant, his reply was that the student body was not yet in sympathy with [reform]." [2] A year later, Whitney described conditions at UC as "worse than ever." [3]

Stagg surely did not fear or oppose the Big Seven's formation in 1896. He probably thought that here was a reform vehicle he could steer and manipulate to his and UC's advantage, through which he could propagate his reputation as the foremost crusader for clean athletics, and in which he could achieve not just regional but perhaps even national athletic glory.

The most significant of the Big Seven's charter rules forbade "professionals" from playing. While Stagg's Chicago team had not been the league's worst violator up to 1896, it was far from clean. That did not

Figure 3.1.   Stagg suited up and played with his first University of Chicago Maroons team in 1892. *Source:* Amos Alonzo Stagg Papers, Special Collections Research Centre, University of Chicago Library.

stop Stagg from proudly staking claim to purity, as with the following statement in 1896 when, as he so often did, he additionally threw all his rivals under the wagon: "We have played a perfectly clean team and no one can bring a charge of professionalism against a single player. No other of the Western colleges are free from taint."[4] The rest of the Big Seven snickered just two autumns later in 1898. Wisconsin—the conference's most consistently strong team in the late 1890s under the coaching of former Princeton star Phil King—officially protested three starters on Stagg's football team, namely, star halfback (and star baseball player) Gordon Clarke and backfield mate J. C. Ewing, both on grounds of professionalism, as well as guard C. J. Rogers for having exhausted his four years of playing eligibility before enrolling at the Midway school. Wisconsin soon publicly questioned the sanctity of six other Maroon players for various transgressions, one on grounds of academic ineligibility. The latter player, starting UC center W. J. Cavanagh, would fortuitously have his season-long suspension for substandard academic work lifted the day before the game against the University of Wisconsin Badgers. The controversy dominated sports-page headlines in the West over the first two weeks of November 1898.[5]

Stagg and UC authorities denied the Badger claims wholesale, going so far as to proclaim Rogers "simon pure."[6] Responding to further charges that some of the targeted nine players were offered financial inducements to enroll at UC, Stagg said, "that is absurd and I do not consider it worth replying to."[7] Yet one member of UW's athletic council countercharged that "Stagg has the highest salaried team that ever played football."[8]

Stagg was livid that Badger authorities would dare point such an accusatory finger anywhere but at their widely rumored corrupt selves. Wisconsin had fed proof of the Chicago trio's ineligibility to the press, which seemed solid, as did that for some of the other half dozen. Only when star halfback Clarke fessed up that he indeed had been a paid coach before coming to UC, which rendered him a professional, did Stagg capitulate and rule him ineligible. Chicago stood by the other eight.

Stagg reacted predictably to the serious charges against his players and program—with a flurry of counterpunches just before the November 12 Chicago–Wisconsin showdown. He (unsuccessfully) protested a Badger player, Harvey Holmes; he threatened to sever all athletic relations between Chicago and Wisconsin; and he announced that he reserved the right to protest any Badger player up to an hour before kickoff, even though the deadline for such action—as stipulated in the game contract—was a week before kickoff. The latter particularly galled the Badger faithful. Commented the *Daily Cardinal*:

> [This] indicates that he has something "up his sleeve" and will resort to trickery to win the coming game. If Mr. Stagg was in the possession of any strong evidence, we are pretty sure that he would have brought it forward, before this. . . . It is impossible to tell just what Stagg's little game is, but it will probably not amount to any more than an attempt to bluff out some of the Wisconsin players just before the game begins.[9]

As it turned out, Stagg did not protest any additional Badgers. Even though he got the last laugh on the field—his Maroons knocked off the Badgers 6–0—Stagg and UC were additionally embarrassed weeks later when news leaked that three of Chicago's other eight accused players had bolted school immediately following the Maroons' season-closing loss to Michigan. One was Rogers, the "simon pure" guard. Stagg grudgingly admitted the "most unfortunate" charge was true.[10]

In December, Whitney slammed Stagg and UC again from his *Harper's Weekly* pulpit, stating that "so far as ethics are concerned, Chicago retrograded. She played Herschberger and Cavanagh, a flagrant breach of the spirit and text of the rules to which Chicago had subscribed. . . . [The] confidence sportsmen reposed in the [UC] faculty, and especially in Stagg, appears to have been misplaced." Whitney also demanded that Chicago fully investigate all of Wisconsin's charges from November.[11]

Wisconsinites rejoiced over Stagg's comeuppance. Months later, the UW junior-class student yearbook, *The Badger*, contained a long poem titled "Some Staggnated Stanzas," which began:

> You've the cleanest team on earth,
> I don't think, Mr. Stagg.
> They've been amateurs from birth,
> *Aber ni't*, Mr. Stagg.
> We were doubtless very mean,
> When we didn't let you screen,
> Their past hist'ry that's so clean,

So we think, Mr. Stagg.[12]

For his part, an irked, defiant, and no doubt embarrassed Stagg wrote *Harper's Weekly* to rebut Whitney's attack and defend UC's questionable 1898 roster.[13] He offered only this sliver of an admission of guilt for having stockpiled so many players with spotty pasts and disregard for academics, players more commonly known as tramps: "I will try to see to it that such a thing does not occur again, and to accomplish this end I will urge the adoption of a rule making it impossible for a man who comes from another institution as a graduate student to play on a Chicago team until he has been in residence a full year."[14]

In reality, Stagg continued to allow graduates of other colleges and professional-school enrollees to play right away, just as the Michigans, Minnesotas, and Wisconsins were doing, within conference rules. But to announce such a stiff self-penalty served two purposes for Stagg: it diverted attention from the fact he had been enrolling and playing such trampish rogues, and it applied the first new coat of gloss to his tarnished halo.

And so it went. None of the conference schools was pure, UC included, but only Stagg kept claiming to be so—a refrain constantly echoed by the mostly sympathetic Chicago press corps, especially the *Chicago Tribune*.[15]

As happened with all conference schools in those years, Chicago players occasionally were accused of professionalism. Stagg always fought such charges with ferocity, even charges leveled by the American Athletic Union (AAU). The AAU formed in 1888 to serve as the nation's preeminent bastion of amateurism—the self-appointed ultimate authority for certifying athletes as clean.[16] Time and again, Stagg had run-ins with the AAU when it refused to certify all of his athletes. This happened in 1897 and 1898, and again from 1903 to 1905, with Walter Eckersall.[17] Northwestern University's track manager in 1897, R. E. Wilson, told the *Chicago Tribune*, "I think that Prof. Stagg, who of all others in the West has apparently been so anxious for purity in athletics, has been a trifle hasty in taking the course he has [with the AAU], as it is exactly opposite to his previously avowed principles."[18]

What's more, the Michigan athletic correspondence files covering the period just before and after the turn of the twentieth century contain many implications, or outright charges, of professionalism at the University of Chicago, some that implicate Stagg himself.

For instance, in early 1901 former star Wolverine halfback John McLean wrote to Michigan athletic director Charles Baird to inquire about returning to the football team, so long as he could get a good paying job. "If I wanted to make money I could play football for other Western colleges of the Big Four, and remain an amateur, on the quiet," McLean alleged, "but if I ever don a football tog again it will be for Michigan." The Big Four of the West, as everyone knew in 1901, included Chicago.[19]

Stagg, like so many all-powerful college head coaches, past and present, demanded not only to know about but to oversee every aspect of his football team, especially when it came to talent procurement. He himself asserted as much in 1903: "No one has any authority to make [illegal] offers without my knowledge and consent and they certainly could not execute them without my assistance. It is my business to keep my department clean." If McLean's charge were true pertaining to UC, then Stagg must have been aware of it.[20]

Other letters in the Michigan files suggest Stagg was leading the way with regard to all aspects of recruiting, such as when Michigan track star Charles Dvorak, who apparently was particularly plugged into the Chicago recruiting scene as a Windy City native, privately claimed he could convince his "old friend" Charlie McMillan to attend Michigan— even though "Stagg had everything fixed for him" already at Chicago.[21] Or the time Dvorak informed Baird that a former Notre Dame football and track man, Kirby, showed up at UC's athletic field and some Maroon players "immediately grabbed hold of him and jollied him" to enroll, "and as much told him that his tuition wouldn't cost him anything. Of course Stagg was behind it all and sent the fellows after him."[22] Or when a UM alumnus from Omaha, hot after a pair of local football recruits, alerted Baird that "Stag [sic] has made them both tempting offers. . . . And if you have any propositions to meet Stag's I will be glad to personally see them and negotiate for you."[23]

Yet in public, no Michigan athletics man ever accused Stagg of cheating. It was likely viewed as a no-win proposition, what with his sterling reputation propagated by virtually the entire powerful Chicago press corps. Stagg knew, as all good football coaches always have, that the most effective on-field schemes amount to nothing without experienced, talented players to execute them. Then, as now, no coach could possibly go to the campus chemistry labs or lecture halls to start filling out his roster. With few exceptions, useful players had to be recruited. From the time the University of Chicago opened in 1892, Stagg had publicly railed against the evils of recruiting. He preferred indirect, subtle, yet hardly unsuccessful means of enticing star athletes. But in the end he would often do whatever had to be done to get good players on his campus.

Stagg found most of his star football players from the high schools in his own backyard. Two of Chicago's best feeder schools—Hyde Park and Morgan Park Academy—were literally in the University of Chicago's backyard: the city's quaint Hyde Park neighborhood.

Stagg's success in recruiting Chicagoans to stay home and play for him should not come as a surprise, considering that up to 1906 he annually scheduled exhibition football games pitting his varsity Maroons against the best Chicago high school teams, or scrimmaged against them as midweek practice fodder throughout the season. In late September 1898, for instance, the *Detroit Free Press* reported that "Stagg began work with his Midway candidates earlier than any others in this section, and they have already played over half a dozen practice games with high school elevens."[24] And Stagg always made sure these encounters took place on his own UC practice field. It was a brilliant, shrewd means of both gauging the abilities of the latest crop of local prep players and coaching them all up and giving the good ones a thrilling taste of what it would be like to be a Maroon. Even better, he did it behind the charitable guise of merely helping out the local youth, of giving a lift to the schools. Perfect cover.

Beyond football, Stagg eventually opened up his athletic facilities year-round to Chicago prep stars in baseball and track and field too, in the hope that getting one foot of theirs through UC's door would soon bring the other. His intense competitiveness and one-upmanship, then, applied as much to the recruiting realm as any other.

Although Stagg once famously said, "Winning isn't worthwhile unless one has something finer and nobler behind it," there often was little noble in Stagg's direct dealings with his athletic rivals in these early years.[25] Time and again, his less-noble side shone as he put the screw to whatever school, or schools, represented the current biggest threat to his and Chicago's athletic success, or which had just handed Chicago a particularly painful defeat. In the late 1890s, that meant Michigan and Wisconsin.

A great example of this is how a series of impetuous Stagg actions following Chicago's loss to Wisconsin in 1897 nearly tore apart the Big Seven Conference by 1899.

Stagg felt that his upset loss to the Badgers in '97—in the game that decided the Big Seven champion—was a fluke. He unsuccessfully challenged the Badgers to an impromptu postseason rematch, so mad was he over the loss, so inflamed over postgame gloats by the Badgers and their head coach, King, and so "morally certain" that he possessed the better team.[26] Stagg's massive offer of a $5,000 guarantee to Badger officials was turned down, UW president C. K. Adams later informed UC president Harper, because "the Wisconsin team could not be allowed to play for a large sum of money, as this would place the team in the class of professionals."[27]

Probably after steaming about it over the winter, Stagg earned a measure of revenge in spring 1898 when he led the charge to try to have Wisconsin's two standout track-and-field athletes—who also happened to be stars on the Badger football team—barred before the conference meet on account of professionalism. Wisconsin refused. Only after the summer, and only after other conference big wheels, Michigan and Illinois, had also sided with Chicago, did Badger officials finally see the merit in the protest. They barred the duo on the eve of the '98 football season.[28]

Wisconsin returned Stagg's volley in early November 1898 by publicly casting suspicion on virtually the entire starting eleven of Chicago's team, as previously explained. "As Chicago has been foremost in the cry for pure sport," UW president Adams said, "we feel that it should make as thorough, impartial and searching an investigation as possible."[29]

Twelve days after Stagg's Maroons topped the Badgers 6–0, they were upset by Michigan 12–11 in the 1898 season finale. For the second consecutive season, Chicago had blown its chance to claim its first Big Seven football title. Stagg sizzled.

Bitter that he could not vanquish his rivals on the field, he apparently resolved to hurt them off it—by giving them all a bold, hard kick in the ledgers.

Through 1898, Stagg had attempted to avoid ever playing his rivals on their home football fields. Michigan, Wisconsin, and Illinois never complained about the arrangement—first, because until 1897, Chicago had not been a serious contender for the mythical title of "Champion of the West," but more than that because Chicago was so much more populous than Ann Arbor, Madison, or Urbana. Michigan, for one, figured a Wolverines–Maroons clash would be three times more lucrative played in Chicago than in Detroit, let alone thirty miles west of Detroit in comparatively tiny Ann Arbor. The home-field shortfall likely was even greater for Wisconsin and Illinois, so everybody stood to lose thousands of dollars apiece by not playing annually in front of the huge crowds of Chicago.

After 1898, it was clear that Stagg's Maroons would now be an annual contender for Western honors. Thus Michigan, Wisconsin, and Illinois wanted home-and-home contracts with UC going forward, regardless of how much less money they'd make every other year when Chicago visited them. Stagg anticipated their moves, and in early 1899, he informed each that a home-and-home arrangement would be fine—so long as either (1) when Chicago made the return trip it would be paid a substantial guarantee, approximately equal to what the Maroons' share likely would have been had the game been played in Chicago (an amount equal to much more than 50 percent of the gate—from a road game!); or (2) that wherever the game would be played, the visiting team every year would receive the same guarantee. In both of Stagg's home-and-home proposals, Chicago would receive the lion's share of the combined gate every two years.

It was a callous, audacious power play by Stagg.

Naturally, representatives from Michigan, Wisconsin, and Illinois gagged at Stagg's proposals. They would never allow Stagg and the University of Chicago to hold either an enormous competitive or financial advantage, especially when Michigan, with so many alumni in and around the Windy City, drew as many fans to games played in Chicago as the Maroons did.

The triumvirate cornered Stagg, and he came out swinging—refusing to meet with the trio's reps jointly in March 1899. Then he shocked the West by suddenly announcing that Chicago would play its marquee Thanksgiving Day game in 1899 against an Eastern team for the first time, Brown University, rather than Michigan or Wisconsin.

Livid, Michigan and Wisconsin countered by cutting off all athletic relations with Stagg's Maroons for the spring and fall 1899 seasons. What's more, the Wolverines and Badgers announced they'd now stage the biggest of their own games each year in Chicago—not caring that

Stagg considered the city to be UC's sacrosanct football ground. The 1899 Michigan–Wisconsin football game would be deliberately played in South Chicago on Thanksgiving Day, to try to steal the thunder from the Chicago–Brown game only a few blocks away.[30]

The widening rift threatened to fracture the Big Seven Conference before it was four years old. But come October 1899, Wisconsin began to blink. The Badgers and Maroons were the class of the conference in football that fall, and the pressure on both schools to mend fences and schedule a postseason game became immense. With Wisconsin publicly waffling, and with Stagg desiring as much as anyone in the West to see his Maroons play the Badgers, he had his face-saving opportunity to quietly back down from his unreasonable stand on home-and-homes. He did by early December, thus ending the standoff. But he avoided public embarrassment by tucking the news behind the much bigger story that his Maroons would indeed play the Badgers in a postseason game to decide the Big Seven championship of 1899, which his Maroons would win decisively, 17–0.[31]

Other actions of Stagg's in those years gnawed even more at his archrivals—primarily, the way he craftily steered Big Seven policy whenever he could, as the only athletic man representing his university at the conference's legislative level. His exalted reputation for honesty and fair play preceded him as UC's faculty representative. Stagg's opinion was more influential than anyone's at those early-years meetings of the Big Seven. While many other faculty reps trusted Stagg implicitly, their respective athletic leaders back home weren't so gullible.

"It is a common criticism among college [athletic] men that every time a change in the rules has been proposed, the University of Chicago seems to have some special benefit in the passing of it," wrote Caspar Whitney in *Harper's Weekly* in February 1899. Whitney in this case was referring to a new conference rule interpretation that would give at least one of Stagg's star players, Walter Kennedy, an additional year of football eligibility.[32]

A former Wisconsin athlete echoed Whitney's criticism, complaining to the UW student newspaper, the *Daily Cardinal*, about the "astuteness and ability of Mr. Stagg to shape things to his own ends. . . . At the present rate it is only a matter of time when Chicago will be too strong for the West. [Conference] teams are simply attending their own funeral by following the leadership of Mr. Stagg."[33]

4

CLOSED FISTS, CLOSED EYES, CLOSED MINDS

Bob Ufer, the radio play-by-play man for University of Michigan football in the 1970s, sometimes melodramatically joked that the action he was about to call would represent "the greatest exhibition of man's inhumanity to man since the Romans threw Christians to the lions."[1]

Seventy to one hundred years earlier, Ufer's wisecrack actually would have been disturbingly accurate. Nineteenth-century football was as troubled on the field as off. Slugfests, bloodbaths, melees—these were the terms used by witnesses, participants, and historians alike to describe the various incarnations of football from its inception in America in 1869 until its most wanton forms of violence were finally legislated out by the 1910s.[2]

As early as 1884, Harvard academic authorities were so concerned with the violence they stationed observers around the field during each of the Crimson's four games. It was quite the eye-opener:

> In all the games brutality had been shown. Blows were stuck and men were knocked down. . . . Among the cries heard on the field were the following: "Slug him!" "Knock him down!" "Break his neck!" "Kill him!" There was fighting with closed fists in all the games.[3]

Amos Alonzo Stagg watched the 1886 Yale–Harvard game as a substitute on the Yale sideline and remembered that Harvard got even for getting raked 29–4 by butchering many of the Yale linemen. One left with a broken nose, another with a deep gash over an eye that required eight stitches, and a third—who'd had the misfortune of lining up against the Harvard tackle that doubled as the school's boxing champion—became a Yale campus "curiosity" for days. "Both his eyes were closed," Stagg said, "and his lips were mangled and hideously swollen."[4]

John W. Heisman, the famous coach, remembered that in his playing days at Brown and Penn from 1887 to 1891, "nearly all linemen, as a rule, lined up squarely against those who played the same position on the opposing team. They didn't crouch or squat or play low. They mostly stood bolt upright and fought it out with each other—hammer and tongs, tooth and nail, fist and feet."[5] The Yale–Harvard game of 1894 was particularly gruesome. Recalled a sideline witness:

> The slaughter was so terrific that there was no [Yale–Harvard] game for three years after that. Wrightington of Harvard had his collarbone broken. Frank Butterworth of Yale had one eye nearly blinded. Practically all the players were bleeding from cuts or from kicks or smashes in the general mauling. Murphy of Yale was unconscious for five hours afterward in a Springfield hospital. I remember when they carried him out of the game. They just dumped him in a pile of blankets, covered him up, and then turned to look at the game again. . . . [N]obody was paying any attention to him.[6]

Some of the kicking was even aimed at the ball. The game associated with all that violence, American football, evolved from English rugby, itself not exactly on par with lawn bowling in terms of participant safety. Americans in the twenty-first century who watch rugby for the first time marvel at its chaos, at its virtual lack of protective equipment, and, especially, at its brutality compared to other contemporary American team sports. And they see the same rudimentary aim in rugby as in their own game of football—namely, to advance an ovalish ball up to about one hundred yards over the other team's goal line. Rugby has its version of field goals and punts as well, but only backward passes are legal, and any form of blocking is disallowed.

Apparently, the elemental nature of rugby that appealed most to these young men was its violence. Americans being Americans, they liked to think they could take anything conceived in England and improve it—with better organization and added flair—as they'd already done in sport by transforming cricket into baseball. The element of rugby most unseemly to these Eastern Seaboard collegians was not the violence; rather, that fumbles and possession-surrendering penalties were far too frequent. So often in rugby a punishing long trek down the field ends on a chintzy, debatable penalty. Nineteenth-century Americans—whose very society was based on the premise that land hard won was yours by god to keep—could not have that.

Order would come in the 1880s, thanks largely to former star Yale player Walter Camp, who would rightly be remembered as the "Father of American Football." Camp introduced the concept of allowing the team in possession of the ball to retain it so long as it advanced it five yards every three snaps, or "downs." He reduced the number of players per side from fifteen to eleven, yet retained the rugby principle mandating that a substituted player could not return. The principle underlying all of the New World rules overhauls, Stagg later observed, was that "the British play a game for the game's sake; we [in America] play to win."[7]

By the late 1880s, "rugby football" had caught on across the East. Yale and Princeton pulled away as the sport's preeminent powers. Yale (mostly) and Princeton made the rules, and everybody else just had to go along. Most prominent among "everybody else" was old adversary Harvard. The next tier of challengers included Penn, Cornell, Army, Navy, Columbia, Dartmouth, and Brown.

Up to this time, football teams were mostly or entirely self-coached; thus, the most powerful person on any college football team, East or West, was the elected captain. Influential alumni obsessed with their alma mater's athletic success might have a say in financial matters, or in scheduling, or in the new art of player recruitment; and in the East, a number of former star players would return annually to help prepare their successors for the coming season, or for a showdown game. But on the team itself the unrivaled authority was the player-captain. He ran practices, determined strategy, meted out discipline, and selected starters.

Change blew in during the late 1880s when lesser schools in the East started to hire outside head "coachers"—some for the entire season, others for just weeks at a time, few for more than a season at a time. By the early 1890s, the practice of hiring these itinerant professional coaches spilled not only into the West but as far as the Pacific and Gulf Coasts, as schools in every corner of America fast began taking up the sport.[8] Most coaches in the East and Midwest were either former Yale Elies or Princeton Tigers, to the extent that Stagg recalled "it was a poor [Yale] player who could not find a job as coach in the early '90s. . . . Coaches were few and in demand."[9]

Yale and Princeton, of course, would never dream of hiring any outsider to coach their teams. Only their men, coaching their systems, would do. Thus, Yale and Princeton were the first colleges to adopt the official policy of hiring only their own graduates as head coaches. Yale's and Princeton's definition of "head coach" and the authority they conferred on him, however, greatly differed from the contemporary and modern definitions.

At Yale, it was Camp who became the Elies' first official head coach in 1888. He won sixty-eight of seventy games over the next five seasons. While Camp may have stepped down as head coach after 1892, everyone in college football knew he continued to run just about everything to do with the sport at Yale right up to World War I, even if almost every year a different former captain or star player would hold the nominal title of head coach. It was Camp who chose Yale's coach and its system of play, Camp who held the purse strings of the Yale Athletic Association treasury, and Camp who ran the de facto national football rules committee through 1905. During the last years of the nineteenth century, the nominal Yale head football coach ranked third on the team in authority—behind both Camp and the captain.[10]

At Princeton, the graduate system of coaching was even more ad hoc—and dysfunctional. In 1894, the *New York Times* reported that "during past years the coaching has been purely voluntary and Princeton has suffered greatly from the lack of efficient coaching. . . . The advantage of having one experienced man to direct the practice is apparent." The new policy in '94 was to have one "head coach" to lead the wave of returning temporary grad coaches—but all under the direction of that year's captain. By 1900, this was still the case. "Capt. Pell has not announced his policy as to the number of coaches he will have to assist him in rounding the men into condition," the *New York Times* reported, "but from what can be learned there will be a head coach and seven or eight transient coaches."[11]

In some years, Yale and Princeton would bring back so many graduate assistant coaches, there would be one mentor for every starter on the varsity squad. Only in this manner were the Elies and Tigers ahead of other schools in coaching.[12]

In the meantime, the country's other football-playing universities were so used to taking Princeton's and Yale's lead on everything that some adopted the graduate head-coaching policy—believing it must be the road to football success and probably to satisfy antifootball academics who saw professional coaching as a particularly evil aspect of intercollegiate football. In the West, Michigan adopted a graduates-only policy from 1897 to 1899, Wisconsin from 1903 to 1904, and others, such as Illinois, Minnesota, and Northwestern, tried it. In the far west, Stanford and Cal adopted the plan in 1901. But such colleges quickly discovered the policy's inherent disadvantages. First and foremost, a freshly graduated player found it more difficult to discipline the same players who had been his teammates only months earlier, whereas a more grizzled outsider whose shortcomings were unknown by his players had no such handicap. In this regard, grad coaches weren't much different than captain coaches. And as a former Michigan star-turned-coach distastefully observed in 1901, "it ruins teamwork to have a player-coach."[13]

Yale and Princeton were too arrogant to see this crucial flaw in their coaching systems. It was the beginning of the end of their stranglehold on football superiority, and it opened the door for the pragmatic West to eventually take over.

The Eastern university that benefited most from Yale's and Princeton's stubbornness was Penn. In 1894, the Quakers hired former Yale star George W. Woodruff as their head coach. He was so successful, so quickly, that Woodruff singlehandedly turned the Big Three into the Big Four—Yale, Princeton, Harvard, and Penn. Through 1898, Woodruff confounded the East with his revolutionary "guards back" offensive system.

Until then, the evolution of offensive strategy in American football had become increasingly narrow-minded—not so much in terms of creativity but, rather, in point of attack. Whereas ball advancement in rugby has always alternated between close-quarters thrusts and widespread flanking attempts, American football by the early 1890s had devolved into a game of mostly mass-momentum attacks aimed right up the gut. The creativity—and extreme brutality—came in the wicked schemes dreamed up to best achieve that purpose. The most effective of these, and most dangerous, were the arrowhead-shaped formations of 1892 and 1893, meant to brutally puncture defensive lines at a single point and at full speed. Harvard debuted the first incarnation of the "flying wedge" or "V-trick" in 1892 at season's end against Yale. Word spread by the next season, and all college teams had adopted some devastating variation of it for both kickoff returns and scrimmage plays.[14]

While in the modern game, seven of the offensive side's eleven men must be on the line of scrimmage when the ball is snapped, back then only one man had to be there—the center. Thus were born schemes in which the snapped ball would be sent far back behind the line of scrimmage, and the carrier would be safely nestled inside a charging V of seven to ten players, which would pulverize the opposing defensive line at a predetermined spot—that is, at one unfortunate player. Commented the *New York Times* in 1893:

> Think of it. Half a ton of bone and muscle coming into collision with a man weighing 160 or 170 pounds. What is the result? The victim is generally sent sprawling with his nose broken or his chest crushed, and if the man with the ball gets through the line for ten or twenty yards the critics all exclaim: "What a grand play."[15]

And that was the problem. At a time when a three-yard gain was considered excellent (remember, teams had but two downs to gain five yards before usually kicking on the third and final down), any play that could reel off a ten- or twenty-yard gain with any regularity was deemed brilliant. As long as it was legal, teams were going to embrace the flying wedge.

Couple that with all the wanton slugging, piling-on, and other barbaric elements of early 1890s football, casualty lists were as long as they were alarming. The *New York Times*, late in the 1893 season, published this cringe-worthy sampling: "Every day one hears of broken heads, fractured skulls, broken necks, wrenched legs, dislocated shoulders, broken noses, and many other accidents of a more or less serious nature."[16] Even deaths were not uncommon. One player from Farmington Athletic Club died in November 1893 after playing Yale. He'd recovered a loose ball, and two Yalies jumped on him, breaking his neck and twisting his spine.

Inevitably and understandably, the public disapproved. "[T]he spectacle of seeing an intelligent youth carted off the field in an insensible condition, with blood flowing from ugly gashes, is anything but a pleasant one," observed the *Times*.[17]

Camp and the rules committee had no choice but to take action before the 1894 season. The committee passed a rule that barred more than three men from being in motion before the snap, or lining up more than five yards behind the line of scrimmage, which effectively killed the flying wedges. But mass-momentum, up-the-gut plays remained the rage, and the brutality of American football subsided only marginally.

The challenge in 1894 for the game's strategists was to somehow find other, legal ways to tap into the flying wedge's big-gain possibilities.[18] Penn's Woodruff wasted no time in devising the first son-of-wedge. His "guards-back" formation was precisely that: he took both guards out of the line, scooched the tackles and ends in against the center, and went with a six-man backfield. Sometimes both guards would be staggered left, sometimes right, or sometimes right behind the quarterback. Regardless, they were always situated in front of the other traditional backfield men (the fullback and two halfbacks).

The guards-back principle was revolutionary in thought and practice. So was Woodruff's idea to pull two linemen before the snap and put them in motion toward the other side, so they could hit the defensive line in conjunction with their opposite-side counterparts. This was termed "flying interference" and shared the same principle as the flying wedge. It was nearly as effective.

If all that didn't confound Penn's opponents enough, Woodruff was the first strategist to take advantage of the rule allowing the punter, or any player aligned behind him, to recover a punted ball. Woodruff made this an integral part of the Quakers' offense, and when successful the play gained yardage in chunks. On defense Woodruff was no less innovative. Foremost was his decision to play his ends in tight, as opposed to out wide, as every other team did to guard against sweeps and end runs. The Penn ends would quickly swing in and smash up the blocking, thus leaving the exposed ball carrier to be tackled by other Penn defenders before the play got going.[19]

Woodruff recruited some excellent players to boot—and his Quakers proceeded to win fifty-five of fifty-six games from 1894 through 1897, a stunning rise to preeminence. Woodruff had convincingly, and

Figure 4.1.   Pre-1906 American football often was pure savagery, with many casualties, as depicted in this unidentified 1905 newspaper clipping. "Every day one
hears of broken heads, fractured skulls, broken necks, wrenched legs, dislocated
shoulders, broken noses, and many other accidents of a more or less serious nature," the *New York Times* reported in 1893. *Source:* Amos Alonzo Stagg Papers,
Special Collections Research Centre, University of Chicago Library.

for all time, legitimized professional coaching. But then Woodruff proved something else about coaching: once other teams figure out your signature innovations, which they always eventually do, you'd better be ready with more. Woodruff wasn't. By century's end, teams began to solve his guards-back plays, and made Penn pay for its interior aggressiveness on defense. Woodruff's countermeasures didn't work. Disgruntled Penn students ran him out of Philadelphia after the 1901 season.[20]

The guards-back formation, meantime, had been picked up and employed by just about every other team in college football by the mid-1890s—except, of course, Yale and Princeton. Proud Yale had to come up with its own distinct variation—the tackles-back formation—and that wrinkle further promoted tightly packed, mass-momentum attacks. In contrast to guards, tackles were always a team's beefiest players, and thus even more effective at knocking defensive heads when blocking or ploughing for yardage when running.[21]

By 1901, the tackles-back was the most popular mode of ball advancement—that is, along with the assistance of a surviving feature of rugby that was now as popular as ever: the pushing and pulling of the ball carrier by his teammates. Heisman explained:

> In [those] days, players of one side were permitted to grab hold of their runners anywhere they could and push, pull or yank them along in any direction that would make the ball advance. Sometimes two enemy tacklers would be clinging to the runner's legs, and trying to hold him back, while several team-mates of the runner had hold of his arms, head, hair or wherever they could attach themselves, and were pulling him in the other direction. I still wonder how some of the ball carriers escaped dismemberment. Some backs had leather straps [or handles], sewed or riveted on the shoulders of their jackets and on the hips of their trousers, so as to offer good handholds for their team-mates.[22]

As the game's strategic breadth contracted, so did the frequency of action. Players usually were not in great physical shape. When the injured weren't requesting a timeout from the referee to regain their senses, which was frequent during the course of these rugged games, all players on offense would be deliberate in repositioning themselves for the next play. (Any form of coaching or signalling in plays from the sideline was forbidden; the game was supposed to be entirely in the players' hands.)

Indeed, in every way football had become a lumbering game by 1901. The high-scoring days of the 1880s and early 1890s were a distant memory. The Big Four now contented themselves to vanquish the small-fry by relatively low scores, in the belief that to leave their starters in to run up big scores was both unnecessary and foolish. Conserving energy and preserving health for those late-November showdowns had become the primary consideration.

In the five seasons preceding 1901, Yale scored an average of only 18.3 points per game, Princeton 20.8, Penn 25.6, and Harvard 18.5. Among the Big Four of the West, Michigan averaged 19.7, Chicago 22.7, Wisconsin 26.8, and Minnesota 16.5.[23]

Man's inhumanity to man was all about to change in 1901. And dramatically.

5

THE HUMAN HURRICANE
Fielding H. Yost

Fielding Harris "Hurry Up" Yost never had a bowl game named after him, like Amos Alonzo Stagg; or a Hollywood feature film made about him, like Knute Rockne; or an iconic trophy named in his honor, like John Heisman; or a national youth football league named for him, like Pop Warner. Even when the Big Ten Conference in 2010 announced a slew of new trophies and awards to pay homage to its most iconic figures, Yost—the coach with by far the best football winning percentage in league history—was snubbed.

Although lasting national fame escaped him, few American football coaches have ever understood the game as well as Yost or been as successful at it. At the University of Michigan in the first quarter of the twentieth century, and at four brief stops before that, he won 83 percent of his games—198 victories against only 35 losses and 12 ties. That's the best success rate of any coach who has lasted more than twenty-five years in the profession, college or pro, and that list includes the likes of Stagg, Warner, Heisman, Joe Paterno, Bobby Bowden, Eddie Robinson, Bear Bryant, Bernie Bierman, Woody Hayes, Lou Holtz, and Bo Schembechler.

Also unmatched are Yost's six national championships[1] and nine undefeated seasons. What's more, the West Virginia native is one of only a handful of coaches to produce dynasties two decades apart, and he built his on either side of the legalization of the forward pass. His first five

Figure 5.1.   Fielding Harris Yost, who "had more personality than any man I have ever met," according to Ring Lardner, and "made the fewest strategical mistakes of any coach I ever met," according to longtime Illinois coach Bob Zuppke. *Source:* Bentley Historical Library, University of Michigan.

Michigan teams (1901–1905) went 55–1–1, won four national championships, and outscored the opposition 2,823 to 42. His final five teams

(1921–1926) won by an average score of 25–2 and bagged four Big Ten titles in going 33–3–2.

As a strategist and innovator, Yost has had few equals. Said his long-time Big Ten rival Bob Zuppke, who coached Illinois from 1913 to 1941: "Yost made the fewest strategical mistakes of any coach I ever met."[2] It was no accident either. While in later life Yost would obsess over his many historical interests—including the Civil War, Custer's Last Stand, Peary's North Pole discovery, World War I battlefield movements—nothing consumed him like football. A college teammate once remarked that Yost played football all day and talked it all night.

Yost the character was no less legendary than Yost the coach. Ring Lardner, the nationally famous sports columnist and jazz-age novelist, observed that Yost "had more personality than any other man I have ever met."[3] Indeed, Yost was a "human hurricane"[4] —a robust man in the mold of Teddy Roosevelt, bearing so much boundless energy and gregarious enthusiasm he often overwhelmed first-time acquaintances. One of his Wolverine players with an eye for detail and a penchant for drama offered, perhaps, the best visual snapshot of Yost during his first decade at Michigan:

> . . . his lumbering frame; his beaming smile; his shuffling, flat-footed walk; the long black overcoat, the derby hat; the short stogie moving back and forth across his nervous lips, punctuating a persuasive drawl, which, on occasion, would swell into a fervent shout; (the) way his eyes twinkled as he told how he outfoxed opposing coaches and teams; his deep concentration; his way of looking through his pockets for things and never finding them; his deadly earnestness in making a point in conversation; the purity of his personal life.[5]

Yost's most fascinating trait was his unabashed penchant for bragging. He was able to harness it when necessary, and he got better at that as he got older, but most times he just couldn't help himself. He once said of the Michigan marching band's tradition of booming the school's famous fight song, "The Victors," after every Wolverine touchdown: "I reckon it's a good thing Louis Elbel was a Meeshegan student when he wrote that song. If he'd been at any other Big Ten school, they wouldn't have had much chance to use it, y'know."[6] This incessant desire to boast endeared him to Michiganders and the working press alike; he was a walking quote machine. But for Michigan's foes, the only thing worse than getting scorched by one of Yost's teams was hearing him openly predict it beforehand or gloat about it afterward.

Yost was able not only to instill his supreme self-confidence into his players, but he ingrained it permanently into the Michigan football program—a swagger encapsulated in his famous pregame motivator: "Who are *they* that they should beat a Meeshegan team?" The unsophisticated southern bumpkin in Yost would radiate whenever he spoke to his team, and that earnest, hokey charm worked, his players said. A backup Wolverine in 1908, J. Fred Lawton, remembered this particular pep talk:

> Up yere on the hill (at the University hospital), the doctors say if a man wants to get aout of a room, it takes three men to keep him in. But, if he's a maniac, it takes seven men to keep him in. Naow boys, the difference between a man and a maniac is that the maniac *thinks* more that he can get aout! Naouw, what I want aout on that field is eleven Meeshegan maniacs, y'know![7]

Yost felt compelled throughout his life to share his football insights with everyone. Didn't matter where—hotel lobby, street corner, barbershop. He'd corral bystanders and relive old plays, or use a nonathlete (often a sports writer) as his tackling dummy to demonstrate how some great play of his worked. "During my college days," Yost's superstar halfback Willie Heston remembered, "we used to get to avoiding him on the campus sometimes. Whenever he met a player, no matter where, he would stop him and start showing him how to block or something, then a big crowd would gather. It embarrassed the boys."[8]

Four decades later, as he approached age seventy and battled internal ailments, Yost didn't exactly back off. "You have to be in ideal condition to talk with Yost," Grantland Rice wrote:

> He hammers your chest with the powerful, stubby fingers of both hands. I introduced Yost to Tex Oliver, Oregon's head coach. Yost at the moment was explaining how to use the hands on a block. At the introduction Oliver stuck out his hand, as per custom. Yost countered by nailing Oliver with the heel of his hand and Tex crashed against the wall, before dropping to the floor.[9]

On Yost's sixty-seventh birthday, he made a United Press reporter his latest unwitting victim. "Yost likes to demonstrate football technique,"

Robert La Blonde wrote after his visit to Yost's office. "As you stand before his desk, he delivers a body block that dumps you into the corner. His stiff-arm, even at quarter-steam, more than hits the spot. If you sneak away from a conversation with Yost without bruised shins, you're a candidate for honors."[10]

It's hard to imagine any football man ever taking the sport more seriously than Yost. Even make-believe football. Famous Players film studio commissioned him in summer 1926 to act as a technical adviser on set of the football movie *The Quarterback*. Actors as well as former players from seventeen colleges were recruited for Yost. Some had been stars, such as Art Garvey of Notre Dame and Jackson Keefer of Brown. But no matter who they were, if they couldn't keep pace, Yost got rid of them. Replacements were constantly being shipped in. "You should have seen the actors they gave me for football players," he later lamented. "A bunch of ping-pong players and dancing boys. They couldn't even catch a football in a butterfly net."[11]

Football rules were sacrosanct to Yost. He was one of those individuals who could memorize a rule book, recite it verbatim, and know instantly whether an action complied, brushed the line, or was flat-out illegal. Perhaps that's what made him something of a football visionary. The sport evolved immensely throughout his coaching career—from that brutal, bunched-up, better-organized form of rugby to the game familiar to all twenty-first-century fans. Time and again throughout his career, Yost was asked his opinion about the latest evolutionary crossroads, and it is uncanny how often he was ahead of the coaching and rules-making packs.

For instance, after the 1904 and 1905 seasons, it was clear at least in the Neanderthal East that something had to be done to open up the game. De facto rules czar Walter Camp suggested changing the allowed increments for advancing the ball from three downs to gain five yards to three to make ten. Stagg and other experts agreed. But Yost predicted that that would result in an even more conservative game featuring little more than punting duels, with outcomes hinging on fortunate bounces and flukes. He advocated four downs to gain ten yards, insisting offenses needed that extra down. But Camp and company prevailed, and starting in 1906 it was three downs to gain ten yards. Even with the addition of rules allowing forward passes, onside punts, and only four men in the backfield, Yost's prognostication proved immediately correct.[12] Just a few weeks into the 1906 season Yost pleaded, "The game is now largely dependable on chance. . . . I think it will be absolutely necessary to reduce the distance to be gained after this season to, say, seven yards, or else to allow four downs."[13] He was ignored. Finally, when critics and fans had howled loud and long enough about the lack of offensive excitement, a fourth down was added in 1912.

Another example: Yost was one of the few coaches at the 1927 postseason American Football Coaches Association (AFCA) convention in favor of retaining the new fumble rule, which stated that a muffed or errant backward pass (a lateral) would be blown dead at the point of recovery by the defense. Notre Dame's Knute Rockne led the overwhelming charge to vote down Yost and the other holdouts, and Rockne attributed his nemesis Yost's position to "some selfish motive or other."[14] But the NCAA football rules committee ignored the AFCA's recommendation and retained the backward-pass rule.[15] Yost later correctly predicted that this rule would eventually spur the most creative coaches to conjure wonderful new offensive wrinkles, what with the concern eliminated of a backfield fumble being returned for an easy touchdown by the defense. Such strategies began to emerge in the early 1930s. "The real use of the lateral pass is just in its infancy," Yost further forecasted in 1934. "Future football players will learn to pass and receive a football with the same proficiency that basketball players handle a basketball."[16] Seven years later, Missouri coach Don Faurot invented the concept of the "option" offense, whose pitch-or-keep principle became the basis of I-formation and wishbone rushing attacks that would become the rage in the 1960s and 1970s. Yost was proved correct again. The dead-ball fumble rule existed in college football until 1992.

It probably surprised no one in 1941 that the NCAA turned to Mr. Football Rules to head up a committee to standardize football statistics from coast to coast. "Until then," recalled Steve Boda Jr., the NCAA's longtime associate director of statistics,

> there weren't any specific rules under which football game statistics were to be recorded. Punting was the worst statistic. Some schools were recording the punt from where it was kicked, not the line of scrimmage. Same with rushing—they'd record the gain from where the runner got the ball. There was no consistency from one school to the next. Starting in 1941 there were 13 rules for football statisticians nationwide. Fielding Yost came up with them.[17]

Unlike Woodruff, Stagg, Warner, Heisman, and the game's other coaching greats who rose to prominence late in the nineteenth century, Yost did not play at an Ivy League school. And from birth he had no association whatsoever with the Eastern establishment.

☙ ☙ ☙

Yost was born in 1871 in remote, north-end West Virginia—in Marion County, coal-mining and farming country. In later life, he would sometimes be called the "Dutchman," but he had only a sliver of Dutch lineage. His surname is German—Bavarian, to be precise—and appears to have been anglicized from Youst by his grandparents' generation. The coach was a fifth-generation West Virginian, and because his male ancestors there had all married Anglo-Saxon women, Yost was of mostly English blood—with additional drops of Irish, Scottish, and Dutch mixed in.[18]

Yost's father, Permenas, was a farmer and merchant in the backcountry town of Fairview. As the Yost family sided with the Confederates during the Civil War, Permenas fought for the South, even though West Virginia separated from Virginia during the war to become a Union state. Yost's granduncle and namesake, Fielding Hamilton Yost, was a regionally famous physician who, for a time, served with Robert E. Lee as surgeon in his Confederate army. By then there were Yosts and Yousts everywhere in the extreme northern counties of West Virginia. Religion was, and remains, a vital thread that ties West Virginians together, and it appears Yost's forebears up both sides of his family tree were devout Wesleyan Methodists. Yost's mother, Elzena, was deeply involved in church activities from a young age, and a well-thumbed Bible was one of the few books in the Yost home.[19] Temperance was a staple of Methodism in the nineteenth century (and indeed through Prohibition), so it is unsurprising that Fielding Yost was a proud teetotaler. "I have never taken a drink in my life," he said upon his arrival in Ann Arbor in 1901. "In fact I cannot even imagine [what] it would taste like."[20]

Yost grew into a man of rugged proportions for the day—six foot, two hundred pounds. Rambunctious and restless upon reaching manhood, he dabbled in teaching and was even a deputy marshal for a time, all before age twenty. After spending two years as a student at Ohio

Normal University in Ada, Ohio, he returned to Fairview and in 1895 enrolled at nearby West Virginia University to complete his training as a lawyer. Yost immediately tried out for the Mountaineers football team and made it, playing in the first game he ever saw under coach Thomas "Doggie" Trenchard, a former Princeton All-American. Yost was hooked.

By 1896, he was a standout tackle and played so well in a trio of losses to Lafayette that that team's coach, Parke "Dink" Davis, took him up as a ringer just a week later for the Leopards' big game against George Woodruff's defending national-champion Penn Quakers. Yost helped the Leopards become the first team to solve Woodruff's lethal "guards back" formation. Lafayette, a small college based in Easton, Pennsylvania, dumped the Quakers 6–4. It was Lafayette's signature victory in an undefeated season that earned the Maroon and White the mythical 1896 national title in some experts' eyes. That it was Penn's only loss from 1894 to 1898 underscores the achievement. For years thereafter, Yost proudly wore his Lafayette letter-winner's sweater, and early in his coaching career he didn't mind one bit that sports writers and rival coaches alike believed he was a Lafayette grad.

After the big win over Penn, Yost returned to West Virginia—"on crutches, head in a bandage," a friend remembered.[21] He resumed his law studies and graduated in spring 1897. Ambivalence clouded his future. On one hand, he was anxious to apply his mineral and property-rights expertise to all the oil, mining, and hydroelectric business opportunities opening up across the Appalachians. On the other, he couldn't bear to leave football behind—coaching held that much appeal. He resolved to pursue both interests, with a plan to quickly work his way to the West Coast because, he recalled, "there was in me the desire to see this great country of ours."[22]

Yost's business career alone allowed him to see substantial portions of it. Until he became athletic director at Michigan in 1921, Yost was based not in Ann Arbor but elsewhere during the winter, spring, and summer months—namely, in San Francisco in 1901, in West Virginia until 1906, and in Nashville until 1921. Over those twenty-four years, Yost ran or helped run myriad nonmining businesses—a cement company, an oil company, a furniture company—and he was even director of a bank and trust. As for mining, he remembered, "I was deeply interested in nearly every type of mineral produced in the country. In fact I actually had a fling at oil, gas, coal, gold, flurospar, silver, bauxite, graphite, asbestos and copper." In oil and gas alone, Yost bought and sold property leases for many years in Kentucky, Arkansas, Louisiana, Texas, Oklahoma, and Kansas.[23] All these ventures made him a wealthy man, yet he gave up most of those pursuits to become Michigan's athletic director in 1921, some seven decades before it would start to become trendy for colleges to hire successful businessmen as ADs.

It is important to point out that Yost wasn't always the hyper bumpkin. In business and as Michigan's athletic director, Yost projected an aura equal to any blue-blooded East Coast urbanite. One can peruse thousands of his correspondences stored in the University of Michigan archives at the Bentley Historical Library and never believe he was anything but an educated man of polish, class, control, and persuasion.

He used that intellect to his advantage as often as possible. Ditto his tenacity. Heaven help you if you ever blocked the "Human Hurricane" on something he desperately wanted done. And if you were an acquaintance of Yost, you soon learned not to bother trying to convince him of anything he opposed, and cringed whenever anyone in your presence tried—be it on business, a football rules matter, Custer's Last Stand, World War I strategic maneuvers . . . anything. "I bet Herbert Bayard Swope, New York's racing commissioner, and a fair talker on his own," Grantland Rice recalled, "that Yost could [outargue] him. Mr. Swope surrendered at 3 a.m. . . . 'It wasn't a fair bet,' Swope said later. 'Yost not only never stopped talking for eight hours, but he never heard a word I said, even when I was shouting.'"[24]

Yost's argumentative coup de grace was getting his dream project, Michigan Stadium, built in 1927. He had to summon all his political favors, politesse, business savvy, work ethic, and personal magnetism to gain favor with everyone of any consequence in the decision-making process—from Ann Arbor to the Michigan state capital and back. In the end, he expertly broke down the resistance of every objector—including a holdout on the university's governing board of regents, James O. Murfin, a former longtime circuit-court judge in Detroit. Upon finally waving the white flag, a bemused Murfin wrote Yost, "You made a mistake when you went in for football instead of law. As an advocate either orally or in writing you have no equal."[25]

Yost liked to think he had no equal on the football field either. And during long stretches of his thirty-year coaching career, he didn't.

That career began just a few months after he graduated from WVU. After being rejected by an Ohio State University faculty member—who evidently was so horrified at one of Yost's football-play reenactments that he screamed, "Get this madman out of here!"[26]—Ohio Wesleyan University (OWU) gave him his first coaching job in 1897. Yost inserted himself into his shorthanded lineup in an early game against the University of Michigan in Ann Arbor, and Ohio Wesleyan tied the Wolverines 0–0—a huge upset. At season's end, the "Battling Bishops" beat Ohio State University 6–0, which gave OWU a 7–1–1 record and its first (and to this day only) "Championship of Ohio." After the season, Yost was recruited to coach and play for the Mahoning Cycle Club Giants of Youngstown, Ohio. The Giants were to play in an early interstate professional football game against the Latrobe Athletic Association of Pennsylvania, the first football team composed entirely of pros to play a full schedule of games. The Latrobe pros had Yost's old WVU coach Doggie Trenchard, and won 19–0.

In 1898, Yost made it as far west as the Plains and coached the University of Nebraska to an 8–3 record, which included a decisive 18–6 victory over archrival Kansas, good enough for a Missouri Valley championship. Yost's salary with the Cornhuskers was to have been $500, but Nebraska evidently was able to pay him only $160 of it.[27]

In 1899, Yost won the same Missouri Valley championship but this time at the University of Kansas (KU), with a perfect 10–0 record. By turning the tables on his former Nebraska charges and beating them 36–20, Yost achieved the adage that decades later would be said only in theoretical tribute by Bum Phillips about Bear Bryant—that he was so good a coach "he could take his'n and beat your'n, then take your'n and beat his'n."[28] The defeated Cornhuskers' twenty points against the Jayhawks came off four field goals (then worth five points apiece) booted by a player Yost had coached up the year before.

A despicable stunt of skullduggery gave Yost a big edge that season. Yost had asked George Krebs, his six-foot-four, two-hundred-plus-pound teammate at West Virginia, to enroll at KU that fall. But Krebs was to pretend he was a football greenhorn from the Kansas boonies, despite having played four years of college ball and at least two years as a pro and having coached West Virginia two years earlier. Yost and Krebs kept the secret even from other Jayhawks players. Early that season, Krebs warmed the bench, but as the Nebraska showdown approached he began to show his true form in practice, until his team-mates begged Yost to put Krebs in against the Cornhuskers. Yost did, of course, and Krebs was a one-man wrecking crew, and was so again in the season finale against Missouri, in which a teammate remembered Krebs "carried our backs over the goal for several touchdowns, like a squaw with a papoose on her back." Because neither Nebraska's nor Missouri's scouts had seen Krebs play, the ruse worked as planned. Immediately after the victory over Missouri, Krebs "got a wire that his mother was very sick" and left campus at once, before final exams. "None of us ever saw Krebs again," the teammate recalled. The Krebs ruse was rumored for decades. Sports columnist Westbrook Pegler got to the bottom of it in 1934, tracking down Krebs, who told Pegler his only compensation for playing at KU was having his expenses covered. Still, the incident stained Yost's reputation for the rest of his life.[29]

A couple weeks after the 1899 season, Yost coached up a team in tiny Coffeyville, Kansas, presumably composed of pros—perhaps including Krebs. Four days before the turn of the century, Yost led the group to an unlikely 35–0 demolition of a team from much more populous Independence, Missouri.

The University of Missouri, which had lost to Yost's Plains teams by the combined score of 81–12 the past two seasons, made a hard pitch to lure Yost to coach the Tigers in 1900, but he was uninterested; Missouri wasn't on the Pacific Coast. Stanford University in Palo Alto, California, was, and when its athletic authorities offered Yost the football post in 1900, he readily accepted. Stanford was desperate to turn around its football fortunes after back-to-back blowout losses to hated Cal, 30–0 and 22–0, and a 2–5–2 record in 1899. Yost promptly led the Indians (now Cardinal) to a 7–2–1 record, capped by a 5–0 Thanksgiving Day victory over most of the same Cal players who had destroyed the Indians in '98 and '99. A crowd of 19,000 attended, thought at the time to be the largest to witness any athletic event staged west of the Mississippi River.

For years thereafter, it was reported that Yost additionally coached three other teams that autumn. One history book says Yost on a daily basis coached Lowell High of Palo Alto at 10 a.m., the Stanford freshmen team at 2 p.m., the Stanford varsity squad at 4 p.m., and the nearby San Jose Normal Teachers College team (now San Jose State University) in the evening.[30] Decades later, Yost was asked if it were all true.

"No," Yost replied. He said he actually coached five teams that fall, the fifth being the Ukiah High team. "According to the clippings, all four of your teams won championships," his questioner continued. "All *five* won championships. Yes, sir," Yost crowed.[31]

After his busy stint in Palo Alto, Yost's four-year college record stood at 31–6–2, with championships won every year. Unsurprisingly, his employers all had given him glowing letters of recommendation, and the local media and student bodies at each stop raved about his coaching abilities. "Success has crowned every eleven that he has coached, and ours were no exceptions," a Stanford student newspaper editorial glowed. "Mr. Yost has been very conscientious throughout the season, and perfectly fair with everyone. Stanford has never had a coach who stands higher in its estimation, or whom it has had more confidence in." That was high praise, considering Walter Camp had coached at Stanford just five years earlier.[32]

Now age twenty-nine, Yost yearned to end his nomadic ways and plant some roots somewhere nearer to the mineral-rich Appalachians, and hopefully at a more prestigious football power. When Stanford and Cal jointly agreed after the 1900 season to adopt the grads-only coaching policy, Yost's return east was sealed. On December 27, 1900, he wrote University of Illinois athletic director George Huff to offer his coaching services, but Huff had already secured Princeton grad Edgar G. Holt for 1901. Huff was about to meet in Chicago with his University of Michigan counterpart, Charles Baird. Knowing Baird was looking for a new football coach, Huff brought along Yost's letter. "Here's a fellow who is looking for a job," Huff told Baird, pulling Yost's letter out of his pocket. "You can answer it for Michigan, if you wish."[33]

A thankful Baird did just that on January 5, 1901:

> Dear sir:
> Mr. George Huff handed me your letter to him of December 27th and requested me to answer for him. Illinois has secured coaches for 1901 but Michigan has not yet selected hers, although we shall do so very soon.
> We won the Western Football Championship for several years, namely 93, 94 and 95. Since then, however, we have won the championship but once, namely in '98. This has been largely due, I think, to unsatisfactory coaching, though I believe our failure this year was

mostly due to the fact that we have a green team, as we had only three old men back.

Our people are greatly roused up over the defeats of the past two years, and a great effort will be made. Alumni everywhere have promised to cooperate, and as we will have three-fourths of the old men back the outlook is splendid. Coaching is the main thing bothering us now.

Would you care to coach at Ann Arbor? What terms? Do you expect to come east soon? If so, could you stop and talk the matter over with us?

If you receive this before you start east, will you please wire me at once whether or not you care to consider the matter and if so, whether you can talk the matter over.
Yours truly,
Chas. Baird[34]

This was Yost's big career break. Michigan might have fallen on lean times the past two seasons, but it was still Michigan, the self-proclaimed "Champions of the West," and one of the perceived "Big Four" football schools of the West, along with Chicago, Wisconsin, and Minnesota.

Upon receipt of Baird's letter four days later, Yost shot Baird a telegram saying he would consider the proposition, and that "full particulars" would follow.[35] The full particulars amounted to a cover letter requesting a salary in excess of $2,000 and fifty pounds' worth of Yost's scrapbooks that were crammed with newspaper clippings chronicling all his coaching exploits, as well as endorsements from former employers.

Yost wasn't the only man Baird was considering. At the same time, Baird and other Michigan athletics leaders were giving strong consideration to Dave Fultz, the former Brown University football star and current pro baseball player with the Milwaukee Brewers of the American League. Fultz was endorsed "by a large number of Michigan alumni," according to a report.[36] But after looking over Yost's scrapbooks, Baird shared them with Michigan's nationally respected athletics trainer and resident de facto assistant football coach Keene Fitzpatrick. "What do you think of him?" Baird asked Fitzpatrick. "I think you had better get him," Fitz replied.

On January 21, Baird wired Yost in San Francisco with the good news: "We accept your offer."[37]

The news leaked out in the press a few days later but wasn't announced by UM authorities until February. Yost would be given a salary of $2,300—more than double what Stanford paid him—plus Michigan would cover all his living and eating expenses while in Ann Arbor from September 1 until the end of the football season.[38] The average American salary in 1900 was $438, and the average salary for a full professor at the University of Michigan was $2,500—but for twelve months' work, not four.

Yost would be the first UM football coach who wasn't either a former star player at Princeton or Yale or a UM grad. In fact, in 1901, Yost would be the only coach among the seven schools good at football at the time who hadn't learned his craft at one of the Big Four universities in the East. That Michigan would hire this gregarious nomad with personal and educational pedigrees unlikely to impress Western athletic men, let alone any easterners, spoke to the heights of Yost's coaching overachievements thus far. Such heights were nothing compared to those he was about to reach at Michigan.

Part II

1901–1905

6

1901 OFF THE FIELD

Coast-to-Coast Yost

By 1901, Amos Alonzo Stagg's pride and ego soared for too long on the glory of Chicago's Western championship of 1899.

His Maroons had played an ambitious fourteen-game schedule in '99 and emerged unbeaten, smashing Eastern middleweight Brown 17–6 and trashing the next best teams in the conference, in the last season before the additions of Iowa and Indiana made it the Big Nine: Northwestern (76–0), Minnesota (29–0), and Wisconsin (17–0). The highlight, though, was a 5–5 tie against one of the Big Four of the East— George Woodruff's Penn team, which had lost but one game over the previous five years. The Chicago press hailed the '99 Maroons as the best team the West had yet produced, and few argued. Seven years after he scrambled merely to field a full, competitive Maroons team, Stagg and his charges finally ruled the West. In denouement, he pulled back.

Stagg now could better entertain the idea of cleansing and curtailing his recruiting efforts after he'd embarrassed his university over the professionalism and eligibility scandals of 1898 and 1899. Letters that Stagg wrote to potential recruits and talent "bagmen" or "bird dogs," as they were called, over the next two years bear that out.[1] Two weeks after the '99 season ended, he wrote this to a wannabe talent-securing bird dog:

> Of course we should be glad to have good players enter the University, but I want them to be genuinely interested in what ought to be

the first purpose in coming to the University. We had a sickening case in '98 with Burnett and this fall in Wellington, both of them men who came of their own accord into the University but apparently with the sole idea of playing football. We do not want any more such cases.[2]

Two weeks later, to another man seeking inducements on behalf of a "Mr. Drees," Stagg wrote, "We cannot and will not bid for the young men to come to Chicago, and if he is on the market, open to offers, it would seem to me very advisable for him to go to some college where arrangements of that sort will be made for him."[3]

A cynic might conclude these merely were examples of how Stagg, when approached by unknown handout seekers, protected and propagated the reputation of incorruptibility he so desperately sought for himself. As usual, though, when Stagg really wanted an athlete whose circumstances left him unable to pay his own way, the coach would spell out precisely what, in fact, could be done for him at UC, as he explained to this friend of a star athlete in March 1900:

> A man is able to work out two-thirds of his tuition[—]that is he could work out $80 of the $120, which he would have to pay. A large number of students here help pay a part of their tuition in this way. The service which they render to the University is in the way of clerical work[—]library work of various kinds, post-office, and messenger service and such work as a student could readily do at the same time not interfering with his studies. We shall be very glad to welcome your friend here and do everything we can to help him make a successful athlete. I am very sure that he will enjoy his life here if he decides to make the University of Chicago his alma mater.[4]

This, in part, is how varsity athletes usually were taken care of at colleges across the nation. That is, find them a barely legit, menial job somewhere on campus to defray some, most, or all of their school-year costs. There was no rule against it, even if it might have outraged some faculty or offended scores of students.

The methods to make up a player's shortfall after the joe job had become even more entrenched by 1901. First, teams fed their best football players ample, healthy meals at a "training table."[5] And if a player was worth the risk, team leaders—on the extreme quiet—might arrange to have a wealthy, football-loving alumnus funnel cash directly into the young man's pockets. Or perhaps, as Michigan began doing in 1896, they'd push the rule barring cash enticements to recruits to its envelope and arrange for alumni to merely loan top prospects cash, to be repaid after the young man left school, as he could afford to.

Common sense suggests it would have been much easier for football leaders to find alumni willing to loan the money, sometimes with interest, rather than give it up forever.

Stagg was far too savvy and careful ever to file away any correspondence that might prove he had knowledge of, or direct involvement with, any such shortfall-covering initiatives at UC beyond job arrangement and the training table. A college football team at the turn of the twentieth century had no hope of being competitive without alumni, or someone, helping many if not most athletes through school in some manner.

❊ ❊ ❊

Like all coaches, Stagg concentrated his recruiting efforts regionally. Occasionally, he'd pull in a stud from the East or from the near or far west, such as Utah. But Illinois, Indiana, Wisconsin, and Iowa appeared to be his prime recruiting grounds through 1901.

By comparison, Fielding H. Yost broke new ground upon his arrival at the University of Michigan in early 1901. UM that summer became America's first coast-to-coast football recruiting university.

Yost had sized up his new charges for the first time at spring practice and came way convinced he needed at least one new dynamic running back and more-effective linemen. Plenty of seasoned talent returned from the young 1900 Wolverine team, which had finished 7–2–1. The defeats were ruinously decisive and, worse, came against Michigan's only marquee foes that season: to eventual Big Nine co-champion Iowa, 27–6, and for the fourth time in five years to the hated Stagg and his Maroons, 15–6.

Because of his nomadic coaching past, Yost now had connections across the country, from eastern Pennsylvania through the Appalachians, across the Midwest, up and down the Plains, and all along the Pacific coast. Yost hit up contacts everywhere. UM's athletic archives from June through early September 1901 are rife with letters sent by

Yost, while still based in San Francisco, to his new boss back in Ann Arbor, Michigan athletic director Charles Baird. Yost constantly provided Baird with updates of his own recruiting efforts, and he implored Baird to help him scour the nation.[6]

Of course, Baird was up to the task. He had been Michigan's chief scourer since 1894, other than in 1896 and 1897 when he'd tried to make it as a lawyer in Chicago. Trainer Keene Fitzpatrick ably assisted him. With each passing year that duo required less and less help from the Wolverine football captain—a fast-fading echo from the times up until the early 1890s when a team's captain ran the whole show.

Fitzpatrick was a Yale man. He'd trained Yale athletes in two stints since 1890. Now he was Michigan's nationally respected track-and-field coach who, each fall, doubled as the football team's trainer and de facto assistant coach. "Fitz" had always aided Baird in his talent determinations, and he even bird-dogged in his home state of Massachusetts.[7] With the help of wealthy, football-loving alumni, Baird and Fitzpatrick had concentrated their recruiting efforts in the Midwest. But in summer 1901, Fitz's recruiting efforts in Massachusetts geographically completed college football's first coast-to-coast recruiting operation.

Yost was relentless. After Baird informed him in July that he'd be taking a trip to Kansas, Yost—having coached at the University of Kansas in 1899—quickly provided his boss with a list of fourteen potential candidates worth looking up along the way.[8] One had quarterbacked Yost's Jayhawks team: Bennie Owen. Come mid-September, Owen quit playing baseball on a pro team in Fort Scott, Kansas, to take a job coaching the Michigan freshmen team for Yost.[9] Owen thus launched a career in college athletics that would soon see him found the Oklahoma Sooners football dynasty, using Yost's high-scoring template.

It was no coincidence that Yost in summer 1901 spent little if any time wooing freshly graduated high school stars; his letters to Baird that spring, summer, and fall contain no mention of any such attempts. Yost wanted college-age men to transfer in. In his seven years in football to date, Yost had gleaned that the paramount ingredient on any football team was experience. Throughout his coaching career he would underscore this point time and again. Talent can win; only experienced talent can win big.[10] Thus, Yost preferred grizzled, grown men with previous college experience to younger, lighter, raw high school grads.

Enabling such a philosophy was the virtually nonexistent rulebook governing all means of talent procurement. Whereas at the turn of the twenty-first century, the NCAA's rulebooks could prop open a steel door in a gale, at the turn of the twentieth century many schools were bound by no recruiting rules whatsoever. Even in the most progressive conferences now sprouting up across America—led by the Big Nine— one could type, single-spaced, all rules covering both talent procurement and eligibility and not fill two pages.

By 1901, the Big Nine had but one transfer rule: only college graduates entering directly into a professional school—such as law, engineering, or medicine—or those who'd previously taken only preparatory courses in college could play right away. All other transfers first had to sit out a school year.[11] Not coincidentally, most transfer grads entering Michigan in this era chose to study law. Medicine and engineering studies were the next most popular disciplines of study.[12]

Yost's recruiting efforts on the Pacific coast winnowed down to two studs, both of whom he'd coached the previous fall at the college level and both of whom aspired to be lawyers, which would allow them to play right away. William Martin "Willie" Heston—out of Grant's Pass, Oregon—was a solidly built halfback with uncommon speed who'd starred for three years on the San Jose Normal Teachers College team, the one Yost had coached on weeknights while coaching Stanford. The other was George "Dad" Gregory, a strong, fast lineman on the Stanford freshmen team. "Heston should develop into an extra good half back," Yost informed Baird, and Gregory "will make a fine guard—210 [pounds] or more and as strong as a bull and loves the game."[13]

Both West Coasters applied to the Michigan law school. Both were accepted. But by August 1 Heston's recruitment hit a snag, as Yost wrote Baird:

> I had a long talk with him. He is very anxious to go to Michigan but his finances are such I am afraid we can do nothing to help him out. I asked him if a *loan* of $100—and his tuition for the year—would help him out: He said, ['W]ell I will just tell you I have about enough to get what clothes I must have and get my ticket back [to Oregon after the school year].' I said[, H]ave you no one of whom you can get money[? A]nd he said, [']I have been trying but have failed so far but might succeed.['] So you see just how it stands. In my opinion we must count him out—I am sorry he can not do more for himself. I

told him I would not promise him a place on the team and that he
might fail to make it. Those were the chances he would have to
take.[14]

No subsequent letter Yost might have sent to Baird that summer regarding Heston survives. Yost, though, loved to tell the following story
for decades thereafter. Shortly after he himself arrived in Ann Arbor
around September 1 for preseason training camp, whom did Yost happen to spot one day standing at the corner of Main and Huron Streets?
One Martin Heston, as he was known then. "Why you little son-of-a-
gun!" Yost shouted as he bear-hugged Heston from behind, lifting the
future star halfback right off his feet. "You made it, didn't you? I always
figured you'd come with me."[15]

   As Heston later explained it, he actually had decided against going to
Michigan, resolving instead to return to his Oregon home. But by
chance, while waiting for a ferry to take him up the coast from San
Francisco, he'd met a visitor from Toledo, Ohio, who wanted to remain
in California. The young man offered Heston his unused return ticket
for twenty-five dollars. Toledo is but fifty miles south of Ann Arbor.
Heston suspected serendipity at work and, on the spot, decided instead
to become a lawyer and a Wolverine, he recalled.[16]

   In addition to Heston and Gregory, Yost's third key recruit in 1901
was Dan McGugin—a player recently graduated from Drake University
in Des Moines, Iowa, whom Yost had seen play once on the Plains.
McGugin was a first-rate blocking guard with uncommon speed, even if
at 180 pounds he was undersized. Yost somehow had tracked him down
to the backwoods of Oregon, where McGugin was working "pretty
hard" at a summer job to try to set up not only himself financially for
school come fall, but his brother as well. A teammate of Yost's from the
1896 Lafayette team coached Drake in football, and he no doubt had
tipped Yost that McGugin could excel at the Big Nine level, too. "I
think he is a good man to have around," Yost informed Baird on June 4,
"so I will turn him over to you."[17]

   This meant Baird would take care of the usuals. He arranged for
McGugin, a Drake grad, to enroll in the Michigan law school, and Baird
lined up some menial job for him as well. Baird must have asked
McGugin at some point to do some bird-dogging while in the Pacific

Figure 6.1. William Martin "Willie" Heston, Michigan's great running back from 1901 to 1904 and the first two-time All-American from the West. *Source:* Bentley Historical Library, University of Michigan.

Northwest because McGugin wrote back on July 20: "Have seen lots of strapping big fellows but none of them ever heard of foot-ball."

By mid-August McGugin's plans also snagged. He needed money ASAP, as he explained to Baird:

> I have received a request that a note of $200 held against me be paid. This was money which I borrowed some years ago with the understanding that it need not be paid until I desired to pay it—until after I had finished school. It is due now because of a financial misfortune to the lender, who was kind enough to not charge me any interest. . . . The arrangement [you and I] made was, as I have it, something like this. It was to be assured me that I should be able to earn $250 during the school year with the privilege of borrowing $150 more if needed. Owing to the busy nature of the fall months $100 was to be advanced at the beginning of the fall term. My summer's work has been more remunerative than I had expected and is netting me money, some of which I will not receive until later in the year. I shall be able to pay this amount and not need to ask any favors from [you] other than this: I need $200 at once. Can you grant me a loan of that [amount]? . . . I realize that this request is both unbusinesslike and unfair to you.[18]

Was the loan one that had seen McGugin financially through Drake? Perhaps. Because McGugin made it to Ann Arbor by mid-September and enrolled, presumably Baird wound up lining up one of his usual deep-pocketed alums to loan McGugin the $200 on the quiet to pay off his debt.

Yost backfilled his first recruiting class with other promising young men, thanks to the help of Baird, Fitz, and bird-dog alumni. D. L. Dunlap from Iowa was one of the players Yost had asked Baird to look up on his trip to Kansas, and he came. But in five years in Ann Arbor Dunlap would barely play and never cracked the starting lineup. While there was no rule forbidding the recruitment of players in the manner of Yost's new coast-to-coast dragnet style, it might have become a scandal if the degree to which he and Baird were scouring had ever gone public. Naïve football fans and even some faculty at the football-prominent schools still liked to believe that the boys sought the school, not the other way around.

For years, all schools across the country had been securing star players in this way. Yost in 1901 merely did it on a coast-to-coast scale.

Now he was ready to apply the same enthusiasm, creativity, and aggressiveness on the field as well.

7

1901 ON THE FIELD

Hurrying Up, Eating Everybody Up

The moment Amos Alonzo Stagg realized his Chicago Maroons team would stink in 1901 probably came on the day he arrived at preseason camp. As the late summer sun fried the back of his neck, cold reality smacked him in the face like a shanked punt. Stagg already knew these Maroons would lack talent at many positions. But now he learned that one of his few veteran reliables—captain Jimmy Henry, a "dashing, brilliant, fearless" halfback, according to the *Chicago Tribune*—had just announced his departure from the University of Chicago to take a job with a wholesale grocery house. Henry had been struggling in his studies.[1]

Newspapers predicted Chicago would bounce back from its below-par 7–5–1 record in 1900. But barring an unlikely influx of talented players, humiliation awaited Stagg's tenth Maroons team. His talent cupboards now shelved little more than crumbs. After captain Henry's departure, four lettermen from '99 remained. Gone were the likes of captain/quarterback Walter Kennedy and backfield stars Frank Slaker and Ralph Hamill. For Stagg, watching his undersized, undertalented players of 1901 attempt quite unsuccessfully to exhibit any promise as a first-rate football team must have burned him far more than the late-August sun ever could.

This was the price of distraction, he must have thought. Also it was the price of his most sincere attempt at purification yet. Neither lesson was lost on him. Stagg surely understood what that meant for him, personally: dismal, long, lonely hours of hard work, not just in the months ahead to wring every drop of success from this clumsy squad, but in the years it might take to return Chicago football to preeminence. At age thirty-nine, Stagg was up for the challenge.

In so sobering a pickle, he probably did not spend even a moment contemplating what thirty-year-old Fielding H. Yost might be doing 240 miles to the east to resuscitate Chicago's archnemesis—the now annually underachieving Michigan Wolverines. Stagg had enough on his mind. But that would change.

❋ ❋ ❋

Upon his arrival in Ann Arbor, Yost learned the sporting press did not give Michigan much chance to win the Championship of the West in 1901. Even rival coaches mostly ignored the Wolverine threat.

University of Minnesota head coach Dr. Henry L. Williams wrote a preseason feature on "Middle Western Football" for *Outing* magazine, and the Yale grad rated Phil King's Wisconsin Badgers (with nine starters returning) as the favorite. Next he ranked Dr. Alden Knipe's Iowa Hawkeyes (with seven), followed by his own Gophers (with seven), and Stagg's Chicago Maroons (with four). Williams listed Yost's Wolverines fifth, with this qualifier: "A successful season this year at Michigan is looked forward to with confidence."[2]

Confidence? Yost oozed it and seldom hesitated to share it. "Yes sir, Michigan is going to beat 'em all this year," he assured a reporter.[3]

Yost had good reason to be so confident upon realizing his own talent cupboard was packed. Eight Wolverine starters returned from 1900, including promising ends Neil Snow and Curtis Redden, guard Bruce Shorts, and tackle Hugh White, that year's captain. While not a single member of the 1901 varsity team weighed more than 190 pounds—a concern, as most coaches preferred at least some linemen upward of 200—most were blazing fast for their size and for their positions.

As would be the case for decades to come, Yost's enthusiasm struck almost everyone he met. "I saw Yost [for] a few minutes the other day," Henry M. Bates of Chicago, the most influential Michigan alumnus on football matters, remarked to Baird on September 6. "He seems to be a determined sort of fellow with a good deal of confidence and leadership. I hope we can turn out a good team."[4]

Having played in football games in three states in the East and successfully coached games played in eight states west of the Appalachians (Ohio, Michigan, Nebraska, Kansas, Missouri, Iowa, Colorado, and California), Yost's confidence was warranted. If he did not know football forward and backward, he sure knew it ocean to ocean.

Yost began construction of his mighty Michigan machine on these four groundbreaking, cornerstone coaching philosophies:

- **A reliance on speed and fast play.** Yost debuted college football's first true hurry-up offense at Michigan. Only fast players in supreme physical condition could achieve it, which Yost discovered eleven decades before twenty-first-century hurry-up gurus such as Chip Kelly, Urban Meyer, and Rich Rodriguez. This factor was crucial to Yost's success and changed the game everywhere but in the stodgy East within two years. The speed at which Yost's Wolverines would run plays, especially in his first two UM seasons, literally swept some opponents off their feet in the opening minutes and often gassed them long before game's end.
- **Intensive off-field instruction.** Yost always liked to boast that his players, more than any others, were "well versed in the fundamental principles of the game in every department."[5] He had discovered this proved a distinct advantage and was best achieved in conjunction with the training table—the place where starters and key backups gathered daily to eat ample, healthy meals. "Yost gives them a fifteen-minute quiz on the rules every day," the *Chicago Journal*'s respected sports editor Sherman R. Duffy wrote. "They know just exactly where every man should be in every play—not only their own positions, but the position of every man on the team, and the position which every man on the opposing team will logically take as each play is started. And they ought to, for Yost gives them checker-board work for half an hour every day."[6] As well, Yost understood that espirit de corps was vital on any football team, and he exploited the training table for that purpose, too.[7]
- **A thick, diverse offensive playbook.** Whereas most of his coaching rivals were devoted disciples of whichever offensive sys-

tem they'd learned as players—usually Yale's, Princeton's, or Penn's—and whereas most coaches asked their players to master only a small number of basic plays with few tricky variations and but a handful of ball carriers, the flexible Yost was betrothed to no such precedents or limits. He happily borrowed schemes from all systems—whatever worked best. He then brainstormed waves of his own unique twists, formations, and plays, all of which he'd cram into a lethal, outsized hybrid offense. Most rival coaches could not even slot it, let alone stop it.[8]

- **Trial-and-error roster tinkering.** Each season, Yost aimed to experiment at every uncertain roster position until he was sure the best possible eleven started, and in the right spots. He did so in the early so-called practice games of late September and early October because there was little time either in spring practice or training camp, both of which were shorter in those days. That leading teams always played creampuffs early in their ten- to four-teen-game schedules enabled such a philosophy. Yost might try a man at end one week, then at fullback the next; or at quarterback, then at right halfback. He would settle on a starting eleven for the toughest games in November.

These weren't Yost's only tenets. Another was his insistence on "every man on every play." It was no cliché to Yost, especially on offense, where every player (legally) "helps to advance the ball either by pushing or pulling," *Michigan Alumnus* magazine said. "Strong individual players he considers very valuable, but experience has taught him that 11 weaker men working together are more efficient."[9] Three other Yost tenets—a sound kicking game, a stout defense, and an aversion to sloppy play and turnovers—would become his new cornerstone credos soon after the legalization of the forward pass in 1906.

Michigan teams for years had kicked off preseason camp at a waterside resort to better cope with the late-summer heat. Yost took his first Wolverine players just north of Ann Arbor, to Whitmore Lake, on September 9. They mustn't have known what hit them. Yost had instructed trainer Keene Fitzpatrick to work the group as never before.

On the field, Yost started off teaching his new charges only signal work, how to properly catch a ball, and how to pass it backward. That's it. Simultaneously, off the field, Yost began hammering into his players the "first principles" of football, captain White recalled. That is, "a thorough study and quiz upon the rules—something which had been sadly neglected in former years."[10]

As Yost then began installing his offensive and defensive schemes, he quickly deduced that much of his talent had been misused, and he began relocating his checkers all over the board. He switched Snow from end to fullback, Shorts from guard to right tackle, Ev Sweeley from fullback to halfback (and later to end), Ebin Wilson from center to right guard, Albert Herrnstein from halfback to right end and back, and so on. Yost tinkered well into November. The addition of Yost's three key imports—halfback Willie Heston, left guard Dan McGugin, and center Dad Gregory—necessitated some of these changes. Sweeley was the team's secret weapon. Few in the nation rivaled his abilities as punter, and his sure open-field tackling made him as reliable a deep man on defense as a team could hope to have.

Probably Yost's most cherished discovery at camp was quarterback Harrison "Boss" Weeks, who'd mostly watched from the sidelines in 1900 under head coach Biff Lea. Weeks was tiny by twenty-first-century standards but an average-sized quarterback for the day at five foot seven, 150 pounds. Quarterbacks could afford to be so small because they seldom ran with the ball; they barked signals and mostly handed off to others—a football coxswain, if you will. Weeks not only radiated the fearless, commanding personality Yost coveted in his field general, he possessed uncommon speed of mind, foot, and action, too.

The pieces all were in place. After two weeks at Whitmore Lake, Yost moved the squad back to UM. On September 23, a thousand students gathered at Regents Field to observe the first Yost practice held on campus. By that session's end, awed students coined their new coach a new nickname, according to the *Michigan Daily*:

> Coach Yost is electrifying the University. His boundless good nature, his ever-ready wit, his straightforwardness and determination [have] not only won the hearts and convictions of his men, but he is at the same time a hard master. [H]e kept his men on the running jump, and he worked as hard as they did. Did a mass play appear slow, there would come a hoarse cry of "Hurry up!" and down the field would come the coach, his red legs flying and an old gray, felt hat's wide brim flapping about his ears.

"Hurry up!" is going to be Coach Yost's title. It struck the students today and hit the right spot. If Michigan hurries up she will
win, is the sentiment. No names could be given by Michigan students more worthy of their dashing coach than his own favorite cry of
"Hurry up!"[11]

The nickname instantly stuck. For decades thereafter, many Americans
knew the coach as much by "Hurry Up" Yost as by his given names. And
pity any Wolverine player who did not hurry up in practice. Immobility
was not an option. "Spectators are not wanted on the field; their place is
in the grandstand," he wrote.[12]

Leading teams, such as Michigan, always played host in the so-called
practice games, and Albion College (located fifty miles west of Ann
Arbor) was first up for the Wolverines on September 28. Such undersized patsies usually left town with their muscles aching, their pride
equally bruised, and, if fortunate, enough cash from the paltry prear-
ranged guarantee—$100 to $400—to fund the trip and help offset some
of their season's expenses. While the rulebook called for thirty-five-
minute halves, usually only late-season showdowns lasted that long. By
contract, or sometimes after bitter bickering just before kickoff, practice games were much shorter—generally twenty- or twenty-five-minute halves.

The Yostmen pounded Albion 50–0 in twenty-minute halves. The
Methodists failed to pick up a first down and never advanced the ball
past their own forty-five-yard line. By contrast, Michigan scored on
almost every possession.

More astonishing to Michigan supporters was the precision and pace
at which the new Wolverines played. "[I]n contrast with the past few
years," the *Michigan Alumnus* noted, "the men did not loaf, played well
together, while not once were they compelled to ask for time because of
exhaustion, nor did they lose the ball on downs. The snap and vim put
into the work was marked."

Left tackle White scored three of Michigan's nine touchdowns on
tackle-back plays, and right tackle Shorts added another. The backs
scored the other five-pointers, two by returning left halfback Walt
Shaw. Late in the game Shaw gave way to his antsy backup, Heston, and
"the latter proved a whirlwind in bucking the line," the *Alumnus* said.[13]

More than a century later, Heston would remain one of the most
prolific touchdown scorers the college game has known, but he rang up

his first TD at Michigan on defense. He shot between Albion's right guard and center, stole the bobbling ball out of the quarterback's hands before he could pass it backward, and was gone. The *Chicago Tribune*'s correspondent praised Heston's "star work" and rated him the "biggest find so far among the newcomers."[14]

On October 5, the Wolverines crushed Case Scientific School of Cleveland 57–0 in twenty-minute halves. Case had not been shut out by anyone in years. Once again, the Wolverine defense was fairly impregnable, surrendering but one first down. The only scare occurred when Case blocked a fifteen-yard field-goal attempt by Michigan, and the visiting quarterback picked up the ball and took off, with clear sailing ahead. But Sweeley, the sure-tackling fullback on defense, tracked him down and rubbed out the threat at the Wolverine forty-five. Heston subbed in for Shaw in the second half, and he and Sweeley continually turned the corner around Case's ends to rip off long runs.

Proving their high-scoring start to the season was no fluke, the Wolverines blanked Indiana University 33–0 the following Saturday, in halves of twenty-five and twenty minutes. And that was in a steady drizzle on a "sea of mud" at Regents Field, which compelled both teams to attempt only the safest of offensive plays most of the time. That is, handoffs up the gut. The Hoosiers scrounged only one first down on the day and, like Albion, failed to advance the ball as far as midfield. Heston got his first start against Indiana and did not disappoint his rapidly growing fan base among the two thousand in attendance. He scored two touchdowns before sitting out the second half. "Sweeley, Snow and Heston are the best set of backs I have ever seen," Indiana coach James H. Horne said.[15]

After three games, newspapers noted that the Wolverines had scored 140 points in 125 minutes of play. Why was Yost going against the time-honored grain and running up such big scores in mere practice games? "Eat everybody up," Yost said by way of explanation. "Big or little, send 'em all the same way. A weak start is likely to end in a weak finish. We have to work all the time in order to do business properly."[16]

Next order of business: C. M. Hollister's undefeated Northwestern team. Determined this year to win the Western championship that had evaded them the year before, the "Methodists"—as they were nicknamed then—arrived in Ann Arbor for the October 19 game having lost only one of their previous fourteen contests dating back more than a year. And Northwestern hadn't been scored on in five 1901 victories.

Hollister's signature offensive brainchild was his "tandem" attack—the original I-formation. With huge, powerful blockers up front aligned in wide line splits (equally unusual for the time), Hollister had been confounding Western defenses with his deceptive new backfield formation. Yost was ready with a scheme to stop it, and Michigan smashed Northwestern 29–0 in twenty-five-minute halves before three thousand at Regents Field. The Methodists never crossed midfield in the opening half. To start the second half, they were awarded the ball at Michigan's ten-yard line on a fluke: Heston inadvertently forward-lateraled to Sweeley on the kickoff return, the penalty for which was a turnover. Down 12–0, Northwestern had a great chance to make a game of it, or at least score, but the Wolverines won the·ball back on downs at their two and punted out of danger. Thereafter, the Methodists crossed midfield only once and never came near scoring range, even for a field-goal attempt. Hollister's tandem was a dud. "Barring a few [six-yard] exceptions, the Michigan line hurled back the ponderous onslaught of purple guards," the *Chicago Tribune*'s correspondent wrote. "The location of the ball was no mystery to the Wolverine tacklers. The runner was picked off as easily as on an ordinary straight buck or end play."[17] Observers across the Midwest took note—Michigan was formidable.

Heston, meantime, lived up to all his newfound attention, scoring three touchdowns against Northwestern. The final two highlighted the game. Long touchdown runs were rare in 1901, yet Heston ripped off ones of fifty-five and forty yards. Long TD runs would become his trademark. At five foot eight, 180 pounds, Heston had world-class sprinter's speed and possessed vision, elusiveness, courage, and power to boot—about everything a coach could ever want in a running back, be it in 1901, 1951, or 2001. Once Heston got around end, or pierced through the line, forget it. He'd usually score because no one could catch him.

For the fourth time in four games, newspapers reported that while Michigan's players appeared in excellent physical condition up to the final whistle, their foes could not keep up. Continually during the second half of the Wolverines' latest win, "time was being taken out for the Northwestern men," according to the *Alumnus*.[18] Timeouts for injury back then were handled like those in soccer to this day: play was held up until the injured man either rose to his feet to resume play or was helped off the field.

UM backers were anxious to see how their Wolverines would fare against the next two opponents, the University of Buffalo (UB) and Carlisle, both respected teams that waged their gridiron wars in the East.

The Buffalo Bisons (later to be renamed the Bulls) had won four in a row, all by shutout. That included a 16–0 win over Lehigh in Bethlehem, Pennsylvania, and—in UB's greatest victory so far in football—a shocking 5–0 upset of Columbia in New York City. Columbia was good, having held the dominant team of the East in 1901, Harvard, to an 18–0 victory. Columbia later would nearly knock off the second best team in the East, Yale, losing 10–5, and would soundly defeat Penn 11–0.

The challenge to Buffalo posed by Yost's Wolverines, who had yet to face any team approaching Columbia's class, did not scare Bisons coach James B. "Turk" Gordon, his eleven Buffalo Bisons starters, nor his four substitutes as they rode the train to Ann Arbor. "Buffalo admirers expressed the opinion that the Michigans would not cross their line during the game," the *Detroit Free Press* reported. [19]

Few across the country believed the final score wired out from Ann Arbor late on the afternoon of Saturday, October 26: Michigan 128, Buffalo 0.

In halves of just thirty and twenty minutes, the Wolverines crossed the Buffalo goal line twenty-two times and converted eighteen of those. "[T]he entire football world is wondering how it was possible for one team to roll up such a gigantic score against the other in the short time given for play," a Buffalo newspaper commented two days later. [20]

Stanford's new coach, C. M. Fickert, wrote to his friend Yost: "I see by the papers that you defeated the University of Buffalo by 128 to 0. I at present doubt the score. . . . Let me know if this score is correct, as I never thought it possible of one team to so defeat another, especially when Buffalo was considered to be so strong." [21]

But the score was real, and every bit reflective of the play that day. Buffalo's players were badly out of shape. They could well get by with a ponderous brand of football in the East, where such was commonplace, but against Yost's supremely conditioned speedsters they were done for. The Bisons knew it early on and quickly lost heart. The Wolverines realized it and ruthlessly exploited the advantage, piling up touchdown, after touchdown, after touchdown.

Enabling Michigan to score so often was one of 1901 football's lingering traditions carried over from rugby, namely, the rule that called for the team that was just scored on to kick it right back to the scoring team, rather than receive the kickoff as in modern football. Teams did not complain about the rule. As in rugby, the thinking was that position on the field was far more important than possession of the ball. And position was more certain than possession in those days because the larger, more roundish ball of the day was harder to handle and nestle, and because the penalty for some infractions, such as holding and forward-passing, actually was a turnover—another rugby staple. Thus, after being scored upon, a team happily kicked off, so as to get the ball as far from its own goal as possible.

Buffalo kept kicking off to Michigan after every score, and many Bisons either were too winded, too incompetent, or too disheartened to bother trying to tackle the Wolverine kick returners; many of the Michigan touchdowns were scored on these well-blocked runbacks. Even when the Bisons did tackle the kick returner, within a few plays a Michigan ball carrier invariably would blast into the open up the middle or around the end and be gone for another score.

By the second half, Buffalo's players were completely gassed, even the four substitutes. Yost then agreed to break the rules in the Bisons' favor, allowing them to reinsert subbed-out players. Not that it helped any, and not that all subbed-out players wanted to go back in. Yost always liked to tell variations of this story:

> The score was about a hundred to nothin' when a Buffalo player comes a walkin' by the Meeshegan bench. He's wearin' patent leather pumps, and carryin' his football shoes. So our team hollers, "Where are ye goin'?" He says, "I'm goin' home! Our coach told us we were comin' daown here to get experience, and I've had enough!"[22]

In the end, Herrnstein scored five touchdowns for Michigan, Snow four, Arthur Redner four, Heston three, Sweeley three, Redden two, and Shorts one. Somewhere in there, the Bisons acquired the ball by penalty-turnover after a Michigan forward lateral inside the Wolverine thirty-five-yard line and attempted a field goal. No good. If not for a poor snap, Michigan's string of defensive goose eggs might have been broken. That hardly would have offset the ridiculous 1,261 all-purpose yards Michigan reportedly racked up that day. The Bisons had never seen anything in the East like the ruthless mix of pace, precision, and power exhibited by Yost's Wolverines.

"We are simply outclassed," Buffalo coach Gordon shrugged afterward. "Our team is stronger than when we rubbed it into Columbia, and it is just a matter of meeting a superior team. I do not think that there is a better eleven in the country than the one Michigan has in the field. I firmly believe that she can put it over any team in the country."[23] He continued: "Michigan has already developed the most wonderful teamwork I ever saw. I think that Michigan could take the conceit out of Yale, Harvard and Princeton, and I would like to see some game of this kind arranged."[24]

For "Hurry Up" Yost, personally, this was a breakthrough moment. For a few days he and his high-scoring Michigan Wolverines became the talk of the nation's sporting press.

Glenn A. "Pop" Warner, the former Cornell star, could relate. He coached the Carlisle Indian Industrial School in Carlisle, Pennsylvania, and he'd already been trumpeted as one of the country's top football coaches. On the day Michigan destroyed Buffalo, Warner's undersized Indians proved no match for the buzz saw of the East, Harvard, falling 29–0 in twenty-minute halves. Seven days later, his Indians would visit the buzz saw of the West, Michigan, at Bennett Park in Detroit. And they'd have to do it without their best player, injured captain/tackle Martin Wheelock—a former All-American in his eighth year (yes) of football. Although not a single Indian weighed as much as 180 pounds, Warner promised nonetheless that his team would not be "Buffalo-ed."

Michigan rooters enthused all week at the prospect of running up an even larger score on Carlisle than Harvard had. To do so might propagate the growing belief in Michigan circles that the Wolverines were the best team in the land. Yost, though, worried. Ever with a firm thumb on the pulse of his team's psyche, he sensed overconfidence. On Friday, Yost "gave them all a bracer in the shape of an old-fashioned tongue-lashing of the 'hurry-up' type," the *Chicago Tribune* reported.[25]

With 8,000 gathered at Detroit's Bennett Park on Saturday, November 2, opening kickoff was delayed as the two future Hall of Fame head coaches, Warner and Yost, bickered over the length of the halves. Warner insisted on twenty-five minutes, Yost on thirty. When neither backed down, they split the difference—twenty-seven and a half.

Michigan won 22–0. One month into the Yost regime, already it had come to this: Wolverine backers bemoaned the result. Harvard had scored seven more points against the Indians than Michigan did, and in fifteen fewer minutes of play. As in previous contests, Michigan dominated the early going and led 16–0 at the half, Heston scoring once. And, as usual, the Wolverines stifled virtually every regular offensive play call of their opponent, whether between the tackles or around end. Warner, though, had a Plan B. As possessor of one of the most imaginative offensive minds football has known, Warner in the second half hauled out his famous "wing shift" plays—"when almost the entire battering force is moved to one side of the line," the *Chicago Tribune* described.[26] For the first time all season, a Wolverine opponent gained ground consistently. Although UM defenders could not solve the Carlisle trick, they did limit its gains. The plucky Indians never threatened the UM goal but retained possession enough to limit Michigan to a single second-half touchdown.

Warner appeared bitter afterward, having been warned and penalized "fatiguingly" frequently by game officials for coaching from the sidelines, even venturing onto the field at times to shout instructions.[27] The easterner growled to reporters, "We had in five green men today. If we had been in the same condition when we met Cornell, I think we would have licked Michigan. . . . As far as comparing Michigan with Harvard I would say that they are not in the same class at all. Harvard can put it all over Michigan." Yost, his pride ruffled by the result, countered by saying "we would have had two more touchdowns in the first half but for bad fumbles."[28]

One week later, a Michigan football team knocked heads with the Ohio State University Buckeyes for the first time in Columbus. Some 375 train-transported UM students joined more than three thousand others at Ohio Field. The Bucks were undefeated, albeit against small fry. No matter, heavier by an average of ten pounds per man, the gallant Buckeyes stymied the Wolverines in the early going on four consecutive forays inside the OSU five-yard line, when UM either ran out of downs or fumbled. The Michigan offense struggled to find its rhythm owing to a tactic many teams would employ to disrupt the Yostmen's onslaught, as the *Detroit Free Press* explained: "On almost every scrimmage some

Ohio man would stretch out on the ground and take the full time [for injury recovery]. This playing for wind was so apparent that the Michigan players finally burlesqued it. The Ohio men could not stand the gag. [T]heir doctors and trainers ran more yards than both teams put together."[29] As halftime approached, quarterback Boss Weeks found the weak spot in the OSU line, its right side, and attacked it repeatedly, if not rhythmically. The Wolverines quickly ran up sixteen points before the break, which included Heston exploding for a forty-yard score. After Snow added an unconverted second-half touchdown, the Bucks attempted a late field goal from the Michigan twenty-five but missed it. The Wolverines won 21–0 in halves thirty minutes.

On Saturday, November 16, it was Stagg's turn next to face a Yost-coached Michigan team—one reaching its zenith of confidence and performance.

✼ ✼ ✼

Stagg's Maroons opened 1901 with five shutout victories, all against pure practice-game piffle: Lombard, Monmouth, Milwaukee Medical, Knox, and Illinois Wesleyan. Stagg still feared the worst and explained why in an October 9 letter to a recruit from Utah who couldn't free himself to come east: "We had a very serious lot of hard luck, in that five men like yourself, whom we felt sure would be here this fall, left us or changed their plans, and we are now battling with a lot of green material, and much of it mediocre, to bring out a team that will not dishonor the University."[30] After the 5–0 start, UC lost thrice and tied twice heading into its last two games: against old rival Michigan, in Ann Arbor, and twelve days later at home on Thanksgiving Day against Wisconsin. Both foes were undefeated—the clear-cut class of the West.

Stagg always kept close tabs on his western foes. His surviving clippings scrapbooks and folders indicate he subscribed to dozens of newspapers, east and west; occasionally, he handwrote notes or corrections onto the clippings. So Stagg knew what awaited his Maroons in Ann Arbor.

There was no overconfidence on the home side. Henry M. Bates, the power-broking UM alumnus in Chicago, for years had known Stagg, and for years had known people in Stagg's inner circle. Three days before the game he sent this warning to Baird, an apt representation of the extent to which the resourceful Stagg—a brilliant football tactician in his own right—had spooked the entire Michigan fan base:

> From a man close to Stagg, I learned today that Stagg feels that our defense has never been tested—and that he hopes by vicious pounding the line, doubtless at tackles, to break us down. He believes that Heston is a good runner, but on the grandstand order and not anxious to take the hard knocks of defensive playing. It is hard to say where his attack will fall, but you can rest assured he has planned especially and shrewdly for what he considers our weak spot. . . .
>
> There is no doubt but that Stagg and his men are [growing] more confident every day. It may sound foolish to say so, in view of the records of the two teams this year, but I tell you it is absolutely essential that every man do his best in that game—or we will lose. . . . We have had experiences with Chicago before, when it seemed as if we could not fail to win, and if we lose this time through overconfidence, words will fail to express the feelings of our alumni. Football experts all unite in saying that Chicago has braced wonderfully and that she is coming very fast this week.[31]

Stagg not only was the equal of Yost and Pop Warner in schematic creativity, he'd been at it for twice as long. Probably because his line was so weak and his backs so unspectacular, Stagg needed a wrinkle in 1901. Thus, he concocted the "Whoa-Back" formation, merely his latest incarnation of something not only permitted but widely exploited before 1910, when a team could drop a lineman into the backfield. In Whoa-Back, a beefy lineman would line up directly behind the fullback and either block for the ball carrier or help to shove him forward from behind.[32]

Whoa-Back didn't help Chicago's cause against Michigan. Nothing did. The Wolverines smacked Chicago by the largest score so far in the ten-year series, 22–0, in thirty-five-minute halves. Conditions at Regents Field were miserable in every respect. The playing surface was a mess, and only 3,500 locals—and a dozen UC supporters—braved the cold, wind, and falling snow.

Almost the entire game was played on the Maroons' side of the field. Only once did Chicago have possession of the ball in Michigan territory, and that was after a short punt; the Maroons then gained only one yard to the Michigan forty-six and punted it back. "It was clearly demonstrated that the only way in which the Maroons could score was on a fluke," the *Detroit Free Press* reported, "and the fluke did not show up."[33]

Chicago picked up only three first downs, one a fifteen-yard gainer off a fake punt—a Stagg invention and one of his pet trick plays. The *Chicago Tribune*'s drive-by-drive game "diagram" reveals Michigan outgained the Maroons 144 yards to 36 in the first half and 258 to 8 in the second, for a final 369 to 44 discrepancy.[34]

For the eighth time in eight Michigan games in 1901, reports noted how only opposing players appeared winded. The second half "dragged out to an almost interminable length owing to the time out taken by the Chicago team," the *Tribune* said.[35] The *Chicago Record-Herald* described it best:

> The tactics of the Chicago team . . . interfered with the rapid style of the Michigan game. The [Maroons] team, of course, was in poor condition, and after every scrimmage, over the ball three or four of them would be lying stretched on the field. Many of these cases of injury were genuine, doubtless, but many more were believed to be pure faking. Michigan almost always lined up on the jump, and then had to allow its ardor to cool while the Chicago players were picking one another up and soothing their bruises.[36]

The score could have been much worse. "If it had been a perfect field Michigan would have scored at will," the *Free Press* observed.[37] As well, the Wolverines fumbled twice deep in Chicago territory, and the final whistle cut short another long Michigan possession at the Chicago two. What's more, the strong play of Chicago's ends, freshman Fred Speik and James MacNabb, plus the slop compelled quarterback Weeks to throw out most of the Wolverine playbook and restrict UM's attacks to between the tackles—effective but deliberate. Yost afterward crowed about the big win, naturally, but wanted a larger score: "We outplayed Chicago at every point, I think. . . . If it hadn't been for [the fumbles] we should have had three more touchdowns." Stagg tipped his cap, although he suggested the conditions hampered his squad more. "On a good field Michigan would not have had such easy work with us," he said. "The Wolverine play was consistent throughout and shows careful training. Chicago's poor offense was a chief factor in the result. . . . I expected the Michigan score to be anywhere from twelve to eighteen points."[38]

Upon his return home, Stagg acted as he usually did after a team clobbered him on the field: he counterpunched as hard as he could off of it.

Days after the game, Stagg filed a protest to UM authorities, charging that starting Wolverine left end Curtis Redden was a professional, for evidently pocketing an eleven-dollar prize as a youth after having won sprint races at a town sports meet. UM authorities mulled the matter while Redden on the following Saturday played in Michigan's fifteen-touchdown 89–0 destruction of Beloit in thirty-minute halves—a near repeat of the Buffalo slaughter.

Upon launching a full investigation the following week, UM decided to hold Redden out of the regular-season finale against Iowa. Why hadn't Stagg protested Redden before Chicago's game in Ann Arbor? Perhaps he hadn't been tipped about Redden in time. More likely, he surmised that his team had no hope of winning in Ann Arbor anyway, and protesting beforehand only would have sent the message to everyone, including his own players, that he was desperate.

Not that Michigan's success against the Hawkeyes hinged on Redden's presence. The Wolverines crushed the Hawkeyes 50–0 on Thanksgiving Day at West Side Baseball Park in Chicago in thirty-five-minute halves. Wolverine fans had hoped their team would put up forty-nine on the Hawkeyes, to allow Michigan to become the first team

Figure 7.1. Stagg watched from the sideline (far right) as Yost's Michigan Wolverines crushed his Chicago Maroons in Ann Arbor in 1901. *Source:* Bentley Historical Library, University of Michigan.

in the West to crash through the 500-point barrier in a season. Yost and the boys obliged, surpassing the threshold by one. It was sweet revenge, too—both for veteran UM players, who'd taken a thorough 28–5 thumping from Dr. Knipe's Hawkeyes the year before, and for Yost, whose Nebraska Cornhuskers in 1898 had been upset 6–5 by Knipe's Iowa charges.

As for Redden, when the UM Board in Control of Athletics interviewed him, he claimed he had never known about the eleven dollars in prize money. If it was offered, he presumed he was guilty nonetheless because his father would have pocketed the money. But Redden's father, apparently a lawyer in good standing, later appeared before the UM board and swore that he'd declined the prize money. Signed affidavits from officials of the games supported his claim. UM thus happily rejected Stagg's protest and reinstated Redden, albeit after the regular season.[39]

Stagg also attempted to hurt Michigan—and Iowa—in the ledger. He still despised it when other schools scheduled games "in his backyard," calling it "the height of impertinence and discourtesy" and "vulgar."[40] Michigan and Iowa authorities had long since set an eleven o'clock Thanksgiving Day kickoff for their game, so that a Chicagoan so inclined might attend both big games staged that day in the Windy City—UM–Iowa followed by the midafternoon Chicago–Wisconsin tilt. A few days before Thanksgiving, though, Stagg moved the Maroons–Badgers kickoff to noon, killing the doubleheader possibility. UM and Iowa authorities were livid, but nine to ten thousand still attended their game, and each school cleared $2,500. About a thousand fewer fans showed up at UC's Marshall Field on the south side to watch Phil King's undefeated Badgers destroy what was left of Stagg's Maroons 35–0.[41]

Football fans and writers across the West, even Stagg, lobbied for a postseason Michigan–Wisconsin game to settle the Championship of the West. There was no chance the game would take place, however. The Badgers might have welcomed it, even if they publicly stated otherwise. But UM authorities and alumni remained mighty bitter toward Wisconsin.

Michigan's beef with Wisconsin athletic leaders wasn't so much because it had suddenly backed out of the Michigan/Wisconsin/Illinois boycott of Stagg and his UC sports teams in 1899, but because UM felt backstabbed in the process. Stagg had split up the triumvirate by convincing UW president Charles R. Van Hise and athletic director John L. Fisher to schedule a postseason game in '99 between their teams to decide Western honors. As further enticement, Stagg dangled two future Thanksgiving Day games at Marshall Field, in place of Michigan, in 1901 and 1902. The Badgers jumped at it, with the two sides keeping the 1902 arrangement secret from Michigan and the press for more than a year.[42]

Michigan athletic authorities could hardly have thought less of their Wisconsin counterparts as late as January 1902. That's when Baird privately remarked to alumnus Bates that it seemed "Wisconsin and Chicago have an understanding [and] are determined to put us in a hole," and when Baird's boss—UM Board in Control faculty chairman Albert H. Pattengill—confided to Bates that while it might be "good politics and good money" to play Wisconsin in football, "they are so nasty, selfish & treacherous that I am in no hurry to make up with them. Let them wait a while."[43]

Stagg could not even bait the Wolverines into a December 1901 showdown against the Badgers when he said, "I am absolutely certain that if a postseason game should be played, Wisconsin would beat Michigan."[44]

Instead, the Wolverines looked forward to the team's first West Coast trip over the Holidays. Stagg had been the first coach to take a college team west during the Christmas break—after the 1894 season, to play Stanford both in San Francisco and Los Angeles. Michigan's venture west had been in the works all year, although details constantly changed. At one point, Michigan considered a full West Coast swing against three teams: the University of Washington in Seattle, Cal in San Francisco, and Stanford in Pasadena. Ultimately, only the latter was arranged, as a sporting spectacle on New Year's Day to follow the annual Tournament of Roses parade—later remembered as the first Rose Bowl game. Michigan's opponent would be Stanford—Yost's team the year before—which had defeated Cal again 12–0 to win the Pacific Coast championship.

The Wolverines' train departed Ann Arbor on December 17 in subfreezing cold with six inches of snow on the ground. Eight days later, the Michigan party of nineteen—fifteen players, Yost, Baird, trainer Fitzpatrick, and student manager Harry Crafts—arrived in Los Angeles. One local paper listed reasons Stanford should win, including the fact that if Heston from San Jose Normal could win a starting spot, then the Wolverines couldn't be that good.

Four days before the game, Yost asked Stanford captain Ralph Fisher if the teams could play twenty-five-minute halves instead of thirty-five because of the heat. No way, Fisher replied. Those who'd bought tickets were entitled to get their money's worth.

On New Year's Day morning, the Wolverines took part in the Tournament of Roses parade, riding in a large carriage. Then they prepared for the afternoon game. The temperature reached the mid eighties— unseasonably hot. Stands had been built to accommodate 2,500 but reported estimates placed the overflow throng anywhere between six and eight thousand.

Stanford could do little on offense but on defense kept Michigan in check for a while. The game was scoreless through fifteen minutes of play. Thereafter, the Wolverines dominated and won, going away 49–0. The heat ultimately did not slow down the Wolverines a bit. [45]

At one point in the second half, Stanford captain Fisher approached Yost on the Michigan sideline to throw in the towel. No siree, Yost replied—the spectators were entitled to get their full money's worth. But then, with eight minutes remaining, Fisher approached his counterpart, White, and pleaded: "If you are willing, sir, we are ready to quit." White agreed. Ball game. [46]

Motivated by digs in the local press, Heston had continually ripped off big gains, finishing with 170 yards on eighteen carries as the Wolverines piled up 527 yards of offense. In his final collegiate game, fullback Neil Snow scored five of Michigan's eight touchdowns—a Rose Bowl record that still stood 111 years later and might never be broken.

Michigan thus finished its first season under Yost with an 11–0–0 record, tied with 9–0–0 Wisconsin for the Big Nine title and the Championship of the West. The Wolverines on the season outscored their foes 555 points to zero, the Badgers 317 to 5.

Official uniform national record keeping for college football statistics did not begin until 1937, so there is no way to verify one official Big Ten history's claim that the 1901 Wolverines "steamrollered for 8,000 yards" in eleven games. [47] As a historical comparison, only two teams in top-level NCAA history entering the 2014 season had ever passed the 8,000-yard barrier in a season: the 2011 Houston Cougars (with 8,387 in

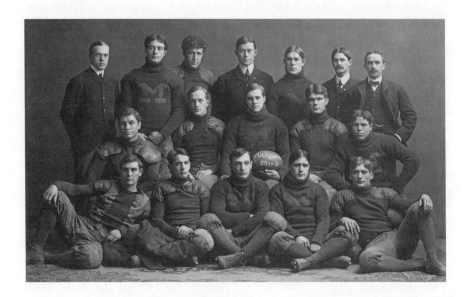

Figure 7.2.   The 1901 Michigan Wolverines, Champions of the West. Front row:
Everett Sweeley, Harrison "Boss" Weeks, Curtis Redden, Arthur Redner, Al
Herrnstein. Middle row: Ebin Wilson, Neil Snow, captain Hugh White, Bruce
Shorts, Willie Heston. Back row: student manager Harry Crafts, Dan McGugin,
George "Dad" Gregory, coach Fielding H. Yost, Herb Graver, athletic director
Charles Baird, trainer Keene Fitzpatrick. *Source:* Bentley Historical Library, Uni-
versity of Michigan.

fourteen games, for an average of 599) and the 2013 Baylor Bears (with
8,044 in thirteen games, for a 619 average). The NCAA record for most
total yards per game in a season was set by the Houston Cougars, but in
1989, with 625. The only other team to eclipse the 600-yards-per-game
mark is the 2013 Baylor Bears. If true that the 1901 Wolverines gained
as many as 8,000 yards, then even 8,000 flat in eleven games would
equate to 727 per game.

As impressive as Yost's hurry-up offense had been, the defense
might have been as impregnable as any in the history of the game—and
not just because of the shutouts. The longest gain Michigan allowed all
season was fifteen yards, and not once on a scrimmage play did a runner
squeeze through the first ten Wolverines so that deep safety Sweeney
had to make a saving tackle; Sweeney's lone touchdown-saving stop
came on Case's return of a blocked Michigan field-goal attempt.

Only decades after the fact did the Helms Foundation, in 1941, rate the 1901 Wolverines number one in all of college football. Over the decades, other college football research foundations that awarded national championships retroactively followed suit. Not until the 1910s, though, would any prominent sports writer in the East have so much as considered awarding the mythical national championship to any team outside the East. In 1901, Harvard was everybody's choice. No polls of coaches or writers existed until the late 1930s. The opinions of a few select but hardly unbiased experts—such as Walter Camp and Caspar Whitney—held sway. So infused were Camp, Whitney, and others in their Eastern bias, Michigan could have scored eight hundred points in 1901 and not been given any more consideration for number one. Only four years earlier, Camp had yet even to deem a football player from the West worthy of a spot on his annual All-America first team, and no western man until Stagg in 1904 was allowed on the rules committee run by Camp.

Whitney ranked Michigan third nationally in 1901, behind Harvard and Yale. "In style of game, in running with the ball, and in punting," Whitney wrote of Michigan and Wisconsin, "these two teams stand up well up towards the very head of American football; in handling of kicks and in highly developed team play, however, they are quite a bit inferior to the eastern leaders."[48] That was an odd comment, seeing as Yost claimed Michigan fumbled but one punt all season.

Ann Arborites felt Michigan was indeed the top team in the land, of course. It was quite a change from twelve months earlier, when the Wolverine football program was in abject disarray, with relations between warring factions so bad that a crossroads meeting of key faculty, alumni, students, and others had to be called.[49] Yost had consolidated everybody with what the *Chicago Inter Ocean* described as his "perfectly organized machine": "There was not a loose screw—not a bearing that needed oil. It worked smoothly, regularly, brilliantly."[50] The "machine" analogy soon would be used so often by sports writers and headline writers it would become passé.

But would the machine's designer and chief manufacturer return to Michigan in 1902? Yost had never spent more than one season at any coaching stop, and Baird had signed Yost to only a one-year deal. By Thanksgiving there already had been rumors that Penn out east was anxious to replace the outgoing George Woodruff with Yost.

Baird didn't wait. By the first week of December he locked up Yost contractually for three more seasons—and raised Yost's salary by $450, to $2,750 per year plus expenses.[51]

With Yost and eight starting Wolverines due to return in 1902—including Weeks at quarterback, Heston and all the halfbacks, and Sweeley, the remarkable punter—the chances Michigan would be all-powerful again appeared strong. As strong as Stagg's newfound resolve to upgrade his talent so that, some day, he could wipe that wide smile right off the face of the gloating, vagabond coach from the hicks.

8

1902 OFF THE FIELD

Stagg's Empire Fights Back

Ever has it been the case, and ever will it be: when a university's most powerful football-boosting alumni raise hell about the state of the team and pointedly suggest solutions, even an iconic head coach and entrenched school president will be all ears. Then all action.

Perhaps the first such example in college football history occurred in 1901, during a Thanksgiving eve banquet at the University of Chicago. It was the night before the Maroons' season-ending, humiliating loss to the Wisconsin Badgers. At one point during the three-hour get-together, the nearly one hundred alumni on hand punted the rah-rah mood and charged forward with their dissatisfactions, in a revolving mass on tackle. One after another, in "very strong" speeches, the alums charged that Phil King's UW Badgers and now Fielding H. Yost's UM Wolverines had left Amos Alonzo Stagg's UC Maroons in the dust—thanks largely to much more aggressive means of talent procurement. Alums argued that Stagg had been far too lax in that regard, according to the *Chicago Inter Ocean*'s look back on the epochal banquet a year later.

> [Alumni] thought the university has still a good bit to learn from the management in other institutions with respect to "rounding" athletic material. It is a well-known fact that Michigan and Wisconsin and other universities to a greater or [lesser] degree make strenuous efforts to get on the good side of as much freshman material as possible. These alumni argued that Chicago has always had a back

seat when the scramble for freshmen began, and that it ought to
wake up and see that prominent freshmen should have just as good
an opportunity to become acquainted with Chicago.[1]

In reality, behind the scenes Stagg hadn't been exactly a backseat rider.
At times, he might even have had the firmest grip on the reins. No
matter, Stagg and UC president William Rainey Harper listened pa-
tiently and intently to the disgruntled.

More than any other, Stagg understood his football situation was
dire. Over the past two seasons his Maroons had won only two of eleven
conference games, and twelve of twenty-five overall. With a mostly
unpromising group of grunts due to return in 1902, an instant talent
upgrade not only seemed a good idea, it was mandatory.

So Stagg and Harper both enthusiastically acquiesced to the alumni's demands. Stagg happily informed the same gathering one year later
that they'd opened his eyes. "In calm and steady tones Stagg admitted
that his previous course had been too strict," the *Inter Ocean* reported

Figure 8.1.   Stagg (left) had a tremendous ally in University of Chicago President
William Rainey Harper (right), perhaps the first American university leader who
was wholly sympathetic to intercollegiate athletics. *Source:* Amos Alonzo Stagg
Papers, Special Collections Research Centre, University of Chicago Library.

in November 1902, "and that [UC leaders were not] ashamed to use reasonable and honourable means to become acquainted with good athletes in high schools."[2] Harper even made it UC policy—a radical concept in an era when universities and their athletic leaders tried to jam the ridiculous concept down the public's throat that the boys sought out the university, not vice versa. A few months following the 1901 banquet, Harper submitted to Chicago's Board of Physical Culture and Athletics a seven-resolution plan—most of it suggested by Stagg—to reorganize the "Physical Culture work," according to UC historian and Stagg scholar Robin Lester. The resolutions, Lester wrote,

> were passed in a form both dignified and vague enough to pass faculty review; their effect was the widespread recruitment of school-boy athletes. Six of the seven resolutions served as Stagg's manifesto to recruit in a more open manner, and they formed an outline of his future recruitment activities.[3]

Harper not only supported the initiative, he led it. Unlike nearly all of his peers, especially Michigan's James B. Angell, Harper was one university president who saw value in a formidable football team, especially the free publicity it garnered nationwide for his fledgling university. Harper had reassured Stagg just the year before that, as president, he'd never "take a step which will seriously disturb the athletic situation. You may be very certain of that."[4]

Harper himself brainstormed one of the resolutions—that nine UC-affiliated prep schools in Illinois and Indiana should become dedicated talent-feeder schools for Stagg, as well as places where ex-Maroons could be rewarded with sports-related jobs. Stagg and Harper did not intend merely to get back into the recruiting game; they intended to win it—decisively. Their key resolution was to identify top-end high school athletes in the Midwest, reach out to them in a mass-mailing campaign, and cozy up to as many as possible.[5]

This ambitious enterprise paid big dividends straightaway. Of Stagg's 1902 football recruits, not only would six start and nine earn letters as freshmen, but three eventually would become All-Americans, at a time when you could count on one hand the number of All-Americans the entire West had ever produced. The trio: rough-and-tumble fullback Hugo Bezdek from Chicago's Lake High School; end Mark Catlin from

West Aurora High School in nearby Aurora, Illinois; and tackle Roswell Tripp from a high school in Pottstown, Pennsylvania. Tripp would transfer and become an All-American at Yale.

While Stagg henceforth concentrated his revitalized recruitment efforts on the high school ranks, he'd long seen the value in Yost's preference of luring older, grizzled players from other colleges. Stagg's big catch of 1902 was John Koehler, who'd helped the University of Nebraska win eight of ten games in 1901 and earn acclaim as one of the best teams in the West. A center on coach Bummy Booth's Cornhuskers, Koehler would switch to tackle under Stagg.

Another resolution in UC's new athletic policy allowed Stagg to level the field in the recruitment of athletes in track and field, the third most popular intercollegiate sport in the West after football and baseball. Conference schools, such as Michigan, Minnesota, and Illinois, for years had been staging spring track-and-field meets for Midwestern high school stars. Now Stagg, too, would host the cream of the young crop for an entire weekend, putting them up in dorms on his campus— only he'd outdo his rivals. Stagg would invite some forty high school teams, featuring virtually all of the best runners, jumpers, and throwers across the Midwest, and treat them like royalty. By 1905, UC would rule the West in track and field.[6]

As explained previously, Stagg for years had been cleverly enticing Chicago-area high school football players onto his UC football field. Each season in early September he'd arrange for either his varsity or freshmen team to play exhibition games against the most talent-laden high school teams of Chicago, including Hyde Park, Englewood, and North Division. He'd even scrimmage midweek against these teams throughout the season rather than exclusively against his own scrubs, as Michigan and other top universities did. Following that epochal alumni banquet of 1901, Stagg expanded on this subtle, ingenious recruiting tactic by immediately allowing all Chicago-area high school athletes the free, unfettered use of UC athletic facilities at least twice a week. "Coach Stagg . . . has been unusually good to all the local high school teams during the winter," the *Chicago Tribune* noted on March 31, 1902. "Stagg's new policy seems to have frightened the outsiders."

Indeed, UW athletic leaders felt compelled to top that one, and far less subtly, per the *Tribune*:

The Hyde Park High School baseball and track teams have been invited to spend their spring vacations at Madison, Wis., as guests of the University of Wisconsin. . . . At present the South Side high school is turning out a fine bunch of athletes, and it is well worth the while of the colleges to "rush" the local boys. . . . The Hyde Park football team played at Wisconsin last fall and reported a good time. The members of the two teams who will make the trip are delighted over the prospects. [7]

Western colleges' all-sports recruiting wars would get far nastier and intense.

☼ ☼ ☼

Western football scheduling for 1902 was held up in January until Michigan, Chicago, and Wisconsin could figure out if, when, and where they might play one another.

Still miffed that Michigan and Iowa had played in Chicago on Thanksgiving Day 1901, Stagg refused to schedule any more games with UM unless it agreed to never again play a team other than the Maroons in Chicago, unless it had UC's blessing. Baird refused. This latest impasse was eventually smoothed over by Chicago lawyer Henry M. Bates, the most influential UM alumnus on athletic matters. Bates and Stagg agreed on a framework for a three-year football contract that would see the Wolverines play the Maroons in Chicago in both 1902 (in mid-November) and 1903 (on Thanksgiving Day), and in Ann Arbor in 1904 (in mid-November). Eventually, Michigan acquiesced and surrendered Chicago turf to Stagg. [8]

Many UM fans were livid at Baird over this, believing he alone controlled Wolverine athletic matters. [9] That was untrue. On broad policy matters, including relations with other universities, Baird surely had a say, but in the end he merely carried out the wishes and decisions of the faculty-run Board in Control of Athletics. That was the case here. The chairman of the UM Board in Control of Athletics in this era—Albert H. Pattengill—dispatched alumnus Bates to mop up the Stagg–Baird mess. When he did so, Pattengill addressed his friend as follows, with tongue poking through cheek: "Mr. Henry M. Bates, Envoy Extraordinaire and Minister Plenipotentiary at the Court of Sir Alonzo de Stagg." [10]

Under what circumstances might Stagg ever agree to allow Michigan to play another team in Chicago? Why, of course, when UC's Marshall Field played host to the game—for a handsome rental fee. When Pattengill and UM athletic leaders decided to bury their ill will toward their Wisconsin counterparts, it only made sense that the first game in three years pitting the Wolverines against the Badgers should be played in Chicago—on neutral ground. With both teams returning most of their squads, there promised to be tremendous interest in the 1902 showdown. When the two sides agreed to play, Stagg gladly allowed his Marshall Field to stage it—for 10 percent of the gate.[11]

If that Michigan–Wisconsin game might decide two Championships of the West—1902 as well as 1901, retroactively—then a Wolverine matchup against the defending Champion of the East, Harvard, might similarly settle two years of national honors. At Yost's urging, Baird tried to convince Harvard authorities to schedule the intersectional showdown. Harvard declined. After a few too many close scares in the 1890s, the Big Four of the East understood they had everything to lose and little to gain by facing a Champion of the West. An even bigger hurdle for any East-versus-West showdown was when to schedule such a game. Eastern powers reserved late November for their rivalry games against one another. And, as in the West, late September and early

Figure 8.2.   Albert H. Pattengill (right), a professor of Greek, was the faculty chairman of Michigan's Board in Control of Athletics. He relied heavily on Chicago alumnus and future UM law dean Henry M. Bates (center) to both draw up and guide UM athletic policy, while athletic director Charles Baird (left) merely enacted it. *Source:* Bentley Historical Library, University of Michigan.

October schedule spots were reserved for practice-game pushovers and middleweight wannabes. That left late October or early November, and playing a difficult game against a Western power in late October would require peaking too early for the easterners' liking, while playing it in early November might take too much out of a squad just before the late November rivalry games.[12]

No matter, Michigan was not done pounding on the Big Four's doors.

✸ ✸ ✸

Yost spent his 1902 off-season back home in West Virginia, which he discovered was "on the boom. I never saw or heard of so many investments," he wrote to Baird. "Millions are being invested in coal lands alone."[13] There just wasn't enough time in one year, or energy in one man, to squeeze out of turn-of-the-twentieth-century America all that Yost could conceive in mining and in football. "If I had been here in the state the last two years I would have made a fortune," he told Baird. "So many opportunities gone by. I ought to quit the football business for good but it seems I cannot bear to give it up."[14]

Predictably, football never was far from Yost's mind during those seven months in West Virginia. From various communities and backwoods posts within the state, he chicken-scratched or typed at least seventeen letters to Baird. Each time Yost implored—no, begged—Baird to help him "hustle" for new first-rate Wolverines.

While at first Yost had only three departing players from his 1901 champions to worry about replacing—the graduating trio of Ebin Wilson (guard), Hugh White (left tackle), and Neil Snow (fullback)—shortly after the Michigan team's return from California, he lost a vital fourth. The other tackle, captain-elect Bruce Shorts, survived an acute case of appendicitis in January, but doctors told him he could never play football again.[15] Walter Camp had called Shorts "the most brilliant tackle the Middle West produced" in 1901.[16]

The bad roster news kept coming for Michigan. Baird soon informed Yost that backup varsity end Arthur Redner was transferring to the Michigan College of Mines for academic reasons, and—worst of all—by March, there was uncertainty as to whether any of quarterback Boss

Weeks, halfback Willie Heston, or Yost's two-star import linemen from 1901, Dad Gregory and Dan McGugin, would return in the fall.

Internal UM letters reveal that Heston and Gregory both encountered money problems in the second semester of the 1901–1902 school year. Yost informed Baird on February 26, just after the start of second semester, that he'd sent Heston twenty dollars, making it fifty total he had "given" him, and that Gregory "wrote me and said he wished to borrow $50 from me. If he had that he could stay in college until June. If not he would be compelled to leave." UM's second semester in those days continued into early June.[17]

This is the only surviving correspondence in the UM files of these years indicating that Yost might ever have directly paid (not loaned) any UM football player a dollar or arranged for the same. For decades, it was believed—even by UM old-timers after the turn of the twenty-first century—that Yost had wantonly paid his point-a-minute players money. One of the big reasons so many faculty members at universities in the West and East, as well as a chunk of the public, fought to stop football's runaway popularity wagon is because it was believed high-salaried coaches would use some of their lucrative earnings to buy players. Surviving letters in the UM files suggest Yost loaned a few bucks here and there, but that seems to be it.[18]

Besides, Yost didn't seem to have much patience or respect for handout seekers. By April 23, 1902, Heston was asking for yet more money, and an exasperated Yost told Baird he suspected Heston's West Coast friend, Gregory, "puts him up to much of it as he wants a slice of it. I should hate to see Heston go as he is a good one, but I really believe it would be best if Gregory is gone."[19]

In that same letter regarding another possible recruit, Yost lamented that "all the good men to be had are so everlasting poor." Remember, there were no athletic scholarships at the time and most young men from the Appalachians westward grew up in rural, lower-class households. Lining up financial assistance of some kind was a necessity for most potential recruits.

All the off-season roster uncertainty shook Yost. He had no intention merely to be a one-year wonder at Michigan, especially after signing his shiny new three-year deal. As his off-season energy and panic gauges redlined, Yost resolved to work ceaselessly on the recruiting front—as he made all too clear in letter after letter to poor Baird. A mere sampling:

> Shall do all I can to locate any good men and turn them our way if possible. Urge all the boys to do this. (January 31)

> We must hustle hard for men. . . . We certainly need to hustle to keep up our end. (February 9)

> Where we can get any lineman I do not know, they are scarce. . . . Shall look out all I can for any good men. I have one or two likely ones in sight. (March 14)

> We truly must hustle if we are to be in the running next season as all our opponents will strengthen and we will be the object of them all. . . . Keep every one on the lookout for good men. (April 19)

> We certainly must hustle for men. Our schedule will be a very hard one to win as some of our opponents will be very strong. (May 5)

> It is up to us [to] hustle for all we are worth, for after all it is on you and I to do the hustling, others will help some but we must do the main work. (June 10)

> That game with Wisconsin will be for blood and I hear from all sides how they are hustling for men and that they are determined to win. Michigan men must wake up and hustle. It is often true that a weak team follows a strong one in nearly all the universities, this is due almost entirely to the fact that every one thinks, oh we will win, and does nothing to make a winning team. Urge every one to hustle, we must do it to win, and if we do it we will win, and if we do not we will meet defeat. (July 15)

> You can rest assured that Wisconsin will do every thing in the world to win and we must be just as determined. . . . Hope to be with you soon and you must hustle every way you can. (August14)[20]

If the above run of excerpts does not reveal how maniacally, relentlessly forcible Yost could become on any issue that consumed him, nothing can.

Not even an angry mule could slow the man down. Somewhere in West Virginia that summer, as Yost hustled and rustled about, "he was kicked by a mule below the knee," quarterback Weeks informed Baird on August 3, "but I guess he can get about. Wonder that the jar didn't injure the mule too."[21]

No doubt adding to Yost's and Baird's off-season concerns were Chicago's reinvigorated recruiting efforts. As early as April, Baird had been tipped that Stagg personally made "tempting offers" to a pair of crackerjack athletes from Nebraska, according to UM alumnus Charles G. McDonald of Omaha.[22]

Michigan, of course, countered UC with its own brand of tempting offers (i.e., loans). In the end, Heston, Gregory, McGugin, and Weeks all returned for the 1902–1903 school year—thanks to menial campus jobs arranged by Baird and shortfall-covering loans provided by wealthy UM alumni.

One such alumnus was Henry J. Killilea, a prominent lawyer in Milwaukee and former Wolverine lettermen himself in 1883–1884. In 1899, Killilea had founded baseball's American League, along with his brother and three iconic baseball figures: Connie Mack, Charlie Comiskey, and Ban Johnson. Killilea had also owned the original Milwaukee Brewers, and from 1903 to 1904 would own the Boston Red Sox. Years later, Killilea bragged that he had helped put Heston through UM, as well as UM's 1904 Olympic gold medalist sprint champion, Archie Hahn.[23] A letter Killilea sent to Baird on August 26, 1902, implied that Boss Weeks—by far the smallest man on the UM team, as quarterbacks were back then—was another of his beneficiaries:

> I certainly am willing to assist in maintaining the high standard established during the past year at the U. of M. and am willing to subscribe the amount mentioned to me in your last letter for that purpose. . . . I have a letter from the little fellow saying he will be unable to return unless assisted as last year. . . . Having started him there, I feel in duty bound to have him continue. . . . I am willing to subscribe the sum indicated for the U. of M. and should it be necessary even to increase it, I will do so if it is necessary to get a winning team.[24]

Letters between Baird and numerous former Wolverine athletes in the UM files circa 1901–1905 indicate these were not wink-wink "loans." They were real. Alumni lenders expected recipient athletes to begin repayment as soon as their college days concluded, whether they graduated or not. Such former players would update Baird on the money they still owed. Sometimes they would enclose partial payment, other times they'd spell out their latest repayment schedule. When hard up, they'd apologetically cite the reason they could not pay down anything on their "note" for a while. An example: "I will pay some on that debt this season," John McLean, a Michigan halfback from 1898 to 1899, told Baird on October 6, 1902, while coaching football at Knox College in Galesburg, Illinois.[25] McLean paid his debt in full one year later while coaching the University of Missouri Tigers.[26]

One ex-Wolverine, James C. "Jim" Knight, attempted to evade repayment entirely. He'd played for one year at Princeton in 1895 before attempting a comeback under Yost in 1901. Knight started a couple of games in September before Yost demoted him to the scrubs by November. Knight left UM disgruntled, apparently. After he became head coach at the University of Washington, Baird hired a UM alumnus lawyer in Seattle to pressure Knight into paying off the loans he'd received, under threat of legal action or garnishment. "I have no compunctions in pressing a man of this type to the utmost," Baird wrote the Seattle lawyer in 1904 after months had rolled by with Knight still holding out. Baird eventually agreed to a reduced settlement of $135.[27]

It's unclear whether the men who actually directed UM athletic policy—Baird's faculty bosses—had any knowledge of these loans to athletes. Probably they did not, as had been the case when the clandestine program began in 1896. The author could find no evidence in UM's archives that Pattengill, Andrew C. McLaughlin, or Judge Victor H. Lane—the faculty triumvirate who oversaw UM athletics in these years—was ever aware.

Letters reveal that in this time Pattengill was especially close to Bates, the influential Chicago alum. The two commented candidly about many sensitive internal sports-management issues—including Baird's and Yost's successes, failings, and personal shortcomings. Yet they did not discuss loans to athletes.[28] And Bates not only knew of the pervasiveness of the loan scheme at UM, he was neck-deep in it, as a future letter would reveal.

✹ ✹ ✹

Yost and Baird secured five impact recruits in 1902. Four were stout linemen, three of them college transfers. Charles "Babe" Carter of Maine had started at Brown University in 1897 and 1898. William C. "King" Cole had played for three years at Marietta College in Ohio. And Joseph "Joe" Maddock had impressed at Albion College for the past two years, and in fact played against the Wolverines in Yost's debut game.

William S. "Billy" Palmer was the fourth lineman, a high schooler from Chester, Massachusetts. In January, a Michigan alumnus in the East, George W. Fuller, tipped Baird about Palmer—a "young man without means"[29] who possessed rare athletic abilities:

> This fellow is in my opinion the most typical football man in the country. He is the fastest two-hundred lb. man I have ever known or seen on the field. . . . Now Charlie if you can arrange some way to furnish him with room and board, tuition and books and keep your hands clean I am almost sure you can get him. Under your training and coaching let me tell you that you would find him a wonder.[30]

Baird informed Yost. The coach investigated Palmer and was told by an old Lafayette man that Palmer "was a wonder"[31] at both football and baseball. Word later reached Yost, however, that Palmer had "played some professional baseball," as so many footballers did each summer, and would do so into the 1920s, to earn easy money.[32] Yost left it to Baird to determine whether Palmer was eligible.

Baird immediately confronted the alumnus, Fuller, with Yost's concern about Palmer's alleged professionalism. Fuller assured Baird that Palmer was clean, or at least as clean as all the college players Palmer had competed with and against circa 1900–1901 in the Northern New York League. These players from "Brown, Yale, Dartmouth, Williams, Amherst, Union, Syracuse, Holy Cross, Georgetown, Manhattan, Middlebury and Univ. of Penn. [all] had such contracts as Palmer had," Fuller said. That is, the club didn't pay them a cent; rather, a "party outside of the Club management" did, on the sly. Thus, a charge of professionalism against any of them could never be proved by any outsider. "I will warrant you that Palmer is alright as to Professionalism," Fuller wrote to Baird. UM ultimately admitted Palmer, presumably on Baird's risky say-so.[33]

Then, as now, no coach ever lands all the prized recruits he covets. Yost and UM had their share of losses. Some turned out to be unmistakable professionals, at which point Yost's and Baird's interest died. Some chose to go elsewhere. And some snubbed everybody, such as Percy Brush. For months in 1902, Yost thought he had a good chance of landing the powerful tackle, who'd just graduated from Macalester College in St. Paul, Minnesota. But Brush brushed off Yost, claiming he had to tend to his ailing father. Eventually, Brush played under coach Dr. Henry L. Williams at the University of Minnesota from 1904 to 1905.[34]

Michigan this year largely ignored the Chicago high school hotbed—at least until September. By the time preseason camps opened early that month, Stagg already had wrangled most of the top schoolboy talent in the Windy City. Startlingly, Wisconsin snared only one Chicago prep star, and not from Hyde Park. UW's outlandish spring break courtship of Hyde Park stars proved a complete failure, and it signaled the beginning of the end of King's run of success in Madison.[35]

One Chicago-area stud remained undecided by mid-September: massive 240-pound lineman Bob Maxwell from Englewood High School. He was still vacillating between Chicago and Michigan. Eventually, he chose to stay home.[36]

As Maxwell mulled, two other frosh-to-be who'd already thrown in with Stagg's Maroons suddenly had a change of heart. Both Fred Hall, primarily a two-miler at Hyde Park whose personal-best time already was far better than any conference man's, and Paul Dickey, a track and football star from South Division High, suddenly left the Maroons camp and announced their intentions to enroll at Michigan. Yost was not in on the raid; Chicago UM alums were behind it.[37]

Remember, there was no national signing day at the time. Verbal commitments meant nothing. And there was no rule, or even unofficial code, against recruiting an athlete already working out at a rival's preseason camp, or even already enrolled. Such raiding attempts happened all the time.

Still, Chicagoans sizzled. So, too, did Stagg. Probably it was he who worked up his loyal supporters among the Chicago press corps into their frenzy—the same journalists who'd written nothing derogatory about Stagg's similar pinching of Koehler from Nebraska. "[C]ertain Chicago alumni of the University of Michigan are guilty of flagrant

violation of both the letter and spirit of amateur rules in offering inducements to Chicago high school athletes to go to the University of
Michigan to play football," one newspaper charged, without offering
proof.[38]

Raiding could go both ways, though. There was nothing preventing a
turncoat from turning back. UC alumni, or Stagg, or both, refused to let
Hall and Dickey go without a fight. A week after the news of their
imminent departures hit the press, a UM alumnus in Chicago—Clifford
Niles—informed Baird that neither player had yet boarded a train
heading east. On September 25, Niles had been "in communication
with Dickey and Hall today and they will leave for Ann Arbor at eleven
thirty tonight—at least they say have promised to, and I believe they
will."[39]

Dickey did. Hall did not. The latter changed his mind again and
enrolled at UC. The former spent but one year at UM and saw mop-up
duty only late in a couple of practice games.

One UM backfield recruit in 1902 who did make the Wolverine
varsity was James Lawrence, a high schooler from just a few miles east
of Ann Arbor in Ypsilanti. Lawrence was a rarity for Yost to this point in
his career—an instant-impact freshman out of high school. In a late-
September column Yost wrote for the *Chicago American*, Yost explained his stance on schoolboy recruitment, and in so doing included a
not-so-subtle dig at Stagg and his new policy:

> I do not think that the high school stars which the Western and
> Eastern teams seem to think are necessary for the welfare of their
> elevens are always what they are cracked up to be. There is always a
> wide gulf between the high school player and a good varsity man, and
> I do not believe in judging any team's prospects from the number of
> high school stars she is able to draw into her squad.
>
> However, the high school man is positively necessary for the
> building up of a team, and his value should not be depreciated. . . . I
> believe that the great improvement in high school teams that is at
> present showing itself all over the country will lead to the picking of
> many college players from their ranks in the next year or so.[40]

9

1902 ON THE FIELD

A Point a Minute

Amos Alonzo Stagg was no dummy. In winter 1902, he lined up an abnormally light football schedule for his Chicago Maroons come fall, and for a good reason: he intended to start mostly first-year players, players he hadn't even recruited yet. Whoever they were, they were going to need the confidence that easy victories would provide. Among potential Big Nine opponents, Stagg declined to schedule championship aspirants Iowa or Minnesota, and he wisely did not line up even a lightweight from the East. A run of victories, no matter how hollow, would be a welcome salve for the past two seasons' worth of welts.

The Chicago greenhorns opened the '02 season by crushing Lombard 27–6, Monmouth 24–0, and Fort Sheridan 53–0 before escaping with a 5–0 victory against Knox University of Galesburg, Illinois. John "Jack" McLean, star halfback on Michigan's 1898–1899 teams, coached the Knox team and sent UM athletic director Charles Baird the following report:

> I want you to whip Stagg to a finish this year. You probably read what we did to him with a bunch of youngsters from here. My center weighed 158, my left tackle 157; right guard 168; right tackle 169; right end 160; and the backs averaged 139. With this aggregation we outplayed him from start to finish. I coached the men on defense for two weeks on how to smash that mass-on-tackle he uses; and he couldn't make it gain. They play the same old game; and it seems to

me if you coach your tackles and backs and guards how to smash it [then] they can't gain on you. With your material you ought to beat him 50 to 0. . . . They have a better team than last year's; that is, it will be better by the end of the season. He has lots of beef, and the men are more experienced than Stagg is willing to admit.[1]

McLean did not elaborate on the last comment. Perhaps he was referring to John Koehler, the transfer from Nebraska whom the press was lumping in with Stagg's first-years straight out of high school.

The Maroons responded to the Knox scare by posting five more shutout victories to close out October—against Cornell College of Iowa (21–0), Purdue (33–0), Northwestern (12–0), Illinois (6–0), and Beloit (18–0). The Illini had an unusually good offense this year, so the shutout by Chicago was an achievement.

Yet nobody was fooled. Stagg's Maroons might have had a 9–0 record entering November, and perhaps even have possess one of the stingiest defenses in the West, but the game everybody expected to decide the Championship of the West did not involve the Maroons, even if it would be played on the Maroons' home field.

❋ ❋ ❋

A few days before Fielding H. Yost departed West Virginia for Whitmore Lake in early September, he still sensed complacency back in Ann Arbor—even in his boss, Baird. Yost did not hesitate to call him on it:

[W]e have very much to do to win all our games. I fear you do not realize what a task we have before us. I do not expect to have such wonderful luck as we had last year. . . . That Michigan team was simply wonderful when considered in the aggregate. I am not in the least discouraged nor shall I leave any thing undone that I can do to bring about success. We face a different proposition entirely from what we did last year and we must meet it differently. Last year the other colleges looked upon Michigan as a game easily won, this season all will realize that they must work their hardest if they expect to win from Michigan. Then again from our side, many will think that we can win and will not do all they can to bring about that success. Last year we started after a season of losses, this after a season of wonderful victories. I tell you it is different.[2]

With Yost's blessing, Baird had lined up one of the most challenging schedules in school history. November included not only Wisconsin and Chicago but both the Iowa Hawkeyes—intent on returning to formidability—and the other member of the West's Big Four, the University of Minnesota. The Gophers would visit UM either in Detroit or Ann Arbor on Thanksgiving Day to close the season. Everybody's game of the year in the West would be played Saturday, November 1, in Chicago, when the co-defending Big Nine champions would square off.

For the Wolverines, a repeat of the near point-a-minute scoring pace of 1901 seemed out of the question. To put that rate into perspective, not since football's highest-scoring era to date —1883 to 1890—had a major college team averaged at least fifty points per game, or scored one hundred in any contest. What's more, Michigan's 128–0 blowout of the University of Buffalo marked the first time any school had run up one hundred points on a respected opponent, East or West. "Michigan can never expect to repeat last year's performance in the way of scoring," Yost observed, "and no Michigan man will look for a repetition of the enormous number of touchdowns."[3]

Yet Yost's Wolverines began the 1902 season even more impressively, destroying Albion 88–0 in a scheduled forty-minute game shortened to thirty-six and a half minutes. It was the usual: fifteen touchdowns for, one first down against. The Wolverines dominated even without two key players: senior left guard Dan McGugin, who'd arrived late at camp and was still rounding back into shape, and senior punter and tackler extraordinaire Ev Sweeley, sidelined indefinitely by the UM Board in Control of Athletics until he removed academic conditions from his literature studies. The bad news from the Albion game was that star running back Willie Heston severely sprained an ankle.

Without Heston in week two, Michigan pounded Case 48–6 in twenty-minute halves. Sweeley's continuing absence led directly to the first score allowed by a Yost-coached Michigan team. Here's how it happened. Following a touchback, backup UM halfback Ross Kidston shanked a punt into a strong wind and Case set up at the Michigan forty-yard line. After a seven-yard gain, Case's left halfback Harry Davidson took a delayed toss around left end. Michigan end Curtis Redden bit on the fake inside and got boxed in. Then right halfback Al Hermnstein, whom Yost moved to Sweeley's spot as fullback on defense (deep safety), made an ill-advised dive, missed, and Davidson trotted across the goal line for a thirty-three-yard score—the "deepest gloom Michigan has experienced on the gridiron since 1900," the *Michigan Alumnus* noted.[4]

The broken string of goose eggs hogged the headlines, and it apparently angered and focused the Yostmen. Through the remainder of October the Wolverines obliterated the following teams: Michigan Agricultural College (the future Michigan State) 119–0 in thirty-eight minutes of play, Indiana 60–0 in forty-five minutes, Notre Dame 23–0 in fifty minutes, and Ohio State 86–0 in sixty minutes. In the latter game, some two thousand scarlet-and-gray-clad Ohioans trekked north to join four thousand Michigan fans at UM's renamed home grounds, Ferry Field.

Heston returned for the Indiana game but reinjured his ankle, then played sparingly against ND and OSU—as Yost no doubt chose to save his limping superstar for the tough November stretch. Herrnstein, the right half, ably picked up the slack. Against Michigan Agricultural, he scored seven touchdowns—still an unmatched Michigan milestone.

Sweeley was reinstated before the Notre Dame game and immediately shored up UM's sometimes shaky defensive play and poor punting. On offense, this year's Wolverines were redefining football fecundity. In six victories so far, Michigan had run up 73 touchdowns and 424 points, in just 269.5 minutes—unheard of numbers with a month still to play.

Inevitably, sports writers and headline writers began to apply the "point-a-minute" nickname to Yost's juggernaut. The much more common description in the press, though, was "Yost's machine" or the "Michigan machine," in honor of the sure precision, power, and relentlessness of the UM attack under Yost.

The new Michigan players ably filled all the holes. Up front on the right side, Charles "Babe" Carter at guard and Joe Maddock at tackle proved every bit as effective as their predecessors. Yost tinkered at left tackle all season, though, trying Moses Johnson, James Forrest, and James Lawrence before settling on Billy Palmer and Wheaton Cole.

The surprise of the year was Paul Jones at fullback. Unrecruited, the Youngstown, Ohio, native had no intention of participating in athletics while studying law at UM. But eagle-eyed Michigan trainer Keene Fitzpatrick discovered him on the regular-student athletics fields and strong-armed him into joining Yost's 1901 team late in the season. Jones quickly became a productive, fearless, center-ramming ball carrier.

The speed of the Yost machine proved no less bewildering in 1902. Yost claimed that in running off plays, "Michigan is faster by 35 to 50 percent than any other eleven." Only fast players enabled such dizzying RPMs. Yost boasted after the season that his Wolverine starters could win an eleven-man relay race against any other team in the country.[5]

According to the *Chicago Daily News*, the two men who keyed the bewildering, rapid-fire Yost attack were Michigan's little field general, quarterback Harrison "Boss" Weeks, and center Dad Gregory:

> Michigan's speed lies, it is believed, in the ability of her center and quarter to follow the ball and of her other line men to follow the play also. It is hard to conceive a team fast unless the center and quarter work together. [If] the center is there the minute the crowd clears off the ball to snap it back, and the quarter ready to give the signal, it will be found that a team's speed has been increased 50 per cent. [Thus] the center should be the one best-conditioned man on the team.[6]

Weeks was so savvy and quick of mind, he usually barked out the signal for the next Michigan play before the untangling even began. Sometimes he'd bark out signals for the next two or three plays, to further accelerate action. Not only that, Heston once remembered that there "was a series of four or five plays we ran without signal. Everyone knew what to do and what play was coming up. Our opponents didn't have much of a chance to get set for us."[7]

One of the nation's best football coaches, Wisconsin's Phil King, scouted the Michigan–Indiana game from the Ferry Field sidelines—along with his fullback, Earl Driver. King was justifiably concerned: "Michigan is playing a very fast game, and the team is much further advanced in the game at this time than is Wisconsin. We realized, and have realized, that we have a very hard proposition to meet on November 1."[8]

✿ ✿ ✿

Under the coaching of King, Wisconsin had become the annual team to beat since the conference's formation in 1896. Entering the 1902 showdown game against Yost's Wolverines, King's Badgers had won fifty-one of fifty-eight games overall, fifteen of nineteen conference games, and three league championships, and were on a seventeen-game winning streak dating back two years.

Eight starters returned from King's undefeated 1901 champs—all but the halfbacks and a tackle. Star ends Allen Abbott and Irving Bush anchored a robust defense, and quarterback Joseph Fogg led a dangerous offense that, outside of Yost's Wolverines, was by far the highest-scoring team over the past two seasons in the West, averaging thirty-four points per game.

The buildup for Wisconsin–Michigan at Marshall Field captivated the West. Never had a game on that side of the Appalachians drawn so much hype for so long, especially in Madison and Ann Arbor. "Undergraduates," the *Chicago Tribune*'s correspondent in Madison wrote, "practically have thrown away their text books for the week, politics has a gallery seat right here at the state capitol and even on railroad trains one hears the well-worn discussion of the opposing teams' chances. It seems as if the whole state was planning to pour in at Marshall Field."[9]

Both schools arranged for abnormally large train excursions to Chicago. With UC's blessing, athletic leaders at UM and UW agreed to construct additional bleachers to accommodate the expected first twenty thousand football fans gathering in the West.

Experts gave Michigan the edge, especially with the speedy Heston apparently fully recovered. In seventeen games, the fewest points a Yost-coached Wolverine team had scored thus far was twenty-one, and the Badgers had been scored on in September by both Chicago's Hyde Park High School and Beloit. King, though, was not about to concede a thing. "The men are all in good condition and will fight the game of their lives tomorrow," he said on Halloween. Yost sounded far less certain than usual: "The man who thinks Michigan has a cinch does not know what he is talking about. If we are defeated it will be mainly due to overconfidence, a spirit that is so manifest I can not break it up."[10]

On an unseasonably warm, overcast day, the seventy-minute game was decided in the first ten minutes, right after Michigan returned the opening kickoff to its thirty-seven-yard line. King had expected Yost to continue attacking with what had been so successful all season for the Wolverines—a heavy dose of end runs (by Herrnstein and, when healthy, Heston) mixed with smashes inside. But Yost instead instructed quarterback Weeks to hammer away repeatedly at the Badger middle, where Yost evidently suspected a weakness existed, and where the defensive impact of UW's standout ends, Abbott and Bush, would be minimized.

The plan worked. Stunningly. On twenty-three consecutive plays to begin the game, mostly smashes up the middle by fullback Jones or tackles Palmer and Maddock, the Wolverines in extreme hurry-up mode bludgeoned and shocked the Badgers by marching seventy-three yards for a touchdown. Maddock ended the drive with a two-yard scoring plunge on the third and final down. Sweeley's successful goal-from-touchdown, or conversion, gave Michigan a 6–0 lead.

These would stand as the game's only points. Only two gallant goal-line stands by the proud Badgers and five missed Wolverine field goals in the second half kept the score from matching the decisiveness of Michigan's victory. The Wolverines contented themselves to mostly pulverize the middle of the outclassed Badger line, while on defense they allowed more than fifteen yards on only two of Wisconsin's fourteen drives and never allowed the Badgers to penetrate past the Michigan forty-eight-yard line.

Michigan outgained the Badgers 273 yards to 75 in the first half and 92 to 48 in the second, for a 365-to-123 final ratio.

Once again, a strong opponent facing Hurry Up football for the first time was flummoxed at the outset, powerless to stop the Wolverine tsunami. A few years later, Yost would pen a long list of "Hurry Up" attestations, one of which was: "Hurry up and score in the first few minutes of the game, before your opponents realize what is going on."[11]

"Michigan showed the most powerful and concerted attack ever seen in western football," the *Chicago Tribune* observed. The *Tribune* continued:

> Few of the immense crowd knew that they were witnessing the acme of modern attack. But the football critics and galaxy of western coaches, drawn from far and wide to see the battle of gridiron giants, marveled at the perfection of unified effort which Yost had taught, and his pupils so ably carried out. It was better offense than the Michigan team of 1901, which registered 550 points without being scored on, showed in its best games last year. This is a bold statement but it was the unanimous opinion of those whose business it is to study football for practical uses.[12]

One such expert in attendance was George Woodruff, the former Yale star and former Penn coach who'd baffled the East in the 1890s with his revolutionary guards-back plays and other wrinkles. Dumped by Penn following the Quakers' unraveling in 1901, Woodruff penned an analysis column for the *Chicago Tribune* off the Michigan–Wisconsin game, and he began it thus:

> For two years I have been curious to see the Michigan team play. I was filled with doubts as to whether it was really as strong in material and in style of play as scores would seem to indicate. My curiosity was gratified yesterday at Marshall field. . . .
>
> That the team is great goes without saying. That it is phenomenal against second class elevens is equally apparent from the scores of the last two seasons. And yet I hesitate to admit that the Wolverines could beat many first class teams which I have seen. As examples I would note the Pennsylvania eleven of 1897, the Yale team of 1900, and the Harvard team of 1901. My hesitancy about the relative merits of Yost's men and teams named above is an evidence that I consider Michigan of both 1901 and 1902 in the front rank of all football teams.[13]

Woodruff was the first respected easterner to name Yost's Wolverine teams the best in football history. His proclamation got almost no play afterward though, probably because he'd buried his lead under wordy, opaque prose. Yet no point-a-minute team of Yost's would receive a more meaningful endorsement.

The entire modern brand of Western football, in fact, impressed Woodruff: "I believe western teams rank well with those in the east. The best here are evenly matched with the best there," and a postseason tournament in 1902 matching up the Big Fours of each region "would probably bring victory to the west."

The tragedy of the day occurred in the stands overstuffed with twenty-two thousand fans. One of several small grandstands erected specially for this game was brought, disassembled, by UW. It measured seventy-five feet long and ten feet high at the back. The day before, two City of Chicago inspectors signed off on its reassembly on the northeast corner of the grounds. The stand was designed to hold four hundred spectators, but according to the *Detroit Free Press*, many more crowded onto it. In the middle of the first half, timbers in the grandstand suddenly began to creak—then snapped. The whole stand swayed to the north then collapsed, dropping hundreds. Incredibly, no one was killed and only a few were seriously injured.[14]

The game was interrupted for fifteen minutes as stunned, scared, and some bloodied spectators flooded onto the northeast corner of the playing field to escape the woodpile wreckage. As police stationed at the barbed-wire fences abandoned their posts to tend to the injured, hundreds of unguarded, ticketless fans outside began pouring inside the grounds. Backups from both teams rushed in to stem that tide and, probably, prevented cancellation of the remainder of the game.

In the days following the game the legal battles commenced. As some of the injured sought compensation, UM and UW authorities together fought their UC counterparts over which party was liable. UC had allowed Michigan and Wisconsin to erect additional stands on Marshall Field but did not commission the work. The incident threatened to hammer another wedge between these schools, athletically. The matter would not be soon resolved.[15]

✿ ✿ ✿

Stagg, of course, had watched in person as Michigan dismantled Wisconsin's pride. Stagg said this Wolverine team was more formidable than most Eastern teams he'd ever seen, and he worried what it might do to his good but green-as-May-grass team in two weeks.[16] Regarding the Badgers, though, Stagg no doubt smelled an opportunity. They were emotionally crushed and might not recover in time for the UW–UC season-closer at Marshall Field on Thanksgiving Day.

On Saturday, November 8, Stagg's Maroons pounded the Indiana Hoosiers 39–0 for their ninth consecutive win by shutout, while the Badgers bounced back to paste Northwestern 51–0.

The Wolverines sure didn't take a step backward after the big win over Wisconsin. With Yost in Minneapolis to scout the Gophers as they defeated Illinois 17–5, the coachless Wolverines faced Dr. Alden Knipe's Iowa Hawkeyes in Ann Arbor. Iowa's hopes of winning their second Big Nine championship in three seasons had dissolved two weeks earlier in a 34–0 loss to Minnesota. The Wolverines made that result look like a nail-biter, putting up thirty-five points on Iowa in the first half alone, stacking seventeen touchdowns in all and converting each one to win 107–0 in sixty-five minutes of play. Quarterback Weeks worked end runs back into the UM offensive mix to killer effect, thanks to Heston's and Herrnstein's running and the outstanding "interference" (the preferred term then for blocking) provided by the rest of the Wolverines. "Michigan's interference on end runs is great, and I cannot see how teams can break it up with a no-gain for Michigan," Ralph Hoagland, the nation's most respected referee and former Princeton star, told reporters afterward. "It is simply the perfection of interference."[17]

Few even in Chicago believed the 10–0 Maroons had much chance against 8–0 Michigan on the following Saturday. UC's prospects appeared to worsen on Monday of game week when Stagg announced sophomore quarterback Lee Maxwell broke his collarbone in practice. Stagg had to juggle his young lineup accordingly, moving his best halfback, Jimmy Sheldon, to quarterback and rearranging his defense, too, for Maxwell guarded Chicago's right end.

History had shown that the more Stagg felt unfairly victimized before a big game, the more he used the press to likewise try to unsettle his opponent. Probably that is why he made the odd decision that week to hold Maroon practices not only in secret but off campus, after sunset, under artificial light, on a field surrounded by a tall wall. Stagg also let it leak he was introducing a wave of newfangled plays on offense to be sprung on the Wolverines.[18]

Then reports of other injured Maroons hit the papers. These were called "bear stories," when a coach deliberately leaked false or exaggerated health reports in hopes of instilling overconfidence in his opponent. Not every Chicago newspaper lapped this one up. The *Record-Herald* ran a cynical two-panel cartoon by John Tinney McCutcheon in which he depicted in the first panel all Maroons players bandaged up in a hospital ward, with the caption, "as Stagg describes the condition of the team before the game." In the second panel, McCutcheon drew eleven fierce, healthy, charging Maroons players on the field with the caption, "as the team really will be during the game."[19]

Stagg knew the best way to improve his chances against Michigan was to weaken it. He attempted to do just that. More than a week before the game, Stagg notified the UM Board in Control of Athletics by letter that a second-year Wolverine was competing illegally in his fifth year of intercollegiate football. On November 6, the chairman of

UM's Board in Control, Albert H. Pattengill, vented to power alum Henry M. Bates:

> Stagg is after us again. This time it is Dan McGugin. Stagg says he has played three years [at Drake] and gives time and place—I went carefully over that when McG. first came and again last spring and decided him eligible under the rules. Of course McG. may have deceived me, but any how I have not been negligent.
>
> We have McG. up at my house tonight to inquire again. Keene [Fitzpatrick, trainer] is coming with him. If we have to throw him off it will make a great difference to the team. There are no more like him. I learned today that Stagg had written to the director at Albion trying to find something against Maddock.
>
> [Stagg's questioning of] purity in Mich. Athletics is most lowly and becoming. [20]

McGugin did indeed appear in games for the Drake varsity team in 1898, 1899, and 1900. But McGugin had insisted all along to Pattengill and the UM board that he was a prep student at Drake in 1898. The Big Nine discounted one year of a student's previous football experience accrued in preparatory study. Thus, McGugin maintained that only two of his three years at Drake should count against him, and the UM Board agreed. This being his second year as a Wolverine, McGugin was competing in his fourth and final year as a collegian.

Desperate to clear his name and remain eligible, McGugin missed practices the week of the Chicago game to travel to Drake University to once and for all obtain written, official proof of his claim.

The Chicago press caught wind of the story three days before the game. Stagg likely leaked it. The *Tribune* hired a correspondent in Des Moines to investigate, who reported that Drake University's official record of student enrolment listed McGugin as a college-level student in each of 1898, 1899, and 1900. What's more, reports said the University of Minnesota also raised with UM athletic leaders the eligibility of McGugin, plus at least two other Wolverines, and Wisconsin authorities had discussed protesting McGugin before the November 1 game against Michigan. [21]

Stagg lied when he publicly denied having brought "any charges against any of the Michigan players," adding,

We stand ready to meet any team which Michigan presents. The eligibility of their men is a matter for their faculty board to decide. It is true that I have heard reports in regard to one of their men, McGugin, reports which would show that he is not eligible. . . . As he played against Iowa [last] Saturday, they have doubtless decided he is eligible. [22]

McGugin returned to Ann Arbor from Des Moines on Thursday of game week. Pattengill immediately updated Bates by special-delivery letter:

McGugin "makes good." We have a certificate from the Registrar of Drake Univ., certifying that "according to the books of Drake Univ. Mr. Dan McGugin was classified as [a prep] student in the Fall of 1898," duly signed.

There is a lot of other material corroborating [including an affidavit from a dean at Drake]. I am more glad to have [McGugin] proven truthful than I am to have him on the team. [23]

The Michigan professor also sent rush letters to Stagg and the press, in which he declared McGugin "as completely eligible under the conference rules as any athlete in the country." [24] Stagg did not comment publicly, but let his feelings be known. "While there is no tendency to doubt the sincerity of the Michigan committee, the feeling was strong at the University of Chicago that McGugin's case was full of peculiar circumstances," one paper reported. [25]

For his part, Pattengill had little respect either for Stagg or his methods. To date, he never shared those thoughts publicly. Privately, however, Pattengill confided to Bates that he was "thoroughly disgusted with [Stagg's] avarice and obstinancy," [26] and slagged Stagg's integrity too. Pattengill also derided Stagg's pompousness, referring to him in letters to Bates as "Sir Alonzo" [27] or "his Majesty." [28] With proof disproving Stagg's latest ineligibility charge in hand, Pattengill gloated to Bates, "I think that smart aleck will henceforth go a bit slow before he bucks the Michigan line again." [29]

On Saturday, before a crowd of only twelve thousand at Marshall Field that included fewer than one hundred UM students, the Wolverines defeated the Maroons 21–0 in thirty-five-minute halves. With Maxwell out, Stagg started seven first-year Maroons: six frosh and

Koehler. Of them, neither fullback Mark Catlin nor right halfback Hugo Bezdek could make it to game's end, having to be subbed out.

What shocked every onlooker was that Stagg's young charges, unlike Wisconsin and every other UM opponent, tenaciously stood up all game long to Michigan's revered between-the-tackles smashes. The Wolverines could not reliably gain ground inside. Boss Weeks soon found that end runs off fake dives worked spectacularly, as did other such trick plays to the outside. Michigan finished with 336 yards from scrimmage, compared to Chicago's 91. Again, thorough domination.

In each half, Michigan scored one touchdown and one field goal. The first TD was classic Heston. On a double pass from the UM thirty-nine-yard line, the halfback was "off like a frightened buck" around left end. George Ivison, subbing at left half for another UC frosh, G. E. Schnur, was stationed at right end on defense—where injured Lee Maxwell normally played—and crashed inside on the fake to Herrn-stein. Heston blew through the hole Ivison left and had only senior captain Sheldon to evade downfield, which he did easily with a sudden

Figure 9.1. At halftime of the 1902 Michigan–Chicago game at UC's Marshall Field, coach Fielding Yost (seventh from right, in dark hat and trench coat) and his bundled-up Wolverines rested on fold-out chairs while posing for a photographer, in this unidentified newspaper clipping. *Source:* Amos Alonzo Stagg Papers, Special Collections Research Centre, University of Chicago Library.

juke to the sideline as Sheldon dived to wrap up legs that weren't there. Heston's touchdown burst covered seventy-one yards.

Sweeley enjoyed one of his best days kicking as a Wolverine. He was good on two of six field-goal attempts. While that would be a lousy percentage in the twenty-first century, it was above average in 1902, as one of four was considered good.[30] It had been only five years since straight-on toe kicks from placement had begun to supplant dropkicks on field-goal attempts. Sweeley missed from 17, 23, 43, and 31 yards out, and was good from 33 and 18.

On defense, the Wolverines had no trouble snuffing out most everything the Maroons ran at them, tricks and all. The Maroons never threatened the Wolverine goal. Late in the game Chester Ellsworth attempted placement field goals from 43, 43, and 50 yards out and missed them all.

Most bettors had put their money on the point spread, not the result, and eighteen seemed to be the consensus line. Michigan thus covered by three. No matter, the ever loyal Chicago press corps hailed the UC mentor. "The showing of the Maroons vindicated Stagg's reputation as a 'wizard,'" the *Record-Herald* observed, adding parenthetically, "but also proved that Yost is crafty."[31]

Surprisingly, Stagg tossed Ivison under the wagon in his postgame statement to the press: "I am surprised at the size of the score, for I do not think the Michigan team so much superior as the result indicates. They earned but one touchdown. The long run was due to a mistake of Ivison, for he had been coached time and again to watch for just such a play as was used to get Heston loose. . . . Michigan played a nice game, but it was their tricks that beat us. . . . Their tricks were very clever. Those same tricks, however, show how green our men were. The men had been coached on these trick plays, and should have sized them up."[32]

Read: The loss was not Stagg's fault.

* * *

In fall 1902, Stagg suddenly had a brother-in-arms raining broadsides of misery down on Ann Arbor. Dr. Henry L. Williams, head football coach and acting athletic director at the University of Minnesota, enraged

Michigan authorities in the weeks leading up to their teams' season-closing game on Thanksgiving Day.

Through his school's faculty rep to the Big Nine, Frederick Jones, Williams privately questioned the eligibility of Wolverine after Wolverine with UM authorities.[33] When UM authorities decided less than two weeks before the game to relocate it from Detroit to Ann Arbor, where for the first time more fans could be safely accommodated, Williams exploded. "Minnesota positively refuses to accept Ann Arbor," he informed Baird, which telegram the *Minnesota Daily* student newspaper published. "You personally agreed with me on Detroit. Play there or no game."[34]

These Gophers were formidable. They had lost only once, early in the season to undefeated Nebraska, and on November 15 with their much heavier lineup they pounded Wisconsin 11–0. On the season, the Gophers had scored 364 points and allowed 11. Experts all quickly recalibrated their assessments and rightly decided that the Michigan–Minnesota game would now decide Western honors for 1902.

As for the game's locale, UM leaders possessed the right under the contract to move the game from Detroit to Ann Arbor, no matter how much Williams, Jones, or anyone else groused about it. The *Michigan Alumnus* later explained that some of the eight-thousand-capacity grandstands at Detroit's Bennett Park were suspect, and after the tragedy at the Wisconsin game UM refused to imperil spectators. Besides, Ferry Field now could accommodate more people, and safely. Countered the *Minnesota Daily* student newspaper: "The contracts for the Detroit tickets had been let and the game had been advertised to be played at Detroit when [Minnesota's] defeat of the Wisconsin team frightened the Michigan men, and they decided that they wanted the added advantage of the home field. . . . The fact of the matter is Michigan is badly scared and is taking every precaution to ensure a victory."[35] In the end, Williams and Minnesota were powerless to convince Michigan to change the venue back to Detroit, and acquiesced.

Apparently, Williams came by his enmity for Michigan and Yost honestly. He had been a teammate and good friend of Stagg's at Yale. In 1894, the two had co-authored the most lauded book on the sport to date: *A Scientific and Practical Treatise on American Football for Schools and Colleges*.[36]

Five days before the game, Pattengill informed alumnus Bates that Jones, the Minnesota faculty rep, would be his guest in Ann Arbor for Thanksgiving:

> I am going to tell him we may stand one Stagg, because we have to, but we simply won't stand two. Williams' conduct about those telegrams can not be easily characterized without large and copious profanity.
>
> Jones has just filled his letters to me all this fall with copious complaints and insinuations concerning nearly all the members of our team from Redden down through the list—Of course it is Williams but I am pretty tired.
>
> His last letter contains a charge of professionalism against Palmer. . . . This may prove to be true—we can not say. But Palmer has gone home and will not be here for the game.[37]

Right, Palmer. It should come as no surprise that Billy Palmer's clandestine professionalism was leaking out mere weeks after he'd cracked Yost's starting lineup in late October. A university's rival athletic leaders, coaches, and alumni always were quick to dig deep into the pasts of sudden midseason lineup crackers such as Palmer. It was an old trick to attempt to hide such studs until the big games, and Yost had shamelessly done it himself three years earlier with Krebs at Kansas. Was he doing it again?

As Pattengill noted, Palmer was no longer with the UM team. He'd suddenly left for his Massachusetts home following his first start, against Ohio State on October 25, supposedly on account of his father's illness. Baird quickly followed Palmer to Massachusetts and brought him back by train in time to play in Michigan's big victory against Wisconsin.[38] But two days after Michigan defeated Chicago on November 15, and five days before UM demolished Oberlin 63–0 in sixty minutes, Palmer sent this handwritten letter and corroborating telegram to Baird—just before leaving Ann Arbor for good:

> Mr. Baird
> I enclose you a telegram which I rec'd from home this morning. Mr Yost thinks that I should stay here and not go home but I am sure you will understand that it would be outrageous for me to do so under the circumstances. I am sure Mr. Pattengill will also see the necessity of the case.

Sincerely Yours,
W. S. Palmer[39]

The telegram, sent to him by Wm. Palmer from Chester, Massachusetts, read simply: "Mother very sick come at once." A month later the
Michigan Daily reported that Palmer's "father and mother are aged
people, to whom any illness would be the end. They live alone on a big
farm. For them Palmer has sacrificed his college work to care for the
farm and to be with them in their declining days. He is a football hero
of the true type."[40] Whether that was the real reason Palmer left, we'll
never know.

It appears Williams never officially protested Palmer or any other
Wolverine, as there is no record of it, private or public.

There was no protesting the final score. Michigan convincingly defeated Minnesota 23–6 in thirty-five-minute halves before a reported
record crowd of 12,000 at Ferry Field (although only 8,635 paid).[41]
Once again, a good team coached exceptionally well proved incapable
in the opening minutes of standing up to the rapid-fire Yost attack.
Williams's Gophers knew what was coming, and had practiced against
it—but no scrub team could hope to match the speed of play of the
Hurry Up machine.

Michigan took the opening kickoff and, in four minutes, marched
eighty-six yards in fifteen plays to go up 6–0. It didn't even matter that
starting fullback Jones was out with a knee injury; backup Herb Graver
gained more than forty-five yards on the opening march. "[Michigan]
dazzled the Minnesotans by the rapidity of her playing," the *Michigan
Daily* wrote. "Much time was taken out for Minnesota players, and part
of this may have been a deliberate attempt to dampen the ardor of a
quick-playing team, which needs to keep in constant action to do its
best work."[42]

Heston scored a touchdown on a nineteen-yard run to give the
Wolverines a 12–0 lead at halftime, then added a thirty-nine-yard TD
late in the game. Minnesota scored on a fluke early in the second half.
Boss Weeks bobbled a punt, and Gopher captain Johnnie Flynn darted
in and grabbed the loose ball, scampering twenty yards for the touchdown.

Michigan controlled scrimmage play throughout, outgaining Minnesota 191 to 73 in the first half and 325 to 126 by game's end. "I have

nothing to say except that Michigan is a better team than I imagined," Williams said afterward. "We put up the best article of football we had."[43]

Eastern football expert Caspar Whitney was on hand and said afterward, "Michigan is certainly a wonderful team, and coach Yost, laboring under the one man coaching system, has done something seemingly impossible. Minnesota played a great game, but there were no questions of Michigan's vast superiority." Yost was filled more with relief than braggadocio afterward, although not by much: "Everything is all right now. We have earned the title of Western Champions. . . . Minnesota was heavy, but slow in charging, and they never would have scored on straight line-bucking because Michigan had the best defense of the year today. There was not a spot or place that Michigan did not outplay Minnesota."[44]

Michigan thus finished the season with an 11–0 record—and was every expert's choice for Champion of the West. That this was the greatest team the West ever had produced few could argue. It was hard to imagine a better team.

The 1902 Wolverines scored 644 points—94 more than the year before. And among top football colleges east or west in 1902, the next two highest-scoring teams were Illinois (389) and Cornell (324). Yale, Princeton, and Harvard *combined* scored twenty fewer points than Michigan. And Michigan became the first team to score more than one hundred points in a game twice in the same season.[45]

The point-a-minute nickname was legit too. Generations later, historians, trying to deduce whether the team indeed scored at that rate, might presume Michigan's games were all seventy minutes long, as the rulebook called for. Of course, most games were far shorter. Michigan scored 107 touchdowns, converted 82 of them, added four field goals and a safety, and piled up all those points in 604.5 minutes of play— 1.07 points per minute. The Wolverines' two-year total under Yost: 1,194 points in 1,207.5 minutes—0.99 points per minute.

No known reports estimated the total yards gained by the 1902 Wolverines. But if it were true that the 1901 Wolverines had amassed some 8,000 yards in the same number of games (11), it would be safe to presume the more offensively prolific '02 team gained even more yardage, perhaps considerably more.

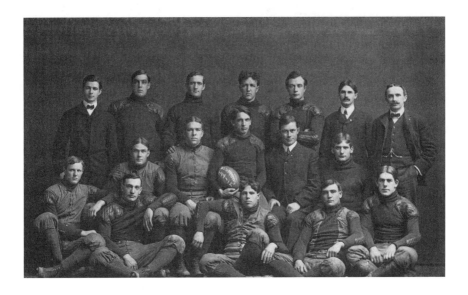

Figure 9.2.   The 1902 Michigan Wolverines, Champions of the West. Front row: W. C. "King" Cole, Curtis Redden, Willie Heston, Everett Sweeley, Herb Graver. Middle row: Joe Maddock, James Lawrence, captain Harrison "Boss" Weeks, coach Fielding H. Yost, Al Herrnstein. Back row: student manager Archibald Smith, Charles "Babe" Carter, Paul Jones, George "Dad" Gregory, Dan McGugin, athletic director Charles Baird, trainer Keene Fitzpatrick. *Source:* Bentley Historical Library, University of Michigan.

On defense, the 1902 Wolverines allowed only twelve points, the fewest of any team East or West. Only two other top teams allowed fewer than thirty: Princeton (seventeen) and Eastern champion Yale (twenty-two). While Yost's 1902 incarnation indeed proved more lethal on offense than its predecessor, it was not quite as suffocating on defense, and not just because of the two scores allowed. Still, "Yost's great eleven represents a perfection of development in which prominent coaches of other university teams say a flaw cannot be found," the *Chicago Tribune* stated. "It is strong in attack, defense, kicking, substitutes, and generalship—in fact, in all the essential elements of modern football."[46]

Michigan's point differential was plus 632. Next best among top colleges nationwide, and the only others with at least a 200-point differential in 1902, were Illinois (+345), Cornell (+286), Yale (+262), Chicago (+223), and Minnesota (+214).

Four Wolverines were consensus All-Western choices: Weeks, Heston, Sweeley, and the new tackle, Maddock. Guard McGugin, end Redden, and fullback Jones also earned first-team All-Western recognition in some quarters. Earl Duffy of the *Chicago American* explained that his choice for an All-Western team "would be the University of Michigan team," because in his view it would defeat any aggregation of Western players that could be brought to face it. [47]

Yet neither Whitney nor Walter Camp named a single westerner to his 1902 All-American team. And as with the 1901 Michigan team, decades later historians might bestow national-championship honors on the '02 Wolverines, but at the time the Eastern press corps mostly ignored Michigan's accomplishments. In the eyes of these football experts, Yale was the champion of the East, therefore Yale was the de facto national champion, period. The *New York Sun*'s final top five: Yale, Harvard, Princeton, Army, and Penn. The *Sun* "was the same paper that gave a seventeen word account of the Michigan–Minnesota game," the *Michigan Daily* huffed. "When will some of those Easterners wake up?" [48]

Only when Michigan could defeat an Eastern power out east. That's still what Yost and Baird aimed to arrange.

❋ ❋ ❋

Stagg's Chicago Maroons closed their 1902 season by upsetting Phil King's Wisconsin Badgers 11–0 on Thanksgiving Day at Marshall Field. Three-hundred-and-sixty-four days earlier, the Badgers had crushed the Maroons 35–0. Now the cleat was on the other foot.

Chicago took second-place honors in the Big Nine with a 5–1 league record and 11–1 overall mark. With so many talented freshmen having cut their teeth in 1902, prospects looked promising for Stagg and his Maroons in 1903.

Yost's other coaching rivals could not say the same. He had raised the bar of expectations so considerably, so quickly, that pressure rose dramatically on the unsuccessful. Following the 1902 season, Doc Hollister quit at Northwestern and Dr. Knipe was run out of Iowa; his team's 107–0 loss in Ann Arbor remains the worst defeat by a conference member in league history.

The shocker came when UW announced that King would not return as coach after seven stellar seasons. According to the *Daily Cardinal* student newspaper, King originally sought a monstrous new $5,000 salary after the 1902 season, but amended the demand to $4,000 plus expenses. Wisconsin alumni wanted King to stay, but not at that salary. If UW was to spend that much on football coaching, alums preferred that a policy of multiple, alumni-only coaches be implemented—modeled along Eastern lines. Obviously miffed, King said "see ya." [49]

Thus the number of great coaches in the West dropped to three: Yalies Stagg and Williams, and Yost.

10

1903 OFF THE FIELD

Football's Greatest Interception

Fielding H. Yost could not possibly crank out another Champion of the West in 1903.

At least that's what Amos Alonzo Stagg and Dr. Henry L. Williams predicted at the Press Club of Chicago's season-wrapping banquet late in 1902. "Both Stagg and Williams firmly believe that Michigan is due for a fall next year," the *Chicago Daily News* reported. After all, three-time champions in college football were more rare than walk-on starters. Williams, the University of Minnesota Gophers coach, explained his reasoning: "It is bound to come. [Michigan] has been successful for two seasons; now there may come the slump. It may be us or it may be Chicago."[1]

For his part, Stagg held firm to his prognostication yet presumed nothing. During his after-dinner speech to the press, the University of Chicago coach tipped his cards and let the world in on his escalating, increasingly unhealthy preoccupation. According to one report, "Coach Stagg said that his sole aim now is to defeat Michigan in 1903."[2]

❋ ❋ ❋

Yost's star now gleamed high in the college football sky. Football men even in the East took note of the quirky West Virginian and his scintillating coaching accomplishments after two years at Michigan.

By January 1903, there were rumblings that Columbia and perhaps even Penn were pushing hard for Yost's services. Ditto Navy, as well as the now King-less University of Wisconsin. Reports said the University of Missouri dangled a one-year, $10,000 contract to Yost—almost quadruple what Michigan was paying him. Despite having signed a three-year contract with UM just twelve months earlier, Yost waffled on returning for 1903.[3]

Was the coaching nomad about to jump jobs again? Or was he merely using the offers as leverage in an attempt to boost his $2,750 salary? Baird wanted his coach to return, as did every UM student, alumnus, or fan who cared a whit about football.[4] Ultimately, the chairman of UM's Board in Control of Athletics, Albert H. Pattengill, summoned Yost to his home on January 26, 1903, to discuss the matter.[5] Pattengill reminded Yost that a handwritten addendum to his contract stipulated: "It is understood and agreed by both parties that if Mr. F. H. Yost desires to stop coaching permanently, he may terminate this contract by notice at the close of [1902 or 1903]."[6] In other words, the only way Yost could get out of his Michigan contract was to quit coaching altogether, and he was wholly unwilling to do that. Bluff called or exodus stalled, whatever the case Yost wasn't going anywhere. Mere hours following his meeting with Pattengill and only four days before Wisconsin would announce alumnus Arthur Curtis as its new head coach at an $1,800 salary,[7] Yost issued a gleeful press release announcing his return to Michigan:

> I realize that I will have to face the hard proposition of making good the extraordinary records of the past two years. It takes more work to keep a successful team winning than it does to develop a losing one into [a winner]. The position which Michigan now occupies in the football world means that every team on our schedule will train for the main purpose of wresting us from our place. It is up to Michigan and every Michigan friend now to work as they never have worked before.[8]

And this started with him. Although he would be permitted to hire Dan McGugin as his first assistant football coach come fall, Yost remained on his own until then.[9] From December to February, before returning to West Virginia to scrounge more business deals, Yost scraped the

Midwest as never before in search of commitments from promising new players.[10]

The need was crucial. Departures were ravaging Yost's roster. To start with, quarterback Boss Weeks, right halfback Al Herrnstein, punter/end Ev Sweeley, left guard Dan McGugin, and left tackle Wheaton "King" Cole had played their four years. Worse, right guard Charles "Babe" Carter had left school before the start of second semester of the 1902–1903 school year because of a nonfootball, nonacademic disciplinary matter, and freshman fullback James Lawrence was not expected to return in September either, probably because he was falling so far behind in his studies. The final devastating blow came when promising fullback Paul Jones, the walk-on who'd supplanted Lawrence as starter, contracted typhoid. Jones survived but doctors forbade him from playing football again. In all, then, seven 1902 Michigan starters and a key backup—gone.[11]

In early January, Yost toured the Plains, including Kansas and Nebraska—ostensibly on pleasure. Even the *Michigan Daily* wasn't biting. "Of course this is only conjecture," the *Daily* wrote on January 15,

> but it might not probably be so wide of the mark to state that Yost was combining business with pleasure on this little western jaunt, and that the real object of the trip will become apparent when the new men report for practice next fall, and it is found that some husky westerners are members of the Michigan squad. Yost is a great football coach in season and out of season, and no small part of his success is due to the fact that he is always to be found looking out for promising new talent and advising them in their choice of universities.

In early February, Yost toured the state of Michigan—an unprecedented recruiting tactic—and didn't even bother to cloak it. "I don't want people to think that I am going about trying to hire boys to come to Michigan and handing over money right and left," Yost told the *Kalamazoo Gazette-News* while in that southwestern Michigan city. "We don't want anyone to come to Michigan and expect to make the team unless he comes in the right spirit, and that spirit must be a good one."[12]

The in-state tour bagged fullback Frank "Shorty" Longman of Battle Creek. He had starred on the Kalamazoo High team in 1901 but a knee injury sidelined him in 1902. There was no rule then barring a college coach from publicly singing the praises of a recruit, and Yost did not hold back about Longman, whom he saw play in a high school playoff game held in Ann Arbor in 1901: "He was a wonder, and despite the fact that he was short-winded I think he would make a good player," Yost told the *Kalamazoo Gazette-News*. "Thorough training would develop him into a handy 185-pounder." Longman would enroll at UM by summer's end.

Even better for Yost, the *Detroit Tribune* reported in mid-February that as many as five crackerjack footballers from Chicago's Hyde Park High School team were likely to attend UM come September, including the Hammond brothers, Tom and Harry. "Full back [Tom] Hammond would be a great addition to the Michigan forces next fall," Yost said. "He is a good line bucker and a great man on defense."[13]

How did Yost know that? Because two months earlier, in December 1902, he'd helped prepare the Hyde Park team for what had been billed as the greatest intersectional football game in American high school history, against visiting Brooklyn Polytechnic Preparatory Institute. Each was hailed as the champion prep team on its side of the Appalachians. A week's worth of buildup heightened the stakes, but the game was no contest. Hyde Park was so overwhelmingly loaded with star players that two months earlier it had lost only 24–5 to Phil King's then undefeated Wisconsin Badgers. On December 6 at the University of Chicago's Marshall Field, Hyde Park showcased the speed and versatility of play now rapidly gaining popularity in the West—thanks to Yost—and annihilated Brooklyn Poly Prep and its meager arsenal of Yale offensive plays 105–0.[14]

While Yost had attended one Hyde Park practice and offered pointers, the college coach who'd leaped at the opportunity to mentor the team throughout game week was, of course, Stagg. He already knew the Hyde Park boys intimately, having opened all his athletic facilities to them for a year, and even scrimmaging his Maroons against the Hyde Parkers during football season.

For more than a year, football and track-and-field coaches in the Big Nine had marveled at the once-in-a-lifetime aggregation of athletic talent at Hyde Park. The University of Wisconsin otherwise would not have shamelessly played host to Hyde Park athletic teams for a free March break getaway vacation back in 1902.

Come February 1903, the *Detroit Journal* reported that Yost had the inside track on securing not only the Hammond brothers but other Hyde Park starters, such as Walter Becker and fleet halfback Marion Wolfe. Oh, and the quarterback too—the most celebrated high school football player and all-around athlete yet produced in the West, if not the nation.

One Walter Eckersall.

❁ ❁ ❁

Of all events, a spring gathering of high school educators sparked the first angry confrontation between Stagg and Yost.

A morning symposium on the evils of schoolboy athletics highlighted the Saturday, April 4, session at the convention of the North Central Association of Colleges and Secondary Schools, held at the University of Chicago. Speech after speech assailed college sport. Professional college-level coaches were particularly "flayed and roasted." The keynote address by Stanford University president David Starr Jordan made headlines nationwide. He told a story about a man he referred to as one of the great coaches of the West:

> [W]e had Mr. Yost, and we won our great annual game with California the year he was with us. That year there came to the university a tall young giant who wanted to study mining engineering. Because of his apparent earnestness he was admitted to college on trial without the usual requirements. He tried for the football team, but could not carry his courses, and was dropped from college the first term without having played on the team.
>
> Yost left us and went East. He went to Michigan, taking with him the young giant who wanted to be a mining engineer. He used that young man as the center around which to build the great team which represented Michigan last year. The young man's name is [George] Gregory. . . .
>
> I hope my Michigan friends will pardon us other sinners in thus pointing out their sin. We are all sinners, I suppose in some way. All of us who have had Yost among us, or any Yost-like men, are bound to be sinners. . . .
>
> The sooner we get rid of college idlers like Gregory, who go to college merely to play football, and of irresponsible, professional

coaches like Mr. Yost, the sooner our college athletics will be pure
and free from the troubles that now assail them.[15]

Stagg was present as Jordan pilloried Yost. Reporters approached Stagg
afterward to ask him what he thought of the speech. The University of
Chicago's professional coach of three sports (football, baseball, and
track and field) said Jordan was right when he pointed to professional
coaching as the primary source of evil in college athletics; what placed
Stagg far above that ilk, he said, was his fulltime membership on the
UC faculty.

Stagg then charged Yost with being "shrewd and clever," telling
reporters, "I have no direct evidence myself of anything against Mr.
Yost, but a great many hearsay statements come to me." Stagg proceeded to disclose publicly for the first time a fast one Yost allegedly
had pulled at the University of Nebraska in 1898, according to the
hearsay—a hidden-ringer stunt almost identical to Yost's Krebs caper at
Kansas a year later.[16]

Ann Arbor sizzled. Pattengill, chairman of the UM Board in Control
of Athletics, bucked the emotion of the moment and issued measured
defenses of both Yost and "Dad" Gregory. The UM board "has confidence in [Yost] as an upright man," Pattengill said. "The greatest difference between Yost and other coaches is that Yost seems to win all his
games." The secretary of the UM Law Department issued his own
statement, saying Gregory "has done good class work ever since he has
been here. His work is so satisfactory that [in three-plus semesters] he
has not received a condition on a single subject, and I was surprised
when I read what President Jordan had to say. The law department at
Michigan is not lenient to athletes. They must be up to standard in their
class work before being permitted to play."[17]

Gregory's second-year law classmates were so worked up they'd have
all signed affidavits swearing to the Californian's good character, integrity, and letter. For his part, Gregory was outraged by Jordan's charac-
terizations. In interview after interview, Gregory refuted in detail almost everything Jordan said about him. "There is absolutely no truth in
his statements," he said. "It is all slander and nothing else. It is a
shame—it is a shame, I say." Gregory insisted he never intended to
become a mining engineer, and actually passed two courses at Stanford
for which he'd been given credit at Michigan. An incident of nonaca-

demic-related mischief got him booted from Stanford, not his grades, he claimed. Gregory said thereafter he earned his diploma from Washburn Prep in San Jose, then passed his entrance exams at UM "without a scratch." Gregory said he always aspired to study law, and Yost had indeed suggested he pursue his degree at UM—but only after Prof. James Ferguson at Stanford, a Michigan grad, had first urged him to do so.[18]

Stagg this time might have realized he'd gone too far in his attack on a rival school. Yet he did not recant what he said about Yost, explaining that he believed he was speaking off the record to reporters at the time.[19]

Somewhere in West Virginia, Yost eventually read the reports. From Clarksburg on April 15, the Michigan coach fired off this letter to his Chicago rival, revealed here for the first time, along with Stagg's reply, both in full:

> Dear Mr. Stagg:
> I think your remarks very unkind to say the least. If I were so disposed I could tell of countless rumors I have heard of you and your men. I have taken no stock in them because I have had no proof although I have had positive statements from fellows who say they know. This rushing into print I think very uncalled for.
>
> In regard to my work at Stanford and what Dr. Jordan said, I have numerous newspaper clippings showing just what they all thought of my work there both as a coach and as to creating the true college spirit as it should be with the University of California.
>
> When I came to Michigan I found a very bitter feeling against you and Chicago University [sic] students, this was also true regarding Wisconsin. I have done everything in my power to change this sentiment and create in its stead a spirit of friendly rivalry, such as exists between Yale and Princeton, and believe they were approaching this rapidly. I fear you have undone it all. I know much of the conditions both at Michigan and Chicago and I honestly believe that Michigan is as clean athletically as any University in America. It is indeed very easy to make accusations. One in the position you or I occupy as coaches can easily pick up idled rumors and hurl them broadcast over the land through the newspaper. I am glad to say I am not guilty of such.
>
> During the past two years there is no one can say that Michigan at any time, in any game of foot ball, took any unfair advantage of any

opponent. I do not believe any [of] our opponents think otherwise unless yourself. We have always tried to play as true sportsmen should.

I am sorry for several reasons that this has occurred, personally not very much. I am not guilty of any unfairness to any one and know it.

I should be pleased to hear from you in regard to this and I assure you I have no hard feelings toward you. I just wished to state how I looked at the matter and have been very frank to you in my statement in regard to it.

Stagg replied on May 5, a carbon copy of which he kept in his files:

My dear Mr. Yost:

Your letter of April 15 received. These are very busy days or I should have written you sooner. I wrote Prof. Pattengill exactly what I said and the circumstances under which I said it. If he will let you read my letter, you will understand the situation better. I have no disposition whatever to rush into print at every rumor or fact which comes to light. On the other hand I would not consider it was always best that good feeling should exist between the different institutions where it must be secured by the concealment of facts which ought to be brought to light. It does not strike me that the good of intercollegiate sport would be conserved, for example, by Chicago or Michigan keeping still if they knew that a foul condition exists in one or the other's athletic department.

It has never been my policy to throw mud at the other fellows and in all my dealings with Michigan, if I knew any facts about any of the men which satisfied me of their ineligibility I presented them frankly to the Michigan authorities, and in the presentation of them I took pains to see that unnecessary ill feeling was not engendered by useless newspaper comment.

You probably will not agree with me, but it does not seem to me for the best interests of college sports for our institutions to have men go out about the country in search for athletic material. As I view the matter, it would have a professional tinge, if I for example, sought to build up the athletic work of my department by making trips around the country for the sole purpose of securing more and better athletic material, and I think that the matter of recruiting, which was well brought out in the papers read before the meeting here in Chicago, is a subject for the earnest consideration of the

Conference. At present it is not a question of blaming this or that University, but it is a question of a frank and honest consideration of every influence which threatens to harm the college sports which we both believe in so fully.[20]

Clearly, Yost's January/February recruiting missions—and their apparent successes—disturbed Stagg greatly. There is no record to indicate Yost replied.

The Chicago–Michigan athletic war thus intensified. Not just between these ultracompetitive men, but involving their entire athletic departments and their universities' zealous, sports-interested alumni, especially on the recruiting trails. Nasty, desperate, disingenuous, cut-throat, immoral—all these descriptions and others would apply to the new recruiting pugilism of the West. The grand prize this off-season? The five-foot-six, 132-pound dynamo from Hyde Park High.

* * *

Walter Herbert Eckersall grew up the youngest of five children to parents of modest means in Woodlawn, the South Chicago neighborhood nestled under the east–west Midway Plaisance. A short walk away, north of the Plaisance in Hyde Park, lay both that community's namesake high school and the adjacent University of Chicago.

Diminutive in height and weight both for the time and for football, "Eckie" became a household name in Chicago by his fourth year at Hyde Park High, 1902–1903. All one had to do was watch him compete in virtually any sport to conclude Eckersall had no equal as an athlete.

In football, Eckersall was able to star at quarterback despite his size because the rules, up to autumn 1903, forbade signal-callers from running; thus quarterbacks could be tiny. Not that Eckersall ever shied away from physical contact. On offense, he called the plays, handled the ball expertly, and proved an ace punter and dropkicker; on defense, he returned kicks and was a surprisingly fierce, sure-tackling safety.

In baseball, Eckersall was a crack shortstop, swung a powerful bat, and could even pitch. In track and field, he exhibited promise as a world-class sprinter, twice ripping off a time of ten seconds flat in the hundred-yard dash, an Illinois schoolboy record that would stand for twenty-five years. At one of his last indoor meets for Hyde Park High,

Figure 10.1. Walter Herbert "Eckie" Eckersall, a five-foot-six, 132-pound athletic dynamo from Hyde Park High School in Chicago, was coveted by every major university in the West. He'd become one of the greatest college football players of early twentieth century. *Source:* Amos Alonzo Stagg Papers, Special Collections Research Centre, University of Chicago Library.

he ran the 220 in twenty-four and four-fifths seconds, only two-fifths off the University of Chicago's gymnasium record.[21]

Eckersall was showered with so much hyperbolic press for so many years that more than a century later it is difficult to cut through it and accept just how peerless and spectacular he often could be in sport— and not just because of his athleticism and uncanny feel for the games. He had flair, too. And daring. Eckersall had the rare courage not only to attempt but pull off incredible athletic feats in clutch moments. He also possessed real humility, at least to this point in his life, which naturally endeared him to teammates. Eckersall liked to lead and was exceptional at it. His Hyde Park High teammates voted him football captain in 1901 and 1902, and he did most of the coaching. "He called signals in a sharp, clear, confident voice," a football teammate would recall. "Whenever we heard his voice, something happened to us. It electrified us. Our spirits seemed to soar and nothing was impossible. It was amazing to see how one man could inspire a whole team."[22]

Having quarterbacked the best high school football team in America in 1902, Eckersall surely would make a fast, virtually seamless transition to the college level in 1903. Stagg wanted him. Yost wanted him. Their alumni wanted him. Every Western college wanted him. Badly. Wisconsin made fervent pitches, probably beginning with that 1902 spring break vacation it hosted. University of Illinois people in summer 1902 attempted to preempt all their rivals by asking Eckersall to enroll at UI.[23] He declined.

Perhaps the first recorded mention of Eckersall's own postsecondary intention came after his junior year at Hyde Park High. It came in a letter Wolverine captain Boss Weeks sent to UM athletic director Baird in July 1902. "Here are the men," Weeks wrote, "that I have heard mentioned as probably U of M men: Thomas Hammond Hyde Park High School . . . W. Eckersall. . . ."[24]

Although Eckersall returned to Hyde Park in 1902–1903, Michigan men continued acting and believing as though their alma mater had the inside track on acquiring him. UM had an ace in the hole, too, and undoubtedly played it. That is, athletic director Baird could relate to Eckersall better than anyone because he himself had been a star, diminutive quarterback at Hyde Park High in 1890, before enrolling at Michigan. Baird's younger brother, Jimmy, had done likewise after him.[25]

As Eckersall's senior year at Hyde Park progressed, recruiters punted subtlety straight into Lake Michigan and went after him, hard.

Stagg probably saw Eckersall several times per week. The Chicago athletic director continued to open up his sports facilities to area high schoolers. Between football, indoor track, baseball, and outdoor track, Eckersall would have used the UC facilities from September through June, probably even more often than most Maroons athletes. Those facilities were only two short blocks from Hyde Park High.

Stagg's creative but sly recruiting approach—that familiarity breeds association—was working. According to the *Chicago Tribune* on October 26, 1902, "The young Hyde Parker at present intends to enter Chicago and throw his lot with the maroons, but other colleges are after Eckersall with all sorts of plans. [Unless] Eckersall changes his mind the maroon coach will carry off the prize." Not that that dissuaded UM supporters. In a particularly brazen ploy in mid-November 1902, on the night before Yost's Wolverines smoked the Maroons in Chicago, two hundred members of UM's local alumni chapter held a "smoker" (banquet rally). According to the *Chicago Tribune*:

> A guest of the smoker was Eckersall, the Hyde Park star. Michigan alumni are "rushing" him hard, and, as one of them said, "If he does not go to Ann Arbor it will be funny." He was seated last night in the midst of a group of prominent alumni who showed him every attention possible. When yells were being given for Yost and [trainer Keene] Fitzpatrick, someone proposed nine 'rahs for Eckersall, and they were given with a will.[26]

Reports in this time said Eckersall had narrowed his college choice to Chicago or Michigan. It must have been awkward for Eckersall then on the day both Yost and Stagg attended Hyde Park's football practice before the squad's 105–0 victory against Brooklyn. Yost offered a few pointers to the Hyde Parkers on Marshall Field. Stagg, having been appointed guest coach for the week, could not have been happy.

Come February 1903, as the *Detroit Tribune* reported, several of Eckersall's Hyde Park teammates appeared ready to commit to Yost. "The only man concerning whom there is the slightest doubt is Eckersoll [*sic*]," the *Tribune* reported. "The parents of the doughty quarter back want him to attend the University of Chicago, also as to be at home, but if the wishes of the man himself prevail, Michigan will secure him. As a quarter back and field general he has no rival in the 'prep' class last year, and many of the most prominent Chicago critics freely compared him with Weeks of Michigan."[27]

By the end of the school year, UC alumni grew wary of the Michigan threat. According to Stagg biographer Robin Lester, a report in June 1903 claimed, "Michigan has had secret embassies calling on Eckersall" and that "rare inducements have been offered." In so doing, the Wolverines "have violated every ethic of intercollegiate sport," a UC athletic management official said, "[and have been] stooping to the lowest practices to steal Eckersall from us." That might well have been true. Or that might well have been just another case of Stagg gutting his archrival with his handy and willing eviscerator, the Chicago press.[28]

Eckersall's indecision continued through summer 1903. That's when the American Athletic Union—the self-appointed national protector of sporting amateurism—discredited the young athlete. The AAU moved to suspend Eckersall merely for the "taint" of having played in one summer baseball game against a team of professionals. An athlete on the take was vermin in the AAU's eyes. Equally as bad, as the AAU saw it, was the athlete who competed against professionals; that athlete thereby became himself a professional, and so did any athletes who subsequently competed alongside him. Critics of the AAU rightly pointed out that that rule, if honestly and fully enforced, would render virtually every collegiate athlete in the country a pro. But the AAU governed amateur track and field in the East, and thus its rulings held weight in the court of public opinion.

Both Stagg and Yost, unsurprisingly, rallied to Eckersall's defense. Neither the Big Nine nor any other college league would suspend any athlete for that dubious AAU reason, and there was no suggestion that Eckersall had ever been paid a penny. He was a professional only by the AAU's draconian code.[29]

As August turned to September, Eckie finally had to decide. UM alumni were convinced he personally preferred Michigan, and that he hesitated to commit only because his parents, friends, Stagg, and crooked UC alumni were all unrelentingly pressuring him to stay home. Conversely, UC alumni were convinced Eckersall personally preferred Chicago, and that he hesitated to commit only because crooked UM alums were hounding him day and night, dangling outrageously illegal, tempting offers.

Each day that Eckie didn't show up at Stagg's annual precamp of sorts in early September—for newbies and out-of-shape veterans—Stagg's anxiety and that of Maroon fans heightened.

Michigan authorities that year had opted to move Wolverine camp far out of town—to Ludington, 225 miles northwest of Ann Arbor along Lake Michigan's upper east coast. Surely Ludington would provide a cooler, less-humid climate for preseason training than the Ann Arbor area. Once there, Yost anxiously pined for Eckersall's arrival.

Ultimately, on the September 12–13 weekend, Eckersall decided to stay home and attend the University of Chicago. [30]

Exactly why he made that choice we might never know for sure. But reports and a pile of sworn affidavits issued over the next two months—and augmented a century later by the author's discovery of a revealing letter at Michigan, and also by Stagg biographer Lester's reporting—provide the following conflicting, fascinating, despicable versions of events, from the UC and UM sides. [31]

Norman W. MacChesney, a close friend of the Eckersall family and a second-generation Michigan alumnus, for months had been offering to assist Walter Jr. through UM in engineering—a discipline Chicago did not offer. MacChesney would claim to have already financially helped at least one of Eckersall's older sisters through college. When MacChesney had heard through the grapevine at some point in early or mid-September that Eckersall was to choose UC, he and another UM alumnus, Clifford G. Roe, visited the athlete and asked him why. In a joint affidavit, MacChesney and Roe later claimed Eckersall "confessed" to them he had been offered the following:

- Assurance he could enter UC without examination or academic conditions, and with the entrance fee and tuition, amounting to $120, waived.
- Salary of forty dollars per month for one to two hours work per day in one of the university's offices.
- Free board year-round and a free room at Hitchcock Hall (the first athletic dormitory in an American college).
- Guarantee of a college coaching position elsewhere after exhausting his UC eligibility.

MacChesney shared this information with other prominent UM alumni in Chicago, including Henry M. Bates (just before Bates moved to Ann Arbor to become a law professor at UM). An alumnus other than MacChesney, probably Bates, reportedly approached Stagg with the charges. Stagg investigated and met with MacChesney directly, informing him that all allegations against Eckersall and the school were without merit. MacChesney believed Stagg insofar as the coach was not involved directly. But MacChesney and Roe stated in their affidavit that "we do believe these offers were made by someone interested in the University of Chicago, or Mr. Eckersall would not have stated them."

Although Eckersall later told the press that MacChesney had been "a good friend of our family, and has always taken an interest in my welfare," the athlete subsequently denied making any of the scandalous statements that MacChesney and Roe claimed. In an affidavit, Eckersall swore that no offer "of any kind" was made to him "by anyone to attend the University of Chicago. I entered the University of Chicago because I preferred this university and because my parents wanted me to be at home."

His parents, Walter Sr. and Minnie Eckersall, themselves issued a sworn statement, denying that MacChesney or anyone else ever financially assisted any of their children through college, and that MacChesney "never spoke to us, or to any of our family, about his defraying the expenses of Walter through college."

Back to that September 12–13 weekend. Suspecting Eckersall was about to join Stagg's team, Michigan representatives had made a last desperate pitch to Eckersall. On Sunday, the *Detroit Free Press* reported that UM alumni had "secured" both Eckersall and Tom Hammond, both of whom had been "counted on as almost certain to attend the Midway school. . . . Eckersall, according to rumors of a rather substantial nature, will soon be in Ann Arbor. Where he is now only a few of his friends know, and they are unwilling to tell."

In fact, UM's weekend efforts failed. When Maroons camp opened on Monday, September 14, Eckersall turned out—to the surprise of almost everyone there. He was given a "hearty welcome," even by the veterans. According to the *Chicago Tribune*, Eckersall spent the morning getting his credits "straightened up" at Hyde Park High, receiving a letter from the school's principal "stating just what credits he had, and it was found they were ample for entrance" at UC.

Still, Michigan alumni refused to lose.

According to after-the-fact reports, four UM grads in Chicago—including MacChesney, Roe, and Phil Bartelme (Baird's unofficial assistant in Chicago)—paid a visit to the Eckersall home later that week to try to yet convince Walter to entrain for Ludington. Unsourced reports said these alumni offered illegal inducements to Eckersall and to another newly enrolled Maroon, Bubbles Hill, to compel them to swap allegiances. The source for this news almost certainly was Stagg.

Although Eckersall later "exonerated" MacChesney from "dishonorable intentions" during the visit, Chicagoans and the Maroons coach erupted in anger. Privately, so did the UM alumni named in the stories, as Bartelme himself informed Baird:

> I suppose you have seen the articles in the Chgo papers regarding the attempted kid-naping of valuable men from the U of C. The newspaper men were after me by the score last night but I kept out of their way. This morning I found [Roe] waiting for me in the office, strong for an immediate reply to the honorable gentleman who makes such reckless assertions. . . . I then advised [Roe and MacChesney] both to keep out of the newspapers' way until the Honorable had a chance to make a few more reckless statements in which he would without question use our names. [Reporters] take it for granted that I [met that day with Eckersall] and even consider my silence as admission that I have. They will now undoubtedly go to the Hon. again and if he doesn't tie a noose around his neck, I miss my guess. It strikes me that McC has a good case of payment of men against the old boy if he only keeps away from the newspapers and permits [Stagg] to do a little more talking.

Bartelme, in fact, did not take part in the attempted raid. Stagg, with neck figuratively in noose, later publicly withdrew his implication and apologized to Bartelme, who in 1909 would succeed Baird as UM athletic director.

Although Roe and MacChesney took great offense to Stagg's public charges that they'd offered illegal inducements to Eckersall, both bit their tongues temporarily, at Bartelme's direction. A month later, all of the above information finally came out in a swirl of headline-grabbing affidavits, countercharges, amended statements, and flip-flops. Not one of the principals on either side escaped tarnish.

Stagg provided a dramatic finale to this opera. In his five-thousand-word diatribe masked as a news release refuting most of MacChesney and Roe's charges, Stagg shed the following light on the alleged kidnapping of Eckersall:

> Behold the spectacle of MacChesney and Roe going to the home of Walter Eckersall at 12 o'clock at night, going to his room, waking him up and working until 2 o'clock in the morning trying to persuade him to leave the college of his choice and go to the University of Michigan. They beseech him to take the first train in the morning. They have his transportation already secured, so they tell him and his mother, and he need not worry at all about his expenses. They are so insistent that they scarcely sleep that night in their haste to get there early next morning. They arrived at 6 o'clock to finish their work.

Stagg refused ever to divulge the rest of the story publicly, but here it is. Stagg aborted the conclusion of that "work" with the shrewdest, boldest recruiting stroke of his career, and certainly by any recruiter in 1903. Evidently, Eckersall did indeed accept that train ticket from MacChesney and Roe, with the intention of enrolling at UM instead of UC. Somehow Stagg found out, because in an interview given some seven decades after the fact, longtime UC sports information director William V. Morgenstern divulged to author Lester the following: "Stagg admitted literally taking Eckersall from the Englewood station platform in Chicago, as he was waiting for the Ann Arbor train."[32] Walter Eckersall thus remained a Chicago Maroon, thanks to the greatest off-field interception in football history.

✿ ✿ ✿

As the Eckersall drama played out in mid-September, Henry M. Bates provided his final, pivotal contributions to Michigan football from Chicago, before becoming a long-time law professor and dean of note.

First, there was the matter of Willie Heston. As the greatest halfback in the West, he might have been money on the field, but he couldn't manage a nickel off it. In clearing his decks, Bates informed Baird of the following after discovering that Heston remained in financial straits:

> I sent Heston $100 about March 1st, 1903, to pay his debts & in
> addition sent him $15.00 per month for March, April, May & June &
> an extra $10.00. These amts were all loaned him & I have his notes
> payable to me as trustee for it all. I told him I could probably loan
> him $15.00 a month for the school year—this year. He said that
> would be sufficient. He also said the $100 squared up all his debts.
> Of course I can do nothing more in the matter now. [Another man]
> will see him through if he is on the square & is not throwing money
> away. I very much fear Heston has gone bad. With what he earned
> during the summer he ought to be in good shape. . . . Please keep my
> part in the matter absolutely confidential.[33]

The devout college football fan at the time—and for decades thereafter—probably believed the rumors and newspaper gossip and concluded Heston was no different than any star football player in the East:
pampered, awash in cash, and wanting for nothing. The above private
letter from Bates to Baird, as with Yost's to Baird in 1901 and 1902,
prove that simply was not the case.

The scrounging Heston and Dad Gregory concocted a scheme with
Yost in late summer 1903 whereby they might sell the new "Hurry Up
Yost" cigars across the country, probably a poor man's attempt to mimic
the extremely lucrative tobacco sponsorship deals in the East that saw a
few college football stars become rich. Heston and Gregory even advised the press at one point they might not return to UM. But the
scheme fell through, and both enrolled again.[34]

The second matter involving Bates was the recruitment and enrolment of Tom Hammond, Eckersall's backfield mate at Hyde Park High.
Stagg desperately wanted him too, almost as much as Eckersall, and
expected Hammond to join the Maroons.[35] But thanks to the efforts of
Bates and others, Michigan had him cold. Hammond wanted to become a Wolverine, as did his younger brother and Hyde Park lineman
teammate, Harry.

The problem was that Tom had only just completed his third year at
Hyde Park High and wasn't yet close to earning enough credits to
graduate. His recruitment by Michigan, Chicago, and others caused a
scandal. Had it really come to this—big-time colleges arm-bending high
school juniors?

In fact, Hammond had completed two years of study at a small high
school before entering Hyde Park High while his family lived in the

East. Even though Hammond now had five years of high school under his belt, Hyde Park High did not recognize any of his previous credits, so he did not yet qualify to graduate. Young Tom was anxious to move on.[36]

In an attempt to throw other schools off Hammond's trail, reports out of Chicago claimed UM convinced the twenty-year-old to let it be known in August he was through with both football and school and was entering the workforce.[37] Meantime, Bates quietly spearheaded the move to prepare Hammond for UM's entrance exams. "We simply must get him in," Bates wrote Baird on September 6. "His tutoring bills should be held until I reach Ann Arbor. I would let as few people as possible know he is there—and particularly the newspapers should not get the news."[38]

After UM admitted Hammond, with conditions, the news got out. Stagg hit the ceiling.

Even though Yost, Baird, and UM's bird-dog alumni lost out on Eckersall, they still hauled in an impressive recruiting class in 1903. In addition to the Hammonds, they acquired two other Hyde Park High starters—halfback Marion Wolfe and backfield man Walter Becker, although neither panned out. Other recruits that did were lineman John "Joe" Curtis from a Pueblo, Colorado, high school; lineman Henry Schulte, a former star for Washington University in St. Louis; Frank Longman, the former Kalamazoo high school fullback; Johnny Garrels, a spectacular all-around athlete from Detroit Central High; and Denny Clark, a prep student from Detroit University High.[39]

All were preps. Just one year after poor-mouthing the practice of loading up on high school recruits, Yost quickly changed tactics and accepted that this was the surest way to go. Probably he realized that high schoolers were (1) far more numerous and easier to locate than unknown, veteran crackerjacks at tiny colleges, (2) likelier to stay for more than one or two years, and (3) far more likely to be eligible, both after a background check for professionalism stains and academically upon entrance.

Ironically, perhaps Stagg's best recruit in 1903 after Eckersall was a transfer—lineman John Tobin from the University of Nebraska. Two high school grads (tackle Edwin Parry and guard Melville "Bubbles" Hill) also would crack the Maroons starting lineup straightaway, but Tobin had college experience.[40]

Tobin's recruitment was scandalous. Not in Chicago, but in Lincoln. Stagg dispatched his previous year's Nebraska pinch—lineman John Koehler, now a Maroons assistant coach—to Lincoln to snatch Tobin off coach Bummy Booth's training-camp field and then personally escort Tobin on a train back to Chicago. That Koehler did. Back in February, Stagg had sent Koehler to Lincoln on a similar raid and he'd nearly convinced Nebraska tackle John Westover, the 1902 captain, and a fullback surnamed Pillsbury to transfer to UC.[41]

Stagg clearly had no qualms about pilfering enrolled, stud players from Nebraska in a manner identical to Michigan's postcommitment pursuit of Eckersall, which had so outraged him. Nor did Stagg hold himself to the same principle on which he'd lectured Yost five months earlier: "As I view the matter, it would have a professional tinge, if I for example, sought to build up the athletic work of my department by making trips around the country for the sole purpose of securing more and better athletic material."

The high-water mark of Stagg's hypocrisy: Koehler and Tobin's train arrived in Chicago from the west in the same week, perhaps even on the same day, that Stagg stopped Eckersall from going east to Michigan.

11

1903 ON THE FIELD

Incredibly, Mich-again

One week into his collegiate football career as a University of Chicago Maroon, it was obvious little Walter Eckersall was going to be special.

After an unofficial warm-up defeat of Englewood High School, the Maroons opened the 1903 season by trouncing Lombard College of Galesburg, Illinois, 34–0. In preseason practice Eckersall had already supplanted last year's quarterback, Lee Maxwell, one of coach Amos Alonzo Stagg's most reliable, first-rate players. "Eckie" played anything like a scrawny, wide-eyed frosh in his debut. Observed the *Chicago Tribune*:

> The Hyde Park lad played his usual star game and was loudly cheered when he went to the side lines [upon being pulled for Maxwell]. He ran the team in good style. . . . He made the most spectacular plays of the afternoon. Once he got the ball on the kickoff and returned it forty-five through a broken field. At another time he played end on a punt, which Ellsworth sent flying sixty yards down the field. The little sprinter was on Cooper by the time the ball reached him and downed him in his tracks.[1]

In the next game, a 23–0 win against Lawrence College of Appleton, Wisconsin, Eckersall "ran the team fast and showed some of the sprinting and dodging ability which characterized his work on the Hyde Park team," the *Trib* noted. That included a fifty-yard run from scrimmage, as quarterbacks this year were now able to advance the ball, so long as they crossed the scrimmage line five yards laterally from where the ball was snapped (the new lengthways line markings at five-yard increments gave the field its "gridiron" appearance). Eckie also returned a kickoff seventy yards, which "brought the crowd to its feet" at UC's Marshall Field.[2]

Following a 108–0 demolition of far-overmatched Monmouth College of Monmouth, Illinois, Eckersall was even more impactful in his first Big Nine game, a 34–0 defeat of Indiana. He ripped off a pair of seventy-five-yard runs, averaged fifty yards on his punts, and his "phenomenal drop-kicking of the last goal from the forty-five yard line filled the hearts of the Maroons with inexpressible joy," the *Tribune* reported.[3]

Three more shutout victories—over Cornell College of Iowa 23–0, Purdue 22–0, and Rush Medical College 40–0—preceded Chicago's tough closing stretch in 1903. Northwestern was first up, now coached by Walter McCornack, a former Dartmouth star. He had been pointing his team to this mid-October game. Chicago was favored by twelve to eighteen points but was fortunate to escape with a 0–0 tie. McCornack's Methodists dominated the first half but fumbled four yards from the Maroon goal line on one deep thrust and missed a field goal by inches on another. Eckersall "did not shine" as in previous games, the *Trib* said, and not just because Northwestern blanketed him on punt returns.[4]

The Maroons played much better a week later in an 18–6 defeat of Illinois, now coached by George Woodruff. The play of the game was turned in by Eckersall, when with Chicago trailing 6–0 he returned a punt sixty yards for a spectacular tying touchdown, on which Eck slithered through more than half the Illini team like an "eel."[5]

Next up for 8–0–1 Chicago was Wisconsin on Halloween in the Maroons' first trip to Madison since 1899. Even though the Badgers appeared resurgent at 5–0, UC fans exuded more optimism than usual. The *Trib* said the "new" and "intricate" plays that the "wizard of the midway," Stagg, had conjured would spell doom for the Badgers and their young new coach, Arthur Curtis.[6] In fact, only one thing spelled doom for the Badgers. Curtis and his crew had defensive answers for everything Stagg threw at them, but were powerless to stop the accurate dropkicking of Eckersall. The frosh made three of five field goals, then worth five points apiece—from twenty, twenty, and thirty-five yards out—and Chicago won 15–6. Eckie made the first kick from a harsh angle. Curtis tipped his cap afterward: "Eckersall defeated us fairly and we have no excuses to offer," the coach said.[7] Perhaps that's what prompted a Milwaukee headline writer to top his paper's game story with: "Eckersall 15, Wisconsin 6."[8]

Just one month into his college career, not only could the little man impact games, he could decide them—single-footedly.

* * *

In Ann Arbor, Fielding H. Yost confidently plugged four of his promising freshmen recruits into the starting Michigan lineup. But he could not find on his squad a reliable quarterback, punter, field-goal kicker, or kick returner. In other words, no Walter Eckersall.

Only three starters remained from his first Wolverine team of two years ago—two-time All-Western halfback Willie Heston, center Dad Gregory, and left end Curtis Redden, the captain. Only one of the four 1902 replacement starters returned: right tackle Joe Maddock. But Maddock would miss the first three games as he made up deficiencies in his academic work. Oft-used 1901 and 1902 backup Herb Graver would take over at right halfback.

The rest of the Wolverine squad was green. At preseason camp in Ludington, Yost and trainer Keene Fitzpatrick drove this team even harder, conditioning-wise, than they had the '01 and '02 predecessors at Whitmore Lake.[9] Yost rightly sensed that this team would need every edge it could muster if it hoped to add much to Michigan's current twenty-two-game winning streak.

For the second straight offseason, Baird could not entice one of the Big Four of the East to schedule Michigan. Probably he did not try too hard this year, what with most of the previous year's team gone and Minnesota, Wisconsin, and Chicago lined up again. A pair of second-tier Eastern powers, Army and Columbia, were willing to play Michigan, but Baird declined their offers.[10] He preferred to keep holding out for one of top-tier powers.

The Wolverines' toughest test in 1903 would come much earlier than usual—on Halloween in Minneapolis against Dr. Henry L. Williams's still-loaded University of Minnesota Gophers. It was prob-

Figure 11.1.   Fielding Yost took a group of mostly green players in 1903 and worked them harder than his two previous teams. He roster-tinkered deep into the season to find a winning lineup and extend his "point-a-minute" dynasty's success. *Source:* Bentley Historical Library, University of Michigan.

ably during preseason camp that Yost learned in the papers that the Gophers had begun practicing three weeks before the Wolverines. By September 16, the Gophers already were playing practice games, and would play ten before Michigan arrived. Inequities perturbed Yost more than almost anything in sport,[11] and that likely was the reason he asked UM athletic director Charles Baird at the last minute to load up even more October practice games than originally scheduled in the spring. Baird managed to jam in seven between October 3 and the Minnesota tilt twenty-eight days later, including two on Wednesdays and one on a Thursday.

To the surprise of nearly everyone outside Ann Arbor, Yost's Wolverine machine kept right on humming in 1903—at least on the scoreboard. Michigan won the seven tune-ups in its now accustomed manner: over Case 31–0 in forty minutes; Albion, 76–0 in twenty-six minutes; Beloit, 79–0 in forty-five minutes; Ohio Normal, 65–0 in thirty-four minutes; Indiana, 51–0 in fifty minutes; Ferris Institute, 88–0 in thirty minutes; and Drake, 47–0 in fifty-five minutes. That was 437 points in 280 minutes. (The referee in the Ferris game later issued a statement saying his ruling of a safety by Ferris had been wrongly presumed by both the press and the Ferry Field scoreboard operators to be a touchback, thus Michigan actually won by two more points, 90–0, but the correct score never made it into the official record.)[12]

Heston was running better than ever through Michigan's first three games. A rough estimate from incomplete newspaper play-by-play accounts suggests he rushed for at least five hundred yards in those games and scored eleven touchdowns. Against Beloit, he scored on runs of eighty, twenty-five, sixty-five, forty, and eighty-five yards and amassed more than three hundred yards—all in the twenty-five-minute first half. But against Ohio Normal, Heston twisted a knee and could not walk off the field without assistance. The injured knee swelled. Yost kept Heston out of the Indiana, Ferris, and Drake games, hoping that under trainer Fitzpatrick's expert mending the star left halfback would heal enough to be effective in Minneapolis.

All the while, Yost kept tinkering with his roster—uncertain he'd picked the right eleven, and uncertain where he should position some starters. For instance, freshmen Frank "Shorty" Longman and ex–Hyde Parker Tom Hammond both were dogged line smashers. Yost threw the fullback bone to Hammond and moved Longman to right end. Hammond's penchant for fumbling the big oval, though, proved vexing.

At the most pivotal position, quarterback, Yost's ambivalence prompted him to vacillate between John "Harry" James and Fred "Norky" Norcross in the practice games. Neither could match the departed Boss Weeks in so many facets, not the least of which was rapidity of play.

Meantime, for weeks leading up to the game at Minneapolis, bad blood again simmered between the Michigan and Minnesota athletic departments. This year, it stayed private. Letters reveal that Gophers coach Williams and Yost (through Baird) dickered over the selection of game officials for the second consecutive year.[13] In big games, Michigan always preferred to have as referee either Princeton's Ralph Hoagland or Lafayette's Charles Rinehart. Hoagland was viewed as perhaps the fairest and best official east or west. Rinehart was a teammate of Yost's on the great Leopards team that had upset Penn in 1896, but he too was popular east and west. Williams refused both men, as he had the year before.

What's more, Williams and his Gophers players had felt victimized by the 1902 game's officials—former Yale All-American Frank Hinkey (referee), Fred Hayner of Lake Forest (head linesman), and Yale's Laurie Bliss (umpire)[14]—and opposed all three for 1903, even though Hinkey and Hayner were practically in Hoagland's class in terms of widespread respect and demand. Replacements that Williams proposed included University of Chicago men, which displeased Michigan. At one point, Baird privately stated UM wanted no one from the "Chicago coaching force" to officiate in this game. In the end, the Wolverines agreed to one UC man: Henry T. Clark Jr., as umpire. He joined Lieutenant Harry M. Nelly of Army as referee and Harold Letton of Yale as linesman.

In another sign that college football popularity was zooming, a record attendance for the West was anticipated at Northrop Field to break the twenty-two-thousand mark set the previous year between Michigan and Wisconsin at Marshall Field. Although some postgame reports would peg the crowd size at thirty thousand, in fact it barely surpassed twenty. Still, hundreds of Gophers fans were stuck outside the grounds, ticketless. Some took to climbing trees or telegraph poles to sneak a peek.

Perhaps the best indication that football fever had infected the general American population by autumn 1903 was that thousands of city folk both in Minneapolis and Ann Arbor demanded some means of following the Wolverines–Gophers game live. This was two decades before the first live college football radio broadcasts and almost five decades before the first telecasts. Telegraph and telephone were the only options in 1903. Some four thousand UM students and other Ann Arborites jammed University Hall to hear a "telephonic" play-by-play account of the game.[15] Similarly, the *Journal* set up five stations throughout Minneapolis to keep interested locals informed, by the play, "in graphic style" on large blackboards. A crowd of twelve thousand alone engulfed the main update board outside the *Journal* building.[16] The *Michigan Daily* student newspaper even published a special game-over bulldog edition—a first.

With the exception of a few hundred Michigan partisans sporting maize and blue on that calm, unseasonably pleasant day, a sea of maroon and gold filled the grandstands and bleachers at Northrop Field.

Wolverine and Gopher players alike got swept up in the enormity of the event, as nervy play punctuated the early going. Little Sig Harris, subbing for injured first-string Gophers quarterback Henry O'Brien, at first showed nothing of the fantastic form that would render him one of the Minnesota's first football immortals. He bobbled the opening kick-off and returned it only to the fourteen-yard line. Six plays later, on the third and final down, Harris fumbled an errant punt snap and was tackled short of a first down at the Gopher fifteen. Such a colossal gaffe usually meant immediate doom against Yost's Michigan machine. But twice the five Minnesota linemen stuffed their Wolverine counterparts—three of whom were playing in their first big game—and right halfback Graver netted zero yards. On third-and-five, Hammond dropped back to the twenty-seven to attempt a placekick field goal. Gregory's snap was uncharacteristically poor, and a Gopher recovered the loose ball at that spot.[17]

A few minutes later, Michigan recovered another Gopher fumble, this one at the Minnesota forty-five-yard line. Heston gained fifteen yards on five carries to help advance the ball to the Gopher twenty-five, but a Heston run on a fake punt failed to make distance.

The defensive stands empowered the Gophers on offense. It helped, too, that the Gophers were gaining field position with virtually every exchange of punts, thanks to Harris's good kicks for them and Maddock's weak ones for Michigan. On five of the Gophers' remaining seven possessions in the thirty-five-minute first half, they drove inside the Wolverine thirty-five-yard line. But three of the drives stalled on downs—at the thirty-, fourteen-, and thirty-three-yard lines. A fourth drive ended with a missed forty-yard field goal attempt by captain Ed Rogers, and a fifth died at the Wolverine thirty when halftime was reached.

The game was scoreless, but optimism permeated Gopher spectators and players alike. Indeed, as Coach Williams had been trying to convince his charges for two months, they could not only stay with the Yostmen, they could defeat them. Now they believed.

Newspaper reports would later underscore that "play was fierce" throughout the game, and that "several men were hurt." That probably explained in part why "after almost every third down a Gopher player might be seen stretched upon the ground," the *Minneapolis Journal* reported. For the second straight year, Williams obviously had instructed his players to continually disrupt Michigan's rapid-fire rhythm on offense by begging the officials for an injury timeout, which the three-man crew obliged.

The problem was, the interminable delays were stretching the game's length considerably, and that had been compounded by Minnesota's dramatic late arrival onto the field at the get-go, which delayed opening kickoff by fourteen minutes, to 2:29 p.m. local time. Sunset would come just after five p.m.

The Gophers had all but shut down the vaunted Wolverine attack. At halftime, Yost did not panic. Rather, he schemed on the fly, drawing up two new plays for quarterback Fred Norcross to call at will. Both were intended for left halfback Heston, to counter whatever the hard-charging Gopher linemen were doing to continually knife through and disrupt Michigan's inside smashes and end runs alike. One antidote was a "quick-opening play straight ahead between guard and tackle," Heston would recall, and the other was a run outside right tackle, off fake "interference" inside.[18]

The Wolverines overcame a huge scare early in the second half, holding on downs at the Michigan twelve-yard line following Norcross's fumbled punt at the thirty. Now it was the Wolverines' turn to siphon energy from a defensive stand.

As Norcross began to mix in the new plays, Heston and Graver took turns smashing the ball forty yards out to near midfield. A quick exchange of punts gave Michigan the ball back at its thirty-seven about midway through the second half.

The Wolverines' superior conditioning began to tell. With Heston lugging the ball on almost every snap, and his blockers gaining in effectiveness, the Wolverines mounted one of the great drives of the point-a-minute era. The Gophers seemed powerless to stop the rising Wolverine surge. According to the *Minneapolis Journal*, an exuberant but nervous Yost "chewed up one cigar after another" on the Michigan sideline as the drive proceeded. Meanwhile, across the field Williams's line coach—his old Yale teammate and all-time great guard Pudge Heffelfinger—shouted some pointed advice to his charges, which Heston heard and never forgot: "Get Heston! Put him out of the game or Michigan will score!"[19]

The *Detroit Free Press* reported that several Michigan players early on heard Heffelfinger "cry out from the sidelines: 'Kill off Heston in the first ten minutes, or you'll lose.' The bleachers took it up and the constant yell went around the field: 'Kill off Heston.'"[20]

By any measure, the blocking and tackling by this point in the game had devolved into pure, desperate savagery. Heston, for one, now sported a mangled face. And yet, after the Wolverines advanced to the Gopher forty, Heston broke free around captain Rogers, the Minnesota left end, and appeared to be sprung on one of his signature touchdown sprints. But Sig Harris, the deep safety on defense, showed his class by bursting out of nowhere from the side to bring Heston down at the twenty. On the next play, Heston failed to gain around left end, and a brutal collision laid him out for one of the few times in his college career. Woozy, he remained in the game. Quarterback Norcross kept calling his number. Heston helped push the ball to the Gopher five-yard line. Plunges by Graver and Hammond shoved the ball only inches from the Gopher goal. Quarterback Norcross was hesitant to call Heston's number again but felt compelled to do so. One Wolverine protested. Decades later, a Michigan sports information director wrote, "Just as Norcross started to bark the signal, big [tackle Joe] Maddock dropped back. His face was cut and bleeding, too. One eye was a deep purple. 'Give me the damn ball!' he growled. '[Heston's] done enough.'"[21] Norcross complied, and on a tackles-back play, Maddock smashed across the goal line. Touchdown. The drive consisted of any-where from sixteen to twenty-three carries (accounts differ). Hammond converted and Michigan led 6–0 with seven minutes remaining as the partisan crowd fell mostly silent.[22]

Back in Ann Arbor, several thousand students and townies took to the streets in wild premature celebration, so sure were they that the game had been won.[23] Williams, Harris, and the Gophers had other ideas. The first was a stroke of savvy rules manipulation by Williams. He kept his head and had his captain ask the referee to receive the ensuing kickoff from Michigan, rather than kick off—as was the custom. This was the first year a team could receive a kickoff after being scored on.

Harris took Hammond's kickoff at the Gopher one and weaved through six Michigan defenders until he was brought down forty-four yards later. Just like that, field position favored the Gophers. "Hope sprang anew in the breast of the Minnesota rooters," the *Minneapolis Journal* wrote the next day.

After having gained only nineteen yards of offense in the half, the Gophers summoned a second wind. They smashed their way to the Michigan thirty-two before an offside penalty forced them to punt. Michigan lost center Gregory to injury on the drive, leaving Maddock as the only veteran Wolverine lineman. Michigan's middle was vulnerable.

Minnesota quickly got the ball back on a punt and advanced as far as midfield before the Wolverines forced them to punt again. About four minutes remained, and the Gophers' chances were disappearing as fast as the twilight. Incredibly, though, Michigan fumbled a punt for the third time in its own end—Graver being the guilty party this time.[24] Yost later echoed newspaper reports in claiming that several Gophers players actually threw their headgears at Graver before the punt reached him, in an effort to make him fumble, which egregious offence the game officials either did not see or did not penalize. Although the Wolverines held on downs inside the twenty, Maddock's shanked punt set up the Gophers for one last drive at the Michigan thirty-eight.

This time there was no stopping the Gophers. Williams obviously had learned plenty from watching Yost's Wolverines the year before. Until then he'd always molded offensive strategy along the stodgy Yale line, but Yost in 1902 had opened his eyes to the benefits of hurry-up play: once on a roll it overwhelms and disheartens a foe. And, when pressed for time, a team can quickly move a considerable distance, even with short gains. So it was that in twelve rapidly run plays, the Gophers scored a touchdown with two minutes remaining. Egil Boeckmann gained the last crucial yard. Captain Rogers kicked the extra point to tie the score at 6–6.

In sheer darkness now, at about 5:30, Northrop Field erupted. Hundreds, maybe thousands, of fans poured onto the field in delirious celebration. What to do now? It would take forever to clear the field, but beyond that, it already was far too dark to continue playing. Both captains agreed to call the game, two minutes early. Michigan's twenty-nine-game winning streak was over, even if its unbeaten string grew to thirty games.

According to statistics published in the *Minneapolis Journal* and verified by that newspaper's game diagram, the Gophers topped the Wolverines in rushing yards gained (237 to 152), punt-return yards (27 to 9), kickoff-return yards (55 to 10), and punting yards (385 to 336). The only significant stat the Wolverines had the edge in was second-half rushing yardage—122 to 96.

"I think Minnesota should have won, as it had the best of it the greater part of the game," Williams said afterward, "but we are satisfied with the result."

Yost was no more gracious a stalemater than he was a loser: "We should have won. The boys played well, but luck was against them. Minnesota has a great team, and I wish we might play them again."[25]

The headline on Frank E. Force's *Minneapolis Tribune* game story the next day summed up the local attitude: "Tie Game; Minnesota Wins." One thing the Gophers claimed for certain that day was the clay water jug the Wolverines left behind on their Northrop Field sideline. It would become known as "the Little Brown Jug"—which the Wolverines and Golden Gophers still play for in college football's oldest trophy game.

While euphoria draped the Twin Cities, some one thousand UM students and as many or more townspeople turned out at the Ann Arbor train depot to honor the Wolverines upon their arrival home on Sunday night. For many of the greeters, joyful cheering soon turned to resentful anger upon seeing the battered faces of many of the deboarding Wolverines, especially Heston's. "By the time we had reached the hotel after the game," Heston recalled decades later, "my right eye was entirely closed and I could see but little out of the corner of my left eye. My face resembled a raw beef roast."[26]

Evidently, Michigan football players never had appeared so beaten up after a game. It didn't take much goading by the local press corps to get players to sound off about it. Heston "bitterly" denounced the Gophers for their rough play. "They not only slugged," Heston said with puffed lips, "but they used their spikes." Michigan trainer Fitzpatrick said the game was "the worst, from the point of foul play, that ever came under my observation. I saw Heston punched any number of times, and once I saw a Minnesota man jump on Norcross after he had caught a punt and knock him out with a blow on the jaw." Said Maddock, "When I went over for the touchdown I was punched in the back of the neck and kicked in the head at least twenty times."[27]

Upon his return to Ann Arbor on Monday, Yost agreed his Wolverines took "terrific bumpings" in "one of the roughest games I ever saw," but he said "I do not say this in a complaining spirit. Our men got the worst of it on general principles for the simple reason that the Minnesota men played that style of game."[28]

The Wolverines were not without guilt. Countered Frank E. Force in the *Minneapolis Tribune*,

> For ten minutes of the play Minnesota put forth all of her strength in attempts to stop [Heston and Maddock], and it is no wonder that they were bruised a bit. . . . Heston did not receive any worse treatment than some of the Minnesota men. I saw Heston after the game and he did not look a bit worse than either Hunk Davies or Jimmy Irsfield. These Minnesota men were pounded in a frightful manner and Davies' face was cut to pieces by blows that could only have come from clenched fists. . . . The charges of Yost and Maddock and Heston are but the wails of disappointed children.[29]

Heffelfinger and the Gopher players to a man similarly denied the accusations. Said Sunny Thorpe, "The only rough play I saw was when a Michigan man booted me in the head and put me out." Thorpe did not learn of the final score until he woke up Sunday morning.[30]

The last of the UM contingent to arrive back in Ann Arbor was athletic director Baird. He was appalled at the bellyaching from his team. Baird not only immediately ordered the team to discontinue it, he compelled captain Redden to issue a statement recanting the accusations because, Baird explained privately, "Michigan has been wont in the past to pride herself on her sportsmanlike conduct and dignified attitude in such matters." That said, Baird charged privately that "we have good grounds for complaint against the Minnesota team. Furthermore I think that Dr. Williams should be held responsible for this more than the Minnesota team as individuals."[31]

What bothered Yost far more than any slugging was the officiating: "We lost [sic] the game through the inefficiency—we'll call it that—of Umpire Clark," he told the press. Yes, Clark—the University of Chicago man. "Graver's so-called fumble, which gave Minnesota the ball before its touchdown, was the plainest kind of interference," Yost said. "There were five Minnesota men jostling him and throwing their headgears before the ball ever came down, and Clark didn't see it, although almost every newspaper report tells about the play."[32]

Clark read about Yost's charges and wrote Baird to inquire if all Michigan men felt likewise about his integrity. Of course not, Baird assured him. Yost obliged Clark's request to write him back directly, and Yost's mind was "still filled with doubt" as to Clark's impartiality, the umpire informed Baird.[33]

Immediately after the game, there were reports Michigan was prepared to cut off all athletic relations with Minnesota, which the UM Board in Control of Athletics denied. The *Michigan Alumnus* magazine, though, correctly reported that the "important matter is that, from whatever cause, ill-feeling exists between the two universities. Whoever may be to blame for it, the distrust is here and must be reckoned with. . . . If it cannot be eliminated, further contests with Minnesota would be intolerable to the spirit of good sport."[34]

From Michigan's perspective, the only practical way the distrust could be eliminated would be if Dr. Henry L. Williams were to leave Minneapolis. And that wasn't happening. Thus, Michigan was unlikely to play Minnesota again any time soon.

* * *

Three teams remained in the hunt for the Championship of the West after Halloween: Michigan, Minnesota, and Chicago. The latter two weren't scheduled to meet in 1903, so if the once-tied Maroons could defeat Michigan on Thanksgiving Day, they'd split the title with the once-tied Gophers, presuming Williams's charges remained unbeaten.

Stagg's undefeated team had but two November games before the home-field finale against Yost's Wolverines. In the first, the vastly undersized Haskell Indians gave the Maroons fits on November 8 before UC escaped with a 17–11 victory. For many Chicago fans, it was an enthusiasm killer. As the *Chicago Examiner*'s football expert Thomas T. Hoyne explained, "Haskell played Michigan football." More particularly, Yost football. That's because Al Herrnstein, the star right halfback on Yost's first two Wolverine squads, now coached Haskell in Yost's hurry-up manner. "Chicago had all it could to do to avoid defeat," Hoyne wrote. "There are many who will say that the Haskell game gave the Maroons great practice against the Michigan style of playing. This, of course, is true, but if such practice is any criterion, it means the Maroons at the present time have no chance at all against the Yost team."[35]

Next up for the Maroons: Army on November 15 in West Point, New York. The Cadets always were just a notch below the Big Four, and a victory for Stagg would open eyes in the East and, more importantly, restore the confidence his squad had lost against Haskell. Chicago led 6–5 in the final minutes, having "outplayed the soldiers in every feature of the game except defense against line bucking," the *Chicago Tribune* correspondent wrote. Then disaster. Eckersall, who'd played "his usual star game," punted from his own fifteen-yard line. It was short. Horatio B. "Dumpy" Hackett, the Army quarterback, settled under the high-arcing kick and motioned for a fair catch at the Chicago forty. The problem for the Maroons is that end Mark Catlin ventured too close to Hackett. The ball landed on the back of Catlin's neck as he slammed into Hackett. Although Chicago's Fred Speik picked up the ball and ran toward West Point's goal, officials blew the play dead and penalized the Maroons fifteen yards for fair-catch interference. From the twenty-five-yard line the Cadets could attempt a free kick, and did. Thomas Doe nailed a placement field goal, and Army won 10–6.[36]

Michigan, in the meantime, beat former Yale star Perry Hale's visiting Ohio State team 36–0 in fifty-five minutes on November 7. Yost inserted James back in at quarterback over Norcross and finally swapped Longman in for Hammond at fullback, moving Hammond to end. The offense seemed to click much better, even though Heston played only briefly in the second half.

On November 14, Yost relied on the same configuration against the visiting Wisconsin Badgers. In another sign that Minnesota had supplanted Wisconsin in the top tier of Big Nine teams, the Badgers proved no match for Michigan. The Wolverines won convincingly in Ann Arbor 16–0 in thirty-five-minute halves before eight thousand fans. Trainer Fitzpatrick said the Wolverine attack appeared 40 percent stronger in this game than in any of the previous nine.[37] Yost had found the winning lineup.

Michigan dominated play in the scoreless first half against Wisconsin before the Hyde Park curse struck the Badgers thereafter. Michigan's own freshman from Hyde Park High, Tom Hammond, made like his former schoolboy teammate Eckersall two weeks earlier and gutted the Badgers with field goals. Hammond's two were from placement, not dropkick—fifteen and forty-five yards out. Hammond also kicked the extra point on Joe Maddock's touchdown. In kicked points against the Badgers, Eckersall edged Hammond 15–11.

A footnote to the Michigan–Wisconsin game: afterward players and coaches on both sides went out of their way to take subtle digs at their mutual nemesis—the good doctor, Minnesota coach Henry L. Williams—by claiming the game was entirely free of slugging. "That was the cleanest, hardest-fought contest ever seen in the West," Wisconsin trainer Pat O'Dea said. "No man on either team violated in spirit or action any of the rules of manly sport."[38]

Three days before Yost's Wolverines crushed Oberlin 42–0 in forty-five minutes on November 21, the coach announced he would return in 1904 to honor the final year of his contract at Michigan. Yost must have loved the *Chicago Tribune*'s headline the next day: "Sad News for Rival Elevens."[39]

More sad news lay just around the corner for one.

※ ※ ※

Six days before the Michigan–Chicago showdown at Marshall Field, Walter Camp typed this letter to Stagg, now the foremost of his players-turned-coaches from Yale: "My dear Lonnie: I expect now in the interest of the sport to be on hand to see your Thanksgiving Day game with Michigan. Will you please arrange so that I shall have a side line badge[?]"[40] Stagg was thrilled to have his old coach attend, of course.

Ties within the Yale brotherhood were strong. As an example, a few days after his Ohio State team had fallen to the Yostmen, coach Hale—a 1900 Yale grad—sent Stagg a few tips for beating this Michigan team, unprompted. "I have never had the pleasure of meeting you, but being a Yale man I feel it my duty to aid you in any way that I can," Hale wrote. "I do want you to clean up on that team."[41]

Yost must have been euphoric upon learning Camp would attend: the father of football, finally on hand to watch one of Yost's own storied teams in action. It was another scrapbook moment in his coaching career. For Stagg, it was all the more cause to work his team, and most of all himself, tirelessly in advance of Yost's arrival.

The previous autumn, Stagg had had electric lights installed over his practice field so that darkness could no longer cut short late-season sessions. He and his team worked well into the evening at the last pregame scrimmage before the Michigan game. Stagg even turned to a dog-eared page from Camp's coaching manual at Yale and invited several former UC players to help prepare the boys before this year's biggest game. But after he "walked wearily off the field," a disconsolate Stagg looked awful and sounded anything but confident in his team's chances.[42]

In Ann Arbor, Yost's biggest problem—for the third consecutive November—was snuffing out the overconfidence he sensed in his team. That seems strange only three and a half weeks after the tie at Minneapolis, and seeing as Chicago had a 10–1–1 record with the only loss coming to an Eastern team. As Thanksgiving approached, the Wolverines too practiced under newly installed electric lights; there simply was no way could Yost could allow Stagg such a practice-field advantage for more than one year.[43]

On game day it was bitterly cold on Chicago's north side, but dry; Evanston was "brown and bare." It was a different story on the south side, where UC was situated. From 10 a.m. until 1:30 p.m., a blizzard dumped five inches of snow. Kickoff at Marshall Field was delayed an hour while an emergency crew that included UC freshmen attempted to clear the playing surface.

Stagg might have grabbed a shovel if he could have joined them, but he'd fallen seriously ill that week. On Monday, he thought he'd come down with just a cold. On Tuesday, just two days before kickoff, he defied his begging wife and proceeded to run practice. "By the day of the game," Stagg recalled in his 1927 autobiography,

> I had an abscess in each ear, both needing to be punctured, influenza had developed and pleurisy and pneumonia were coming on. . . . I was driven to the game and onto the snowy field in a carriage, in fearful pain from my ears and a sinus headache—two of the most exquisitely painful aches, it is said, to which man is heir. I was swaddled in bedclothing and Mrs. Stagg sat beside me as nurse.[44]

Compounding this "physical torture," Stagg also recalled, was the "mental agony" of watching what transpired on the field. Yost's Wolverines obliterated his Maroons 28–0 in an ostensible seventy-minute game cut short fifteen minutes by three things: the weather, approaching darkness, and the foregone conclusion.

Michigan led 22–0 at halftime, having dominated play as wholly as that score implies, and as much as any Wolverine team ever had in any big game. No less than the weather, this Wolverine onslaught "froze into silence" some twenty thousand fans who'd made it to Marshall Field, blizzard and all.

Michigan possessed the ball for almost the entire first half and marched at will: sixty-three yards before turning it over on downs, fifty-two yards for a touchdown, eighty-three yards for a touchdown, fifty-three yards for a Tom Hammond field goal, thirty yards before a punt, and forty-five yards that set up another field goal—for 318 yards rushing by the break. By contrast, Chicago ran nine offensive plays in the first half for fourteen yards. The second half was superfluous. From his carriage, Stagg subbed out seven players. Yost kept all his starters in until the bitterly cold end.

The Maroons played "like a lot of calves in a cow pasture," one teary-eyed player summed up.[45] The only highlight for the Maroons was the defensive play of the freshman the *Chicago Tribune* already was calling the "most spectacular figure in western athletics."[46] Eckersall prevented several Michigan touchdowns by fearlessly slamming his small body time and again into the streaking Heston—textbook, last-chance tackles.

For his part, Heston showed again why, when healthy, he had no equal on any football field as a ball carrier. Newspaper play-by-play accounts suggest he ran for at least 180 yards, and Heston scored two of

Michigan's three touchdowns. "He can scarcely be referred to (on the football field) as a human being," the *Trib* reported. "He appears to be three parts pile driver and two parts kangaroo."[47]

The latter description refers to a Heston play that became legend. On one of his last breakaway runs, he decided to foil that bothersome Eckersall once and for all. Rather than try to evade him, as he'd been doing unsuccessfully, this time Heston chose to sprint right at him. Eckie waited, waited, then dived at the proper instant at Heston's knees. But all he grabbed was air. Heston timed his "kangaroo" leap perfectly and bounded right over and past the embarrassed freshman. Heston stumbled as he regained his balance, and that was enough to allow Fred Speik to gain an angle and haul him down thirty yards later. "The crowd, Michigan and Chicago alike, roared its applause," the *Trib* said of Heston's leap.

Yost afterward smiled as never before, barely able to contain his elation. "Michigan played its best game of the year," he crowed. "In three years I have never seen them get into the plays better, or pull more together."[48]

Figure 11.2.   In this unidentified newspaper clipping, Michigan halfback Willie Heston breaks into the open at snow-covered Marshall Field on Thanksgiving Day in 1903, with Chicago Maroons (including Walter Eckersall, far right) in pursuit. *Source:* Bentley Historical Library, University of Michigan.

Northwestern coach McCornack was in attendance and wrote for the *Tribune* that "the Michigan team of this year is possessed of general football knowledge the equal of any I have never before seen. Combined with this was the ability to use such knowledge in a big game."[49]

An impressed Camp published his observations in the *Yale Alumni Weekly*, including these:

> In the first place, any eastern football man who believes that the play of the best teams in the Middle West is crude should go out and watch one of the important contests there and become convinced of his error. Some of the teams carry the development of the play, particularly in methods of attack, to a point fully as high and even more complicated than the eastern teams. . . .
>
> The Michigan team, coached by Yost, was one of the best drilled teams the writer ever saw, the men getting into their play with remarkable speed and working hard for every inch. In Heston they had a man at halfback of the build of Shevlin of Yale, although four or five pounds lighter; extremely fast on his feet, a good dodger, and an unusually hard man to stop in a broken-up field.
>
> There were several other individual players of note, but Heston was the best the writer saw.[50]

Camp named Heston to his 1903 All-American team—the first time he'd so honored a running back from the West.

❋ ❋ ❋

Yost's coaching accomplishment in 1903 ought to stand as one of the great feats in the early history of the profession. Stagg and Williams were right to doubt the West Virginian's ability to produce another championship team in '03, especially after Yost in September threw in with four freshmen starters who had never played a down of college football, as well as two other starters who'd never played a meaningful minute. The year before, Stagg had wrung every drop of ability from a similarly green roster and came up twenty-one points short in the championship showdown against Michigan.

Yet this Wolverine team went 11–0–1 and outscored opponents 565 to 6. The only score allowed was the touchdown by Minnesota—the similarly undefeated co-champion of the West—on the last play of the game, set up by a disputed fumbled punt by Michigan. And all this while the Wolverines' best player, running back Heston, missed four games entirely and most of two others because of a swollen knee—almost half the schedule. What's more, one of Yost's pet plays on offense, tackles-back smashes, had been banned between the twenty-five-yard lines in 1903. That was sixty of the field's 110 yards, in the area where most of a game was played. And yet by season's end this (not quite) point-a-minute Wolverine team arguably was on par both offensively and defensively with its two more celebrated predecessors, especially in line play.

One of Yost's secrets to success in 1903 was his invention of a real-life machine—football's first blocking sled for linemen. The *Michigan Daily* described it in October:

> The machine is in the shape of a platform, twelve by five feet in dimensions, mounted on four wheels. The front, twelve feet in width, is heavily padded. Four men are placed on the platform and a

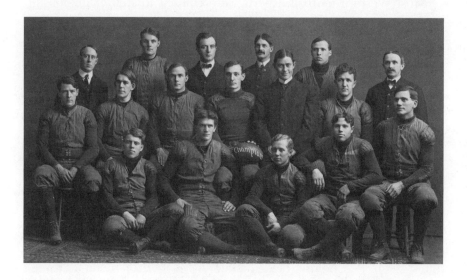

Figure 11.3.   The 1903 Michigan Wolverines, Champions of the West. Front row: Fred "Norky" Norcross, Frank "Shorty" Longman, John "Harry" James, Willie Heston. Middle row: Tom Hammond, Herb Graver, Joe Maddock, captain Curtis Redden, head coach Fielding H. Yost, George "Dad" Gregory, Henry "Dutch" Schulte. Back row: student manager Thomas Roberts, Cecil Gooding, assistant coach Dan McGugin, athletic director Charles Baird, John "Joe" Curtis, trainer Keene Fitzpatrick. *Source:* **Bentley Historical Library, University of Michigan.**

squad of five players are stationed four feet from the machine. When Coach Yost gives the signal, the squad charges forward against the padded bulwark. The machine is constructed so that when the five men strike it at the same instant it will give way, but if they straggle even a little it remains stationary.[51]

Although both Cal and Southern Cal on the Pacific Coast invited Michigan to make a holiday-season sojourn along the lines of the one two years earlier, Baird answered privately that neither he, Yost, nor trainer Fitzpatrick had the energy after the grueling season to even contemplate it—well, unless the money was too good to turn down, which it apparently wasn't.[52] One thing was certain, however, as UM Board in Control of Athletics chairman Pattengill even said publicly: despite all the clamoring, a postseason rematch against Minnesota was out of the question.

The Gophers finished the season with a 14–0–1 record, climaxed by a 17–0 defeat of the Badgers in Madison in a game that devolved into a slugfest. Minnesota outscored its opposition 581 to 12 on the season.

Most Western football experts were content to split championship honors between Michigan and Minnesota, while others gave the nod to just the Wolverines. The *Chicago Tribune* observed that

> no one who saw Yost's great machine plow through Chicago on that snow-clad, windswept gridiron at Marshall Field will deny that he demonstrated beyond appeal that under the conditions no team in the west, at least, could have stood before it. . . . [T]he Michigan team improved far more between the game with Minnesota and the end of the season than the Minnesota eleven did in the same interval. In other words, it seems fair to say Yost's team would be the logical victor if they had met again this year.[53]

Even better for Yost at the end of the 1903 season? Eight starters, including the great Heston, were due to return in 1904.

✻ ✻ ✻

More embarrassed than Eckie or anyone connected to the University of Chicago by the turkey of a performance the Maroons served up on Thanksgiving Day was Stagg. The twenty-eight-point margin of defeat was the worst of his fourteen-year coaching career to date, and, more galling for Stagg, it came in a championship game, with his old college mentor watching. Vexing Stagg too was that this was his most talented team since 1899; former Illinois star Fred Lowenthal said it might have been the most star-studded team in the nation.[54] It just didn't mesh.

"[F]or the first and last time on any field, I was disgraced," Stagg recalled in *Touchdown!*, his 1927 autobiography. "Not even the brilliant work of Eckersall could obscure that." Stagg placed much of the blame for his 1903 team's collapse on two unnamed starters, who had "quit under fire" against Michigan. "[B]ut what of the coach who had let such a crop come to harvest? I grew more and more morbid in my weakened physical state. . . . I came down with pneumonia after the game, my mental depression offset the staunchness of my body, and I came very close to death."[55] Indeed, on December 3, Stagg battled high fever and had difficulty breathing. He was also hard of hearing as a result of his punctured ear drums. "Four trained nurses have been called in and every precaution is being taken to prevent the spread of the disease to unaffected parts of his lungs," the *Trib* reported. Stagg's doctor told the *Trib* that the coach "does not realize how sick he is, but worries a great deal."[56]

Among Stagg's chief worries was the sudden disappearance of Eckersall from the UC campus following Thanksgiving. By the second week of December, Eckie still hadn't returned. Rumors spread that UM alums again were dogging him to transfer to Ann Arbor. Untrue, Eckersall said, upon his return to school before Christmas. Stagg publicly attributed embarrassment and disappointment over the loss to UM for his star player's lengthy withdrawal from school. Exactly how Eckersall would make up those missing weeks of study, Stagg did not say.[57]

The coach spent the holidays in Chloride, New Mexico—"brooding during my convalescence over the disgrace that had come to the university under my aegis." He cut that rest period short, though—a "foolhardy mistake," he admitted in 1927, "that I am not yet done paying for."[58]

But there was work to be done—so much work. Because somehow, some way, Stagg just had to defeat Yost and Michigan in 1904.

12

1904 OFF THE FIELD

Alabaster Alonzo Stagg

The three Rs that mattered most to Lonnie Stagg in 1904 were raidin', recruitin', and retainin'.

Raidin', as in raiding rosters of lesser colleges for impact replacement players.

Recruitin', as in intensely wooing prep stars.

Retainin', as in keeping all his players happy enough, prosperous enough, and most importantly academically interested enough to remain both on campus and eligible to play.

In 1904, Stagg would earn straight A's in all three disciplines.

His acumen in the ignoble third R, retainin', was especially uncommon and perhaps unprecedented. That's because, unlike all other coaches, Stagg had two secret weapons: first, a school president, William Rainey Harper, wholly sympathetic to athletics; and second, he possessed academic influence within his university not only as a member of the UC faculty but as a department head—of Physical Culture and Education. Before, during, and after the 1904–1905 school year, Stagg unhesitatingly employed both weapons to admit new players, and then to keep his entire flock eligible.

With ethical standards across college sport seen to be in a disturbing, nationwide free fall in 1904, Stagg committed many of the worst "three R" sins of his athletic career—with his desperation never higher and his competitive ferocity never more inflamed, courtesy of archrival Field-

Figure 12.1.   Stagg loaded up on new recruits in 1904 to an unprecedented level, picking the luscious Chicago prep orchard almost clean and raiding lesser universities as far away as Washington state. *Source:* Amos Alonzo Stagg Papers, Special Collections Research Centre, University of Chicago Library.

ing H. Yost and his indomitable Michigan football machine, unbeaten now in thirty-four games.

All the while, Stagg's health was a mess. Six weeks after his 1903 team's cowering collapse at the hands of Yost's Wolverines on Thanksgiving Day, Stagg told an acquaintance he was only "gradually making improvement" from his near-death pneumonia scare. That he was "able to walk nearly a hundred yards now without much pain" qualified as an accomplishment worth sharing, yet he admitted he still had to do "most of my walking with bicycle."[1]

As spring neared, Stagg's health "became sharply worse," as he explained in his 1927 autobiography:

> [It came] as a result of leaping a flooded gutter with Alonzo, Jr., in my arms. I was running off three track meets in one day. A heavy fall of snow in the morning had melted rapidly when the sun burst through, and the streets were so sloppy that I had to carry the five-year-old boy en route from my home to the gym. Near the gym I took a run to clear a broad pool, landed on ice on the far side, and in a desperate effort to recover my balance I threw certain bones in my lower back out of place, discovered over fifteen years later.

Bravely but unwisely, Stagg continued to actively coach the Maroons baseball and track-and-field teams that spring while still tending to his myriad office duties as department head and athletic director—"until I had irritated the sciatic nerve fearfully," he recalled. "Sciatica drove me to Colorado that summer, without relief."[2]

The relief Stagg sought most probably had nothing to do with his limited stamina or ailing back. Ergo, the three Rs.

On raiding, Stagg's actions suggest his golden rule was, Do unto others as has been done unto you. One year after Yale cherry-picked one of the best linemen he'd ever recruited, Roswell Tripp,[3] and in the same summer that Swarthmore College in Pennsylvania enticed two Maroon linemen away—Robert "Big" Maxwell and Sherburn Wightman—Stagg in turn raided for replacements.[4] As he probably saw it, if the ruthless Eastern schools could successfully mine his roster for gems, and if his rivals, too, had been doing it to others, there was nothing wrong with him raiding Midwestern lesser lights and regional powers farther west—in the Plains and, this year, all the way to the Pacific Coast.

In August, Stagg lured one of two players he targeted on the University of Washington roster: captain and star lineman William Speidel, who returned to his hometown to study postgrad medicine at UC.[5]

Three other impact transfers for Stagg included William "Dan" Boone, a superb lineman from Hillsdale College in Michigan, plus a pair of world-class sprinters who played football too, both from Lewis Institute in Chicago: George Varnell and Bill Hogenson. Stagg also raked in transfers from the University of Arkansas, Bethany College in Kansas, Grinnell College in Iowa, and Armour Institute of Technology in Chicago.[6]

Incredibly, Stagg had the temerity to raid the University of Nebraska roster for the third consecutive year. Nebraska wasn't yet a nationally respected power, but it sure wasn't Hillsdale, Grinnell, or Lewis Institute. The Cornhuskers could be counted on annually to be as formidable as any team in the West after the Big Four (Michigan, Chicago, Minnesota, and Wisconsin). That Stagg would raid Nebraska again revealed how bold and desperate he'd become.

After snagging John Koehler in 1902 and John Tobin the year before, Stagg wooed Nebraska center Charles Borg in 1904. He practically gloated about the acquisition in the press once the Maroons' preliminary camp opened in September. Borg worked out for a full week with his new teammates.[7]

Then Bummy Booth suddenly showed up at Marshall Field. The Nebraska coach chatted amicably with Stagg and showed no signs of bitterness at having watched three of the best linemen he'd produced on the Plains plucked away by the Old Man in as many years. According to the *Chicago Chronicle*, Booth shared with Stagg "all of the good points about Borg," and congratulated Borg "for selecting what he termed 'the best law school in the West.' He explained that he would have to hasten on to Lincoln that night and, after wishing well his friends on Marshall Field, left."

Booth, in fact, had no plans to leave Chicago until doing unto Stagg what Stagg had done unto him. After darting back to his hotel room, Booth sent a message summoning Borg. There, the coach went to work on his lineman. "It took Coach Booth two nights and a day to convince the curly-headed Nebraskan that he could not afford to desert his alma mater just to get the glory of playing on the maroon team," the *Chicago Chronicle* followed up. After making his decision, "Borg sought out

Coach Stagg . . . and told him that he just had to go back to Lincoln." Later, Stagg told the *Chronicle* he didn't say a word to Borg. He just let him go. "I didn't ask him to come and I didn't ask him to stay," Stagg said. Booth escorted Borg onto a train and the pair headed back to Lincoln.[8]

Stagg lamented that he had "lost the most valuable acquisition of the year."[9] But he didn't hesitate an instant to summon a replacement. Probably even before Booth and Borg deboarded in Lincoln, another grizzled interior college lineman had already telegrammed Stagg to say he was on his way: Louis Scherer of the University of Washington— Speidel's linemate. Scherer was said to be one of the best guards ever to play on the West Coast.[10]

Of course, the raidees in most cases behaved just as deplorably as the raiders—jumping schools the instant a more appealing offer arrived. The less honorable even played their pursuers off against one another. Such as James Lightbody.

Lightbody had opened eyes across the Midwest in the 1902–1903 school year as a middle-distance runner and football player at DePauw University in Greencastle, Indiana. Stagg had been tipped that Lightbody was looking to step up the intercollegiate athletic ladder, and the coach did not hesitate to write him this nonsolicitation solicitation in July 1903: "It would not, of course, be proper for me to suggest your leaving De Pauw, and I should not now write you, were it not that Mr. [Frank] Allen writes me that you are planning to leave and enter some medical school in October. In that event, of course, we would be more than pleased to have you come to the University of Chicago."[11]

Lightbody indeed took off for Chicago. As an undergrad transfer, he had to sit out the 1903–1904 school year but became a track-and-field superstar nonetheless. At the 1904 Summer Olympic Games in St. Louis, Lightbody won three gold medals and a silver (more than any other competitor), all in middle-distance events.

But before he'd departed for St. Louis, Lightbody sounded out Michigan on August 5, 1904, about transferring there, writing directly to UM athletic director Charles Baird. Reports later said Princeton also wanted Lightbody.

Baird replied to Lightbody on August 6 with a nonsolicitation solicitation of his own: "While we do not wish in any way to try to influence you to leave Chicago, yet if you have finally decided to do so we shall be glad, of course, to welcome you to Ann Arbor." Because he'd sat out the previous school year, Lightbody could compete in 1904–1905 at any university, even if he transferred again.

Baird and Lightbody discussed the matter briefly in person at the Olympics, to no resolution. Unsure if Lightbody was sincere and yet anxious to snag him if available, Baird assigned UM track captain-elect and Olympic champion and world-record-holding pole-vaulter Charles Dvorak to investigate further back in Chicago, Dvorak's hometown. "I would suggest that you casually drop in on him so as not to excite the suspicion of any Chicago University [sic] people," Baird advised Dvorak on September 14. "Do you think that he would keep the peace and not tell the Chicago people that we were talking with him, in case I meet him and have an interview in Chicago?"

Baird got an emphatic answer two days later, in a story in the *Chicago American* under this sensational headline: "Accuses Coach Yost of Bribery." Lightbody publicly charged Yost and UM "with systematic violation of the amateur rules," the *American* reported, adding that Baird "made the proposition of free board and room, and when Lightbody refused, Yost, according to the sprinter, added [a $3] weekly allowance." The public never knew that Lightbody had initiated contact with Michigan.

Why Yost would be involved in the recruitment of a track-first athlete at all, let alone as point man ahead of track coach Keene Fitzpatrick (who was in St. Louis, too), was not explained by the *American*. Charged Lightbody: "They coaxed me, begged me, and held out every inducement imaginable to get me to leave Chicago. . . . I didn't accept for many reasons, but principally because I don't believe in that kind of athletics." Baird's surviving correspondence in the recruitment of Lightbody appears complete, and in two letters to Lightbody, Baird made no such offers. At least in writing. [12]

Stagg declined to comment publicly on Lightbody's charges against Michigan. "His stand on the subject, however, is so well known that his silence, it is believed, does not require explanation," the *American* included in its bombshell charge from Lightbody. "He is said to be so rigid in enforcement of amateur restrictions that he will not even permit his athletes to accept employment about the university." That wasn't true, of course. Stagg by 1904–1905 was telling recruits in letters, such as to Carl M. Bair of Des Moines, that "there is no question but

what you can make your board by working at the commons at meal-
times, and you could also work out your tuition; and you would thus
reduce your expenses to a minimum."[13]

Come late September, Lightbody still had not informed Baird or
anyone from Michigan that he for sure would remain in Chicago. On
September 23, with the start of the first semester at UM only days away,
Baird asked captain Dvorak to inform Lightbody that "if he is still
inclined and really wants to come to Michigan and would like to see me,
I shall be pleased to come over and talk over the situation with him. . . .
You must be very careful and not let him lead you into a trap laid by the
Chicago University [sic] people. They might try to catch us."

They did. Lightbody was in on this second trap. On September 26,
he wrote Baird again, asking, "What can you do for me at Michigan?
You told me you would write about the 15th of Sept. That has passed.
Would like an early answer." Lightbody added this postscript: "Address
me in plain envelope if you write."

Nine days later, Dvorak reported back to Baird: "Nothing doin' in
the Lightbody case. I wrote to him asking him to come into the city and
see me Friday, but he never showed up. Then several of the papers had
accounts of attempts to kidnap Lightbody. The best thing is to cut it
out."

Finally, Baird agreed. Lightbody remained at UC for the 1904–1905
school year. On October 25, Dvorak informed Baird, after further
snooping, that it was "as I thought. Lightbody is a poor student. He has
been made keeper of the Grounds (so I was told) in the effort to make
him stay at Chicago."

* * *

As for the recruitment of high schoolers, Stagg's 1904 haul was unlike
anything ever seen in the West in sheer talent and number.

Official recruiting lists were not publicized in those days, but from
reports it can be gleaned that Stagg added at least twenty frosh football
players from the high school ranks, and perhaps as many as thirty. That
would be the early twenty-first-century recruiting-class equivalent of
about one hundred, when the annual new-scholarships limit is twenty-
five. Most of Stagg's recruits were two- or three-sport stars, and most
came from the luscious football-talent orchards of Chicago, which in

1904 bore more college-worthy fruit than ever. Stagg bagged almost the entire crop.

Whereas bountiful Hyde Park High had been picked practically bare the year before, it was North Division High's turn this year. Stagg wooed nearly the entire North Division backfield: halfbacks Leo De-Tray and Carl Hitchcock and fullback Ed Hill. Stagg's other top Chicago-area recruits included Art Badenoch, a 190-pound guard from Englewood High; Fred "Mysterious" Walker from Hyde Park High; fleet halfback Lester Larson from West Aurora High; and guard Burt Gale from East Aurora High. From outside Chicago, Stagg recruited at least four high schoolers, including Fred Noll of Henry, Illinois; Charles Wondries, a Californian originally from the Chicago suburb of La-Grange; and Clarence Russell from Oskaloosa, Iowa.

In all, between high school recruits and college transfers, Stagg added somewhere in the range of twenty-five to thirty-five new players in 1904 (again, no official list exists)[14]—a whopping stockpile in an era when ten new recruits would be an uncommonly high number in the West. Indeed, Stagg recruited in 1904 as if he'd never be able to do it again.

❊ ❊ ❊

Getting all these new players onto the UC practice field was one thing. Getting them all admitted to the university and thereafter keeping them academically eligible—that is, retaining them—was quite another.

While Stagg in public always espoused the highest of academic ideals, behind the scenes he relentlessly, unrepentantly, and unhesitatingly advocated for the continuing eligibility of his academically struggling star athletes. Harper helped him.

In their early years at Chicago, Harper had scolded Stagg on at least two occasions for particularly galling examples of scholastic corner cutting. After the 1896 season, Harper asked Stagg in a letter, "Please explain to me how [V.] Sincere was permitted to play in the Autumn Quarter with three demerits in previous quarters uncancelled on the Examiner's books. Please let me know to-day how this happened."[15] Two years later, Harper asked Stagg "how it was possible for [football captain and sprinter Walter] Kennedy to run Saturday night, in view of the fact that he has not been doing his [academic] work since Christmas."[16] There is no surviving record that Harper wrote such a letter to Stagg after 1901, following implementation of their paradigm-shifting policies to aid football. As Stagg biographer Robin Lester discovered in the UC archives generations later, Harper surely would have had good reason to chastise Stagg. Lending more credence to that theory is that Stagg drew up a master list of dozens of instances when a UC athlete from 1892 through 1901 was rendered ineligible because of deficient studies. That the archived lists discontinued after 1901 might not be a coincidence.[17]

The most galling case was that of Walter Eckersall himself. The star quarterback was as incompetent in the classroom as he was competent on fields of sport. And yet, undoubtedly with Harper's continual blessing, Stagg ensured that Eckie was given every conceivable break academically at UC after yanking him off that train platform in September 1903. As Lester revealed in shocking detail, Stagg convinced president Harper and the UC faculty to perpetually overlook the fact that Eckersall was barely cracking open a book or attending classes.

When Tom Hammond snubbed Stagg to enter Michigan in 1903, the Chicago press corps made a huge deal of the fact that he hadn't yet graduated from Hyde Park High after three years of study there. Neither had Eckersall—after four years. Lester discovered that even though Eckersall was enrolled at UC in his first quarter merely as a sub-freshman, to make up his shortfalls, his academic work still proved "disastrous." Eckersall's three-week departure from campus after Thanksgiving surely contributed. It only got worse after 1903, as Lester wrote:

> Eckersall led his teammates off—as well as on—the field in failing grades and total absences from classroom work. He registered for courses with the same instructors the next quarter (winter 1904), but his political science instructor, Charles Merriam, reported that "he never appeared in class" during the quarter. His work in English showed a C average, although he again led the class in absences. Eckersall continued to participate in athletics. . . . In fact, he and six other first-year students who were flunking participated in intercollegiate track meets for freshmen. Their participation and the press coverage prompted an embarrassed University Council to reconsider the basis of eligibility for freshmen, but the inquiry petered out when

Harper assumed responsibility with Stagg for the involvement of the errant students.[18]

One of the conference's charter regulations stipulated that "no student shall be permitted to participate in any intercollegiate contest who is found by the faculty to be delinquent in any of his studies."[19] Stagg and Harper by 1904 were all but mocking that rule, especially with Eckersall. According to Lester, in an attempt to steer Eckersall at least toward the vicinity of eligibility for his second year, Stagg arranged for him in the third quarter to be enrolled in low-work classes normally taken only by upperclassmen and taught by athletics-friendly professors. Eckersall still struggled to make grade.

Word did leak out about Eckersall's scandalous academic record. The Chicago press corps mostly glossed it over. In September 1904, the *Chicago Journal* stuck out its neck and addressed UC's "black eye"—its "remarkably small percentage" of prominent athletes who graduate.[20] Nationally, *Collier's* magazine later slammed Eckersall as "simply an 'athletic ward'" of the university.[21] UC authorities endured the embarrassments without comment.

Eckersall wasn't the only prominent Maroon athlete whom Stagg had admitted through the side door. Another was Hogenson, the internationally ranked sprinter. Following the Olympics, Hogenson sought more glamorous college laurels than Chicago's Lewis Institute could provide, and that summer in St. Louis he entertained recruiters' offers. Michigan and Chicago led the charge. After Hogenson chose to attend Chicago, Baird confided to UM track captain-elect Dvorak that he had pulled Michigan out of the Hogenson sweepstakes. Baird privately explained that he'd personally traveled to Lewis Institute, examined Hogenson's academic record in detail, "and concluded that he could not enter any first-class University without more preparation,"

> unless he was shown favor. . . . My own judgment is that he can not carry college work anywhere. I understand the methods adopted to take him to Chicago and wish to say that much as we need him, we cannot afford to compete with Chicago in the manner by which they secured this man. His case is analogous to that of Eckersall.[22]

For Baird to say this in private is quite an indictment. In a letter to UM track-and-field coach Keene Fitzpatrick, Baird stated flatly, "If Stagg keeps loading up with men of this class he will get himself in hot water."[23]

* * *

Not even the team of Yost and Baird could touch Stagg in any of the three Rs in 1904. And for the third consecutive off-season, the duo had more work to do in that regard than they'd originally expected because of another health tragedy. After losing tackle Bruce Shorts to career-ending appendicitis in 1902 and fullback Paul Jones to career-ending typhoid the year before, right guard Cecil Gooding contracted typhoid immediately after Michigan's '03 season-ending win in Chicago. Unlike Jones, Gooding could not shake the disease. He died on January 5.[24]

What's more, a promising tackle, Leigh Turner, had been a second-team Walter Camp All-American at Dartmouth in 1903 and enrolled at Michigan in February 1904 to continue studying law. He even played on the Wolverine baseball team that spring. But probably because he was a nongraduate transfer, he was ineligible to play football in fall '04. He served as Yost's coaching assistant instead.

In their 1904 talent searches, Yost and Baird all but abandoned raiding. The only three eligible transfers were two backfield men with little college playing experience (prep students Theodore Stuart from the University of Denver and Paul Magoffin from Marietta College in Ohio) and a reserve end, T. J. Smull from Ohio Northern.[25]

Yost and Baird for the second straight year focused their talent-acquisition energies on high school recruiting, with the same coast-to-coast ambition as before—as much out of necessity as anything, because Stagg and UC alumni had all but cornered the Chicago market. "[E]very boy in Chicago has been offered inducements," Baird confided to trainer Fitzpatrick on July 18, "and it seems almost impossible to get a man out of that city unless we do far more than we wish."[26] A month earlier Baird claimed to have discovered Stagg's secret recruiting weapon—a man named Bell. "[T]his man is a rank partisan of Chicago and is the man they use as a go-between when they are inducing students to enter Chicago University [sic]," Baird wrote to a prominent UM alumnus in the Windy City. "He is the man who had charge of the Eckersall deal and also made the arrangements for several other athletes who went to Chicago. These are facts of which I am certain."[27]

Baird's and Yost's searches for high school talent in 1904 were rich only in quality, not quantity. This even after losing one of the most promising verbally committed Michigan recruits of the point-a-minute era—George Cook of Cleveland—to Cornell.[28] The three recruits of prominence Yost and Baird did land were husky linemen loaded with potential: Adolph "Germany" Schulz, a 220-pounder from Fort Wayne High in Indiana; 190-pound Walter Rheinschild of Los Angeles High; and a behemoth from Healdsburg, California—six-foot-five, 230-pound Ralph Rose, already a world-class shot-putter as a high schooler.

Scandal surrounded the recruitment of both Californians.

Rheinschild was one of the nation's most sought-after recruits in 1904. Nine years later he would tell the *Los Angeles Times* that Southern Cal coach Harvey Holmes offered him seventy-five dollars a month to play for the Trojans, and that Wisconsin recruiters trumped that with a one-hundred-dollar-a-month pitch. "Twelve hundred looked big to me, but I wanted a winner," he would recall. Similarly, Rheinschild said he declined an offer of $2,200 a year to attend Dartmouth. A Wisconsin newspaper reported in September 1904, just before Rheinschild departed California, that he "declares openly that [Baird] offered to pay all his expenses during the season and finally offered him remunerative employment" at Michigan.

Quietly securing a menial job on campus for top athletes was standard recruiting procedure everywhere. The *Los Angeles Times* in 1913 reported that the Eastern press corps at the time decried Rheinschild's decision to accept a "Ty Cobb salary at Ann Arbor." Rumors that Rheinschild was being paid $50,000 a year to attend UM, or that he was "the highest salaried amateur athlete in the business," were similarly preposterous.[29] In one off-season, Michigan's now long-entrenched, clandestine recruitment program did not accelerate from offering metered, shortfall loans with interest to needy top recruits and arranging for a campus joe job so as to help a top recruit make ends meet, to outright paying players one hundred times more than the average American salary. Indeed, surviving letters on recruitment efforts by Baird in UM's correspondence files circa 1904 suggest nothing had changed. An argument can be made that irresponsible journalism was as much to blame as reality for the public's perception in 1904 that the entire college sports enterprise reeked like a late-summer bog.

Then there was Ralph Rose, whose enormous body accommodated far more than the average man's share of stupidity, or at least naïveté. In December 1903, he wrote to UM intending to follow in his father's footsteps to Ann Arbor and asked about financial assistance. Baird replied he would do what he could to secure Rose a job by the start of second semester on February 15 and informed Rose how much UM students normally pay for room and board. On January 8, Rose replied that he indeed would need help "from a financial point of view," so he was looking to "get something to do so that I could defray my expenses in whole or in part." Rose wasn't asking for a handout, nor did Baird even mention the loan option, let alone dangle any cash. Rose's father was a well-to-do UM grad, after all.[30]

And yet, after actually asking Baird in the above letter if it were "very cold in Michigan this time of the year," Rose decided by the end of January to attend UM. Then he immediately bragged to friends that Michigan had offered him far better inducements than either Cal or Stanford, including a lucrative salary at the college library. In reality, Michigan had no lucrative jobs for students in any library, let alone one for Rose.

Rose's comments became a nationwide scandal. West Coast sports followers howled. Yost got hammered. Even if true, how could Rose not have known how dumb it was to brag about such things? Baird had no choice but to publicly refute the charges when his and UM's policy was to remain silent when such accusations hit the press (usually the Chicago press).[31]

While Rose broke the world record in the shot put and won the Olympic gold medal that summer, the rube proved incapable of taking his studies seriously or refraining from spouting nonsense (such as challenging world heavyweight boxing champion James J. Jeffries to a fight),[32] or bragging again about special treatments he was accorded at Michigan whenever rival athletes or reporters were around. "Can you not put a muzzle on that man Rose?" a former football player asked Baird.[33] The UM Board in Control forbade Rose from playing football in fall 1904 because of his poor academic showing after one semester, but probably also to keep him away from reporters. By January 1905, less than a year after he'd enrolled at Michigan, Rose was kicked out of school. Baird could not have been happier.[34]

As for Michigan's recruiting efforts in Chicago, by the second week of September 1904, it appeared Yost and Baird would actually be shut out this year in the Windy City. But just before preseason camps opened, one of North Division's star prospects—235-pound lineman Walter "Octy" Graham—chose Michigan over Chicago. Graham had been expected to throw in with his three high school teammates under Stagg's tutelage. But he explained to a reporter that he wanted to study engineering, and UC didn't have an engineering program. The usual charges of improper influence by UM alums flew about in the Chicago papers. Yet Graham did wind up studying engineering at Michigan, and in spring 1908, he would graduate with a bachelor of science in mechanical engineering.[35]

Graham's case raises an important point. Although it was a scandalous era rife with dubious acts, many college football players—including stars—actually did care about their studies and did want to major in more than just eligibility. These players might seek loans or even receive money outright to help see themselves through each school year, but they had in mind long-term career ambitions, not just short-term athletic glory.

A study by the author of the point-a-minute years at UM reveals that the majority of the top prospects recruited, or raided, by Yost and Baird wound up earning their degrees. It is virtually impossible to compile a definitive list of all players Yost and Baird might have targeted to bring to Ann Arbor because, as everywhere then, new recruits were never officially announced or identified; among the "scrubs" there might be any number of recruits who'd failed to pan out, mixed with players who'd risen from the class-team ranks of the general student population.

Of the twenty-three new men Yost and Baird added from 1901 to 1905 who earned their letters on the varsity squad, fourteen graduated and nine did not. Of the nine, one did not have a chance to graduate: Gooding, the starting right guard who died in 1904.

Most impressively, each of the thirteen varsity members on Yost's 1901 Wolverine team wound up earning a degree, twelve at UM (eight in law, three in liberal arts, one in engineering) and one at the Michigan College of Mines, whereto Arthur Redner transferred in 1902 and wherefrom he graduated in 1905. So the team with the perfect record

(11–0–0) and perfect defense (zero points allowed all season) also had a perfect graduation rate.[36]

Yost and Baird did bring in some borderline students—especially as their desperation level rose circa 1903–1904 to try to match Stagg's talent hauls. But those football players who did not pay proper attention to their studies paid for it with short- or long-term ineligibility. Punter extraordinaire Ev Sweeley missed the first two weeks of the 1902 season as he eliminated conditions. All-Western tackle Joe Maddock was cut at least one break—a summer 1903 condition was eliminated[37]— until getting the boot from school in spring 1904, when he had two years of eligibility remaining. And when Charles "Babe" Carter from Maine, the right guard in 1902 who'd bolted after the first semester, decided to come back in 1904 after more than a year off, he missed the first two games while he apparently eliminated dust-covered academic conditions.[38] A leading faculty member of the UM Board in Control, Judge Victor Lane, in January 1905, would assert that dating back to 1899 there had been "but one or two cases in which a man has been permitted to play on a varsity team who had a condition in his work, and then by reason of peculiar conditions in the particular case which were thought to justify it."[39]

For his part, Yost saw more value in academics than the average itinerant professional coach, despite his guttered reputation as a coach who cared only about football. Yost privately indicated to Baird while talent-wrangling in 1901 that he opposed having "any worthless fellows around—only good college men. Others are nothing but [demanding] ringers at best." In another letter Yost informed Baird that one standout player he had a line on was "anxious to come, but as he would come entirely for football, I think we had better drop him."[40]

But, like any coach, when such high-mindedness might cost him a victory, out the window went that thinking. Indeed, come autumn 1904, Yost groused publicly that "we are hampered this year by having four men who are great players [but] barred from the team by the faculty. Two of these are [letter-winning] 'M' men and the other two could make this varsity in a minute if the faculty would let them play." One of the latter two was the big lug Rose. The former two were Harry James, the quarterback Yost had finally settled on in 1903, and James Lawrence, a halfback who hadn't been academically eligible since 1902. Neither would play another down for the Wolverines, although James would graduate in 1905 with an engineering degree. Yost furthermore claimed that four backup Wolverines in 1904 also were barred on account of academic shortfalls. Embittered, Yost fired off this public shot at his archrivals during the '04 season:

> I wish Michigan's critics would point out one other school in the West where football players are out of the game this year on account of their studies. I have never heard of any Chicago or Wisconsin or Minnesota players being out of the game on that account since I began coaching at Michigan. At least they are all ready to get into the game when it comes time to play Michigan.[41]

Knowing what happened behind the scenes as we do now, some eleven decades later, the inescapable conclusion must be that the faculty who ran UM's Board in Control of Athletics—chaired by Pattengill—took academics more seriously by far than their counterparts at the University of Chicago, meaning Harper and Stagg. Yost and Baird believed this to be true. While Baird apparently never shared that opinion publicly, he did so privately in 1904 with his track captain-elect, Dvorak: "[I]f Mr. Stagg continues to secure men so poorly prepared and kept at the University in the manner in which [Hogenson and Eckersall] are, it seems to me that he will experience much difficulty in holding them together."[42] Although Baird probably never knew it, the following summer his prediction would prove startlingly correct.

❊ ❊ ❊

Stagg, in the meantime, had a public image to uphold. The more he actively fed the notion that his morality was as unimpeachable as it was unrivalled, the more he believed it, the more the press and the public gobbled it up, and the more untouchable he became. And yet the more hypocritical he appeared in the eyes of his in-the-wise nemeses. The Michigans and Wisconsins continued to privately and sometimes even publicly roll their eyes at "Alabaster Alonzo Stagg"—as a *Michigan Daily* editorial labeled him[43]—or "his Honorable," or "Sir Alonzo."

Despite all that he himself had done this off-season to raid, recruit, and retain so many outstanding football players, Stagg purported to be at his own wit's end over all the highly publicized evils infecting college football in 1904. He told the *Chicago Evening Post* on September 27:

I can't stand it. I'll simply throw up my position and quit the college athletic world if it continues. There is small reason for trying to keep athletics perfectly pure when your rivals are beating round the bush, using all sorts of reprehensible tactics and reaching out in all directions to get great material for the football squad. The public will become sickened over the plethora of criticism and suspicion, and the best and most engaging amateur sport—college football—will fall by the wayside. I'm completely discouraged.[44]

Those comments were published just hours after the mother of one of Stagg's players who'd bolted to Swarthmore College, Robert "Big" Maxwell, said this in the *Chicago Journal*:

Mr. Stagg talks about the high standard of amateurism at the University of Chicago, and I know athletes at that college who spend their summers at swell resorts and have apparently unlimited funds. They do no work, nor can their parents give them any such supplies of money. Where do they get it? A good many people know.[45]

13

1904 ON THE FIELD
Authentication Denied

In turn-of-the-twentieth-century America, news traveled fastest by wire. But that was merely to one recipient: the telegraph operator at the other end. Newspapers still delivered news fastest to the masses, thanks to passenger and commercial trains running everywhere day and night. Bundles upon bundles of dailies would be dumped off at hundreds of stops by the ever-passing trains crisscrossing the country. Bundles weren't light, either. In 1904, Chicago alone boasted ten dailies; Detroit, five.

As in any business, those in college athletics kept tabs on their competitors via myriad newspaper subscriptions. That's how, in the first days of September 1904, Fielding H. Yost in Ann Arbor learned that his football rivals already had begun pre-camp training sessions, or were about to—when he and his Michigan Wolverine were prevented from doing likewise.

For years, such preliminary practices had preceded the official start of a university team's training camp and could stretch out the preseason to a month, starting as early as late August. That was too long for professors at Big Nine universities offended by intercollegiate athletics—which meant most of them. Undoubtedly, to appease them, the nine faculty reps who ran the conference passed a new rule before the 1904 season to limit preseason training to the two-week period immediately preceding the first day of classes at each university.[1] It was another high-minded edict that, no doubt, sounded proper and read well in the paper but, in reality, proved unfair and merely the latest inept attempt to crack down on the football beast.

Or perhaps there was something more behind the new rule. As the *Chicago Record-Herald* reported, "Michigan opens its doors later in the season than most other conference universities."[2] Autumn semester at the University of Minnesota, for instance, began September 6, so Dr. Henry L. Williams began working out his Gophers at a lakeside resort on August 26, well within the new two-week window.[3] Two other members of the unofficial Big Four of the West—Chicago and Wisconsin—ignored the new rule. By September 2, second-year coach Arthur Curtis had arranged for his Badgers to begin practicing, despite the fact that UW classes did not begin until September 29.[4] Similarly, even though his Maroons' training camp should not have begun until September 17 (because the first day of the fall quarter at the University of Chicago was October 1), Stagg had his two assistant coaches, Jimmy Sheldon and Floyd Harper, welcoming old and new players alike for preliminary workouts starting September 5.[5]

At Michigan, the first day of classes fell on September 27. Thus, by the new rule, Yost and his Wolverines could not begin practicing until September 13. UM's Board in Control of Athletics insisted the team abide, regardless of what other Big Nine rivals might be up to. On September 3, athletic director Charles Baird informed his boss, chairman of the UM board Albert H. Pattengill, that Yost was not a happy pre-camper: "You will note that all of the universities are paying no heed to the two weeks rule in regard to early training. We shall get started ten days after everybody else and Yost is stewing because we are so late."[6] As Yost stewed, Lonnie Stagg brewed. While supposedly resting for three weeks in Estes Park, Colorado, to relieve wretched sciatica, Stagg brainstormed ways to use his thirty-odd outstanding new prospects. His backfield was three-deep with good players, and his line almost as well stocked. "Chicago will have a great team this fall—much better than in 1903," he told the *Record-Herald* upon his return on September 11. "Michigan will be Chicago's hardest opponent again this year. Coach Yost will surely turn out at least as strong a team as he did last year."[7]

Six days after Stagg's return, the Maroons opened with a 40–5 win against Lombard College. To see what his new crew could do, Stagg started eight first-year players, subbed in six more, and held out some returning starters until the second half, including superstar sophomore quarterback Walter Eckersall.

In subsequent games into late October, Stagg tried players at different positions, penciling in an ever-changing depth chart. In the backfield, quarterback Eckersall and third-year starting fullback Hugo Bezdek were locks, but the left and right halfbacks changed practically by the week.

Eckersall suffered no sophomore slump. He executed plays even more crisply and in faster succession, he had few rivals as a punter or dropkicker, and he remained a blazing fast and elusive runner in the open field. Eckie stood out in Chicago's victories against Lawrence (29–0), Indiana (56–0), Purdue (20–0), Iowa (39–0), and Northwestern (32–0), which set up the Maroons with a 6–0 record heading into an expected tough game on October 30 against Illinois.

The Illini indeed proved stingy, allowing only one touchdown in a 6–6 tie. Chicago's championship aspirations wobbled. But, looking ahead to November, a defeat of Texas and season-closing victories in Ann Arbor on November 13 and on Thanksgiving Day against Wisconsin surely would give Stagg's Maroons a co–Championship of the West, along with Minnesota, which appeared a lock to go undefeated through thirteen mostly easy games, what with neither Michigan nor Chicago on the Gophers' schedule.

✱ ✱ ✱

Athletic director Baird had had a huge dilemma in filling out Michigan's 1904 schedule. Who to play on Thanksgiving Day? Chicago and Wisconsin already were paired for that date, and Minnesota wasn't an option because nobody at UM wanted the headaches—Baird from dealing with Doc Williams, and Wolverine players from knocking heads with the roughhousing Gophers. Thus, Baird looked east.

Immediately after the 1903 season, Michigan announced its desire to find a marquee Eastern opponent to play somewhere in a big Eastern city on Thanksgiving Day 1904. "Our principle object," UM Club of New York treasurer T. H. Owens told the *New York Times*, "[is] to show the football public in the East that the University of Michigan can turn out an eleven to play the game just as scientifically and with just as good results as any of the elevens in this section of the country."[8]

Michigan people weren't alone in their desire to see how Yost's Wolverines would fare against a beast of the East. On December 6, 1903, the director of physical culture for the coming 1904 World's Fair in St. Louis, James E. Sullivan, attempted to woo the defending champions of the West and East, Michigan and Princeton, to play in a world championship football showcase.[9] Michigan surely would have jumped at the chance, but only two days later George Coughlin, assistant manager of the Princeton football team, idled such chatter by announcing the Tigers would not play the Wolverines anywhere in 1904.[10]

Neither Yale nor Harvard was interested in playing Michigan either, for the same reasons as in previous years, as UM athletic director Baird explained in 1904 for *The Inlander*, UM's monthly student magazine:

> In arranging their schedules the managers of Yale, Princeton and Harvard plan to play two big games, and eight or ten practice games, each season. For years Yale has played Princeton and Harvard; Princeton has played Yale and Cornell; and Harvard has played Yale and Pennsylvania. The coaches and trainers plan to develop and perfect their teams for these games. All other games are looked upon as practice contests. . . .
>
> Having in mind Michigan's record in the past, no coach or captain of Yale, Harvard or Princeton is apt to consider a game with Michigan as a practice contest. Therefore to arrange a game with the western team would necessitate the abandonment of [one of their big] games, which has become a fixture in the schedule. This they are unwilling to do. . . . Therefore as long as Michigan develops such strong teams she will have difficulty in securing a game with Yale, Princeton or Harvard.[11]

The same was not true of Columbia University in New York City. The Lions traditionally played football one or two notches below the Eastern heavyweights. A year earlier Columbia had sought a game against Michigan.[12] Bill Morley, Columbia's coach, was an old Wolverine himself in 1895, before moving on to Columbia to become a two-time consensus All-American back in 1900–1901.

When Princeton, Yale, and Harvard declined UM's Thanksgiving Day overtures, Columbia jumped in. Morley wrote Baird in December

1903 to say he looked "favorably" upon a game against Michigan and "shall consult the entire [Columbia athletic] board at its next meeting."[13]

A few months later, Morley met with his old pal Baird in Ann Arbor to discuss details of the proposed game. In May, Morley told the *New York Times* the game was all but a lock, pending "consent of the graduate advisers of the Columbia team."[14] According to a later report in the *Detroit Free Press*, it would be the first time "in the history of college football for a western eleven of consequence" to play in New York City.[15] An official announcement was expected within days, the *Times* reported. It did not come.

All through summer 1904, Michigan officials remained "confident" the game was in stone.[16] Yost announced as much on August 26.[17] Seven days later, Baird privately informed guard Babe Carter in a letter that the game "is now practically assured, and I expect to be in New York about Sept. 10th" to finalize details in a contract.[18]

That didn't happen either, but Morley and Baird did meet in the second week of September, either in Ann Arbor or Detroit. The two men discussed eligibility rules for the game. Top universities in the East at the time forbade graduate transfer students from playing without first sitting out a year, whereas in the West these men could play right away. Disagreement on this point—specifically, over which region's rule would apply—had been the source of the long delay in working out a contract, the *Detroit Free Press* reported. Baird capitulated, although exactly how was not made public. Morley told Detroit-area reporters that all obstacles were now removed; the contract signing was a mere formality. With that, Morley hopped on a train home.[19]

"The game in New York will be the great East and West contest and thousands from the West will go down to see this game," Baird wrote privately in September.[20]

Indeed, UM alums across the nation anxiously awaited vindication day for the Yost Machine. Columbia wasn't Michigan's first choice, nor even its fourth—Penn would have been—but the Lions would do. The venue was the clincher: uptown Manhattan, where college football zealotry had been born in the early 1890s thanks to wildly popular Yale–Princeton games at the Polo Grounds. The Wolverines' thirty-four-game undefeated streak was sure to hit forty by late October, and victories at Wisconsin on October 29 and at home against Chicago on

November 13 would set up what Wolverine fans hoped would be the greatest achievement in UM's football history: a point-a-minute steam-rolling of Columbia in the Big Apple before the eyes of the enormous, and enormously influential, East Coast press corps. No wonder Yost was so anxious to get going.

The *New York Times* listed the 1904 season's biggest games in its September 12 edition and placed Michigan at Columbia ahead of all other Thanksgiving Day matches in the East, including archrivals Penn versus Cornell at Philadelphia.[21] The setting for the Wolverines–Lions game would be American League Ballpark in Manhattan's Washington Heights, more popularly known as Hilltop Park, home of the American League baseball franchise known then as the Highlanders but soon to be renamed the Yankees.

By late September, Baird became seriously concerned. "I have seen Morley twice this summer," he confided to 1901 team captain Hugh White, "and he swears that he is in favor of the game but I cannot get him to sign the contract."[22] This was highly unusual nine months after the sides had tentatively agreed to the game, four months after general terms had been agreed to, and more than a week after final impediments presumably had been removed. Intercollegiate football contracts in the first decade of the twentieth century were usually drawn up and signed immediately after terms were agreed to, and for big games that always happened by early spring, at the latest.

Baird was vexed. Finally, on October 4, upon realizing "that the time had come for a final answer one way or another," he wrote to Morley asking for a "definite decision."[23]

Meantime, the fourth model of the Yost Machine had fired up instantly, without backfire, per usual. Michigan smeared Case (33–0 in forty minutes, zero first downs allowed) and Ohio Northern (48–0 in thirty-five minutes). Two days before Kalamazoo College came to visit on October 8, word got out that antsy Michigan authorities had no idea what was going on with Morley and Columbia. Then Morley's return letter arrived:

> My Dear Charlie:
> It seems ill-advised at the present time for Columbia to add another hard game to her already difficult schedule. Playing Pennsylvania, Yale, and Cornell is in itself a bigger undertaking than any other varsity team in the east attempts. I am, therefore, very sorry to have

to tell you that just now I think Columbia had better not add another game, as the football situation does not warrant her doing so.

Very truly yours.

Wm. R. Morley[24]

Enraged, Michigan authorities announced the news unilaterally on October 11. Southeastern Michigan deflated. By explanation, UM's athletic management released a long statement containing Morley's letter in full, plus much of the backstory (excluding the eligibility disagreement), concluding: "We greatly regret to disappoint the thousands of Michigan supporters who wished to see this game played."[25]

UM's unilateral announcement angered Morley and the Columbia side. Morley told the *New York Times* that "as far as he knew the whole matter was still undecided."[26] On October 18, "Columbia management" finally announced, too, that the game had been "officially declared off." Morley even told the press the game had never been arranged, that Columbia merely had had the proposition under advisement. "This is hardly borne out by some of the [Columbia] notices sent out in the first part of the season," according to a special report out of New York for the *Michigan Daily*. "[Tickets were] being quoted with an extra amount when the Michigan game was included." W. E. Metzenthin, Columbia's star quarterback, shot back at UM with this statement:

> We don't think we should be made the scapegoat for the eastern colleges. Michigan is an unknown quantity, but admittedly dangerous. We understand that the proposition made us by the Ann Arbor management was submitted to several of the big teams in this part of the country, all for the same date, and that Columbia was the only one of the lot that looked upon it favorably. When we found that Michigan was sending out challenges like a merchant would send out circulars, we called it off, and personally I'm glad of it.[27]

In fact, Michigan hadn't approached any other Eastern teams since December, and Columbia football leaders knew it. What's more, the precarious "football situation" at Columbia that Morley had cited to Baird appeared to be just fine before the season. The *New York Times* had predicted that Morley's Lions would be "pretty nearly as good as that of last season, which was believed to have been the best that ever represented the blue and white."[28] Apparently, that wasn't the case. Listless practice-game victories concerned Morley.

On October 12, one day after Michigan announced the cancellation, Swarthmore College of Pennsylvania lost to Columbia by a surprisingly close 12–0 score. Two days later, Swarthmore's newly lured star lineman Robert Maxwell—who went by the literal nickname "Big" at the University of Chicago in 1902 and 1903, and by the ironic nickname "Tiny" upon transferring to Swarthmore—penned a column for a Chicago daily. Maxwell was asked for his assessment on how Morley's Lions would fare against Yost's Wolverines. Maxwell was unequivocal:

> Having played against both Columbia and Michigan, my opinion is that if these two teams should meet, Michigan would be the victor by over thirty points. . . . [T]here is not in my mind the shadow of a doubt as to the result. In the first place, Michigan's whirlwind attack would completely run Columbia off her feet. The plays would come so fast and regular, and with such precision and variety, that Columbia would be used up before the end of the first half. . . . [T]he only man on the Columbia team who can be considered in the same class with Michigan players is Metzenthin, one of the fastest runners and best dodgers in the East. The rest of the team is inferior. . . . The only department that Columbia outclasses Michigan in is in dirty playing. . . . With Michigan's attack and Columbia's weak defense, the game would be a walkover for the Ann Arbor boys. I think Columbia did a wise thing to call off the game.[29]

Columbia proceeded to play so poorly in a 12–0 defeat to Amherst a week later that the *New York Times* said the Lions "showed scarcely an element of first-class football ability."[30] That prompted the *Michigan Daily* to rub in this salt regarding its one-time Thanksgiving Day opponent: "There would be little glory for Michigan in beating a third-rate team."[31] Columbia subsequently lost 16–0 to Penn and 34–0 to Yale, and finished its disappointing season with a 7–3 record, having defeated only one team of any consequence, Cornell, 12–6.

Michigan was left in an unthinkable predicament: no game on Thanksgiving Day. Brown, Cincinnati, and Amherst all offered to sub in for Columbia.[32] But Baird, Yost, and UM alums had too much pride to stoop any lower than the Lions. They'd rather play nobody on turkey day than a football nobody. And Minnesota was still out of the question.

Thus, the Wolverines would end the 1904 season on November 13 at home against Stagg's Maroons.

* * *

The Wolverine player who probably took news of the canceled New York trip the hardest was captain Willie Heston. His one career shot at dazzling the skeptical East Coast press corps—gone.

Despite graduating with a law degree in the requisite three years, Heston returned for a fourth and final season as a Wolverine in 1904. He studied literature in the tag-on semester.[33] Stagg had had players who similarly squeezed out every drop of eligibility, and he himself played sports for six years at Yale, and he suited up for the Maroons in their inaugural 1892 season too, but he couldn't resist slamming Michigan and Heston in the *Chicago Evening Post* on September 27: "The maroon coach cited the case of a rival institution that had a graduate return to take a post-season law course [sic] so that his great value could be utilized in the football eleven this fall."[34]

Stagg's hypocrisy aside, this was after all Heston's seventh season of college football, after three previous at a California teachers' college now known as San Jose State University. But that experience at San Jose Normal never counted against Heston's four years, presumably because of the conference rule that discounted any experience a student might gain at a college whose academics, or even just its football, were of a particularly low order. The conference arbiter in these years, Clarence Waldo, tabulated the Big Nine's official list of colleges that did make the academic or football grade, and evidently San Jose Normal wasn't on it.[35]

Despite being injured in an elevator in St. Louis that summer, Heston was probably healthier in his senior season than he'd been since 1901. As Michigan's opponents lamented.

In Michigan's third game, a 95–0 obliteration of vastly overmatched Kalamazoo College in just forty minutes, Heston might have rushed for more single-game yards than any running back before or since, at any level of college football. "As usual, Willie Heston's performance was the headliner of the matinee," the *Michigan Daily* reported. "A review of the game shows that the captain advanced the ball during the afternoon 515 yards—considerably more than a quarter mile." Heston continually broke away on long gains and scored six of Michigan's sixteen touch-downs, four on runs of sixty-five, seventy, eighty-five, and sixty-five yards.[36]

How fast was Heston? The fastest man in the world in 1904 just happened to be a fellow UM student—Archie Hahn. At the Summer Games in St. Louis that year, the "Milwaukee Meteor" became the first man to win the Olympic sprint double: gold medals in both the one hundred and two hundred meters. Back then, there was a sixty-meter dash, too, and Hahn won a third gold in that race. Two years later, Hahn won the Olympic one hundred meters again. In 1901, he had tied the world record in the hundred-yard dash (nine and four-fifths seconds) and set a world record of 21.6 seconds in the two-hundred-meter straightaway dash, a race long since discontinued.[37]

Michigan's nationally respected track-and-field coach, Keene Fitz-patrick, doubled as the Wolverine football trainer. He marveled at Heston's breakaway speed and had this idea to help Hahn with his: pit the two men against one another in one-hundred-yard match races on campus. Fitz did so some two hundred times. Heston led Hahn at thirty to forty yards every time. "At that point," Heston recalled, "I could hear him go by." Heston occasionally pressed Hahn to the finish but never beat him.[38]

By 1904, Heston had refined his abilities as a running back that would have made him a standout in any era. His stiff-arms were vicious-ly effective, with either arm. At five foot eight and 180 pounds, he was stout enough to be an effective inside power runner. Perhaps best of all, and to a "remarkable degree" as a Michigan sports historian wrote in 1948, Heston was able to "maintain his feet" upon being hit while leaping, spinning, or making a harsh cut. "Willie Heston always ran low, with a wide-spread, pumping knee action. He had a cat-like ability to land on his feet, no matter how hard he was hit, his legs still driving forward."[39] He was unafraid to hurdle sprawled players or low-charging tacklers—such as Eckersall in the 1903 game. Heston first coined the phrase that became a mantra for running backs in the first half of the twentieth century: "Use your searchlights and jump the dead ones."[40]

By 1904, Yost had tired of defending Heston's strong play on the other side of the ball. Asked by a reporter in October if Heston was as good on defense as he was on offense, Yost "without thinking" quipped,

"Why, really, I don't know. None of my backs has made a tackle this year."[41]

On October 12, Heston scored three touchdowns in Michigan's 72–0 defeat of the College of Physicians & Surgeons in just twenty-two and a half minutes. A week later, Heston scored three more times in a 31–6 defeat of Ohio State in sixty minutes. Two minutes into the second half of that game, Michigan fell behind on the scoreboard for the first time in the Yost era. The Buckeyes led 6–5 after cashing in a fumble by fullback Frank Longman. That snapped the Wolverines out of their lethargy. Four days later, the Wolverines beat the American Medical School 72–0 in just twenty-three and a half minutes—a worthless outing, as many of the med students appeared unfamiliar with the game.

It was hoped West Virginia—Yost's alma mater—could provide a much stiffer test. But being a team rooted in glacial, doleful Eastern football, the Mountaineers had no idea what hit them in a 130–0 loss in Ann Arbor in forty-three minutes. *The Daily New Dominion* of Morgantown wrote that the Wolverines appeared to the Mountaineers as "giant forms which seemed to be clad in football togs, but which acted as no football players ever seen in West Virginia." Somewhat more seriously, one Mountaineer said this when asked how his team could possibly be beaten 130–0:

> Well, they had a long ton of meat and bone and the thing moved with an average velocity of about eight yards a second. When it collided with West Virginia, West Virginia scattered and the thing went on. Why, I played against a man that weighed 245 pounds stripped. He was faster than the fastest man on our team. Once he carried the ball two yards across the goal line for a touchdown with two of our men hanging on his legs. I had about twenty-five yards to run across the field once to catch Heston. He had at least fifty yards to run to escape me. When I got there he was gone. . . . All we could do was to line up down the field and wait until the bunch came along. Sometimes we would get them, and sometimes we wouldn't—mostly wouldn't.[42]

The point-a-minute machine screamed into unseasonably warm Madison on October 30. Yost figured Arthur Curtis and the Badgers would provide the best test of the year. The Badgers, now three years removed from their last Big Nine title, appeared formidable again. They'd won their four previous games of 1904 by a combined 218–0.

With eleven thousand boisterous supporters cheering them on, the Badgers twice held on downs after the Wolverines had carried the ball nearly the length of the field, and the first half ended scoreless. But then Yost's machine kicked into a higher gear and could not be stopped. Michigan scored five touchdowns in the second half, while the Badgers could barely gain a yard against the stout Wolverine defense, and UM won 28–0 in seventy minutes.

The Chicago dailies dredged up those old machine allusions to underscore Michigan's impressiveness in their next day's editions. The *Tribune* ran a page of photos of star Wolverine players under the header: "Cogs in Yost's Great 'Machine' at University of Michigan."[43]

For the third consecutive year, Michigan knocked Wisconsin out of the championship race before Thanksgiving. Only a warm-up foe (this year Drake) and Stagg's Chicago Maroons stood between Michigan and an unprecedented fourth consecutive Championship of the West.

✿ ✿ ✿

Before the game in Madison, Yost had fired this shot toward the Windy City, probably intentionally: "Wisconsin always plays us a hard game. They are the hardest team in the West to beat, much harder than Chicago. We have never had a great deal of trouble beating Chicago."[44]

Stagg surely saw the story because it remains in one of his archived 1904–1905 clippings scrapbooks. The *Inter Ocean* kicker headline that labeled Yost the "'Hurry Up' Genius" probably rankled Stagg as much as that quote below it.

Yost thus splashed another dash of kerosene on the Michigan–Chicago rivalry, and worked up Maroon partisans to set the stage for one of the oddest, most entertaining spectacles ever to take place at a Midwestern college football game—not the Chicago–Michigan game at Ferry Field, but the Chicago–Texas game at Marshall Field the week before.

As the Maroons lassoed the Longhorns 68–0, who did fans and reporters recognize sitting high up in the Marshall Field bleachers? Why, none other than Fielding Harris Yost and William Martin Heston, scouting the Maroons in person. Yost had left assistant coach King Cole in charge as the Heston-less Wolverines faced Drake. Word of the dynamic duo's presence spread fast. A Chicago newspaper described this one-of-a-kind festivity:

> Of even more interest to Chicago students than the progress of [the game] was the presence of Coach Yost and Captain Heston of the Michigan team, who closely studied every move Chicago made to aid them in beating the maroons at Ann Arbor next Saturday. Yost was the center of attraction on Marshall field, and as he viewed the game from a section packed with Chicago enthusiasts he was made the object of much good-natured fun. Long yells with Yost's name on the end were given, and he was continually prodded with witticisms as to what Chicago would do to Michigan next Saturday.[45]

Yost just smiled. A cartoonist on hand captured the scene for one Chicago daily. He depicted the game as purely secondary attraction, with all heads spun in reverse, looking up at Yost and Heston.

The press box even got in on the fun. Troublemakers sent bogus scores of the Michigan–Drake game to the public-address barker, "to the effect that Drake had scored twice on Michigan," the *Tribune* reported. At that, the catcalls really rained down on the Michigan duo— or up, as the case was. "Yost's face was a study as he heard the 'news,'" the *Trib* said.

"Well, what do you think of that?" Yost told the masses. "When the cat is away the mice will play. We should have known enough to stay at home, eh, Martin?'"

In fact, Drake kicked only one field goal, whose value this year had dropped from five points to four, in a 36–4 Wolverine win in fifty minutes. Not that that would have mattered to the thousands of Chicagoans having the time of their lives at the expense of their archnemesis Yost.

Finally, when one jeering Maroon fan asked the Michigan coach aloud, "Why don't you smile?" Yost could no longer resist. He quickly shot back, "We'll smile enough next Saturday to make up for it."[46]

* * *

Willie Heston, the last active varsity member of Yost's 1901 championship team, suited up in a college football game for the last time before a

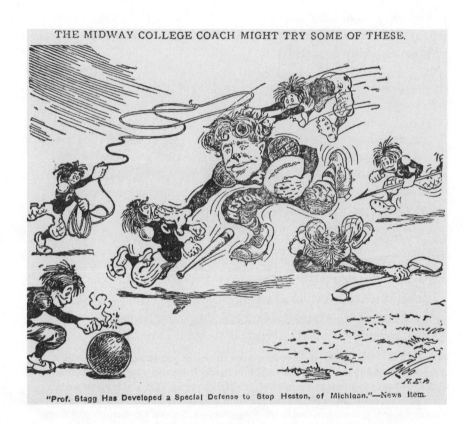

THE MIDWAY COLLEGE COACH MIGHT TRY SOME OF THESE.

"Prof. Stagg Has Developed a Special Defense to Stop Heston, of Michigan."—News Item.

Figure 13.1.   Willie Heston was not an easy runner to bring down, a point humorously made by this unidentified newspaper cartoon circa November 1904. *Source: Amos Alonzo Stagg Papers, Special Collections Research Centre, University of Chicago Library.*

record crowd of 13,125 at sun-soaked Ferry Field. Before kickoff, a film crew from the American Kinetograph Company of Orange, New Jersey, captured establishing shots of the crowd, and the starting Wolverines even posed while a cameraman panned the line, then shot game action. The filming worked—said to be the first successful film footage (and oldest surviving) of an American football game.[47]

Few thought Stagg's Maroons had much of a chance to beat the Wolverines. That included UC students, fewer than fifty of whom signed up for the school's official trip package when hundreds had been expected.

Despite his public digs, Yost wasn't overlooking the Maroons. He and Stagg liked to throw strategic curveballs at one another, and the

Figure 13.2. One of the strangest, most entertaining spectacles ever to take place at a Big Nine football game happened away from the playing field at the Chicago–Texas football game in 1904. It all began once Yost and Heston were spotted in attendance, scouting the Maroons, as depicted in this unidentified newspaper clipping. *Source:* **Amos Alonzo Stagg Papers, Special Collections Research Centre, University of Chicago Library.**

Michigan coach had a doozy this year. Throughout his UM career, Heston played left halfback and almost always wrought his damage on runs around Michigan's right end—or the opponent's left end. For Heston's swan song, Yost intended to run him more than usual around the opposite side, in part to stay away from Chicago's All-American end Fred Speik. The new plays for Heston might have been run in a new formation Yost debuted in 1904, among dozens in his arsenal.

The new formation looked like an arrowhead of sorts, and it featured a novel means of attack. Behind either a balanced line, or a line staggered right with a tackle over, the three backs stationed behind the quarterback lined up not parallel with the line, as in "regular" formation—known by Woody Hayes acolytes seventy years later as the "fullhouse T"—but rather in an unparallel line "aiming" just outside the right end. From this formation, as the *Chicago Journal*'s football strate-

Figure 13.3.   A panoramic photograph capturing the opening kickoff between Michigan and visiting Chicago at jammed Ferry Field in 1904. *Source:* **Bentley Historical Library, University of Michigan.**

gy expert Thomas T. Hoyne explained, Yost debuted a style of attack "setting an entirely new example in aggressive football for the country." Particularly, it was the manner in which the backs hit the line. Rather than the ball carrier physically helped forward by the other two backs, in unison—to smash into the line as a conjoined threesome for maximum penetration force, as was done heretofore—Yost conceived this "repeater game" of sorts, Hoyne said. "The man with the ball hits the line, and just as he is being stopped, perhaps another one of the backs plunges into him from behind and drives him forward a little farther. A few seconds later the third back strikes the bunch and drives him farther still. This is an entirely new idea in football outside of the University of Michigan." Indeed, it was the debut of the one-man ball carrier—albeit a sore ball carrier, no thanks to all those smashes from behind. Still, it presaged the sport's future. Old-time football men who watched the Yostmen execute these one-man runs against Wisconsin were stunned at their repeated success.[48]

Stagg's surviving strategic notes of 1904 contain formations he intended to use to defend against this new Yost brainchild.[49] The Michigan coach must have seen something during the Texas game to be convinced that Stagg would overload his defense to match Michigan's strength on formations tipping to the offensive right side, thereby leaving the Maroons' other side vulnerable. Stagg's notes reveal that very intention. Yost was ready for it. In the week before the Maroons game, he installed new plays for Heston to run left, to Chicago's vulnerable side, from right halfback as well as from his usual left. Yost's only concern: Heston was uncomfortable and unsure carrying the ball in his left arm after forty-three games of mostly tucking it into his right arm.

Apparently, Yost instructed quarterback Fred "Norky" Norcross not to use the new plays right away. The Wolverines didn't need to. On their first possession, starting from their thirty-eight-yard line, they drove seventy-two uninterrupted yards for a touchdown in fourteen plays to go up 5–0.

After Eckersall pinned Michigan at its fifteen with a long ensuing kickoff, the Wolverines kept right on marching. Ten plays later, from the Chicago fifty, Norcross finally called one of the new plays for Heston around left end. The ruse worked. Heston circled the right side of the Maroons defense and burst for forty-two yards, down to the eight after Eckersall finally shoved Heston out of bounds. On the next snap, Tom Hammond scored for the second time and Michigan led 10–0 after another failed conversion.

Urgently needing to stem the Wolverine's momentum, Chicago chose to receive the ensuing kickoff this time. Michigan forced an immediate punt. Eckersall then kicked the Maroons right back into the game. Burt Gale snapped him the ball from Chicago's twenty-two-yard line, and Eckersall launched a mammoth punt. Wherever the ball landed—one report said it arced all the way to the Michigan ten—it bounded into the end zone, downed for a touchback. An eighty-eight-

Figure 13.4.   Michigan's Tom Hammond breaks free around the Maroons' right end during the 1904 game in Ann Arbor. *Source:* **Bentley Historical Library, University of Michigan.**

yard punt from scrimmage and about one hundred yards from Ecker-sall's foot.

On the next play, Eckersall ran back Joe Curtis's return punt eight-een yards to the Michigan thirty-seven. From there, the Maroons achieved something only one other team had done to a Yost-coached Michigan team in four years—they repeatedly smashed the ball right through the Wolverines, and in eight plays scored a touchdown. Ecker-sall successfully targeted plays at Michigan's freshman right tackle, Octy Graham. Fullback Hugo Bezdek carried the ball the final seven yards. It was the Maroons' first score of any kind against UM since 1900. Ed Parry converted, and the Maroons trailed 10–6 with three-quarters of the game yet to play. "The Chicago university band broke into *Hot Time* and the Maroon contingent went wild," the *Detroit Free Press* re-ported.[50]

Michigan kicked off and forced an immediate punt, and that's when Eckersall's bravado—Yost would have called it recklessness—got the best of him. Eckie never lacked for gall on a football field and here he called for a fake punt. But Michigan stymied fullback Bezdek short of the first down. It was a tide-swinging blunder. From the Chicago twen-ty-six, the Wolverines quickly ran off eight gaining plays and scored on a Heston four-yard run. Tom Hammond's conversion made the score 16–6, which Michigan took into halftime. In the interim, the Maroons had lost four of their best players, three to injury (left tackle Parry, Bezdek, and right half Mark Catlin), and right tackle Dan Boone was ejected for slugging. The Maroons appeared done.

Yost instructed Norcross to run more plays for Heston around left end in the second half. Norky barked out such a signal on the first scrimmage play after the kickoff—and it ended in disaster. Heston bob-bled the ball and lost it. Eckersall sprinted up, scooped it up, and scored on a forty-yard fumble return. University of Washington transfer Bill Speidel converted, pulling the Maroons to within four points again, 16–12. New life for the sky-high Maroons.

No team had scored twice on Michigan since 1900, before Yost's arrival, and no college team had scored twice on a Yost-coached squad since 1899, when Yost's Kansas Jayhawks surrendered twenty points to the formerly Yost-coached Nebraska Cornhuskers.

Despite the fact that Speik, Chicago's senior captain, was now sur-rounded by nothing but first- and second-year Maroons, Michigan appeared in real danger for about the next fifteen minutes of play. One fluke turnover and Chicago could take the lead. The teams proceeded to exchange punts and fumbles in the middle of the field. Heston fumbled twice without major consequence, both times while running to his left.

But, as the Wolverines did the year before at Minnesota with the score tied 0–0 and momentum wearing the wrong colors, they mounted a tenacious, long drive late in the game. This one covered ninety yards, climaxing with Hammond's third touchdown. His conversion was the final score in a 22–12 Michigan victory.

From a yardage standpoint, the game was no closer than in the three previous Yost/Stagg games. The Wolverines outgained the Maroons 280 to 60 in the first half and 268 to 12 in the second. Other than the opening drive of the game when the Maroons moved thirty yards and their first-half touchdown drive of thirty-seven yards, Chicago advanced the ball but five yards on the day. Michigan's one hundred yards in penalties and fumbles helped to keep the Maroons in the game.

The Chicago youngsters—starters and inserted backups alike—put forth a plucky effort that won the admiration of the press and fans from both sides afterward. UC president Harper sent a message of hearty congratulations to the team, closing with: "Never did an Alma Mater have more reason to be more proud of its sons."[51]

Said Stagg afterward, "I am proud of the team. There is not a quitter on it and all the men played a magnificent game against fearful odds. It seems strange the fatality that pursues us when we play Michigan. I wish we could meet them again with a whole team and let the twenty-two men fight it out. I would not be afraid of them."[52]

Yost said the final score would have been about 40–6 had his team not made so many blasted mistakes.[53] When it was suggested to him a few days later that, per some reports in Chicago, the Maroons had been the equal of the Wolverines before all those key player losses and bad luck, Yost all but laughed: "Do you know how much ground they gained in actual scrimmage? Just about 65, while we gained over 500. . . . They claim we were outplayed but being outplayed like that will win us games right along." As for the claim of "hard luck in having their regulars put out of the game," Yost pointed out that Michigan scored two quick touchdowns at the outset with all of the Maroon starters in. "For my part, I wish the regulars had stayed in," he said.[54]

Heston was hailed as the hero of the game, despite his fumbles. He gained 239 yards on thirty-eight carries, many around the left end. He thus finished his Wolverine career without ever experiencing defeat; Michigan went 43–0–1 in his four years. A Michigan alumnus at the time wrote to Walter Camp to sing Heston's praises and claimed that "detailed statistics will show that in each of the past four football seasons, Heston gained more ground than any other two players in the country." No such statistics survive to verify the claim. [55]

There is no way ever to know how many yards Heston rushed for at Michigan. Official statistics weren't kept in college football until the late 1930s. Newspapers never published complete play-by-play accounts of Michigan's practice-game victories, and even if they did there were occasional discrepancies between the dailies as to the identities of ball carriers on various plays, lengths of runs, and so on. Nevertheless, long runs usually were mentioned in every game report. The author has gleaned from them that Heston in his Michigan career had at least forty runs of more than twenty yards in length, and probably more. Of those forty, at least twenty-two runs were more than thirty-five yards long, and thirteen were more than sixty yards long.

As the years went by, estimates as to how many touchdowns Heston scored kept rising, to as high as 110. Decades later, he claimed the correct figure was 92. [56] But contemporary newspaper accounts were quite reliable in this regard and usually agreed on touchdown scorers. Occasional mistaken identities were understandable, considering players didn't wear numbers and touchdowns were scored perhaps half a field from the press box, usually amid a thicket of collapsing players. The author's findings nearly match the research conducted in 1958 by Steve Boda Jr., the NCAA's longtime associate director of statistics. Boda counted seventy-one touchdowns for Heston. [57] The author could not be so definitive. Depending on which discrepant accounts you choose to believe for two games—against Wisconsin in 1902 and American Medical in 1904—Heston scored 69, 70, or 71 touchdowns. [58] The NCAA officially credits him with 72, based mostly on Boda's research. Boda furthermore concluded that in the seventeen games for which he could deduce rushing statistics, Heston gained 2,339 yards and averaged 8.4 yards per carry. [59]

What's more, because of injuries and—in that one instance in Chicago—scouting, Heston played in only thirty-seven of Michigan's forty-four games from 1901 to 1904, and he played minimally in at least four. Thus, Heston averaged nearly two touchdowns per start. Entering the 2010s, the only player in NCAA history to average fully two touchdowns per game was Marshall Faulk of San Diego State from 1991 to 1993.

To put Heston's TD total in further perspective, no other player from the pre-forward-pass era (i.e., before 1906) is believed to have scored anywhere near 71 touchdowns. Thereafter, colleges across the country by World War I enacted the three-year eligibility rule, after having permitted four or more years before 1906. The only player who came close to Heston's mark until after freshmen became permanently eligible again in 1972 was the great Jim Thorpe of Carlisle. He scored 70 touchdowns in 44 games in 1907, 1908, 1911, and 1912, according to the NCAA. No player after Thorpe scored as many as 60 career TDs until the 1980s.[60]

Consider these additional facts when comparing Heston's TD total to the moderns: the ferocity of pre-1906 football (his face was a bloody mess at the end of at least two games); he played both ways; there was no passing attack to loosen a defense; and protective equipment outside of a leather helmet, optional nose guard, shin pads, and ridiculously large knee pads was almost nonexistent.

What cannot be disputed: Willie Heston was one of the most dominant players of any era in college football history. He was the first player to be named All-Western four times, and the first from outside the East to be named a two-time All-American.

※ ※ ※

With no Thanksgiving Day game to prepare for, on the Saturday following their victory over Chicago, Yost, Baird, and Fitzpatrick traveled east to take in the Harvard–Yale clash at New Haven. Incredibly, it was the first time Yost had seen either team play, even though he knew their systems, as well as Princeton's, from top to bottom. The Elies beat the Crimson 12–0 to claim the Championship of the East. The UM trio could hardly believe the brand of football on display: slow, uncreative, conservative, and uninspired. Each Michigan man said as much publicly.[61]

Yet Eastern-based experts continued to slag the quality of football played west of the Appalachians. Caspar Whitney placed Michigan at number eight in his final national rankings in *Outing* magazine.[62] A year earlier, the self-appointed chief justice of athletic amateurism had censured Yost's and UM's ethics but, as usual, overreached due to sloppy research. For instance, Whitney cited Paul Jones's mid-school-year departure from UM in 1902–1903 as one of the chief outrages, when Jones in fact did not return for second semester because he was recovering from a long bout of typhoid that nearly killed him.[63] It must have been more difficult than usual for Yost to bite his tongue after the '04 season. He must have thought that if the Columbia game had come off as planned, Whitney would be dining on crow until Christmas.

As it was, while Yost and all UM supporters reveled in a fourth consecutive undefeated championship season, it rang strangely hollow. And not because despised Minnesota went 14–0–0 and again claimed a half-share of the Western title. Rather, it was because no one could quite get over the letdown that followed the cancellation of their planned Thanksgiving Day coming-out party in Manhattan. Authentication in the eyes of the East mattered greatly to Yost and company, but it continued to elude them.

Michigan's whirlwind attack would have wowed the easterners. Fitzpatrick, the Michigan trainer, could not believe how slow Yale and Harvard continued to play. "They wait until everybody gets line up, then the quarterback looks cautiously around for a weak spot, then he drawls out his signals, so as to give everybody a chance to absorb them thoroughly and then there is a line smash for two or three yards, and sometimes not even that," he said. "I think our end runs would startle them a little, for they use mass plays and close formations almost entirely. Yale moved so slowly that we could execute three plays to her one."[64]

Ann Arborites and Detroiters asked Yost countless times upon his return from the East if he thought Michigan could defeat the Yalies. "All I want is a chance to play them," he said. "I wasn't afraid to put my boys against them before I went east and saw their play, and I am less afraid now than I was before. Is that an answer? If it is, you're welcome."[65]

※ ※ ※

Stagg had been barely able to accompany his Maroons to Ann Arbor on November 13. He'd all but exhausted himself by then, and as in the

Figure 13.5.   The 1904 Michigan Wolverines, Champions of the West. Front row:
Ted Stuart, Fred "Norky" Norcross, Harold Weeks. Second row: Harry Ham-
mond, Denny Clark. Third row: assistant coach W. C. Cole, Tom Hammond,
Frank "Shorty" Longman, captain Willie Heston, athletic director Charles Baird.
Back row: student manager A. H. Montgomery, Walter Graham, Charles "Babe"
Carter, trainer Keene Fitzpatrick, Adolph "Germany" Schulz, head coach Fielding
H. Yost, Henry "Dutch" Schulte, John "Joe" Curtis. *Source:* Bentley Historical
Library, University of Michigan.

previous winter, he could barely walk without experiencing shooting
pain in his back. "I hardly lasted out the season," Stagg recalled in his
1927 autobiography.[66]

On the team's trip home from Ann Arbor, he stopped at the Battle
Creek Sanatorium health resort for forced rest and comfort. After
coaching the Maroons to a season-ending 18–11 defeat of Wisconsin on
Thanksgiving, in which Eckersall returned a punt 105 yards for a touch-
down, Stagg sought longer-term relief in the famous mineral baths of
Mount Clemens, Michigan, on the northwest shore of Lake St. Clair.
He convalesced there for weeks.[67]

Yost telephoned Stagg in Mount Clemens in late November to wish
him well. "I'll tell you what," Yost told reporters after the call, "this
coaching business does a man all up if he isn't careful."[68] He'd know.
Yost was so run down and underweight following the grueling 1903

season, he put twenty-five pounds back on by the first week of January.[69]

Word of Stagg's health reversal had leaked just days before the Michigan game. After the loss in Ann Arbor, praiseworthy pieces on Stagg appeared in Chicago's sports sections—on his Herculean efforts to coach up his young squad, on how he had battled poor health all season long, and, mostly, on his unmatched ethical standards. UC president Harper led the hagiographic charge, releasing a long statement full of testimonials, such as this one:

> His intense love for pure sport, his incorruptible spirit, his indefatigable effort, his broad minded zeal and his absolute fairness of mind and honesty of heart have exerted an influence upon western university and college athletics that has been felt far and wide and produced results of which we may all reasonably be proud. . . . In the reforms that still require to be worked out he will be one of the leaders. [W]hen these reforms have come about the world will begin to appreciate some of the ideals toward which many, and among these Mr. Stagg, have been working. I am confident that it is the universal wish on the part of college and university men that Mr. Stagg may see these and many other reforms carried into effect.[70]

The *Chicago Tribune* nearly trumped that: "Doubtless no man in America connected with the field of athletics occupies quite so high a place in the esteem of the better class of amateur sportsmen as Coach Stagg."[71] In a separate editorial, under the headline "Coach Stagg's Unusual Burdens," the *Trib* worried that Stagg might have to give up college athletics for good. After pointing out that there "are not so many leaders in the field of college sports who possess his high ideals and sportsmanship," the *Trib* stated that "no athletic director or coach in this country attempts to do as much work as Stagg. In football alone, for instance, he has done the work which in Michigan is shared by Coach Yost, Trainer Fitzpatrick and Graduate Manager Baird. And Stagg does not work on football alone, as does Yost. . . . Students and faculty alike are urging him to leave Chicago for a long rest, in order that he may be ready for strenuous times next year."[72]

Stagg was one step ahead of them. On both counts. Even if his preoccupation with getting the better of Yost and his point-a-minute Wolverines was practically killing him.

14

1905 OFF THE FIELD

The Nadir

All those nationwide reports in 1904 of nefarious recruiting practices soiled college football's reputation worse than even the violence on the field, even if some of the muck was raked by green, or yellow, journalists whose claims were often exaggerated, bogus, or dubious.

Enough of it was real, and enough of the worst evils unreported— safely hidden as they were from the rumor-mill press—as to warrant the universally shared conclusion that something had to be done to clean up the whole rotting enterprise. "[N]ever in the history of athletics has there been so much soliciting for new men in the West as this year," Michigan athletic director Charles Baird said.[1] The *Chicago Tribune* observed that recruiting "has been conducted more openly than usual this year by leading universities," and in deplorable manners.[2]

In autumn 1904, Big Nine presidents pounced. They did not wait for the annual day-after-Thanksgiving legislative meeting of their faculty representatives. In previous years the reps would debate further crackdowns but usually stop short of agreeing to anything substantive. The presidents this year met before the reps did, in St. Louis, and "urged" reps at their coming meeting to approve college sports' first residency rule, that is, a rule barring freshmen from playing any intercollegiate sport in their first academic year. This rule, it was naively believed, would prevent the enrolment of any young men who cared more about sports than books, and thus would end the deplorable, out-of-control recruitment of such "students." As well, the presidents hoped the rule would halt the occasionally successful, outrageous pursuit of star high school undergraduates such as Tom Hammond (by Michigan) or Walter Eckersall or Leo DeTray (by Chicago). Conference leaders had mulled the residency rule since the league's formation in 1896. The drastic measure sat on table's edge as an ace in the hole, ready to be turned over when really needed.[3]

The catalyst for action had come in February 1904 when high schools in Chicago passed a rule forbidding schoolboy freshmen from participating in athletics within their first six months of enrolment.[4] Reform-minded faculty in the Big Nine simply could not be outreformed by high schools.

The climate for change gained further momentum practically by the week as 1904 wound down. Brown University's outspoken reformist president, Dr. William H. P. Faunce, both lectured and wrote about the devolution of college athletics from "the period of genuine recreation" thirty years earlier to the present "period of prevarication."[5] The University of Chicago's president, William Rainey Harper, floated the concept in a feature for *Harper's Weekly* of actually endowing college athletics, as a means of reducing or eliminating the public's role in funding through ticket sales, "one of the most serious administrative problems of higher education."[6]

Although other crackdowns were murmured, including the elimination of highly commercial Thanksgiving Day spectacles, it would be enough for Big Nine reps at their 1904 meeting to pass the one-year residency rule because not all reps were on board. Even before their November 25 meeting at the Chicago Beach Hotel, the University of Minnesota's rep, Fred Jones, hedged. He spoke for most athletic men in the conference when he told the *Chicago Journal*,

> I have this question to ask. Would not such a rule tend to drive western athletes into the big eastern schools, where such rules would not prevent them from participating [immediately] in athletics? I believe that the result would be that more and more of our good athletes would go east. It would be putting a penalty on athletic skill. [T]here is no reason why they should not be permitted to play in their freshman year.[7]

The one-year residency rule indeed proved too contentious. Iowa's faculty rep argued against it even more vehemently than Minnesota's. The rule as proposed did not have support to pass. Before day's end, however, reps instead agreed to a compromise—a watered-down "one semester" residency rule.[8] Specifically, the rule would read: "No student shall participate in any intercollegiate contest who shall not have been in residence a semester and shall have full credit for a semester's work previous to the term or semester in which the student participated."[9] Big Nine schools more successful in spring sports, such as Illinois, preferred the amended rule because freshmen could still compete in baseball and track and field in the second semester; the rule would essentially bar freshmen football players only.

Before the meeting concluded, the University of Chicago's faculty rep, Lonnie Stagg, argued that the rule should apply not only to incoming high school graduates but to incoming graduate transfers as well. As Stagg stated publicly before the meeting, "I consider that there is just as much evil in a graduate changing schools as for the man who has not yet received his [high school] diploma."[10]

The truth probably was that in Stagg's mind, the even greater evil would have been if his football coach archrival, Fielding H. Yost of Michigan, reverted to intensely wooing grizzled college grads to immediately fill his roster holes, what with former high schoolers having to sit out a year. Eliminating both options for Yost and other rivals, Stagg surely figured, would mean that no conference school would be able to play a single newly recruited football player come September '05. Stagg convinced his fellow reps to so broaden the rule.[11]

To go into effect, the rule had to be passed within sixty days by each of the conference's nine faculty boards in control of athletics, per a Big Nine bylaw. Minnesota's and Iowa's rejected it. Most coaches and athletes across the league echoed the Gopher/Hawkeye argument, that the best Midwestern high school footballers seeking to play right away would merely go east to do so. After six months of arm bending, however, both Minnesota and Iowa caved. The one-semester residency rule was unanimously passed at a June 2, 1905, conference meeting.[12]

Thus no incoming freshmen or transfers would be allowed to play football come fall. Except one. The *Chicago Journal*'s critique of the new rule back in November addressed exploitable loopholes. One pertained to the University of Chicago. That school was on the quarter, or quadmester, system. Three quarters of study at UC—fall, winter, and spring—equated to two semesters at other conference schools. That meant two quarters of work amounted to more than one semester. Thus, at UC, freshmen could enter in the spring quarter and continue studying in the summer quarter, the *Journal* noted, "and do enough work to make them eligible for the football team in the Fall." Big Nine schools on the semester system would have to enroll a recruit months earlier—by the end of January or early February for the start of the second semester—to make him eligible by September.[13]

The freshman exception was Gerry Williamsen. A high school football and track standout in Milwaukee, back in September 1904 he had begun working out with Stagg's Maroons. But after he was denied admission to UC for having insufficient high school credits, Stagg parked Williamsen at Morgan Park Academy, a prep school run by UC. There Williamsen studied up and starred at fullback for one more season. His second attempt to enroll at Chicago proved successful in the spring quarter of 1905, which began April 1. Williamsen also studied during the summer quarter, June 17 to September 1. When he showed up on Stagg's practice field on September 25, a week before the opening of fall quarter, he'd satisfied the equivalent of the residency rule and became eligible to compete right away—through the very loophole the *Journal* had prefigured. Stagg immediately anointed Williamsen as one of the favorites to fill one of the only deficient positions on his 1905 team—the two ends. Although Williamsen would not become a starter, he'd play enough in 1905 to earn his C as a member of the varsity squad.[14]

Reports back in November 1904 did not say whether it was Stagg who'd suggested the one-semester compromise, nor did anyone publicly accuse Stagg or Chicago of gaining an edge because of its term system. Regardless, Stagg was anything but desperate to add Williamsen or any other new players. The Maroon coach already possessed far more top-flight players than he knew what to do with. Legally, too. Stagg had loaded up on so many new high school recruits and transfers in September 1904—perhaps more than thirty, the majority of them prep stars—that he had to park many on the reserves and freshmen teams. Six of those players would earn their first letter as second years in 1905, and four would start: Burt Gale at center, Merrill Meigs at left guard, Clarence Russell at right guard, and Fred "Mysterious" Walker at left halfback; halfbacks Lester Larson and converted lineman Lewis Scherer (the second University of Washington transfer from a year ago) would fill vital backup roles. Today, we'd describe these six as having been "redshirted." They joined six returning letterman from the 1904 first-year class who, we'd say today, had played as "true freshmen"—including three starters. All told, Stagg's massive 1904 recruiting and raiding hauls would produce seven first-rate starters in 1905, five quality backups, and more than a dozen others still parked on the reserves.[15]

Such success from one recruiting class was far beyond anything ever seen in the West. It was as if Stagg in 1904 knew the residency rule would come into effect before the next season and accordingly wrangled two classes' worth of recruits (and then some, actually). Lending credence to this theory, Stagg's school president and close friend, Harper, was among the leading advocates of the residency rule among Big Nine presidents. Harper knew its implementation likely was imminent because University of Wisconsin president Charles R. Van Hise had lobbied hard for the rule's adoption at a spring 1904 meeting of conference presidents, and Harper likely shared that privy insider information with Stagg.[16]

With his football team already so stuffed with "redshirt freshmen," Stagg appeared far less engaged than usual at that November 1904 meeting of Big Nine faculty reps, when discussion raged over the divisive residency rule. Per the *Minneapolis Journal*, "Stagg was not greatly interested in the question and was willing to vote with the majority."[17]

* * *

The issue that did anger Stagg—and Harper—by early 1905 was the long-unresolved legal mess over the 1902 grandstand collapse at the Michigan–Wisconsin game on UC's Marshall Field. Chicago finally informed both schools that unless the matter was resolved imminently, the Maroons would schedule neither the Wolverines nor Badgers in football in 1905.[18]

For more than two years, Wolverine and Badger athletic leaders had jointly argued that UC alone was liable for financial restitution sought by twenty-five to thirty of the injured victims that day. Apparently, the law was on UM and UW's side, as neither school's unincorporated athletic association—under whom the game was contracted—had "any legal status," but of course the University of Chicago did. Edward W. Washburn was the victim who sought the most restitution: $2,500. That amount, perhaps not coincidentally, equated to UC's 10-percent share of the $25,000 gate. The core of Chicago's position was that UC had absolutely no say in the management of the game, to the point that UM and UW did not even have the courtesy to consult Chicago leaders before erecting additional temporary stands on UC's own field, one of which collapsed—thus, 100 percent of the liability should be theirs.

Michigan and Wisconsin further complicated the matter by demanding compensation from Chicago, with interest, for having contributed money in 1898 to the construction of permanent grandstands at Marshall Field, from which UC had benefited financially at dozens of subsequent home games. Stagg and UC balked, charging that six years had gone by before either side lodged an official complaint, and besides, both schools had since benefited financially themselves from the construction of those stands—Wisconsin in 1900, 1901, 1902 (twice), and 1904, and Michigan in 1900, 1902 (twice), and 1903. Indignation escalated and entrenchment deepened with each exchanged letter and meeting, to the point where by February 1905, a collision of these iron-willed athletic leaders again seemed imminent—a break off of relations as sure and as ugly as that of 1899.[19]

Then news that Harper was dying of cancer reached his counterpart at UM, James B. Angell. On February 21, UM's negotiators on the matter—athletic board members and law faculty Judge Victor Lane and Henry M. Bates—sent UC this matter-closing letter:

> We have [just] learned from President Angell that President Harper is very seriously ill. He has also informed us that President Harper was very anxious, particularly on account of his illness, that the matters we had been considering should be speedily settled. Moved by these considerations, [we] withdraw our objections to your proposition [and] will recommend its acceptance by our Athletic Association at an early meeting.[20]

Harper's tragic personal predicament immediately closed the fast-widening breach and cleared the way for Stagg and Baird to conclude terms on a home-and-home football contract for 1905 and 1906. Stagg's fifth attempt to defeat Yost's Wolverines would come on Thanksgiving Day, November 30, at Marshall Field.

∗ ∗ ∗

In the final weeks of 1904, UM athletic director Charles Baird re-signed Yost to a five-year contract that would pay the coach $3,500 in 1905, $3,750 in 1906 and 1907, and $4,000 in 1908 and 1909.[21]

It was an outrageous sum in the eyes of academics, who earned anywhere from $2,000 to $7,000 for nine months' work at leading universities, whereas coaches coached full-time for three months, tops. But Yost's new contract was not outrageous compared to his peers. Arguably, it was a bargain.

In the East, Harvard's head coach William T. "Billy" Reid was pulling in $5,000. According to the *Chicago Record-Herald*, Yale's annual brigade of returning football alumni coaches—who helped prepare the Elies in training camp, or just for big games—earned $1,000 apiece, some for only six days' work. George Foster Sanford at Columbia at the turn of the century had earned $5,000 a year. In the West, Northwestern's Walter McCornack was set to earn the same as Yost in 1905—$3,500—while Dr. Henry L. Williams at Minnesota earned "more than Yost," the *Record-Herald* said. Phil King surely did not return to coach Wisconsin by accepting less than that minimum $4,000 salary he'd demanded in 1903.[22]

The *Record-Herald* could only speculate that Stagg's salary was "something like" $4,000 at the University of Chicago, where he multitasked as coach of the intercollegiate football, baseball, and track-and-field teams and also acted as both athletic director and faculty director of the Physical Culture and Athletics Department.

"My multitudinous duties required continuously long hours of work, day time, evenings and Sundays, which I have been able to do only through the unpaid, voluntary and sacrificial efforts of my devoted wife," Stagg recalled in his 1927 autobiography. "While it was within my power to compel a larger salary, I have never used it and have accepted the salary of my faculty colleagues in corresponding positions. I have talked, written and lived for the principle of faculty position and faculty salary grade for coaches, which I regard as the safest and soundest principle for developing and maintaining healthy conditions in intercollegiate athletics."[23]

In fact, Stagg summoned every bit of his power on July 6, 1905, when he asked UC President Harper for a 33-percent raise to his $4,500 salary. In a letter to Harper, Stagg prefaced his cap-in-hand request by stating it was because he had been "absolutely loyal to the University" that he'd turned down "scores of opportunities for personal gain" elsewhere over the years:

> My home obligations supported by my recent physical condition have led me to reflect upon the exactions of my work and the financial returns, and I feel that I am justified in asking the University for a salary of $6,000.00, part of which could very properly come from the Athletic fund. . . . For several years there has rarely been an hour, day or night during residence which I have devoted to personal enjoyment, and Mrs. Stagg has worked hundreds and hundreds of hours helping me without financial reward.[24]

Stagg listed six further justifications for the raise, including one eye-roller ("The worry of carrying on satisfying intercollegiate contests with limited material and the strictest of scholarship eligibility rules is burdensome") and one candid admission ("The struggle to secure a fair proportion of athletic material from high schools and preparatory schools is a continuous moral as well as nervous strain"). Thirteen days later, the weakening Harper sent Stagg this short note: "The Trustees authorized me to set apart an additional $1,500 for you from the Athletic Fund, making your salary $6,000. This will go into effect July 1st."[25] By comparison, Michigan in 1905 paid its football coach, athletic director, track-and-field coach, and baseball coach upwards of $10,000 total. By that barometer, Stagg was a screaming bargain at $6,000, even if—among college football coaches nationwide—his salary now far and away topped the profession.

* * *

Significant college football reform seemed inevitable after *McClure's*, a popular national monthly magazine, published a blockbuster two-part exposé on the sport's sins in June and July 1905. Henry Beach Needham, a former college football player himself and friend of U.S. President Theodore Roosevelt, laid bare all the off-field evils perpetrated up and down the Eastern seaboard, especially by the Big Four.[26]

In part 1 in June, Needham detailed how recruiting practices were no more deplorable anywhere than those centered around America's top two prep football factories: Phillips Exeter Academy in New Hampshire (where Stagg prepped) and Andover Academy just north of Boston. "It is high time that the public were made to realize the extent and viciousness of this practice," one school principal told Needham.

How bad and widespread was college football recruiting in the East in 1905? A top recruit shared with Needham a letter he'd received from one of the reputed "cleanest" universities in the East, Williams College of Williamstown, Massachusetts, in which he was told, "[If] you are in need of financial aid, there are plenty of scholarships here to be had for the asking. There are good jobs about town, and no money matters will worry anybody."

As on the field in the East, no one could compete over the long term with the Big Four off the field. Princeton's schemes at the time would awe the most resourceful Western recruiter. The Tigers captain himself would visit prep schools on a weeklong recruiting tour and balk at having to make up his lost study time. One football-loving former student became Princeton's unofficial proselytizing coordinator. Every year he'd set up a "recruiting station" at hotels in both Exeter and Andover and during a week spent at each school would "send for athletes of promise and achievement." He'd even offer inducements to a nonathlete friend of the star, if that would land the star himself. It didn't matter how far from graduating the prep athlete might be academically; this lead talent wrangler "sent into the Princeton entrance examinations boys one, two, even three years away from college. 'Go in and try it,' he told them. 'There's no harm in trying; you might get through.'"

Once at Princeton, the recruit would be provided with a menial job and free food at the training table (athletes in the West were expected to pay for training-table board). Beyond that, a potential "scholarship abating all tuition" was available—as well as the conscience-easing assurance that all Tigers players were similarly being taken care of.

Inducements turned to rewards once a recruit became a star in the East. Needham examined the sweet deals given to the foremost football players in the country at the time: captain and right tackle James J. Hogan at Yale, captain and left tackle James L. Cooney at Princeton, and fullback Andrew L. Smith at Penn. The most egregious, and lucrative, bounty received by athletes at Big Four schools was the entire proceeds from the sale of scorecards at their college's baseball games, worth "thousands" of dollars at Penn alone. Hogan's gifts and favors at Yale also included an all-expenses-covered ten-day postseason trip to Cuba in 1903, free tuition, and commissions from cigarette sales as the local agent for the American Tobacco Company. Needham claimed that even more flagrant violators of the amateur spirit than Hogan, Cooney, and Smith were "readily nameable."

In concluding part 1 of his exposé, Needham cited outrageous examples of the continuing problem of tramp athletes—those who hopped from small school to big school at the first opportunity, even in midseason. He also pointed out how the other member of the Big Four of the East, Harvard, was hardly above reproach.

McClure's published part 2 in its July edition. Needham cited summer baseball as probably the most odoriferous enterprise staining college athletics at the time. That had been true since the 1880s and would continue, East and West, well into the 1920s. As so many college football players also were standout baseball players, joining one of the innumerable summer pro or semi-pro teams in America provided easy summer money to a football player, and, bonus, it kept him in shape. By 1905, the practice of collegians playing summer pro baseball was decried in every corner, especially with the AAU's binoculars focused on virtually every pro or semi-pro ball team. Needham cited all the dishonest means by which a collegian was paid covertly: from playing under an alias and receiving money directly, to having the money sent to dad back home, to having the money paid to some other second party, to being paid directly by a phony employer other than the baseball team. Anything to uphold the collegian's amateur status. Summer baseball reeked, and everyone everywhere knew it.

Needham examined college sports financials in the East. The principle ledger at Harvard University in 1903–1904 showed a deficit of nearly $31,000, but the Crimson athletic association enjoyed a surplus of more than $33,000. It was the same at Yale: a $31,000 athletic association surplus, while the university itself showed a $42,000 deficit. "There is no sane excuse for the luxurious expenditures in athletic management at the large universities," Needham wrote. "Nothing is too good for the men who fight and bleed for their university. The money pours in, and it is the natural thing, perhaps, to squander it."

A Yale alumnus followed up Needham's findings by claiming the Eli football association maintained a slush fund for athletes of $100,000—the equivalent of $2.5 million in 2012.[27]

Needham distributed blame for college sports' evils but asserted that "much of the evil . . . is rightly attributable to the coaches."

Needham's was merely one of many such "muck-raking" exposés to hit newsstands that summer. Others tackled issues far more serious and impactful to Americans than college athletics. Even so, the *McClure's* revelations made it impossible for the rotting enterprise of college sport to continue as it was much longer.

In the West, the *McClure's* series might have provided a thin measure of vindication of sorts; athletic leaders and plugged-in alumni there had been maintaining for years that, despite what Eastern apologists such as Caspar Whitney in the mainstream coastal press had always propagated, conditions east of the Appalachians in virtually every manner exceeded transgressions taking place in the West.

No one in the West gloated. A "matcher" series on conditions in their section of America was inevitable.

❊ ❊ ❊

In an era when a college football team seldom relied on more than fifteen to eighteen core two-way players each season, or seldom had as many as twenty-five serious varsity candidates, seventeen returning varsity-caliber University of Chicago Maroons in summer 1905 faced academic ineligibility. Baird's prognostication a year earlier—"if Mr. Stagg continues to secure men so poorly prepared and kept at the University . . . he will experience much difficulty in holding them together"—proved correct.

Seven of the seventeen UC academic delinquents had made the 1904 varsity team. Eight had played against Michigan and comprised much of the nucleus of the returning team: quarterback Walter Eckersall; linemen Bubbles Hill, Art Badenoch, and Fred Noll; and halfbacks Leo DeTray, Ed Parry, Fred "Mysterious" Walker, and Carl Hitchcock. The other nine players ranked among the cream of the shelved 1904 crop, who awaited their chance in September '05 to crack the Maroon varsity.

Stagg attacked this crisis as any other. His surviving papers contain a chart listing all seventeen players. For each, Stagg listed the player's summer address, reason for ineligibility and in what course or courses, the names of the instructors, and "remarks on how it can be straightened out: When? Who will be in charge?"[28]

Much work had to be done. Hill was deficient in four courses, Noll and Lewis Scherer in three apiece. Eckersall's latest alarming academic shortfall amounted to dropping an astronomy class, one of only two he'd been taking in the spring quarter. That hardly constituted "doing full work," as required in Rule 1 of the Big Nine code since 1896.

By rule, all academic deficiencies ostensibly required elimination before these players would be allowed to compete come September. Probably it would have been too scandalous internally for Stagg to have asked President Harper at the outset to make all those problems for seventeen athletes just go away. Besides, Stagg had internal influence and experience in working out such problems on his own, even if he had to appeal to President Harper at times to get his way.[29]

No less than six of the summer 1905 delinquents were allowed to take special makeup exams, according to Stagg's chicken-scratched notes on his ineligibilities action chart. But by September 11—with the start of the fall quarter exactly three weeks away, and with the Maroons' preseason camp opening that very day—Stagg had become desperate. He informed President Harper in a letter that ten players remained ineligible, and that he was "considerably worried" after having spent "the whole summer working on this difficulty." Although Stagg said he thought that "all of the men will eventually become eligible," he very clearly appealed to Harper for immediate, last-ditch help in the matter.[30]

He got it. All seven of the returning varsity men were reinstated, including Eckersall. Of the other ten, one dropped out by summer's end and another reportedly was to transfer to Princeton. The remaining eight—Gale, Hitchcock, J. R. McCarthy, Lester Larson, Horace Tarbox, William Hewitt, W. W. Magee, and Norman Barker—all made it to Stagg's preseason practice field, too.

Ten of these remaining fifteen players would earn their C in 1905. Seven would start by November.

* * *

In November 1905, *Collier's Weekly* magazine provided the matcher exposé on college-sport scandals in the West, released in four parts and written by a University of Wisconsin grad student, Edward S. Jordan. Titled "Buying Football Victories," the series' aim was to provide a "description of the unacademic and demoralizing methods which are being employed by the athletic directors, coaches, students, alumni, and friends of the six largest Middle-West universities in their mad chase for victory."

Jordan took Chicago, Illinois, and Northwestern to task first, in the November 11 edition. In subsequent weeks, one at a time, he addressed conditions at Wisconsin, Michigan, and Minnesota.[31]

The problem with Jordan's series was no different than what Caspar Whitney had discovered a decade earlier in his perforation of Western collegiate athletics. Indeed, it is a time-honored ideal of investigative journalism. As the *Washington Post*'s secret FBI informant "Deep Throat" would lecture one of the paper's Watergate reporters, Bob Woodward, seven decades later, "You build convincingly from the outer edges in, you get ten times the evidence you need. . . . If you shoot too high and miss, then everyone feels more secure."[32]

Jordan broke some startling news in the *Collier's* series, but overall, he shot too high and missed. The publication of his series at the end of football season suggests it might have been rushed. There were enough factual errors and unsupported hearsay allegations for athletic men at the profiled universities to point to, and thus to render their denials credible.

Jordan did not unearth the Michigan loan scheme to star athletes; no one has until now. It was the crux of the school's recruiting operation, and a conscience-clearer for boosting UM alumni and athletic men alike, what with professional reputations and careers at stake. Jordan made several glaring errors in his Michigan exposé that anyone familiar with the operation of athletics in Ann Arbor would have spotted and probably compelled them to discredit the entire series. Especially wrong were Jordan's assertions that over "the Michigan athletic board, Baird holds a supreme and controlling power" and that Board in Control chairman Pattengill "is known among Michigan men as a man who loves a winning team." In fact, while Baird might scheme with loan-providing alumni behind Pattengill's and other Board in Control members' backs, he could not order so much as a bag of grass seed for Ferry Field without Pattengill and the board's say-so. And "Old Pat," the Greek professor, personally cared little about football. He didn't even attend all the big games. Before the 1902 contest against the Maroons in Chicago, Pattengill confessed to his friend and future faculty colleague Henry M. Bates that, "No, I do not expect to see the Chicago game. I don't care much about football anyhow."[33] These and other errors by Jordan in his Michigan exposé alone undermined the good reporting that he otherwise did, mostly on other schools.

On UM, Jordan reprised the published scuttlebutt of the past few years. He dredged up the 1903 allegations against Yost and center Dad Gregory by Stanford University president David Starr Jordan and implied that Michigan's effective recruitment efforts by alumni was the result of paying players outright. That key error notwithstanding, Jordan was elementally correct in his conclusion that the "path of Michigan has been blazed by her alumni. . . . The alumni serve as an athletic clearing house and supplement the field agency work of the Yost school of victory."

As for Stagg's school, Jordan summarized UC's transgressions by charging that "Western educators . . . place the University of Chicago first among the violators of the trust which rests upon all universities for the conservation of academic ideals." And, furthermore, that UC

> possesses and makes use of larger official resources for the maintenance of athletes than any other university in the West. To athletes sought after in the annual bidding contest between friends of the rival colleges, the resources of Chicago appear most seductive. In devoting those funds, endowed for "needy students," to the maintenance of athletes and in providing for a remission of tuition for athletic qualifications alone, Chicago commits an offence which no other university would dare testify to.

Chicago's easy-job program and means of financially assisting athletes were deplorably systemic and efficient, Jordan wrote.

> Many are given scholarships, fellowships and a remission of tuition for student service. It is through the instrumentality of this "student service" that Chicago has found it possible to "check" the bids of the scrambling colleges. Over one hundred persons are employed as

messengers, library attendants, monitors, telephone operators and ground marshals, and in return for three hours' service daily, full tuition is remitted. In some instances no work is required of athletes, and in others the athletes really do little in return for the remitted fees.

Stagg released a statement discrediting the *Collier's* attack. While allowing that the magazine "had a good motive in projecting the series of articles on athletics in the middle West"—a shot at his rivals—Stagg accused Jordan of depending largely "upon the words and suspicions and rumors" of rivals and "enemies," and that in "the literary structure of his article the effort is always made to have the reader draw a strong inference of wrongdoing" on UC's part, when several "of the statements I know positively to be false."[34]

As Stagg blowbacks went, this one—to borrow another reference from *All the President's Men*—was largely a nondenial denial.[35]

∗ ∗ ∗

It was fitting that one of the most galling and appalling cases of football player recruitment ever in the Midwest occurred during the nadir of college scandals: autumn 1905. Walter "Wally" Steffen had been a hot-shot football commodity in the schoolboy ranks of Chicago since 1902. That year the diminutive quarterback from North Division High was named captain of the mythical All-Chicago second team, behind first-teamer Walter Eckersall at Hyde Park High.[36]

Thereafter, everyone projected Steffen to be the next Eckersall. His recruitment followed the same arc as Eckersall's too. But Steffen was far more brazen and took greater control of his own postsecondary destination than did his uber-star predecessor. Steffen intended to leave the high school ranks in 1904. One of his leading suitors was Michigan. "We are striving to secure Steffen and hope you can help us," Baird wrote on July 18, 1904, to his track captain-elect Charles Dvorak in Chicago. "I think that he can do the college work satisfactorily and that we can secure him without offering him inducements. I hope we may be able to get him."[37]

Steffen wrote to Baird on July 21 in answer to a previous letter from Baird, an outgoing copy of which does not exist at Michigan. Apparently, Steffen had accepted an offer from Michigan before informing Baird that he preferred another school's offer more:

> In your letter you wrote that I would make myself bound by accepting any offer, but I fail to see your point. I have talked the matter over with my father and we agreed that it would be best [to] take advantage of [the other] offer and I am sorry to think that I can not go to Michigan, but I am using my best judgment and don't think I can change my mind. . . . Hoping you are having a pleasant vacation and that you will not think I am acting foolishly in doing as I have written.[38]

Baird and Michigan weren't alone in thinking they had had the inside track on acquiring Steffen. According to the *Chicago Tribune*, by September 1904, so did recruiters from Chicago, Northwestern, and Wisconsin. The problem, it turned out, was that Steffen was short an entire year of study at the high school level. Steffen apparently chose to become a Badger, but attempts by UW recruiters to get him successfully enrolled failed. When that news went public, no other Big Nine school could dare afford—because of the 1903 Hammond and Eckersall scandals—the awful backlash that surely would follow enrolling a student who everyone now knew was so far short of earning his high school diploma. So back to North Division High went Steffen for another school year.[39]

The delay meant Steffen would not be able to play football at any Big Nine university in 1905 because of the new residency rule. Phil King had revitalized Wisconsin's talent procurement efforts upon his return earlier in the year, and he pursued Steffen ceaselessly. So did Stagg. So did Northwestern again, and so did Lafayette and Princeton in the East. Michigan remained out of the hunt.[40]

In June, Steffen chose Chicago.[41] He finally showed up on the Maroons practice field by the first week of October and proved an immediate athletic wonder on Stagg's freshmen football team. In an October 5 scrimmage between the frosh and the loaded UC reserves squad, "Stagg's new Eckersall" dazzled with touchdown runs of seventy and forty yards, and he kicked one extra point—accounting for every point as the frosh tied the livid reserves 11–11.[42]

Wisconsin's King did not give up. He brought two of his star players with him to Chicago, ostensibly to scout the Maroons against Iowa on

October 7. But afterward the trio attempted to charm Steffen into accompanying them back to Madison. One of the players was a high school friend of Steffen's. The trio succeeded. The next day at four p.m., "New Eckersall" became "Formerly New Eckersall" when Steffen hopped a train up to Madison with the Badger men. The story topped sports sections the next day. Chicagoans seethed. But after less than twenty-four hours as a Badger, Formerly New Eckersall already was on a train steaming back down to the Windy City, where he resumed his apprenticeship as New Eckersall for good. Steffen's explanation was that he grudgingly lived up to a promise he'd made to the incessant Badgers to visit the UW campus.[43]

Of course, in reality there was more to it than that. Much more. Wrote Jordan of *Collier's* in his most shocking revelation:

> In the spring of this year, [Steffen's] school coach, Charles Daly, a Northwestern enthusiast, approached Steffen and asked him to go there. He answered, "You fellows can't get me at Northwestern, and they can't get me at Wisconsin. You haven't got the money. I am going to Chicago. I tell you they won't get me there for what they gave DeTray. I know what he got."[44]

15

1905 ON THE FIELD

Equal to the Task

Officially, for five months after the 1904 football season, Lonnie Stagg suffered from rheumatism and sciatica as he lay in pain recuperating, and barely working, in the spas at Mount Clemens, Michigan, and Hot Springs, Arkansas.[1] "It is known that the trouble has developed into a nervous affliction in the back, and the use of the lower limbs has at times been threatened," a report claimed in April 1905. "The trouble does not seem to yield to treatment."[2]

In reality, nothing "in the world caused his sickness but his constant worry over the achievements of [Fielding H.] Yost and Michigan," Stagg's friend Jesse F. Matteson wrote in the *Chicago American* later that year. "But," Matteson added, Stagg "knew what he could do if he could get the men with which to do it. He knew that he could beat Yost and would some day do it. So he kept 'pegging away.'"[3]

Stagg now had the talent. "Pegging away" meant exhaustive planning to an unprecedented degree, even for him. Exhibit A: his pregame and postgame football notes to himself he kept on opponents. Stagg's notes for Michigan in 1905 far exceed those for any other game of this era. Apparently, for years Stagg carried with him everywhere a blue or black pencil, and either a small stack of blank paper or index cards. He'd jot down ideas as they came to him as to how to beat an upcoming opponent. Notes could be as brief as these for Michigan in 1905: "Practice blocking place kicks a lot. Tom Hammond is deadly," or "Our ends must look out for a fake kick when they try a drop." Other notes might contain detailed Xs and Os as Stagg brainstormed ways to meet certain formations. For this year's Michigan preparations, Stagg scribbled dozens of such notes. He listed seventeen "Don'ts" for his players, specifically for the '05 Michigan game—finger-wagging reminders that included "Don't let Mich ever see you weaken."[4]

Whereas Stagg was never as driven, focused, or intent as at the opening of preseason training camp in September 1905, Yost was never so distracted. His otherworldly success after eight years as football coach had landed him a book contract. Yost's instructional *Football for Player and Spectator* hit bookstores in September. Glowing reviews nationwide earned him more praise and fame than did even his 43–0–1 record thus far at Michigan or his eight-for-eight career championship tote.[5] His "Hurry Up" nickname was so ingrained by now that the *Michigan Daily* took to referring to him as "H. U. Yost."[6] But as Wolverine preseason camp opened at Whitmore Lake on September 11, someone was missing, per the *Chicago Tribune*:

> Another Michigan record has been broken. Yost was not out for the first day of practice of the year. He always has been the first one on the field and the last to leave it, but some business matter in connection with his book called him suddenly to Detroit this morning, and he did not show up at Whitmore Lake.[7]

Yost returned the next day. But two weeks later, the *Trib*'s correspondent raised concern again. "At Whitmore lake the course of events has been one that would seem to indicate either that the coach had grown careless and overconfident, like the undergraduates, or that he had decided that his men were so good they needed little attention from him. Yost quit the camp for a trip to Nashville and almost as soon as he got back, jumped away again to Ann Arbor."[8]

In Nashville lived the two most important figures now in Yost's life: Dan McGugin and Eunice Fite. McGugin, Yost's formidable left guard at Michigan in 1901 and 1902, apprenticed the next year as Yost's assistant coach before becoming Vanderbilt University's head coach in 1904. McGugin had already installed the hurry-up brand of football in Nashville and was far along in constructing the South's first powerhouse, with Yost's continuing help. Fite was Yost's sweetheart, the twin sister of McGugin's love, Virginia Fite. By spring 1906, the football coaches would marry the Fite sisters, thereby becoming not only lifelong friends, business partners, and ideas-sharing coaching comrades but brothers-in-law, too. Until 1921, Yost would reside with wife Eunice in Nashville each off-season, and he'd base his business ventures there.[9]

But that Yost in 1905 would leave his Michigan training camp for a single second, let alone a second time, for any reason, no matter the crisis or draw in Nashville, is as shocking now as it apparently was then. The sunburned man in the floppy felt hat in 1901, who'd run about the field attending to every detail in his maniacal zest to prove himself on the largest stage of his life, could now appease distraction. True, it was early days of preseason—when more of the workouts were conditioning-based under trainer Keene Fitzpatrick than football-centric under Yost. But it revealed a weakness. Stagg surely smelled it.

Vulnerability.

* * *

With almost all of his Wolverines back from 1904, Yost possessed the team to beat in the Big Nine in 1905. Confidence did not lack among the other three of the West's Big Four, especially the one in Hyde Park. "It is conceded on all hands," the *Tribune* observed, "that the Midway coach has the best material in his career," and that Stagg's veteran players "freely predicted" that the greatest season in Maroon history awaited.[10]

By dusk on November 4 the Championship of the West already was down to a two-team race. Old master Phil King had indeed summoned that old Badger swagger, but Stagg vexed him again when Chicago beat Wisconsin 4–0 thanks to a dropkicked field goal by—who else?—Walter Eckersall. Two weeks later, the Badgers rebounded to upset the Gophers 16–12 in Minneapolis, effectively ending Doc Williams and Minnesota's bid for a third straight championship.

Before upending Wisconsin, the Maroons had smacked Lawrence (33–0), Wabash (15–0), Beloit (38–0), Iowa (42–0), Indiana (16–5), and Northwestern (32–0). Despite bustling with backfield talent, Stagg's offense stumbled far more often than rooters or critics could understand. Stagg had been especially secretive this year, too, practicing behind a tall fence and forbidding any spectators during preseason camp because, he said, he wanted neither UC students nor any other outsiders memorizing the Maroons' new signals before the Maroons did.[11] The offensive shortcomings seemed to cloak the fact that the UC defense had been simply brilliant thus far.

Michigan, in the meantime, won all eight of its September and October games, all in the usual two-pronged fashion: by blowout, by shutout. On offense, the beefiest Yost squad yet appeared a step slower than its four predecessors. The usual precision on offense was there, but it masked shortcomings at every position in the backfield, and quarterback/captain Norky Norcross still could not run off plays as rapidly as Boss Weeks did in 1901 and 1902. Norcross's play calling at times could be suspect, too. As well, a knee injury hampered the shifty Norcross's effectiveness on runs around end. Shorty Longman, last year's All-Western fullback, aggravated an old knee injury in preseason and played both sparingly and far less effectively than in either 1903 or 1904. Perhaps worst of all, Yost could not find within his squad a game-breaking replacement for Willie Heston at left halfback; Harold "Hal" Weeks (younger brother of Boss) was the best of a merely adequate lot. Tom Hammond still proved magnificent on plunges from right halfback, but the Wolverines struggled to hurt teams on end runs. As a result of this predicament and the injuries, left tackle Joe Curtis proved by far the surest and most often used ground-gainer—on tackle-back plays.[12]

And so, with defenses paying far less attention to end runs from this Wolverine team, Michigan's offensive output scaled back accordingly: no more scores in the eighties, nineties, or one hundreds. Entering November, UM had defeated Ohio Wesleyan 65–0 in thirty-three and a half minutes, Kalamazoo 44–0 in thirty-five minutes, Case 36–0 in forty minutes, Ohio Northern 23–0 in twenty-nine minutes, Vanderbilt 18–0 in forty minutes, Nebraska 31–0 in seventy minutes, Albion 70–0 in forty-five minutes, and Drake 48–0 in forty-five minutes.

When Michigan visited Urbana to take on Illinois on November 4, a large group of visitors from Chicago, all sporting fresh carnations on their lapels, sat up high in the stands to watch the Wolverines carve the Illini, 33–0 in seventy minutes. For more than a decade, it had not been uncommon in the West for a coach to bring along a star player or two to scout a formidable coming opponent—such as when Stagg brought two players to Ann Arbor in 1894, or when Yost and Heston the year before observed the Chicago–Texas game. But in Stagg's latest monuments to

obsession and one-upmanship, he, trainer Hiram Conibear, and fourteen Maroon regulars hopped a train down to Urbana and sat in the east
bleachers to scout the Wolverines, the *Tribune* reported. "Each had a
big notebook, and copious notes were taken on the failings and strength
of Michigan."[13] Stagg demanded that each of his fourteen players pay
acute attention to the specific Wolverine he would line up across from
on Thanksgiving. Maroon players later shared their notes with Stagg
and one another.

Michigan did not allow a single first down, let alone a serious scoring
attempt by Illinois that day. On offense, despite appearing "25% slower" in rapidity of play compared to previous point-a-minute teams, the
Wolverines embarrassed the best team Illinois had fielded in years with
successful plunge after plunge into the line.[14] Stagg piled on his praise
for Michigan publicly, but privately he told an acquaintance, "If we can
withstand their attack on our line, I think we have a fair chance for
victory."[15]

After crushing Ohio State a week later 40–0 in seventy minutes, the
Wolverines played host to the suddenly hot Wisconsin Badgers. Experts
now thought so much of the Badgers, what with six veteran players in
their fourth years and King having out-generaled Minnesota's Dr. Henry Williams in the Badgers' 16–12 win over the Gophers,[16] that the
November 18 game at Ferry Field was billed as UM's toughest remaining game. Yost and trainer Fitzpatrick fuelled the belief. "The chances
of Michigan's winning from Chicago are better than of winning from
Wisconsin," Fitzpatrick told the *Chicago Inter Ocean*.[17] "Yost is a much
worried coach," the *Chicago Daily News* added. "This he has confided
to several of his Chicago friends, for he fears the Badgers as he has
never feared a football team before in all his career."[18] Matteson of the
Chicago American wrote that Wisconsin, as well as Chicago, was so
strong that the "opinion of practically every football man in the West,
unless he be a Michigan man, is that Yost will have to sacrifice one of
the games for the other, and even then he may not be able to win
either." One expert told Matteson, "If Michigan wins from Wisconsin
and then defeats Chicago it will be one of the most sensational perfor-
mances ever recorded in the history of all football."[19]

Before a record home crowd of seventeen thousand, Michigan defeated Wisconsin 12–0 in seventy minutes. Both teams struggled offensively. The first half would have ended 0–0 had Wisconsin not fumbled

away a placekick missed short by Hammond. As it was, UM recovered at the four-yard line, and three plays later Hammond smashed over for the touchdown. Hammond converted, thereby giving Michigan a 6–0 lead at the intermission and providing more proof that former Hyde Park High stars held some kind of hex over UW. Michigan mounted a near-perfect eighty-yard drive for another touchdown in the second half. Wisconsin missed three long field goals, each barely sailing wide of the goalposts. Fortune was with the Wolverines all the way on this day.

Marring the proceedings at a Michigan–Wisconsin game for the second time in four years was that one large section of stands collapsed, this time early in the second half. A long platform able to accommodate two thousand standing spectators had just been built, engineers having approved of the soundness of construction. But after too many rooters piled onto it and continually stamped their feet in unison to various cheers, or perhaps merely because of cheap timbers or improper fastenings, the stand began to wilt in the middle. Police begged rooters to evacuate it. Some did. Finally, the stand slowly teetered forward until collapsing "with a dull, grinding crash," the *Michigan Daily* reported. Front-row spectators were jammed against the wire fence that surrounded the playing field.[20]

Remarkably, as in 1902 in Chicago, few people were hurt beyond scratches and bruises—only four, reportedly, and none seriously. The game was delayed half an hour as starters and subs alike from both teams helped with rescue efforts, especially in tearing down the wire fence to relieve those crushed against it. (Eerily, almost nine decades later, a third tragedy involving fans at a Badgers–Wolverines game would occur at Camp Randall Stadium in Madison. Some twelve thouasnd UW students surged the field to celebrate a 13–10 victory over Michigan in 1993, but the wave of descending humanity jammed against a low chain-link fence separating fans from the playing field; seventy students were injured in the crush, eight seriously. But again, incredibly, no one was killed.[21])

As for Michigan's victory, Yost knew his team had benefited from more than its fair share of the bounces against the Badgers, and it concerned him. "We will have to improve our work to defeat Chicago," he said afterward. "[T]he worst part of the Michigan spirit is displayed in the expectancy to gain a certain victory, and the failure really to enjoy it when it does come."[22] Actually, Michigan fans and players enjoyed it too much. An easy 75–0 defeat of Oberlin in forty-four minutes the following Saturday did nothing to ward off a winning football team's most dreaded infection: overconfidence. It acts as a shield against such self-questioning and, thus, improvement. It didn't help that Bummy Booth, Nebraska's coach, had said this after his strong Cornhusker team fell 31–0 in Ann Arbor, "I don't believe there is a team anywhere that can withstand that whirlwind attack. . . . I never saw such a combination of weight and speed in all my career."[23] Fred A. Wenck, one of the leading football critics in the Eastern press corps, had piled on with this glowing assessment:

> In my humble opinion, the highest Western football standard, as represented by the University of Michigan for the last five years, has been far better than anything we have ever seen from Yale, Princeton or Harvard, with the possible exception of the Yale eleven of 1900 [and] even that aggregation—big powerful and impregnable as it seemed—moved as a snail compared to the speed of Michigan.[24]

Many facets of the Wolverines' play concerned Yost, including their continuing propensity to fumble.

Stagg's Maroons prepped for the Wolverines with two more impressive victories by shutout: Purdue 19–0 and Illinois 44–0. The problem was that powerful lineman-turned-right-halfback Dan Boone, a second-year Maroon, had been declared ineligible. Purdue successfully protested him before their game. The Big Nine's new arbiter of eligibility issues, the University of Minnesota faculty rep Fred Jones, ruled that Boone's three years of playing experience at Hillsdale College should count against his four years of eligibility because that school's academics and athletics warranted inclusion on the conference's so-called list of first-tier colleges for such determinations.[25]

Almost immediately, the accusatory finger for Boone's disbarment was pointed at Michigan. A report claimed Yost tried to have Northwestern coach Walter McCornack protest Boone, failed, and instead convinced Purdue head coach Al Herrnstein—Yost's former UM halfback—to do it. "There is not a word of truth in it," Yost replied to the charge. "As far as I am concerned I had just as soon see Boone play. I want Chicago to have its best team. Michigan has not made a move to get Boone protested."

Eventually, the proof provider was found to be Jimmy Nufer, Purdue's trainer. He was a rival athlete at Albion when Boone competed at Hillsdale, and Nufer was "acquainted with all the facts. Nufer [then transferred] to Michigan and was protested from the track competition in his senior year and the protest stood good. His case was identical with Boone's."

Stagg believed Jones's ruling against Boone to be a "deep injustice." The Chicago coach cited the similar background of Yost's current back-up left halfback, D. L. Dunlap, who remained eligible. He'd entered UM in 1901 from Iowa as one of Yost's first recruits, never played for two years while languishing on the scrubs, and only this fall was seeing meaningful action. "It is not my intention to lodge a protest against Dunlap," Stagg said. "Dunlap played on the Lenox College team [of Iowa] four years, and his team beat the University of Iowa one of those years. It was, of course, a much stronger team than the Hillsdale eleven was at any time. Dunlap's case was brought up three years ago and it was decided that Lenox did not rank as a college team. Therefore the same decision probably would be given again, even were I to make a protest." UM athletic authorities said nothing.[26]

No matter, the power showdown was set: Michigan at Chicago for the undisputed Championship of the West on Thanksgiving Day.

✿ ✿ ✿

Like a sparking, smoking, grinding carousel, the out-of-control college football centrifuge was about to spin right off its pin in the waning days of November 1905. A more apropos musical accompaniment than a calliope would have been some turn-of-the-century version of the orchestral glissando from the end of the Beatles' "A Day in the Life"— with its rising, intensifying, cyclonic, symphonic crescendo just before the dramatic cutoff.

A college football scandal a day hit the press as the '05 season approached its end. On the field, off the field—it was all bad news, and across the country. Edward S. Jordan's exposé in *Collier's* describing the rot in the West was arriving in mailboxes each week in November. Penn and Harvard were in a snit and about to break off athletic relations. And coverage of in-game brutality grabbed headlines as never before. The early-season Wesleyan–Columbia game had "degenerated into a brawl" involving players, at least one coach, and fans. An egregious piling-on incident triggered the melee. U.S. President Theodore Roosevelt, already aroused over his friend Henry Beach Needham's summer revelations in *McClure's* magazine about the rot in the East, had summoned reps from the Big Three on October 9. Roosevelt expressed to them his support for the game and ordered the reps to issue a joint statement saying they intended to do something to clean it up. Three days later, the Harvard, Yale, and Princeton reps pledged to "do their utmost" to honor the "obligation" of playing the game by the rules "relating to roughness, holding, and foul play." In reality, no one intended to change a thing.[27]

Then the music finally stopped, and the carousel crashed. Saturday, November 25, became the most infamous day yet in man's inhumanity to pigskin.

The New York press howled after Union College's best player—right halfback Harold Moore—died in Fordham Hospital after suffering a cerebral hemorrhage in a game in Manhattan against New York University. Moore had tackled an NYU ball carrier too high, an observer said, and a teammate—simultaneously rushing in to help stop the advance—kneed Moore in the chin. The weight of the other two men slammed Moore's head to the ground. Moore never regained consciousness. A month earlier, he'd been forbidden from playing after suffering a head injury against Wesleyan; unconfirmed reports said that that injury had left Moore with a weak heart, or perhaps a blood clot on the brain.[28]

On the same Sunday front page, the *New York Tribune* similarly informed its readership that an eighteen-year-old in Rockville, Indiana, died instantly in a game when a broken rib punctured his heart. A day later it was learned a third football player also had died on Saturday, bringing the sport's nationwide death toll since October 9, at all levels, to eighteen according to the *Chicago Tribune*, and sixteen according to the *New York Tribune*. The *Chicago Trib* itemized the deaths as eleven high school players, three college players, one "girl" player, and three others, with eleven of them aged seventeen or under. Causes of death included body blows (four), spinal injuries (four), concussions (six), and blood poisoning (two). That nearly all of the deaths were suffered by children or teenagers—who played at a level where there could be huge disparities in player weights, and where coaching as to the safest ways to tackle, run, and block was either poor or nonexistent—was not addressed in the sensational reports.[29]

As it happened, a violent incident in the same day's Harvard–Yale game stirred the wrath of Harvard alumni, including President Roosevelt. Crimson punt returner Francis Burr signaled for a fair catch but got creamed by sprinting Yale tackler James Quill. Referee Paul Dashiell called no foul. Dashiell just happened to be chairman of the rules committee. This followed an ugly incident two weeks earlier when a Harvard player had struck a Penn player in the face, openhanded, after getting kicked in the groin.[30]

University of California president Benjamin Ide Wheeler spoke for many of his academic comrades that weekend—and for millions of Americans—when he said, "The great trouble is that the game is in the hands of a self-appointed, self-organized committee[:] Mr. Camp and his associates. They have promised reforms, but have done nothing. Now the college presidents have lost patience. We will revise the rules ourselves, and the changes will be radical."[31]

Events moved quickly. Two days after that tragic Saturday, Columbia let it be known it planned to abolish football. A day later, New York University followed suit, and NYU president Herbert McCracken invited reps from nineteen prominent eastern universities and colleges to meet on December 8 to discuss whether the widespread abolition of football was in order.[32]

The climactic E-chord had sounded, and it not only kept ringing throughout the short week leading up to Thanksgiving Day, but well into the new year, until wholesale change both on and off the field would go into effect.

* * *

Against that backdrop, the Michigan Wolverines and Chicago Maroons concluded preparations for the nation's last big game of the year—to determine the Champion of the West. Fittingly, off-field turmoil raged in both camps in the short week preceding the Thursday, November 30, game.

On Saturday the 25th, the Michigan Board in Control of Athletics ruled Yost's starting left halfback, Hal Weeks, ineligible for having skipped too many of his engineering classes. Publicly, Yost bemoaned

Weeks's loss, but internally he did not protest nor complain about losing so important a player in that, of all weeks, according to board chairman Albert H. Pattengill. It was a bold move by Pattengill, who made the decision to shelve Weeks in consultation with Judge Victor Lane, the next most influential faculty member on the board.[33]

On the same day, Chicago dailies carried the news that Stagg's own left halfback, Leo DeTray, would not play against Michigan. A retina injury he'd suffered in the Northwestern game on October 28 proved more serious than first believed. With his blurred vision worsening, eye specialists ordered DeTray to bed for two weeks of "absolute quiet," the *Chicago Chronicle* reported. "Stagg says that he does not suppose that Yost and the Michigan team will believe this is anything but a bear story and added, 'but unfortunately it is true and Leo will not be in the game.'"[34] Stagg told the *Chicago Examiner* that he "had expected great things from DeTray in this game. He is the greatest halfback Chicago has had since Ralph Hamill" from 1896 to 1899, and Stagg added that "under no circumstances" would he imperil DeTray's eyesight and play him against Michigan.[35]

Reports the day before the game suggested DeTray, in fact, had been up and about all week, had even practiced with his Maroon team-mates and would play.[36] No one took those reports seriously.

The purported loss of DeTray left Stagg without his two starting halfbacks (Boone being the other) for what surely loomed as the most important athletic contest of his life. Was Stagg fated to lose yet again to Yost and Michigan, after all he'd done, and sacrificed, and endured over the past four years, especially the past two? His observation the previous November about "the fatality that pursues us when we play Michigan" was wrapped more in melancholy than frustration then.[37] If he'd said it now, it'd be through gritted teeth.

On Monday the 27th, Stagg surprisingly filed an official appeal of the ruling that banned Boone. Each of the Big Nine faculty reps would immediately vote by mail. Illinois and Wisconsin were rumored to be in Chicago's corner, and optimism pervaded the Windy City. "I have every hope in the world that Boone will be reinstated before nightfall," Stagg told the *Chicago Examiner*. "With this star back in the game and the new plays we have learned, I hope to spring a big surprise on the Michigan eleven."[38]

In his appeal, Stagg cited the similar case of Michigan's Dunlap. He also cited another case—of Michigan's starting left guard for the past three years. Henry "Dutch" Schulte had played three years at Washington University in St. Louis before coming to Michigan, Stagg charged. UM authorities had long known about it, too, Stagg said. Washington U was far more prominent an institution than Hillsdale or Lenox College of Iowa, so how, Stagg asked, could Boone be banned when Schulte remained eligible at Michigan?[39] On Tuesday the 28th, the Big Nine denied Stagg's appeal. Four faculty reps—Michigan's, Chicago's, Minnesota's, and Iowa's—abstained, and the other five all voted to uphold Jones's original decision. "Chicago had no new evidence, as alleged," said Illinois rep Herbert J. Barton, "but instead sought to prove that there were parallel cases on the Michigan team. There was nothing new brought out."[40]

Chicagoans flipped out. So did the Chicago press. "Schulte should be kept out of the game until he can positively clear himself of the charges of having played more than his four years," the *Journal* ranted. "Michigan owes it to its reputation to see that the matter is cleared up and the facts presented by Stagg disproved or the player barred."[41]

Stagg did not officially protest either Schulte or Dunlap. He all but couldn't. One year earlier, the Big Nine faculty reps, in an "unwritten law," underscored their aversion to the "practice of protesting players at the eleventh hour," and they restated that "no protests should be filed within two weeks before games, at least," according to the *Minneapolis Journal*.[42] Throwing Schulte's name into the shark pool served an equitable if hardly sportsmanlike purpose, though. "It is up to Michigan to decide whether or not Schulte will play," Stagg told the *Record-Herald*. "I brought out the fact of Schulte's six years of competition as an additional argument in favor of Boone. I have received proof that my charge is true."[43]

It must be pointed out that the West's sordid history of last-minute attempts to bar star performers on other teams probably were not all originally motivated by purity or fairness of competition. A Michigan alumnus had shed light on this in 1903, in sharing letters with Baird about the past of William S. "Billy" Palmer, the tackle who'd bolted UM twice (the second time for good) during the 1902 season. In investigating Palmer's athletic history, the alum wrote that he believed it was "some Eastern" bettor desiring to place a wad down on the Wisconsin

Badgers before their '02 showdown against Michigan, with the thought he "could succeed in disqualifying" a UM player or two, who anonymously informed UW authorities of Palmer's professional-baseball past.[44] No athletic man in the conference would have cared about such betting ramifications, just the competitive ones involving their own team. Still, gambling undoubtedly played a role in how some of these last-minute revelations about players' supposed checkered pasts came to light. It's unknown if bettors played any role in the Boone, Dunlap, or Schulte revelations, but the line on the 1905 Michigan–Chicago game in Western betting parlors surely bounced around amid the roster uncertainties.

For his part, Schulte denied having played more than two years on the Washington U team. The issue was complicated, not least because Schulte was not a student at WU when he played on its hybrid school/townie football team. UM authorities counted no more than one year at Washington U against his four years of eligibility. Regardless, Michigan had no intention of dropping Schulte at this late hour.[45]

Some Chicago dailies dug more into Schulte's past, one claiming he collected a portion of the gate while playing for Washington U, thus rendering him a professional.[46] Other reports, in Chicago and across the West, flat-out slagged the integrity of UM's athletic authorities for not barring Schulte.

Pattengill finally had had it. For ten years he had refrained from telling the world just what he and his fellow UM athletic leaders thought of Amos Alonzo Stagg. But upon his and the Wolverine team's arrival in Chicago the day before the Thanksgiving showdown, and seeing the depths to which Michigan's reputation had sunk and been sullied in the Windy City and Midwestern press, Pattengill let loose all his pent-up anger in releasing this statement to the *Record-Herald*:

> To the Editor:
> Mr. Stagg has adopted his usual tactics and is trying cases in the newspapers. His motive in this case is perfectly obvious. No other member of the conference, so far as I know, ever resorts to this method of procedure. When Mr. Stagg gets into a tight spot he usually resorts to an attack on Michigan.
> . . . Not one word of complaint in regard to Mr. Schulte's ineligibility has come to our ears from any source. If Mr. Stagg had any evidence concerning Schulte's standing in his possession, common

courtesy and the relations between the two universities demanded
that he should communicate it to the Michigan board.

[In his Boone appeal] there were some allegations made by Mr.
Stagg reflecting on Mr. Schulte's position, on the strength of which
Mr. Stagg in the newspapers ventures to pronounce on *ex parte*
testimony Mr. Schulte ineligible.

I venture to assert that no member of the conference except Mr.
Stagg, and no arbitrator or arbitration committee, on the strength of
this evidence would vote to disqualify Mr. Schulte. In 1901, on the
strength of charges presented by Mr. Stagg, a very few days before
the Thanksgiving day game with Iowa, the Michigan board disqualified [Curtis] Redden from participation in that game. It was afterward discovered that Mr. Redden had not committed the fault with
which he was charged.

Mr. Schulte is entitled to be considered innocent until he has
been proved guilty.

We have no desire to play an ineligible man on our team. The
Michigan board has taken in this case all reasonable precautions to
ascertain the truth. We have no evidence to convince us that Mr.
Schulte is not eligible. It may turn out that we are mistaken. But to
bring up a case and make charges two days before the Thanksgiving
day game against a man, not to the Michigan board but to a group of
Chicago student reporters, shows only too well the quality of Mr.
Stagg's sportsmanship.[47]

✿ ✿ ✿

Hay two feet deep had been strewn across the turf at Marshall Field all
week, to protect the grass from the wintry elements along Lake Michigan. Bales of it had to be cleared off on the morning of the game.

Even though more fans would be accommodated than at any previous football game staged in the West, these were the toughest sports
tickets of any kind to score in Chicago history through 1905, maybe in
American sports history to that point. While UC alone received more
than fifty thousand official requests, the university's counsel and business manager, Wallace Heckman, informed president Harper that it
"looks as if 200,000 or 300,000 people want to go."[48]

The 12–0 Wolverines had won twenty-six games in succession since
the 6–6 tie at Minnesota in 1903 and hadn't lost a game in five years—a

string of fifty-six games, the longest undefeated streak so far in the history of the sport. What's more, a shutout victory over the Maroons would be the fifty-first of the Yost era at Michigan, and would give the coach his second season of defensive perfection at UM, since the '05 Wolverines thus far had outscored the opposition 495–0 in 591.5 minutes of play. Through nearly five seasons, the "point-a-minute" sobriquet was legit. Combined, his teams were but a tiny fraction from averaging exactly that: they'd scored 2,821 points in 2,827.5 minutes of play, or 0.9977 points per minute. Of the forty points allowed by Yost's Michigan teams since 1901, twenty-six came off flukes. [49]

The 9–0 Maroons had not lost a Big Nine game to anyone other than Michigan since the season-closing blowout loss to Wisconsin in 1901. In outscoring their '05 opposition 243 to 5, Stagg's 1905 Maroons efficiently if not dynamically manhandled every foe. "Every player on the team is heart and soul in the game," Stagg said before the campaign, "and the result will be a surprise to many."[50]

Most of the 25,791 paying fans arrived early at Marshall Field. It was bitterly cold, ten degrees, with only occasional flurries expected. Fans obliged warnings published in all the papers that day, and repeated in the constant pleadings of the 100 guards, 200 ushers, and 150 policemen stationed inside the grounds: no stomping your feet in unison![51] That's what caused the disasters at the Michigan–Wisconsin games, it was speculated. Michigan rooters filled most of the massive west-side grandstand, which ran the length of the field. Among the Chicago partisans filling the other sections was seventeen-year-old Chicago high school student Knute Rockne, who worshipped Walter Eckersall.[52] Among the absent was University of Chicago president William Rainey Harper, who lay in a nearby campus bed, dying of cancer, too weak now even to sit up, let alone attend.

The pressure on the three game officials—referee Horatio B. Hackett of West Point, umpire Charles Rinehart of Lafayette, and linesman Bill Roper of Princeton—had to have been immense, and unprecedented. Either West or East, officials seldom called a game precisely by the book in terms of rules preventing rough play. But after President Roosevelt had personally written Paul Dashiell a few days earlier to complain about his work in the Harvard–Yale game,[53] and with new stories every day on football reform and cleanup efforts splashed on page ones across the country, the mood of the week compelled Hackett,

Reinhart, and Roper to call a strict game. Before kickoff they so informed Wolverine captain Norky Norcross and Maroon captain Mark Catlin. No rough play would be tolerated, and the guilty would be ejected.

Before kickoff, Stagg reportedly pleaded with his Maroons, "Don't let Yost cram this one down my throat."[54]

At 1:45 p.m., Ted Stuart, in at left halfback for Hal Weeks, kicked off for Michigan.[55] Starting from their thirty-three-yard line, the Maroons' foul luck picked up right where it had left off at Ferry Field in 1904. With the Maroons facing third-and-three on their thirty-five-yard line, the great Eckersall dropped to punt. He apparently meant to fake a fake punt but fumbled. Michigan recovered at the twenty-eight. "Yost's great machine was within striking distance of the goal, inside of three minutes, and maroon rooters groaned in despair," the *Chicago Tribune* reported. "It looked as if history must repeat itself and Michigan would score right at the start, as usual."

But two plays later, quarterback Norcross fumbled—the bugaboo for the Wolverines all season. Chicago recovered. Even a pair of Michigan runs for no gain would have set up Tom Hammond nicely for a medium-range field-goal attempt. Perhaps sensing that the blown op-

Figure 15.1. A *Chicago Journal* cartoonist dressed up this game photo, showing the formal wear that male and female spectators alike always donned when attending football games in this era. The *Chicago Chronicle*'s next-day headline is inset. *Source:* Amos Alonzo Stagg Papers, Special Collections Research Centre, University of Chicago Library.

portunity signaled the change in fortune they'd been awaiting for five years, the emboldened Maroons marched out to their forty-eight before Eckersall punted.

Peeved at their blown scoring chance, the Wolverines took over at their nineteen and immediately began an attempt to smash up the field. Was Yost's machine this time on its way to another of its famous early-game, relentless, will-crushing drives? "The watchers were too intent to sing or even yell," the *Trib* noted. "The game hung on the developments of the next few minutes. Everything depended on whether Stagg's defense could stop that gruelling assault."

It did, at the Michigan thirty-seven-yard line. Eighteen yards is all this Wolverine machine could grind out. Indeed, the Maroon defense proved formidable. The longest carry for UM so far was three yards.

Johnny Garrels punted. Two plays later, senior Maroon fullback Hugo Bezdek fumbled, and Michigan recovered at the Chicago thirty-nine—teeing up another easy scoring opportunity. On first down Hammond made a yard. On second down, the Maroon line stoned fullback Frank Longman for no gain. Hammond tried a placement field goal from forty-nine yards out, but he mis-struck it. Eckersall grabbed the ball at the UC fifteen and returned it ten yards. Another blown scoring chance for Michigan.

The Maroons could not move on offense either. Neither Carl Hitchcock subbing for Boone at right half nor Mysterious Walker (in for DeTray at left half) could gain. Bezdek, the West's best fullback this year with Michigan's Longman on the limp, couldn't gain either, nor Art Badenoch on tackle-back plays, nor captain Catlin when he'd drop into the backfield from end. The only Maroon player who posed any threat to this ruggedly stout Yost defense was the elusive, tricky, speedy Eckersall.

And so it went. Back and forth, Eckersall and Garrels punted. On their next thirteen possessions in the first half, the two sides scraped but thirty-four yards of combined offense. Experts could barely believe that Garrels was matching Eckersall in punting distance. Because Eckie was such an exceptional punter, the Maroons normally would gain considerable yardage on so many exchanges and move into scoring range. Chicago, though, never advanced inside the UM fifty until late in the half, and never as far as to allow Eckersall to attempt one of his famous dropkick field goals.

It was early in this series of exchanges, about midway through the first thirty-five-minute half, when fate intervened on the Maroons' behalf. Michigan's Joe Curtis, hailed in all quarters as the best tackle in the West for the past two seasons, charged hard to block one of Eckersall's punts. Curtis left his feet, dived, arrived too late, and slammed all of his six feet and 216 pounds into the five-foot-six, 142-pound junior quarterback. "Eckersall fell prostrate and was almost unconscious from the assault," the *Trib* reported.

The umpire—Yost's old teammate at Lafayette—did not hesitate to rule. "Instantly Rinehart blew his whistle," according to the *Trib*, "and disqualified Curtis for his all too apparent effort to put out of the game entirely the man on whom Chicago pinned its greatest hope."

The grandstand packed with Michigan fans "went wild" in outrage, the *Minneapolis Journal* reported.[56] The majority of fans, though, unleashed "a storm of hisses and angry groans as Eckie lay where he had fallen," the *Trib* said. "Coach Yost frantically threw up his hands and tossed his arms about in derision at the umpire's ruling, but it made no difference. Curtis had to leave the game with the hisses of thousands accompanying him."

In the climate of that week, there was no other ruling Rinehart or any other official could have made. Whether or not Curtis intended to pulverize Eckersall, he did. As he walked off the field to all those catcalls, Curtis was inconsolable, bawling in shame. His teammates and fellow UM students later would swear that Curtis was the last player who'd ever deliberately take out an opponent in such a manner.[57]

No matter, out went not only the man Walter Camp had rated the year before as "undisputedly" the best tackle in the West but, more particularly this season, Michigan's best blocker on offense, best lineman on defense, and—just as importantly—its best ball carrier that season. A huge loss. "The whole team became confused and bewildered," a team member later wrote.[58]

After at first appearing knocked out from Curtis's hit, Eckersall remained in the game. The back-and-forth kicking exhibition continued until the half ended scoreless. The Maroons outgained the Wolverines in yardage sixty-five to sixty and picked up six first downs to Michigan's four. "A great burst of joy and applause rang out from Chicago's stands," the *Trib* said. "Stagg's men had done what few expected they could do. They had played the great Michigan scoring machine absolutely to a standstill . . . and demonstrated that they had at least an even chance to win."

As Stagg congratulated his charges at halftime and offered additional instructions, a message arrived. It was from UC President Harper. His son, watching the game across 57th Street from an upper-level window in Hitchcock Hall, kept the forty-seven-year-old Harper informed by telephone. At the half, Harper dispatched an attendant carrying an urgent message for the players—that they "must win this game." Stagg then carried that inspirational message over the goal line, pleading with his Maroons "to win for the dying president's sake."[59]

Yost made one substitution at halftime, a crucial one as it turned out: benching left half Ted Stuart for William Dennison "Denny" Clark, a strong, fearless third-year man from Detroit. Clark had aggravated a knee injury a couple weeks earlier, otherwise he might have started over Stuart, in Weeks's place.

The offensive stalemate and punting duel continued after the intermission, with Garrels continuing to surprise everyone with his distances. But that's how talented these teams were. Indeed, Garrels was an incredible all-around athlete in his own right. He would win Olympic medals at the 1908 London Summer Games in both track (silver in the 110-meter hurdles) and field (bronze in shot put). He additionally would break the world record in discus four times, unofficially.[60]

Early in the second half, Stagg made a shocking substitution. He removed left half Walker and replaced him with Leo DeTray, who'd watched the first half in street clothes but had changed into his togs at the intermission. Whether the eye specialists who had been treating DeTray for two weeks approved of his playing—such as Dr. Brown Pusey, who had been due to examine DeTray's eye on game-day morning merely to see if he was well enough to leave bed to watch the action—was not noted.[61] By all reports, DeTray played a strong half.

About midway through the second thirty-five-minute stanza, Chicago recovered a muffed punt by Norcross at the UM forty. Again the Michigan defense proved immovable, and on third down Eckersall attempted his first dropkick field goal, from more than forty-five yards out and at a bad angle. Eckie mis-struck the ball low, and the Michigan line partially blocked it. Norcross retrieved the ball at the UM ten, returning it seven yards. "Michigan rooters at once gave Eckie the laugh with their 'Gee hee, Gee ha, Gee ha-ha-ha, A-ha, Eckersall'" taunt, the *Trib* noted.

By this point, it had become clear to everyone at Marshall Field that, barring a fluke or ruinous gaffe, this game was destined to end in a scoreless tie. The defenses were that strong, inside as well as on the ends.

With about twelve to fifteen minutes remaining, fortune appeared to swing farther to Michigan's side. After another booming Garrels punt and subsequent UC penalty, the Maroons were pinned back at their seven-yard line. Eckersall dropped back behind his goal line to punt. There, he summoned the daring that so often augmented his elite athleticism, which Stagg decades later called "the most daring play I ever saw in a championship game."[62] Eckersall faked the punt, took off around end and found enough open space to pick up the first down before being crowded out of bounds at the Chicago twenty-two. Garrels himself had faked a couple of punts already, so it wasn't so much the fake that surprised the Wolverines as the circumstance. No one but Eckersall would have had the gumption to call that play for himself while standing behind his goal line, late in a 0–0 championship game.

After an exchange of punts and twenty-one yards of hard-earned gains, the Maroons advanced to the Michigan forty-seven. The Wolverines stiffened and forced another punt, to the UM nineteen. Yost was always more conservative than most coaches when in possession deep in his own end; in such field position his preference through the remainder of his career would be to punt on first down. Garrels lined up to do so, and the Maroons undoubtedly expected it, only Garrels faked it again and ran around right end. Ed Parry, Chicago's left end, had got sucked into the middle. "With a clear field now," the *Trib* said,

> the tall Michigan end shot across [yard marker after yard marker], edging toward the side lines to get past Eckersall, who was all that stood between Chicago and defeat. Twenty-eight yards Garrels had covered when the maroon quarter gathered for his spring. Diving low, he grabbed the runner firmly, but the shock nearly tore him loose, and only by clinging to one of Garrels's feet could Eckersall stop his foe.

Just like that, Michigan had all the momentum again. And then, just like that, gave it right back—for good. Because on the next play, at midfield, fullback Longman fumbled. Chicago recovered.

The Maroons picked up one first down and Eckersall punted. Garrels tried another early-down fake punt, this time unsuccessfully, and then booted it back to Eckie at the UM forty-five. Chicago gained three yards in two tries, and that set up the deciding play.

On third-and-two from the UM forty-two Eckersall lofted a beautiful punt just over the UM goal line. Sub left-half Clark grabbed the ball. If he'd kneeled down there, it would be a touchback and Michigan would begin a series at its twenty-five. Instead, Clark attempted to run it out. Immediately, he realized his colossal error. There, bearing down on him, were Chicago's right tackle Badenoch and captain Catlin, the latter playing through cracked ribs—and the surest tackling lineman on the team. Clark slipped past Badenoch and over the goal line, but Catlin "tore into him," the *Trib* reported, "and hurled both man and ball back across the fatal chalk mark," pinning Clark there.

There was no forward-momentum rule for ball spotting in 1905. A runner wasn't deemed down until it was clear he was held down, or until he himself yelled, "Down!" The officials, upon not hearing Clark cry down, ruled a safety. Clark swore afterward that he indeed had "cried down" but referee Hackett was "up the field" and did not hear him. Yost later said he heard Clark's cry.[63]

No matter, it was a safety. "[T]he man who ran the scoreboard could not believe his eyes, or knew nothing of the rules, for he failed to post the '2' to Chicago's credit," the *Trib* reported. "The rooters hesitated and guessed. . . . All doubt was set at rest, however, when Referee Hackett held up two fingers, and several side liners rushed toward the scoreboard to wake up the man in charge." About five minutes remained. "Chicago's stands nearly fell down [with] unheard of joy," the *Trib* reported.

There was little chance Michigan could score any points now, barring a fluke.

Even though Yost subbed out Clark for Paul Magoffin with instructions to run the gamut of UM's arsenal of trick plays, none worked; the Wolverines never advanced as far as midfield in the waning minutes.

The long, final whistle ended the suspense, with Michigan in possession at its fifty-two-yard line. Final score: Chicago 2, Michigan 0.

Figure 15.2.   As brilliant as he was a field general, an open-field runner, and a dropkicker, Walter Eckersall also was an excellent punter, as depicted here in an unidentified newspaper photograph. A long, lazy Eckersall punt began the decisive play in the 1905 Michigan–Chicago game. *Source:* Amos Alonzo Stagg Papers, Special Collections Research Centre, University of Chicago Library.

❉ ❉ ❉

Figure 15.3. In this panoramic newspaper photograph, a record crowd of more than twenty-seven thousand crammed Marshall Field to watch Chicago upend Michigan 2–0 and end Yost's point-a-minute dynasty. Various headlines from the next day's Chicago dailies are inset. *Source:* Amos Alonzo Stagg Papers, Special Collections Research Centre, University of Chicago Library.

A "mad" scene that "cannot be adequately described" ensued, the *Trib* said. Hundreds of Chicago fans tore down the interior fence and rushed the field, some to surround the disconsolate Wolverines and jeer them, but most to mob the victorious Maroons:

> [A]s fast as they could be reached, the players were lifted on the proud shoulders of their admirers and carried in triumph from the battlefield. The maroon band started a triumphant march around the gridiron. . . . [E]ager were Chicago sympathizers to get a glimpse of or touch the head of those men who had beaten Yost's team at last, those men who were undisputed champions of the west, who had fought their fight desperately yet cleanly [and] had overthrown their bitterest foe, and avenged the insult publicly offered their coach by [Pattengill] only a few hours before.

Up in the jammed press box, a budding young sports writing legend and future nationally renowned jazz-age humorist and novelist, Ring Lardner, wept. A former UM student, he would recall that no one had seen him cry in public before.[64]

Yost was particularly gutted. It was the first time in nine years of coaching college football that he'd ever been beaten out of a championship—a disappointment that has yet to be experienced by any other man. "I can say little more than that Michigan was defeated in one of the best and hardest fought games I ever witnessed," said Yost, about as magnanimous as he'd ever be after a Michigan loss. "The two teams as a whole were about equal,

> but I believe Garrels had the better of Eckersall in the kicking part of the battle. . . . The Michigan team fought a good fight and I am satisfied with its work, even if our five years' record of victories has been shattered. In regard to the ruling which put Curtis out of the game, I would like to say something had we won. As it is, we have no sour grapes to offer except that the action hardly seemed warranted. Curtis always has played a clean game. But we are beaten and we congratulate Chicago on the victory.

That victory indeed was earned by Stagg's Maroons. While a tie score might have been the fairest result for these evenly matched teams, the Maroons avoided killer mistakes after the first few minutes, whereas the Wolverines could not. And the Maroons outgained the Wolverines 146 yards to 131 and picked up more than twice as many first downs, seventeen to eight, according to play-by-play accounts. Eckersall punted twenty-three times, Garrels twenty.

While every Wolverine player despaired, Curtis, Longman, and Clark felt particular anguish. Curtis was shamed over his ejection. Longman failed most times on smash after smash to gain so much as a yard, and his second-half fumble was critical; yet, with a knee so injured, he probably should not even have been playing. Clark, meantime, was mortified by his decisive error. The *Trib* reported that he was overheard saying, "[This] is horrible. . . . I shall kill myself because I am in disgrace. I can't live and bear to look at any one again." Clark did not attend the team dinner at the Hyde Park Hotel afterward, nor did he join his UM mates at the theater that evening. Instead, "he merely sobbed and remained alone in his room," the *Trib* said. Later that night, Clark "was in a state of mental collapse and threatened to take his own life." Two teammates stayed with him.

The next day, however, Clark termed reports that he'd contemplated suicide "absurd."[65] Before hopping a train back home he wired his minister father in Detroit: "Don't believe anything you see or hear. Will be home to dinner."[66]

Critics, including Walter Camp, plus many Michigan fans, pilloried Clark for his "rank blunder" of running the ball out of the end zone on the decisive play.[67] Months later, captain Norcross absolved Clark

NEVER MIND, CLARK; IT TOOK MICHIGAN TO BEAT MICHIGAN.

Figure 15.4. In this unidentified newspaper cartoon, Yost consoles a distraught Denny Clark, whose immense gaffe provided Chicago with its winning two points. *Source:* Amos Alonzo Stagg Papers, Special Collections Research Centre, University of Chicago Library.

somewhat by stating in the *Michiganensian* student yearbook that "it is unfair to throw all the blame upon Clark. He was told to run the ball out by one of the team mates and in the intensity of the excitement, he blindly followed the advice. Certainly no one has ever censured him for the error half so bitterly as he blamed himself."[68] Indeed, there was something to the *Trib*'s unsettling next-day story. "Before that game," a report later claimed, "'Denny' Clark was one of the most popular boys on the campus. He was a leader in school activities, was a brilliant scholar and greatly beloved. He returned [from Chicago] silent, baffled, fear-stricken [and] he became almost a recluse."[69]

In sharp contrast, those victorious Maroons players who'd been hoisted onto the shoulders of fans were taken on a victory ride right out of Marshall Field, and all the way to Bartlett Gymnasium, the team's indoor athletic headquarters and football locker room. Along the way, some students sang a song, whose lyrics had been penned for them by half-blind halfback Leo DeTray, which concluded:

> O, Fielding Yost! Poor Fielding Yost;
> Of Michigan now you cannot boast.
> We knew you'd meet your Waterloo;
> The maroon would down the maize and blue.
> And now as champions of the west,
> We'll hang up our suits and take a rest.

The *Trib* said that the "greatest" postgame celebration began when Stagg "was discovered in the act of slipping quietly from the field." Not so fast. Stagg was raised aloft, too. Nothing "less than the entire circuit of the field could satisfy the hundreds who followed him, and when he finally was set down at the steps of the Bartlett gymnasium, with battered hat and breathless, he looked as if he, too, had been through two thirty-five minute halves of fierce scrimmage."

Once Stagg was able to pull himself away from the fans, bedlam awaited him in the basement of the gym. Old grads, former Maroons players, and UC professors alike were there together, "clasping hands, laughing, shouting, and throwing arms about one another." Upon seeing the old man, his closest friends "pounced upon" him. Prof. Oliver Thatcher, one of Stagg's most ardent supporters on the UC faculty, "embraced him, and the two did a cross between a double shuffle and a cakewalk," the *Trib*'s witness reporter wrote. Stagg then repeated the dance with Frank Bell, passenger agent for the Wisconsin Central, described by the *Trib* as "another of the faithful"—and the same man whom both Michigan athletic director Charles Baird privately and Edward S. Jordan (author of the *Collier's* exposes) publicly had identified as the bag-man talent wrangler who did Stagg's dirty work in securing players, however necessary.

When Stagg spotted his fullback, Bezdek, still in grimy uniform, the coach rushed over, hugged him, and shouted, "Beautiful, Bezdek—beautiful!" Stagg repeated the congratulatory embraces with his other weary players.

That evening, the Champions of the West feasted on turkey at a sumptuous Thanksgiving dinner and banquet. Stagg had much to be thankful for. Health-wise he had barely got through the season, again. Indeed, in six weeks' time he'd be hospitalized for rheumatism before convalescing for the remainder of the winter and a chunk of the spring in Miami, Florida.[70] On this victorious night though, Stagg could relax, contented. Four years of exhausting, soul-taxing, even life-threatening toil had produced this victory. Every savvy recruiting initiative he'd brainstormed and installed with Harper's blessing, every sly enticement tactic, every roster raid, every athlete he got admitted into UC through the side door, every professor's or administrator's arm he twisted to keep all those players eligible, every regulation he may have coyly

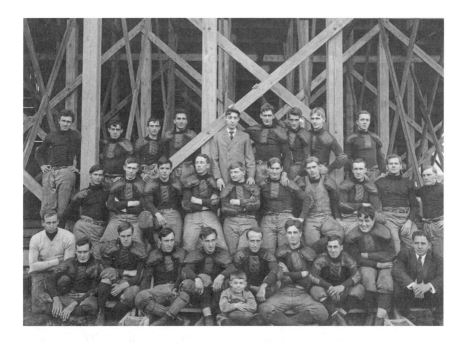

Figure 15.5.   The 1905 Chicago Maroons, Champions of the West. In the bottom row, Stagg is pictured far right, Eckersall third from right. *Source:* Amos Alonzo Stagg Papers, Special Collections Research Centre, University of Chicago Library.

steered past the Big Nine faculty reps to aid his cause or hurt his rivals, every smear of Yost or Michigan in the press, every night he lay awake brainstorming novel on-field schemes—each and every one of those actions, plus an injection of overdue good fortune, did Stagg require to finally, barely, beat Yost and his Wolverines. The great machine, disabled.

After turkey dinner came the speeches. A joyous Stagg closed his remarks with this memorable gloat: "Last spring, when we won the conference track meet, Coach Yost promised me a stomachful this fall. He certainly has given it to us today, but I find tonight that my appetite has been equal to the task."

A banner headline in the next day's *Chicago Journal* served up one last dish of crow to the vanquished braggart from Ann Arbor: "Yost's Reign of Terror Is Over and Stagg Is King Again."[71]

Figure 15.6.   In this *Chicago Journal* cartoon, Stagg prepares for his long-awaited Thanksgiving feast. *Source:* Amos Alonzo Stagg Papers, Special Collections Research Centre, University of Chicago Library.

Part III

Aftermath

16

FULLY DISMANTLED

The will on the part of college educators to massively reform football only hardened as 1905 turned to 1906. Harvard took the lead from Yale and Princeton in reforming rules on the field.[1] Michigan, surprisingly to many in the West, took the lead in reforming rules off it.

At the urging of James B. Angell, UM's football-agnostic president, Big Nine faculty reps met in Chicago on January 19 and 20 to draw up a set of drastic crackdowns, ostensibly based on three general aims advocated by Angell: (1) a great reduction in the number of games played, (2) a great reduction in the amount of money spent on coaches and maintaining players, and (3) reformation of the game's playing rules.[2]

With regard to the third aim, Big Nine reps quickly agreed that the current incarnation of football be abolished at their universities and that it be left to a pair of dueling rules committees back east to reform the game. If their revamped rulebook insufficiently curbed violence, then the Big Nine would draw up its own.

Two days of bitter, contentious debate followed over how to specifically address aims one and two. Michigan's faculty rep, Albert H. Pattengill, had the unenviable task of supporting his university's longtime president in urging the harshest reform measures, while realizing that UM students, alumni, and fans probably would scream to the heavens in outrage. Ultimately, the faculty reps settled on fourteen new conduct and management restrictions, pending ratification by each university's senate, the most impactful of which were these:

- That the six-month residency rule be extended to one full year;
- That athletic eligibility be reduced from four years to three and be limited to undergraduates;
- That the football season be limited to five games, with preseason practice beginning only after the start of fall term and the season ending well before Thanksgiving, and with high schools, academies, and independent professional schools no longer scheduled;
- That freshmen and second teams not play intercollegiately;
- That ticket prices not exceed fifty cents, after tickets to big games had been selling for as high as three dollars;
- That the training table be abolished;
- That students be required to pass all university entrance requirements, all intervening school work, and take a full workload in the present semester;
- And that "hereafter there shall be no coaching except by regular members of the instructional staff appointed by the trustees on the recommendation of the faculty, and that the salary attaching to the position shall be no more than that paid to other members of the faculty of the same rank."[3]

The last rule proved most incendiary.[4] Of the conference's nine head football coaches, only faculty members Amos Alonzo Stagg at the University of Chicago and Dr. Henry L. Williams at the University of Minnesota would be allowed to continue in their jobs. Fielding H. Yost at Michigan and the six other football coaches would be banned. In other sports, only Illinois athletic director and baseball coach George Huff would be retained. Midwestern press outside of Chicago, Minneapolis, and Urbana railed at the coaching rule, especially in Detroit and Ann Arbor. "Yost is a university graduate," the *Detroit Free Press* fumed, "the same as the 'Great-I-Am' of Chicago, the foxy doctor of Minnesota, and the big fat boy from Illinois. The only difference is that Stagg, Williams, and Huff have the right to prefix 'Professor' in front of their names through the grace of the powers that be at their institutions."[5]

UM students and alumni denounced the coaching rule in the strongest terms. Chicago's 2–0 victory was only weeks old, and Stagg's actions against Schulte in the days leading up to that game still burned the UM faithful. Stagg was immediately suspected of being behind the coaching rule. That was untrue, even though most in Ann Arbor would never believe it. Pattengill even publicly expressed support for the rule in principle.[6]

Although Stagg announced, while recuperating in Miami, that he thought some of the Angell Conference reform measures went too far, he did not cite the coaching rule as one of them.[7] Since at least 1903, Stagg had pointed to the nonfaculty professional coach as the root of most evils in college athletics, and no one in Ann Arbor forgot his evisceration of Yost on that point three years earlier. What's more, any rule that might bar Yost would have received some measure of instantaneous support among other conference reps, especially Minnesota's.

The counterpoint to Stagg's view on professional coaches, which had been emphatically raised and argued not just at the Angell Conference but for years, was that it was Stagg's very arrival in 1892 as the West's first prominent, permanent, paid coach that compelled everybody else to follow suit in the first place.[8]

UM students held a mass rally in support of Yost. Pattengill returned to Ann Arbor having to defend measures he'd voted to support in Chicago, while expressing his genuine admiration for Yost. Soon it was argued that UM could not honorably abrogate any man's contract, and surely shouldn't do so in Yost's case. His contact ran through 1909. Therein lay the germ of a potential modified measure: apply the rule at each institution only after the current coach's contract ran out. But the UM senate, while mulling passage of the conference reforms in February 1906, went a step further. It proposed and passed a version of the coaching rule that would be even more stringent than the Big Nine's: dispensing with all paid coaches entirely, whether on the faculty or not, "as soon as existing conditions and contracts make such action possible." Deadpanned the *Detroit Free Press*, "Now maybe Chicago will sign up Stagg as a professor for the ensuing ninety-nine years."[9]

Ironically, this action wound up saving Yost. Perhaps the UM Senate passed its harsher modification in earnest, in support of Angell's reform-minded wishes. More likely, someone of influence and power—almost certainly Pattengill—informed the Senate that such a rule would also soon bar Stagg, Williams, and Huff. And the faculty reps of their schools would never endorse such a proposal, especially Chicago's, whose rep was Stagg himself.

Sure enough, when Big Nine reps met again on March 9 to consider amendments to the Angell Conference proposals, Pattengill suggested just such a stiffening of the coaching rule. Fully "four hours of stormy debate" ensued, the *Chicago Tribune* reported. In the end, and unsurprisingly, all teeth were extracted from the coaching bite down. The rule was amended to merely "recommend" that only faculty members serve as coaches, and only "as soon as existing contracts in the several institutions permit."[10] Everyone proceeded to ignore that recommendation. Likely this was Pattengill's plan all along. If so, it was a brilliant stroke—his greatest off-field victory over "Sir Alonzo de Stagg."

Of the Big Nine's other reform measures, one of the most contentious was the new three-year limit to participation. It would bar at least four Wolverine starters if all chose to return: Tom Hammond, Shorty Longman, Fred Norcross, and Joe Curtis. Paranoia more than anything compelled some UM students and alumni to believe this rule was another orchestrated by Stagg and Chicago, solely aimed at further disassembling Yost's football machine. But what those people apparently did not consider is that the rule similarly would bar Walter Eckersall from competing in his fourth and final year at the University of Chicago, and Stagg would never allow that to transpire. Sure enough, at the March meeting of Big Nine faculty reps, a retroactive clause was added to the three-year rule so as to not deny such athletes—in 1906 only—their fourth year of eligibility. The other Big Nine reforms all passed, more or less as originally written.[11]

Yet that wasn't enough for many reform-minded faculty leaders. Wisconsin nearly abolished football. Northwestern actually did, for two years.[12] Stagg's good friend and interference-running UC president William Rainey Harper successfully staved off an abolition movement at the UC senate, mere weeks before he finally succumbed to his cancer.[13]

But UC faculty succeeded in another hurtful way, by ordering the cancellation in the short term of Chicago's publicly popular but ceaselessly contentious athletic rivalries with the Universities of Michigan, Wisconsin, and Minnesota. Stagg mightily disapproved but could not prevent it. The Wolverine–Maroon football, baseball, and track-and-field rivalries were dead for the foreseeable future. Harper's interim replacement as UC president, J. P. Hudson, had to talk Stagg off the ledge after the athletic director, while still convalescing in Miami in late

March, informed Hudson that he was "greatly hurt by the actions of our faculties in taking such extreme attitude in the recent discussions implying to the public by so doing that the university was among the worst offenders athletically."[14]

As for the game of football itself, by April a newly amalgamated, reconstituted, singular national football rules committee passed a wave of sport-changing initiatives to reduce or eliminate brutality. Among them:

- The introduction of the forward pass, albeit with ridiculous limitations;
- Barring tackles or guards from dropping into the backfield;
- The reintroduction of the live punt;
- And, more significant than anything else, increasing the yardage needed to gain a first down from five yards to ten, with the number of downs remaining at three.[15]

The formula with which Yost had practically mastered the sport of college football—as few college-sports coaches ever have—wound up having almost as short a shelf life as the dozens of diagrammed plays in his instructional book of 1905. The game on the field would now completely change as much as the conditions and regulations off it. From so many standpoints, Yost had to start over, along with every other coach. You couldn't blame Yost if he felt unfairly targeted or picked on through all the rules changes of recent years.

Yost never admitted that his focus on coaching Michigan football seriously began to wane in 1906. But there were indications behind the scenes it surely had. Whereas each of Yost's offseason letters to athletic director Charles Baird in 1901 and 1902 had dripped with purpose, energy, and forcefulness, especially pertaining to talent searches, in contrast football was an afterthought in his letters to Baird on June 29 and July 5, 1906. Rather, Yost mostly discussed some coal-business deal in Eastern Kentucky that he and Baird were cooking up—at the very time his beloved football machine was falling to pieces because of player departures and looming ineligibilities.[16]

Probably by then Yost already had grudgingly accepted what would become apparent to everybody come November: his point-a-minute machine had been fully dismantled.

＊ ＊ ＊

As fate decreed, it was only two months after the Big Nine passed its debilitating reforms that Michigan finally convinced one of the Big Four of the East to begin a home-and-home football rivalry: Penn. The timing could not have been worse from a Michigan standpoint. Come fall, departures and academic casualties indeed ravaged the 1906 Wolverine roster. Opting not to return for their fourth years were right half Tom Hammond, fullback Frank Longman, and quarterback Norky Norcross. Academic ineligibles included star linemen Adolph "Germany" Schulz and Walter Rheinschild.[17]

Considering those losses, and the inability to immediately replace them because of freshmen ineligibility, it was an accomplishment for Yost's 1906 Wolverines to win their first four games of the newly abbreviated five-game schedule. Prospects for the climactic game against Penn darkened further when UM captain Joe Curtis broke a leg in practice. That game, played in Philadelphia, proved as disastrous as Ann Arborites feared. Penn pulverized Michigan 17–0. It was no less bitter a defeat for Yost and Michigan than the previous year's in Chicago. In the eyes of the East, who surely did not understand how threadbare this Wolverines roster had become compared to its five predecessors, the result further discounted the accomplishments of Yost's point-a-minute powerhouses.[18]

Resentment over all the debilitating conference reforms thus deepened in Ann Arbor. The short schedule impeded the squad's overall development and limited Yost's well-known proclivity for roster tinkering deep into a season. As well, Yost bemoaned the loss of the training table for its many assets. At the December 1906 Big Nine meeting of faculty reps, UM argued for elimination, or easing, of these restrictions, as well as for the continuation of the retroactive feature of the three-year rule. That's because Michigan would lose several star athletes set to enter their fourth years in 1907–1908, including football captain-elect Paul Magoffin, track captain and star football end Johnny Garrels, and baseball captain Roswell Wendel. Two-thirds, or six, of the Big Nine reps had to approve any rule change. Michigan's motions were voted down.

The snubs convinced the majority of UM students, alumni, and regents—if not the faculty—that membership in the Big Nine conference now proved harmful to the university's best interests. UM announced it would ignore some of the conference crackdowns in fall 1907, which in turn compelled a football boycott of the Wolverines by other conference schools. The last straw likely came when Michigan ended the 1907 season with a narrow 6–0 defeat to reloaded eastern power Penn before 19,500 at expanded Ferry Field. Yost did not attribute the loss so much to his crafty, long-pass touchdown play that officials called back, but rather to the "full force" of Big Nine regulations that were now hamstringing his Wolverines—particularly the limit on games. Penn played twelve games in 1907 and twelve the year before; Michigan played eleven games over both seasons, fewer than half of Penn's total. "The best coach in the world supported by the best athletes cannot counteract [this] disadvantage," the *Michigan Daily* asserted.

Even though the Big Nine voted to increase the length of football schedules to seven games starting in 1908, Michigan officially left the conference that January.[19]

Three years later, Yost gave a speech in Chicago to UM alumni in which he tried a little too hard to justify the benefits of Michigan's status as an athletic independent, and downplayed the loss of UM's hot rivalry with Stagg's UC Maroons. Yost concluded with this shot at his nemesis: "In my opinion, there never has been a time when we could resume athletic relations with Chicago, which is to be regretted, for one thing, because usually its team was easy picking."[20]

* * *

Through 1916, UM competed as an athletic independent. It looked east for its big athletic contests, especially in football. Penn, Syracuse, and eventually Cornell replaced Chicago, Wisconsin, and Minnesota as the Wolverines' chief football rivals. The door appeared to open in 1909 and 1910 for Michigan's return to the conference, when the Gophers scheduled a football home-and-home with the renegade Wolverines. Minnesota was the runaway conference champion both years, but Yost and Michigan defeated Doc Williams's Gophers both times. The defeats stung conference leaders almost as much as Doc Williams, and the "Big Eight" soon passed a rule preventing members from competing against former members. That cannonade infuriated Ann Arbor and only hardened UM's resolve to remain independent.[21]

After more or less swapping football victories against Penn, Syracuse, and Cornell for a decade, and tired of playing the jilted rebel, Michigan chose in 1917 to return to the conference. Ohio State had joined in 1912, so UM's return gave the league its Big Ten name. Starting in 1918, the Wolverines and Buckeyes would play annually; starting in 1935 they'd close their seasons against one another; starting in the '40s the Buckeyes would join the Wolverines as a national power; and by century's end their fierce rivalry would be regarded more than any other as football's foremost.

As for the Maroons, Walter "Wally" Steffen—the "New Eckersall"— proved as effective and dynamic as his superstar predecessor. Stagg surrounded him with almost as much talent as he did Eckie, and Chicago won conference championships in 1907 and 1908. While the Maroons after that would win only three more titles over the next sixteen years, Stagg's 1913 team ranked alongside the 1899 and 1905 Western Champions as his best; it won all seven games, relying on speed and on Stagg's continuing cutting-edge development of forward passing schemes. The 1913 team even earned national championship recognition.[22]

A year earlier, Stagg had lost the tool of power he'd wielded at the conference level since the formation of the league. In 1912, faculty representatives at long last voted to effectively oust Stagg from their group, passing a rule that read, "The faculty representative of each university in the conference must be a person who receives no pay for any services connected with athletics or the department of physical culture."[23]

Stagg and Yost coached head-to-head only three more times, in 1918–1920. The Wolverines won two. Thereafter, the Chicago–Michigan series went back on ice. By the time it resumed in 1927, the fates of the two storied football programs were barreling down markedly different roads: Michigan, screaming along after four Big Ten titles in five years, with others not too far down the highway; Chicago, plummeting downhill on the rocky road of de-emphasis to incompetence. The Wolverine–Maroon rivalry suddenly had become as much a football relic of yesteryear as bulky leather noseguards, bushy moustaches, and moleskin jackets. Stagg's Maroons would never beat Michi-

gan again. Talent-procurement obstacles impeded him as never before.[24]

Speaking of recruiting, Michigan's clandestine loan-to-athletes program continued long past 1906. In the Board in Control's annual report
to the UM regents in 1928–1929, chairman Ralph W. Aigler explained
that a "small, unofficial" loan scheme "was discontinued, at Mr. Yost's
suggestion," five years before the launch of the Carnegie investigation
into nefarious recruiting practices at America's foremost football-playing universities. That investigation began in 1927–1928,[25] so by Aigler's
timeline and testimony Michigan recruits purportedly stopped receiving loans in 1922–1923. "Since that time," Aigler wrote in his report, "so
far as we are aware, there has been no alumni loan fund for athletes,
official or unofficial, in Detroit or elsewhere."[26]

By 1939, the Big Ten modified its charter rule barring remuneration
to athletes, from "No student shall be admitted to any intercollegiate
contest who receives any gift, remuneration or pay for his services," to
much more detailed language, including, "No scholarships, loans, or
remissions of tuition shall be awarded on the basis of athletic skill, and
no financial aid shall be given to students by individuals or organiza-
tions, alumni or other, with the purpose of subsidizing them as athletes."[27]

Inevitably, hell had been raised. So the rulebook thickened. And so
on and so forth, nationwide, with regard to all the other clever recruitment ploys and advantages, new ones of which were always being discovered—to the point where, by the second decade of the twenty-first
century, some forty-six thousand words' worth of rules and regulations
crammed the NCAA manual.[28]

Perhaps one sage, anonymous Michigan alumnus got it exactly right,
for all time, when in 1903 he remarked on U.S. academia's ever hope-
less, dual pursuit of caging the football beast and enforcing amateurism:

> If the athletic tail, they say, does not already wag the University dog,
> it is trying to—and with some success. . . . College athletics [have
> developed at] such a rate and have grown into an organism so big and
> so many-sided that nobody knows exactly what to do with it. . . . In
> the essence of the thing, the receipt of money is really not important;
> the important matter is whether athletics are a man's business or his
> play, his reason for being here or an accident of it. The rules on this
> point should be revised? Doubtless; but how? Try to draw a line that

shall justly separate the professional from the amateur. Write out a
rule that will work. Hundreds of men will welcome your success
should the miracle occur.[29]

17

FATES

Fates of notable principals in this story:

Several UC Maroons who played in the 1901–1905 era got coaching jobs at Stagg's referral, from coast to coast. As examples, Hugo Bezdek, Chicago fullback from 1902 to 1905, enjoyed a long, successful career as head football coach starting in 1906 at Oregon, Arkansas, and most notably Penn State from 1918 to 1929; and Mark Catlin, captain of the 1905 Chicago team, coached at the University of Iowa from 1906 to 1908 and at Lawrence University in Appleton, Wisconsin, from 1909 to 1918 and 1924 to 1927.[1]

Yost's point-a-minute players were in much higher demand. The majority of his 1901–1905 starters and many backups—an incredible thirty-two players in all, plus two assistant coaches—landed coaching jobs at universities and colleges in every region of America except the upper East Coast: in Michigan, Indiana, Illinois, Iowa, North Dakota, Montana, Washington, Oregon, California, Nevada, Utah, Colorado, Nebraska, Kansas, Oklahoma, Texas, Arkansas, Louisiana, Mississippi, Tennessee, North Carolina, Virginia, District of Columbia, Pennsylvania, and Ohio. Most, if not all, got their jobs at Yost's craved referral. These men, some of whom had barely played in games, spread Yost's coaching doctrine far and wide. Some lasted for only a few years in the profession. A few became icons themselves.[2]

Bennie Owen, Yost's freshmen-team coach in 1901, established the Oklahoma University football dynasty in 1905. Through 1926, his Sooner teams became synonymous with high-scoring wins, racking up 5,031 points to the opponents' 1,470. Oklahoma likes to boast that its football program is the highest scoring of all time, and it was Owen who set that course. Including earlier coaching stops at Washburn and Bethany College of Kansas, Owen retired with a career winning percentage of .677. He was a charter inductee into the College Football Hall of Fame as a coach in 1951, and the playing field at OU's football stadium remains named after him.[3]

Dan McGugin is remembered as the father of Southern football. After starring at left guard for Yost on the 1901–1902 Michigan teams, and serving as Yost's assistant coach in 1903, McGugin established the South's first college football dynasty at Vanderbilt University. With the exception of one year, from 1904 through 1934 he coached the Commodores to unparalleled success in the South. McGugin's winning percentage of .762 ranks behind only Gil Dobie, Joe Paterno, and Woody Hayes among NCAA top-division coaches whose careers exceeded thirty years. Fifteen of McGugin's teams lost fewer than two games. His early Commodores teams destroyed most southern teams and in 1910 shocked the nation by tying defending national champion Yale 0–0.[4] McGugin remains the only coach in NCAA history to win his first three games by more than sixty points. He and Yost always shared football notes, and for years even ran systems "identical in plan and practically so in detail."[5] McGugin famously roused his Commodores before playing Yost's Wolverines to a scoreless tie in the 1922 dedication game of Nashville's Dudley Field, the South's first large football stadium. McGugin railed, "Yondah, my pore boys, lies a Confederate cemetery. . . . You are going against Yankees, some of whose grandfathers killed your grandfathers in the Civil War!" McGugin conveniently did not mention that he grew up in Iowa, the son of a Union officer. Yost later snickered, "That McGugin and his phony accent. Before he came to Vanderbilt, he'd never been farther south than Toledo."[6] McGugin died in 1936. He was a charter inductee into the College Football Hall of Fame in 1951.

Frank "Shorty" Longman, Yost's fullback from 1903 to 1905, coached at Arkansas and Wooster College before leading Notre Dame to its greatest athletic triumph by far prior to the famous 1913 win at Army—a 1909 win at Michigan over one of Yost's greatest post-1905 teams, which earned ND its first acclaim as Champion of the West. Longman thus became the first Yost pupil to beat the master.[7]

Figure 17.1.   In this team photo of the 1899 Kansas University Jayhawks, coach Fielding H. Yost (upper right) is pictured with his quarterback and future founder of the Oklahoma Sooners football dynasty, Bennie Owen (lower left). *Source:* Bentley Historical Library, University of Michigan.

Al Herrnstein, Yost's star right halfback in 1901 and 1902, coached the Haskell Indians and Purdue Boilermakers before moving on to Ohio State from 1906 to 1909. He compiled the best winning percentage (.731) of any Ohio State coach with at least a four-year tenure before Woody Hayes. Herrnstein's Buckeyes nearly beat Michigan twice in an era when Yost never lost to Ohio State, and he led the Bucks to their two biggest wins since taking up the sport in 1890—at perennial southern champ Vanderbilt in 1908 (17–6) and at home against Vandy in 1909 (5–0). Ohio State's football success under Herrnstein was an important step toward gaining approval to enter the conference in 1912.[8]

Fred "Norky" Norcross, Yost's quarterback from 1903 to 1905, to this day owns the best winning percentage of any head coach in Oregon State history, having gone 14–4–3 (.738) from 1906 to 1908. According to Wikipedia, "the 1907 season was by far his best and possibly the school's best ever. In the 1907 season, the team went 6–0, scored 137 points, and gave up 0 points. The team won the unofficial championship of the Western United States."[9]

W. C. "Bill" or "King" Cole, Yost's left tackle in 1902, coached Nebraska from 1907 to 1910. In 1909, he led the Huskers to a 7–1–0 record and Nebraska's first-ever unshared Missouri Valley Conference crown.

Tom Hammond, Wolverine fullback/end/halfback in 1903–1905, coached only one year at Ole Miss (1906) but became the first Rebels coach to defeat that school's two archrivals in the same season: LSU (9–0) and Mississippi State (29–5).

Joe Maddock owns the best winning percentage of any University of Utah football coach not named Urban Meyer. Maddock, Yost's right tackle from 1902 to 1903, went 30–10–1 (.744) from 1904 to 1909. His first Utes team lost its opener to Colorado, then ran the table in Yost-like fashion, outscoring foes 295–0 to finish 7–1.

Henry Schulte, the derided Michigan left guard from 1903 to 1905 who, according to Stagg, had long since used up his eligibility before the 1905 Michigan–Chicago game, became the first Missouri Tigers coach of any tenure beyond twenty-five games to sport a winning record. He went on to coach the Nebraska Cornhuskers.[10] As for the verdict on Schulte's eligibility status in 1905, immediately after the season the Big Nine assigned its longtime arbiter of such cases, Professor Clarence

Waldo of Purdue University, to conduct an investigation into Schulte's past. Waldo pursued the case for months. On March 12, 1906, he announced his ruling. To Chicagoans' surprise, Waldo supported Schulte's and Michigan's contention that he'd played only two years for Washington University, not three as Stagg had charged, and that only one of those two years at WU should count against his four. Thus, after having played in 1903 and 1904 as a Wolverine, Michigan in fact rightfully had played Schulte in 1905, his fourth and final year of eligibility. All the aspersions cast by the press against Schulte and Michigan, it turned out, were unjustified. Stagg issued no apology.[11]

John "Joe" Curtis, the Wolverine tackle kicked out of the 1905 game at Chicago for roughing Walter Eckersall, received a public reprieve from Eckersall himself a few days later. "I do not believe and never have believed that Curtis had any intention of playing dirty football when he struck me after that punt," Eckersall said. "I wish to exonerate him from all charges of deliberate design to injure me or put me out of the game. . . . He has been too harshly censured."[12] Curtis's teammates elected him captain for 1906. Late that season, in a scrimmage against the Wolverine scrubs, he broke his left leg and, thus, would miss Michigan's long-awaited game against an eastern power, Penn in Philadelphia. For Curtis, it was a second consecutive tragic, premature end to a season. Stagg sent him a heartfelt letter to "express to you and to Coach Yost my personal sympathy & the sympathy of the Chicago team in your great misfortune." A month later, when he could finally sit up, Curtis wrote Stagg to thank him for his thoughtfulness.[13]

George "Dad" Gregory coached only one year, at Kenyon College in Ohio. But in 1907, he had to endure another round of grief from Stanford University president David Starr Jordan, who repeated his charges of 1903 against him and even dragged Willie Heston into it. This time, Jordan asserted that Gregory while on the West Coast in 1901 was offered, for starters, "$1,500 a year . . . from Yost through a local agent." Yost and Gregory issued hot denials. Pressed to name his informant, Jordan would say only that in 1902 he had spoken to someone in Chicago in whom Gregory purportedly had confided.[14] Jordan's charge almost certainly was a falsehood. To believe it, you'd have to believe that Gregory burned through that $1,500 (more than three times the average American's salary in 1900) after just one semester, because it was at that point—as letters cited in chapter 8 of this book reveal—that Gregory tried angling in desperation with Heston to borrow additional small amounts of money from Yost to help see themselves through the remainder of the 1901–1902 school year. Gregory, by the way, earned his UM law degree on time and was never held out of football on account of his studies.

Denny Clark remained at Michigan for the duration of the 1905–1906 school year, then departed for the Massachusetts Institute of Technology, presumably to continue his engineering studies. His football days apparently ended at Marshall Field. He never got over his gargantuan gaffe in the 1905 loss to Chicago. In 1925, according to a syndicated story in the *Chicago Herald-Examiner*, Yost "noted that a year previously he had met the middle-aged Clark in Portland, Oregon. Clark recalled his error constantly during their reunion and Yost tried to set him at ease. Yost concluded that 'only Dennis still feels the pain of it.'" Clark couldn't shake it. In 1932, he shot himself through the heart. In the suicide note he left for his wife, Clark hoped his "final play" would help to atone for his error in 1905.[15]

Willie Heston coached Drake in 1905 and North Carolina A&M (now NC State) in 1906 but won only seven of seventeen games and gave up coaching thereafter. He played in one big football game as a pro. Heston commanded five or six hundred dollars (reports disagreed) to play for Canton against host Massillon on Thanksgiving Day 1905 in a showdown of loaded Ohio pro teams. No one until Red Grange in 1925 would be paid more to play in a single game. But Heston showed up vastly overweight. On his first carry, he ran to his favorite side, the right, and attempted to cut upfield on a hay-covered portion of the field. The Massillon hosts had strewn hay to cover spots of pure ice, and Heston didn't see the ice. He wiped out, snapping a leg bone. Massillon won 14–4. Heston's football career was finished.[16] Thereafter, he pursued a law career in Detroit, rising to assistant prosecutor of Wayne County. He then became a judge on Detroit's Recorders Court criminal bench for seven years. Heston ran a half mile a day into his seventies, entered the 1960s as one of the oldest living All-Americans, and died on his eighty-fifth birthday in 1963.[17]

Walter Eckersall captained the 1906 Chicago Maroons and thanks to Stagg's creativity and teaching became one of the game's first expert forward passers.[18] At his last game at Marshall Field, in November 1906, UC showered him with gifts and honors. One month later, how-

Figure 17.2. Denny Clark never got over his fateful mistake in the 1905 Michigan–Chicago game. He killed himself in 1932, hoping somehow that that "final play" would atone. *Source:* Bentley Historical Library, University of Michigan.

ever, school officials booted him out of school—for cause. In another shocking revelation from Stagg historian Robin Lester, by private order of interim school president H. P. Judson, Eck was never to be re-admitted. Lester reported that after four years of study, Eckersall had earned only fourteen of thirty-six credits required for a degree in commerce, and that it would have taken him "many more years" to have graduated. What's more, by December 1906, Eckersall had left a trail of dishonor across the campus in his personal dealings, to the extent that a close friend admitted to Judson in confidence that the star quarterback was "a grafter as well as a monumental liar."[19] A wag suggests that those traits, combined with his academic portfolio, trained him perfectly for his chosen profession: sports writing. The *Chicago Tribune* hired him in 1907 to be its foremost expert on college football, which influential role he enjoyed through the 1920s. On the side, he became just as prominent a football figure as a game official, and he juggled the dual, if conflicting, roles—as some other sports writers did—until his premature death in 1930 from health woes brought on by his hard-partying lifestyle.[20] Like Heston, Eckersall was always sure to make any all-time or all-century team into the 1950s.[21]

Henry M. Bates, the powerful Michigan alumnus in Chicago who joined the UM faculty in 1903, became dean at the UM Law School in 1910, a post he held until his retirement in 1939. Bates became a widely published national expert on constitutional law and was even called to testify in 1937 before the Senate Judiciary Committee on President Franklin D. Roosevelt's proposed reorganization of the U.S. Supreme Court. One of his students in the early 1930s was Gerald R. Ford, starting center on the 1934 Wolverine team and the future U.S. president.[22]

Keene Fitzpatrick remained at Michigan until 1910. The Big Four of the East had been taking runs at him for a decade, but Princeton finally pinched arguably the nation's best track-and-field coach for an $8,000 salary—a $5,000 raise. For the next twenty-two years, "Fitz" continued to turn out top-rate teams and athletes with the Tigers and is remembered as one of America's preeminent track-and-field coaches before World War II.[23]

Charles Baird remained Michigan's athletic director through the next three tumultuous school years. Baird left Michigan and collegiate athletics for good in spring 1909. His wife reportedly inherited one million dollars upon the death of her father, a wealthy bank president in Kansas City. The couple relocated there, and Baird himself became an influential banker.[24] In 1936, he donated $70,000 to his alma mater— the equivalent of $1.1 million in 2012—for the purchase of a fifty-three-bell, forty-three-ton carillon in the new Burton Tower on campus. Dedicated as the Charles Baird Carillon, its largest bell still chimes on the hour.[25] Whether Baird knew that Stagg three decades earlier had contributed $1,000 to the installation of chimes in Mitchell Tower on the University of Chicago campus is not known.[26] Baird was succeeded as UM athletic director by Phil Bartelme, the active UM alumnus in Chicago on athletic matters during the point-a-minute years.

Albert H. Pattengill died suddenly of heart disease on March 16, 1906. By seven days he lived long enough to maneuver the Big Nine coaching-rule amendment through, and by just four days he lived long enough to see his and Michigan's vindication by Big Nine arbitrator Waldo in the Schulte eligibility matter. Pattengill's sage, measured leadership was sorely missed in 1907 and 1908 when emotion overwhelmed events and pushed Michigan out of the conference. "Professor Pattengill seemed to have the unique charismatic appeal that made him the spokesman for both students and faculty," Yost biographer John Behee observed.

> His early interest in student athletics, his important role in prompting Dexter Ferry to donate those 17 acres used for athletics, and his tireless efforts as chairman of the Board in Control of Athletics had endeared him to students and faculty alike. With emotion and deep suspicion ready to replace reason, this was a time when charismatic personalities were in great need. No leader of similar stature emerged.[27]

❉ ❉ ❉

"H. U." Yost remained Michigan's football coach through 1926, except for 1924 when he temporarily stepped aside. In 1921, Yost successfully schemed to succeed Bartelme as athletic director, and in adding those hefty duties he was compelled finally to live year-round in Ann Arbor. Yost remained AD until 1941, upon reaching the university's mandatory retirement age of seventy. He died five years later.[28]

The first four of Yost's point-a-minute teams of 1901–1905 eventually earned national-championship recognition. According to the NCAA, the 1901 Michigan team was retroactively named national champion by the National Championship Foundation, the Houlgate System, and the Helms Athletic Foundation, while Billingsley Report gave the honor to Harvard and historian Parke Davis to Yale. All of those selectors awarded Michigan the national title in 1902, although Davis split the honor with Yale. Billingsley rated the 1903 and 1904 Michigan teams number one, and the National Championship Foundation split its titles between Michigan and Princeton in 1903 and Michigan and Penn in 1904; the other selectors picked Princeton in 1903 and Penn in 1904.[29]

Which of the four championship point-a-minute teams was best? The 1901 team possessed the most team speed, the hardest-hitting fullback in Neil Snow, and perhaps the best punter in America in Ev Sweeley and was the best defensively. It probably earns a slight edge over the 1902 squad, which had the most prolific offense of the four teams and many of the same players, a year more seasoned. By season's end, the 1903 team's defensive play rivaled even the '01 squad's and was beefier than its two predecessors, and the '04 team was heavier still and almost as formidable offensively as the '02 team; but both years' lines had youthful weak spots, and neither team had Harrison "Boss" Weeks at quarterback. Thus, the team with the perfect record, uncrossed goal line and perfect graduation rate, 1901, should get the nod.

Yost's final four years as coach provided an impressive coda to his Hall of Fame career. Those Wolverine teams went a combined 28–2–1 and won Big Ten championships every year (1922–1926), employing Yost's much-derided but highly effective "kicking game," also called the "punt, pass, and prayer." It was a game plan of extremes: be super conservative in your own end, punt it away on early downs (on first down deep in your own end), wait to gain field position on punt exchanges by virtue of your stout defense and better punter, then wait for your defense to inevitably force the opposition to fumble either a punt or a carry or throw an interception. Then, turn super aggressive in the other team's end and unleash a dizzying array of scoring plays, especially through the air.[30]

From 1921 onward, Yost attempted to follow the career arc of Stagg off the field. He gave hundreds of speeches across the country, each oozing righteousness. He loved it that by the Great Depression, he too was beatified in some corners for his high sporting ideals, his commitment to purity, and his devotion to and promotion of such admirable causes as the Boy Scouts, Prohibition, and "athletics for all" university students.[31]

Even still, despite actually teaming with his former archrival Stagg in the late 1920s as the Big Ten's resident purity partners of sorts, and despite receiving such glowing endorsements later in his career as this gem from Big Ten commissioner John L. Griffith in 1929—"You have built your own ideals into Michigan's athletics [and] everything is on a sane and sound basis. [Universities] may well look to Michigan as an ideal"—Yost could never shake his early reputation as a scoundrel. Deplorable incidents such as suiting up as a key ringer for Lafeyette in 1896, his Krebs sequestering at Kansas in 1899, and all the sensationally bad press he got during the point-a-minute years dogged Yost to the grave. Decades later, noted sports historian Murray Sperber provided compelling evidence to support the 1929 Carnegie investigation's finding that Yost, as his Roaring Twenties archrival Knute Rockne always privately charged, was deeply involved in recruiting chicanery at Michigan and that he hadn't reformed one iota.[32]

Considering all he accomplished in his Hall of Fame career, it's surprising that Yost's name seldom is mentioned anymore among the game's all-time great coaches.[33] Perhaps his ever-present braggadocio eventually alienated his contemporaries. An anonymous man who once had been "fairly active in the administration of athletics at Ann Arbor" made the following pointed observation to sports columnist Joe Williams in 1938: "[Yost] was the best coach of all time with the possible exception of Knute Rockne. Most people would be inclined to grant him this distinction if he did not always insist on assuming it himself. I have known few men as vain as Yost [but] in his heyday, I'll grant you, he did something to be vain about."[34]

Yost might have acquired the lasting fame of a Rockne, Warner, Heisman, or Stagg had he and his point-a-minute teams secured the chance to show off their dazzling, cutting-edge power in front of the East Coast press corps. Rockne and his Notre Dame Fighting Irish achieved that very goal a generation later, and it garnered "Rock" and Notre Dame more fame by the late 1920s than any coach or football team in the sport's history. Yost waged a bitter off-field war against

Rockne and Notre Dame from 1923 until Rockne's death in 1931, and Yost's jealousy on this point probably was no small contributing factor.[35]

However pure or hypocritical Yost had become by the 1920s and 1930s, the following fact is indisputable: Yost for the rest of his life unfairly carried the cross for all the sins committed at Michigan and across the West in the reckless era of 1901–1905. More than anyone else, Stagg anchored it there.

For that reason, perhaps the most appropriate last words on Yost should go to Yost. After *Collier's* skewered his integrity in 1905, he observed, "The friends of Michigan will know that it is a lot of lies without any statement from me, and her enemies will believe it, and if I piled up denials mountain high it wouldn't make any difference."[36]

* * *

Stagg remained a college football head coach and icon for generations—into the nuclear age, 1946. But at the University of Chicago he fell victim to William Rainey Harper's collective inverse—increasingly reform-minded presidents, culminating with Robert Maynard Hutchins. First, Harry Pratt Judson devised the plan in the mid-1920s to handcuff Stagg's talent-procurement efforts and player-retention ability, according to Stagg biographer Lester. Following a Big Ten title in 1924, the Maroons' football fortunes quickly fell off a cliff. By the time Stagg turned seventy in 1932, Hutchins was in power and refused to waive the university's mandatory retirement-age rule. Stagg had to go. With all of the academics-first ideals he had been espousing for decades finally in actual operation, Stagg's last eight teams won just twenty-five and tied five of sixty-nine games (.399).[37]

Across-the-board de-emphasis at UC ramped up yet more after Stagg left, and by the late 1930s the Maroons had become a joke on the gridiron. The Maroons lost their last game against the Wolverines 85–0 in 1939. Hutchins put UC's intercollegiate football program out of its misery following that season, and the University of Chicago withdrew as a member of the Big Ten in 1945 due to inability "to provide reasonable equality of competition." Michigan State filled the void in 1949.[38] By the late 1930s, a professional team, the Chicago Bears of the National Football League, already had taken over as the most popular football team based in the Windy City. In 1962, the Bears would adopt a serif C logo similar to the one Stagg's UC Maroons wore starting in 1899.

With no desire to retire, Stagg in 1933 became head football coach at the University of the Pacific, and he held that position until being forcibly retired again after the 1946 season. For the following six years, he co-coached Susquehanna University in Pennsylvania with his son Amos Alonzo Stagg Jr., then from 1953 to 1958 he coached the kickers at Stockton College in California. He finally retired at age ninety-six, remaining in Stockton for the last six years of his life. [39]

On the field, Stagg innovated like few men who ever strolled a sideline. In his 1927 boasts-filled autobiography, he claimed to have originated everything from the onside kick, to what we now know as shotgun snaps, to assigning jersey numbers to players. Indeed, Stagg invented myriad plays and formations. While he probably was given too much credit for pioneering shift plays, he has never been given nearly enough for his advancements in the passing game starting in 1906. [40]

As for the way Stagg conducted himself off the field, the praise heaped on him is unparalleled in the annals of American sport. Pick any decade since the 1890s and you can find such assessments of Stagg as these:

- "Doubtless, no man in America connected with the field of athletics occupies quite so high a place in the esteem of the better class of amateur sportsmen as Coach Stagg."—*Chicago Tribune*, 1904. [41]
- "Perhaps no other individual has contributed so largely to the standards and ethics of American college sports, or done so much for high standards in them."—*Yale Alumni Weekly*, 1931. [42]
- "His character and career have been an inspiration since his undergraduate days for countless Americans of all ages."—U.S. President John F. Kennedy, 1962. [43]
- "The one consistent thread in the tapestry of Stagg's character was his unbelievable commitment to honesty and fair play. . . . The 'Grand Old Man' epitomized all that was fine and decent in intercollegiate athletics."—Joanna Davenport, professor of sport history, Auburn University, 1988. [44]
- "Amos Alonzo Stagg is the concrete example of what a man, what a teacher, what a coach, what a husband, what a father should

be."—Stagg biographer John Greenburg, on WTKA radio in November 2011.[45]

As a young man, Lonnie Stagg did not always live up to those ideals.
By the Roaring Twenties, Stagg may or may not have genuinely reformed and metamorphosed into the "Grand Old Man"—the supreme
paragon of virtue that everybody claimed he was. But in those early
years, especially during Yost's point-a-minute reign, the surviving
record reveals that Stagg was not. He became so creative at recruiting
talented athletes, so successful at getting them admitted, and so unapol-
ogetically aggressive in keeping them academically eligible as to impress even the most resourceful coaches today. What's more, Stagg
devised for all time the college coaches' playbook on how to expertly
manipulate the press to his every advantage.

Perhaps most slyly, Stagg used his position as the only coach or
athletic director on the faculty body that ran what would become the
Big Ten Conference to legislate advantages for his Chicago Maroons
sports teams, and saddle Chicago's most dangerous athletic opponents
with disadvantages.

This is not anything like the portraits of Stagg that were painted for a
full century, until Lester's myths-busting exposé. It's not as though
there weren't contemporary accounts of Stagg's dishonest or manipulative actions. His foes didn't always sit by quietly and take it as Stagg
snookered them again and again. Even sportswriters slagged Stagg from
time to time in those early years.

But dissonant voices eventually were engulfed by the rivers of gush
that perpetually flowed from Stagg's publicity volcanoes—that is, the
many Chicago dailies in existence at the time, and eventually the entire
nation's sporting press. The Krakatoa proved to be Stagg's self-serving
autobiography, released in 1927 at the height of sport's so-called Gold-
en Age and the zenith of gee-whiz sports journalism. Once all the ooze
hardened, all anyone could see in any direction was a vast plateau of
igneous, impenetrable Stagg mythology.

In that boasts-strewn 1927 autobiography, Stagg said perhaps more
than he meant when he contrasted the difference between the British
and Americans in the matter of rules compliance. "The British, in general, regard both the letter and the spirit," Stagg wrote. "We, in general,
regard the letter only. Our prevailing viewpoint might be expressed

something like this: Here are rules made and provided for. They affect each side alike. If we are smart enough to detect a joker or a loophole first, then we are entitled not only in law but in ethics to take advantage of it."[46]

That clearly was Stagg's early-career MO. He didn't think he was doing anything unethical in manipulating, or apparently even building into the rules, loophole after loophole.

However much he had to live down or make up for in his later pious years, Stagg eventually was given a free pass—for life. Unlike longtime college coaching "saints" such as Penn State's Joe Paterno, Ohio State's Jim Tressel, and Tennessee basketball coach Bruce Pearl, all of whom were shown the door in disgrace early in the twenty-first century, Lonnie Stagg never spent one minute of his retirement years wondering how the hell his meticulously forged armor of supreme sainthood had ever been pierced. Even long past his death in 1965 at age 102, Stagg's reputation for honesty and sportsmanship remained unquestioned, unparalleled, unsullied.

Most people in college athletics today still believe that to be the case.

In November 2011, the Big Ten conference removed Paterno's name from the new football championship trophy it now presents annually, after Penn State fired him in the wake of the enormous Jerry Sandusky child-sex scandal. "We believe that it would be inappropriate to keep Joe Paterno's name on the trophy at this time," Big Ten commissioner Jim Delany said in a statement. "The trophy and its namesake are intended to be celebratory and aspirational, not controversial."

The other coach's name was not removed—it remains the Stagg Championship Trophy.[47]

NOTES

By section and chapter, the following notes list where information was gathered for this book. Primary sources include hundreds of correspondences of the principals, found in the athletics-rich archives at both the University of Michigan (UM) and University of Chicago (UC).

UM's extensive athletic archives are in the Bentley Historical Library on North Campus. Cited correspondences are referenced by date, folder description, box number, and collection, followed by the abbreviation BHL-UM (for Bentley Historical Library, University of Michigan). The following collections are cited:

BICIA (Board in Control of Intercollegiate Athletics)
CB (Charles Baird)
FHY (Fielding Harris Yost)
HMB (Henry Moore Bates)
HOC (Herbert Orin Crisler)
JFL (James Frederick Lawton)
UMAD-IF (University of Michigan Athletic Department–Individual Files)
UMARNF (University of Michigan Alumni Records Necrology Files)

UC's archives are in its Special Collections Research Centre, located on the first floor of the Joseph L. Regenstein Library, which, in a dissonant or fitting coincidence (depending on your point of view), sits directly on the south end of old Marshall Field. The massive Amos Alonzo Stagg collection fills 339 boxes that stretch 384 linear feet—longer than even a pre-1912 football field. Cited correspondences are referenced by date, folder number, box number, and collection, followed by the abbreviation SCRC-UCL (for Special Collections Research Centre, University of Chicago Library). Two collections are cited:

AAS (Amos Alonzo Stagg Papers 1866–1964)
PHJB (Office of the President, Harper, Judson and Burton Administrations Records 1869–1925)

The following secondary sources proved just as vital in piecing together this story:

1. Daily newspapers and periodicals of the day. Most stories referenced from long-defunct dailies were found as clippings in the vast, meticulously compiled scrapbooks collection of Stagg at UC and, to a much lesser extent, of Yost at UM. As for still-publishing dailies, those with searchable, online, digital story archives—primarily the *Chicago Tribune*, *Detroit Free Press*, and *New York Times*—were invaluable. So were bound annual editions of the UM student newspaper (*Michigan Daily*) stored at the Bentley Library, as well as digitized editions (provided online by the HathiTrust at http://babel.hathitrust.org/cgi/mb) of UM's student monthly magazine (*The Inlander*), student yearbook (*Michiganensian*), and monthly alumni magazine (*Michigan Alumnus*). Without online access from one's home office to these old publications and many others, and without the twenty-first century ability to search these digitized chronicles for names and subject matter, on dates and times convenient to a researcher with a consuming day job, this story probably could not have been told to this level of understanding.

2. Books on the early history of college football in general and on Stagg, Yost, and UM football in particular, as cited in each chapter's notes.

3. The following sources for game, season, coach, and statistical information:

- For NCAA statistics and records: *Official 2014 NCAA Football Records*: http://fs.ncaa.org/Docs/stats/football_records/2014/FBS.pdf.
- For game scores, season records, and head coach names for major colleges and Ivy League schools: *ESPN College Football Encyclopedia* (New York: ESPN Books, 2005).

- For year-by-year profiles of University of Michigan Wolverines teams: the Bentley library's football pages, starting at http://bentley.umich.edu/athdept/football/football.htm.
- For year-by-year records of Stagg's University of Chicago Maroons teams: the *UChicago Football Records Book*, starting at page 11, http://athletics.uchicago.edu/sports/fball/record-book-fb.pdf.
- For game accounts, unless otherwise noted: next-publication stories in the many daily newspapers in both Chicago and Detroit, as well as in the *Michigan Daily* student newspaper, the monthly *Michigan Alumnus* magazine, and occasionally the *New York Times*. In most cases, lengths of halves were consistently reported; when there was no unanimity or consensus, *Michigan Alumnus* reports filed days or weeks after the fact were used.

INTRODUCTION

1. Quoted in Bob Considine, *The Unreconstructed Amateur: A Pictorial Biography of Amos Alonzo Stagg* (San Francisco: Amos Alonzo Stagg Foundation, 1962), 160.

2. "Eat 'Em Up, Big or Little," unidentified clipping, October 15, 1901, 1901 clippings scrapbook, Box 45, BICIA, BHL-UM.

1. THE PRAYING PITCHER

1. Geoffrey Blodgett, "The Day Oberlin Beat Michigan, or Did We?," *Oberlin Alumni Magazine*, Winter 1999, http://www.oberlin.edu/alummag/oamcurrent/oam_winter99/atissue.html.

2. John T. Ellis to Baird, 24 June 1894, "Correspondence, June-July, 1894" folder, Box 1, CB, BHL-UM; and Sherrill to Baird, 24 October 1894, "Correspondence, October 1894" folder, Box 1, CB, BHL-UM.

3. "Thinks Signals Were Known," *Chicago Inter Ocean*, November 30, 1894; "Michigan 6, Chicago 4," *Michigan Daily*, December 3, 1894; *Detroit Free Press*, November 25 and December 2, 1894; "Three Football Victories," *Michigan Alumnus*, December 1894, 46–47.

4. L. C. Hull Jr., "The Michigan-Chicago Games—Past and Present," *The Inlander*, November 1904, 79–80.

5. Amos Alonzo Stagg (as told to Wesley Winans Stout), *Touchdown!* (New York: Longmans, Green and Co., 1927), 57.

6. "Maroon Is on High," *Chicago Tribune*, November 27, 1896.

7. Henry M. Bates to Ward Hughes, 11 October 1897, "1897 October (1)" folder, Box 1, CB, BHL-UM.

8. John A. Jameson to Hughes, 28 October 1897, "1897 October (2)" folder, Box 1, CB, BHL-UM.

9. Online ancestry researcher Ruthann Lumb of Windsor, Ontario, painstakingly traced Stagg's lineage for the author, in part through Ancestry.com and the Sons of the American Revolution website. Patricia Kryk, the author's mother, found lineage confirmations online as well as helpful background information about Stagg's early life. For David Condit's background, see http://www.condit-family.com/ps01/ps01_382.html.

10. Stagg and Stout, *Touchdown!*, 106.

11. *Biographical and Genealogical History of the City of Newark and Essex County, New Jersey: Illustrated* (New York: Lewis, 1898), 321.

12. Stagg and Stout, *Touchdown!*, 45–47.

13. Ibid, 48.

14. Ibid, 108.

15. "University of Chicago's Great Athletic Instructor," *Chicago Tribune*, November 20, 1904.

16. Allison Danzig, *Oh, How They Played the Game* (New York: Macmillan, 1971), 53.

17. Stagg and Stout, *Touchdown!*, 77.

18. Ibid., 102–9; Robin Lester, *Stagg's University: The Rise, Decline, and Fall of Big-Time Football at Chicago* (Urbana: University of Illinois Press, 1995), 9–11.

19. Stagg and Stout, *Touchdown!*, 130.

20. "Tribute by President W. R. Harper," *Chicago Tribune*, November 20, 1894.

2. JUDICIOUS EXPENDITURES OF MONEY

1. Murray Sperber, "College Sports, Inc.: How Big-Time Athletic Departments Run Interference for College, Inc.," in *Buying In or Selling Out? The Commercialization of the American Research University*, ed. Donald G. Stein (New Brunswick, NJ: Rutgers University Press, 2004), 17.

2. The first twelve rules proposed by the new Big Seven Conference on February 8, 1896, fit on one page, typed, single-spaced; a draft in that form is in "CORR., Jan–Mar 1896" folder, Box 1, CB, BHL-UM; the so-called Western Conference, or Big Ten, in the 1920s annually produced a tiny handbook to contain its ever-broadening rules, and the 1925 version is in "UM Board in Control of Intercollegiate Athletics; Papers, Misc." folder, Box 7, HOC, BHL-UM; *2012–13 NCAA Division I Manual* (Indianapolis: NCAA, 2012).

3. Ronald A. Smith, *Pay for Play: A History of Big-Time College Athletic Reform* (Urbana: University of Illinois Press, 2011), 11–12.

4. Mark F. Bernstein, *Football: The Ivy League Origins of an American Obsession* (Philadelphia: University of Pennsylvania Press, 2001), 52.

5. Smith, *Pay for Play*, 13–17; "College Work and Play; Yale Making Charges against Princeton Athletes," *New York Times*, May 4, 1890.

6. For biographical background on Caspar Whitney, see a paper by John A. Lucus for the International Society of Olympic Historians: "Caspar Whitney," Journal of Olympic History 8, no. 2 (May 2000): 30–38, at Ancestry.com: http://wc.rootsweb.ancestry.com/cgi-bin/igm.cgi?op=GET&db=dfitchett&id=l4682. On his amateurism zealotry, see a paper by John A. Lucus for the International Society of Olympic Historians: "Caspar Whitney," *Journal of Olympic History* 8, no. 2 (May 2000): 30–38, http://library.la84.org/SportsLibrary/JOH/JOHv8n2/johv8n2h.pdf. See also Whitney's Wikipedia page: http://en.wikipedia.org/wiki/Caspar_Whitney. Some of Whitney's *Outing* writings are available online courtesy of the LA84 Foundation at http://www.search.la84.org. See also "Say Whitney Is Amusing," *Chicago Tribune*, December 29, 1903.

7. "Hirelings in the Teams," *Chicago Tribune*, November 25, 1895.

8. "Basis for the Charges" and "Ann Arbor Men Are Indignant," *Chicago Tribune*, November 26, 1895.

9. "Whitney Stirs Them Up," *Chicago Tribune*, December 27, 1895.

10. "Are Not New to Football Players," *Chicago Tribune*, January 14, 1895.

11. David O. Whitten, "The Depression of 1893," Economic History Association, http://eh.net/encyclopedia/the-depression-of-1893/.

12. John C. Rolfe, "A Symposium on Professionalism in Western Athletics," *The Inlander*, January 1896, 157–58, http://babel.hathitrust.org/cgi/pt?id=mdp.39015071372331;view=1up;seq=181.

13. Will Perry, *The Wolverines: A Story of Michigan Football* (Huntsville, AL: Strode, 1974), 30–32; *UM Catalogue of Graduates, Non-Graduates, Officers, and Members of the Faculties: 1837–1921*, 85; and "A Symposium on Professionalism in Western Athletics," *The Inlander*, January 1896.

14. Jerome C. Knowlton, "Purity in College Athletics," *Michigan Alumnus*, January 1896, 58.

15. "Boys Must Not Slug," *Chicago Tribune*, January 12, 1895; "To Govern College Athletics," *New York Times*, January 13, 1895; "Are Not New to Football Players," *Chicago Tribune*, January 14, 1895; "Chicago University Athletics," *Chicago Tribune*, March 3, 1895; "Draw the Line Close," *Chicago Tribune*, February 9, 1896; "Adopted New Rules," *Michigan Daily* clipping, undated but likely February 9 or 10, 1896, in "CORR., Jan–Mar 1896" folder, Box 1, CB, BHL-UM; Kenneth L. (Tug) Wilson and Jerry Brondfield, *The Big Ten* (Englewood Cliffs, NJ: Prentice-Hall, 1967), 50–53 and 446; John Kryk, *Natural Enemies: Major College Football's Oldest, Fiercest Rivalry, Michigan vs. Notre Dame*, updated ed. (Lanham, MD: Taylor Trade, 2007), 25–27, 35, 37.

16. Three folders in Box 1 of the CB collection at BHL-UM (January to March, April to July, and August to September) contain all of the pertinent 1896 correspondences of UM principals referenced in the notes that follow.

17. Baird to "Buck" [Richards], 1 February 1896.

18. Baird to H. Mortimer "Mort" Senter, undated but some time in January 1896.

19. Senter to Baird, 1 May 1896.

20. Baird to Richards, 1 February 1896.

21. Baird to B. M. "Bert" Carr, 28 March 1896.

22. Richards to Baird, 1 April 1896.

23. Frye to Baird, 11 May 1896.

24. Baird to Richards, 6 June 1896.

25. Carr's loan/playing contract with Baird: 8 June 1896.

26. Baird to Ferbert, 18 September 1896. See also Baird to Ferbert, 14 September 1896.

27. Average American salaries since 1900, by decade: http://usa.usembassy.de/etexts/his/e_prices1.htm.

28. Report with detailed chart in *The Inlander*, June 1896, comparing costs of attending leading universities in the West, reprinted as "University Fees," *Michigan Alumnus*. November 1896, 15–21.

29. Wilson and Brondfield, *Big Ten*, 52; *Michigan Daily*, undated clipping but likely February 9 or 10, 1896, "CORR., Jan–Mar 1896" folder, Box 1, CB, BHL-UM.

30. Roger Sherman and Baird both attended Hyde Park High in Chicago and played football together there before both enrolled at the UM in 1890. Sherman eventually starred for the Wolverines at end; Baird played varsity football for just one year. Both became lawyers, and both expended considerable effort in their immediate postgraduate years in aiding the Wolverine football cause: Baird as undergraduate team manager, then as graduate manager of athletics and by 1898 as UM's first full-time director of athletics; Sherman as an influential Chicago alumnus and talent bagman. Indeed, Whitney exposed

Sherman's talent-securing acumen in his initial screed against Western football.

31. Roger Sherman, "A Symposium on Professionalism in Western Athletics," *The Inlander*, January 1896, 164–66.

3. THE CLEANEST TEAM ON EARTH

1. Oil magnate J. D. Rockefeller donated $80 million in 1890 to establish the University of Chicago—the equivalent of more than $2 billion in 2013.
2. "Whitney in Chicago," *Chicago Tribune*, September 28, 1897.
3. "Hirelings in the Teams," *Chicago Tribune*, November 25, 1895.
4. "Stagg Approves the New Rules," *Chicago Tribune*, November 29, 1896.
5. See myriad clippings, circa the first two weeks of November 1898, from the many Chicago dailies, as well as a few from the University of Wisconsin student newspaper the *Daily Cardinal*, in Athletic Scrapbook No. 9 (November 1898), Box 131, AAS, SCRC-UCL. The nine Maroons players questioned by UW, per various newspaper reports: Rogers, Clarke, Ewing, Clarence Herschberger, P. Knolla, Orville Burnett, T. W. Mortimer, Walter S. Kennedy, and J. R. Henry.
6. "Clarke Is Off the Team," *Chicago Chronicle*, November 2, 1898.
7. "More Protests Made," unidentified clipping, likely November 5 or 6, 1898, in Athletic Scrapbook No. 9 (November 1898), Box 131, AAS, SCRC-UCL.
8. "Ugly Rumors from Wisconsin," *Chicago Record*, November 6, 1898.
9. "His Little Game," *Daily Cardinal*, November 9, 1898.
10. "Stagg's Challenge to Whitney," *Chicago Record*, December 17, 1898.
11. Whitney, *Harper's Weekly*, December 3, 1898.
12. "Some Staggnated Stanzas," *The 1900 Badger* (University of Wisconsin junior class yearbook), 1898–1899, 124, http://digital.library.wisc.edu/1711.dl/UW.UWYearBk1900.
13. "Stagg Hits Whitney," *Chicago Post*, December 16, 1898.
14. "Stagg's Challenge to Whitney," *Chicago Record*, December 17, 1898.
15. Here's one of the innumerable examples—on October 14, 1898—of how the *Chicago Tribune*, circa 1895 to 1906, acted as Stagg's seldom-questioning reputation polisher: "Stagg is strict in his scrutiny" of his athletes' background and would "not allow men to play if their records are not all right."
16. John Lucas, "The Hegemonic Rule of the American Amateur Athletic Union 1888–1914: James Edward Sullivan as Prime Mover," *International Journal of the History of Sport* 11, no. 3 (December 1994): 355–71.

17. "Michigan Favors Stagg," *Chicago Tribune*, March 11, 1897; "Ready to Leave A.A.U.," *Chicago Tribune*, March 20, 1897; "Will Keep Up the Fight," *Chicago Tribune*, September 20, 1898; Lester, *Stagg's University*, 56; "Capt. Ellsworth to be Protested," *Chicago Tribune*, September 5, 1903; "Battle for Life Now On over Eckersall Dispute," *Chicago American*, October 21, 1903; "Charges Made Known," *Chicago Record-Herald*, October 22, 1903; "Charges Cause Stir," *Chicago Record-Herald*, October 23, 1903; "Chicago–A.A.U. War Over," *Chicago Tribune*, December 17, 1905.

18. "Michigan Favors Stagg," *Chicago Tribune*, March 11, 1897.

19. John McLean to Charles Baird, 2 February 1901, "Correspondences, August to September, 1898" folder, Box 1, CB, BHL-UM.

20. "Stagg's Hot Words," *Chicago Chronicle*, October 30, 1903.

21. Dvorak to Baird, 16 August 1901, "Papers, July and August, 1901" folder, Box 1, BICIA, BHL-UM.

22. Dvorak to Baird, 8 September 1903, "Correspondences, 1903, September to December" folder, Box 1, CB, BHL-UM.

23. Chas. G. McDonald to Baird, 4 April 1902, "Papers 1901 March–April–May" folder, Box 1, BICIA, BHL-UM.

24. "The Other Leading Westerners," *Detroit Free Press*, September 25, 1898.

25. Considine, *Unreconstructed Amateur*, 14.

26. Stagg and Stout, *Touchdown!*, 207. See also "Chicago's Chance," *Detroit Free Press*, November 16, 1897.

27. Memorandum A, in C. K. Adams to William Rainey Harper, 16 July 1898, Folder 9, Box 20, PHJB, SCRC-UCL.

28. "Look Up Their Records," *Chicago Tribune*, September 17, 1898; "Accepts Chicago Conditions," *Chicago Tribune*, September 23, 1898; "Game Will End All," *Chicago Record*, November 8, 1898.

29. "Ewing Is Suspected," *Chicago Record*, November 4, 1898.

30. Sources for Stagg's bold, hard kick in the ledgers of Michigan, Wisconsin, and Illinois and the nearly yearlong athletic war in 1899 that ensued: (1) an attached stack of official documents and communications (letters and telegrams) both received and sent between the combative parties circa 1899, in Folder 1, Box 88, AAS, SCRC-UCL—which includes lengthy, typeset summaries of both Stagg and UC's position as well as that of the rival trio's; (2) clippings circa March 14–21, 1899, in Athletic Scrapbook No. 10 (December 1898 to March 1899), Box 132, AAS, SCRC-UCL; "Michigan's Position," *Detroit Free Press*, March 26, 1899.

31. "Timely Sporting Gossip," *Detroit Free Press*, April 16, 1899; "Chicago and Wisconsin," *Chicago Tribune*, October 25, 1899; "Colleges Reach Terms,"

Chicago Tribune, December 2, 1899; "Sporting News of the World," *Detroit Free Press*, December 6, 1899.

    32. "Again Criticises Chicago," *Chicago Tribune*, February 18, 1899.

    33. "Chicago Too Powerful," *Chicago Tribune*, February 21, 1899.

4. CLOSED FISTS, CLOSED EYES, CLOSED MINDS

    1. Bob Ufer recordings courtesy of Ufer archivists Steve Sapardanis and Art Vuolo Jr.

    2. Bernstein, *Football*, 32–37.

    3. "Trying to Save Football . . . ," *New York Times*, December 6, 1884.

    4. Stagg and Stout, *Touchdown!*, 94.

    5. Danzig, *Oh, How They Played the Game*, 71.

    6. Ibid, 63.

    7. Stagg and Stout, *Touchdown!*, 57.

    8. For more on the roots of coaching, see Kryk, *Natural Enemies*, 24–25, 34.

    9. Stagg and Stout, *Touchdown!*, 141.

    10. "Coaching the Yale Team," *New York Times*, November 6, 1892; "Yale Hard at Work; Preparing for the Football Game with Princeton," *New York Times*, November 16, 1896; "Yale's Football Players," *New York Times*, October 3, 1897; "McBride to Coach Yale," *New York Times*, August 13, 1900; "Yale's Football Plans," *Boston Evening Transcript*, July 12, 1900. On Camp's traditional role, see "Rafferty at New Haven," *Boston Evening Transcript*, July 30, 1903.

    11. "Football at Princeton," *New York Times*, April 11, 1894; "Football at Princeton," *New York Times*, August 11, 1900.

    12. By 1910, fifteen coaches worked with the Yale squad, with "eleven taking a player each and leaving four to watch the scrubs" (*New York Times*, October 20, 1910).

    13. Former halfback Gustave Ferbert served as Michigan's head coach from 1897 to 1899; "Coach King at Wisconsin," *Michigan Alumnus*, March 1905, 276; Fielding Yost could not have returned to Stanford as head coach in 1901 if he'd wanted because both Bay Area universities switched to this grads-only system of coaching; "Professional Coach System Is Superior," *Los Angeles Times*, November 27, 1904; John McLean to Charles Baird, 2 February 1901, "Correspondences, 1901" folder, Box 1, CB, BHL-UM.

14. Scott A. McQuilkin and Ronald A. Smith, "The Rise and Fall of the Flying Wedge: Football's Most Controversial Play," *Journal of Sport History* 20, no. 1 (Spring 1993): 57–64.

15. "Change the Football Rules," *New York Times*, December 2, 1893.

16. Ibid.

17. Ibid.

18. See also David M. Nelson, *Anatomy of a Game: Football, the Rules, and the Men Who Made the Game*, 2nd ed. (Newark, DE: University of Delaware Press, 1994), 70–74.

19. Danzig, *Oh, How They Played the Game*, 112–20.

20. "Woodruff May Resign," *New York Times*, January 9, 1901; "Penn's Staff of Football Coaches," *New York Times*, August 14, 1901; "In the Football World," *New York Times*, October 16, 1901; "Quakers Face the Crisis of Their History," *Philadelphia North American*, December 1, 1901.

21. Nelson, *Anatomy of a Game*, 83–84.

22. Danzig, *Oh, How They Played the Game*, 72.

23. Deduced from these teams' annual results.

5. THE HUMAN HURRICANE

1. According to the National Championship Foundation: http://www.cfbdatawarehouse.com/data/national_championships/champ_results.php?selector=National%20Championship%20Foundation.

2. Unidentified clipping circa August 1946, subheaded "Made Few Mistakes," in "Newspaper clippings (2)" folder, Box 7, FHY, BHL-UM.

3. Ring Lardner to "Carl," 23 May 1921, "1921 May (2)" folder, Box 4, BICIA, BHL-UM.

4. "Yost," *Minneapolis Tribune*, September 18, 1905.

5. Draft manuscript, J. Fred Lawton , *'Hurry Up' Yost in Story and Song*, in "Yost, Fielding H. (1)" folder, Box 2, JFL, BHL-UM.

6. Perry, *Wolverines*, 47.

7. Lawton, *"Hurry Up" Yost*.

8. *Detroit Times* clipping, August 21, 1946, in "Clippings folder (3)", Box 7, FHY, BHL-UM.

9. Grantland Rice, "The Sportlight; the End of a Long Trail," *Detroit Free Press*, April 29, 1941.

10. Robert La Blonde, United Press wire service story, *Pittsburgh Press*, April 30, 1938.

11. Unidentified clipping on Yost's work on the movie, circa November 1926, outsized Yost scrapbook 1924–28, FHY, BHL-UM; John Dennis McCallum, *Big Ten Football since 1895* (Radnor, PA: Chilton, 1976), 225.

12. "Yost in Favour of Changes," *Chicago Tribune*, December 16, 1905; "Views of Yost on Rules," *Chicago Tribune*, December 22, 1905; "Yost to Retire," *New York Times*, November 14, 1907; "Coach Yost on Football Rules," *New York Times*, February 24, 1912; "Yost Wants Four Downs," *Michigan Daily*, January 9, 1907; "Don't Change the Football Rules," *Chicago Tribune*, November 26, 1906.

13. "Hard Football Games during Rest of Year," *New York Times*, October 16, 1906.

14. Knute Rockne to Jesse C. Harper, 7 January 1928, "Harper, Jesse C. 1928/01-06" folder, University Athletic Director's Records, 1909–29 (UADR 13/34), University of Notre Dame Archives.

15. "College Coaches Get Bigger Voice on Rules Board," *Daily Illini*, December 31, 1927; "Rules Body Places Gained by Coaches," *New York Times*, December 31, 1927.

16. *Atlanta Georgian*, April 3, 1928; *Monroe (La.) News Star*, January 18, 1934; *Atlanta Constitution*, February 11, 1934.

17. Telephone interview by the author with Steve Boda Jr., July 7, 2009.

18. Patricia Kryk, the author's mother and an online ancestry researcher, helped the author trace Yost's lineage and family history back many generations.

19. Various unidentified newspaper clippings in Yost's files provide information about his mother, namesake uncle, and other family members, stored in a family clippings scrapbook, Box 7, FHY, BHL-UM.

20. "Coach Yost Doesn't Touch Liquor," *Washtenaw Times*, September 24, 1901.

21. John Richard Behee, *Fielding Yost's Legacy to the University of Michigan* (Ann Arbor, MI: Uhlrich's Books, 1971), 22.

22. Yost, "Lasting Values in Athletics," speech transcript included in a special bound gift book given to Yost upon his fortieth anniversary at Michigan, Box 7, FHY, BHL-UM.

23. Behee, *Fielding Yost's Legacy*, 29.

24. Rice, "Sportlight."

25. Kryk, *Natural Enemies*, 83.

26. Wilson and Brondfield, *Big Ten*, 133.

27. Details of Yost's first coaching jobs circa 1896 to 1900, especially the one-off professional games: Behee, *Fielding Yost's Legacy*, 22–25; many clippings in two Yost scrapbooks, one covering his Ohio Wesleyan, Nebraska, and

Kansas stops (in Box 7, FHY, BHL-UM), the other his time in the Bay Area (in Box 45, BICIA, BHL-UM).

28. Dale Robertson, "Remembering with Fondness the Great Bum Phillips and His Place in Houston History," *Houston Chronicle*, October 18, 2013.

29. Westbrook Pegler, "Pegler Recalls Mysterious Grid Star Who Ripened Rapidly for Crucial Game," *Pittsburgh Press*, November 13, 1934, and "Fair Enough," *Reading Eagle*, November 20, 1934.

30. Wilson and Brondfield, *Big Ten*, 133.

31. Perry, *Wolverines*, 45.

32. Editorial, *Stanford Daily*, December 6, 1900, clipping in Yost's 1900 Bay Area clippings scrapbook, Box 45, BICIA, BHL-UM.

33. "Landing Yost a Lucky Trick," *Detroit Free Press*, March 5, 1905; "How Illinois Sent Yost to Michigan," *Urbana Daily Courier*, November 6, 1919.

34. Baird to Yost, typewritten copy, 5 January 1901, "Papers, 1901 January" folder, Box 1, BICIA, BHL-UM.

35. Yost to Baird, telegram, 9 January 1901, "Papers, 1901 January" folder, Box 1, BICIA, BHL-UM.

36. Henry J. Killilea to Baird, 11 January 1901; Walter E. McCornack to Baird, 13 January 1901; and Fred W. Murphy to Baird, 15 January 1901, all in "Papers, 1901 January" folder, Box 1, BICIA, BHL-UM.

37. Baird to Yost, telegram, 21 January 1901, "Papers, 1901 January" folder, Box 1, BICIA, BHL-UM.

38. Contract between Yost and UM, October 4, 1901, "Correspondence, October 1901" folder, Box 1, BICIA, BHL-UM.

6. 1901 OFF THE FIELD

1. Letters Stagg wrote to recruits circa 1899 to 1901, including the following three examples, are in Folders 2 and 3, Box 13, AAS, SCRC-UCL.

2. Stagg to H. H. Everett, College of Physicians & Surgeons, 21 December 1899, Folder 2.

3. Stagg to Benjamin I. Salinger, 9 January 1900, Folder 2.

4. Stagg to J. V. Cole, 7 March 1900, Folder 2.

5. Lester, *Stagg's University*, 54; Keene Fitzpatrick, "Michigan's Football Training," *The Inlander*, November 1904, 82–83.

6. Yost-to-Baird letters circa 1901 are split between two locations at UM's Bentley Library: Box 1, CB, and Box 1, BICIA, BHL-UM.

7. On Keene Fitzpatrick's integral role in the football program, see *Michiganensian*, 1903, 158; *Michiganensian*, 1906, 163–64. Letters from Fitzpatrick to Baird circa 1897 to 1901 reveal Fitz's deep involvement in recruiting:

26 January 1897, "Correspondence, 1897" folder, Box 1, CB, BHL-UM; 15 July 1901 and 16 August 1901, "Papers July & August 1901" folder, Box 1, BICIA, BHL-UM.

8. Yost to Baird, 6 July 1901, "Correspondence, 1901" folder, CB, BHL-UM.

9. Owen to Yost, 16 September 1901, "Papers September 1901" folder, Box 1, BICIA, BHL-UM.

10. Kryk, *Natural Enemies*, 86, 93–95.

11. "Changes in Athletic Rules," *Detroit Free Press*, December 2, 1900; "Plan New Rules for Athletes," *Chicago Record-Herald*, November 27, 1903.

12. Of the twenty-one players on the 1901 Wolverine varsity squad—as listed in "News: Athletics," *Michigan Alumnus*, October 1901, 23–24—twelve studied law, five medicine, three engineering, and one (an end named L. N. Udell, a presumably unrecruited student who'd previously played only on a class team at UM) studied literature.

13. Yost to Baird, 3 June 1901, 27 July 1901, 31 July 1901, and 1 August 1901, "Correspondence, 1901" folder, Box 1, CB, BHL-UM.

14. Yost to Baird, 1 August 1901, "Correspondence, 1901" folder, Box 1, CB, BHL-UM.

15. Perry, *Wolverines*, 50.

16. Ibid, 49.

17. Yost to Baird, 4 June 1901, "Correspondence, 1901" folder, Box 1, CB, BHL-UM; McGugin to Baird, 20 July 1901 and 10 August 1901, "Papers July and August 1901" folder, Box 1, BICIA, BHL-UM.

18. McGugin to Baird, 16 August 1901, "Correspondence, 1901" folder, Box 1, CB, BHL-UM.

7. 1901 ON THE FIELD

1. "Maroons Lose Captain Henry," *Chicago Tribune*, August 26, 1901.

2. Henry L. Williams, "Middle Western Football," *Outing*, November 1901, 206–8.

3. "Yost Is Going to Win All Games," *Washtenaw Times*, September 6, 1901.

4. Henry M. Bates to Baird, 6 September 1901, "Papers September 1901" folder, Box 1, BICIA, BHL-UM.

5. "Why Michigan Is Great," *Michigan Daily*, December 10, 1902.

6. "Yost the Greatest Coach of Them All," *Chicago Journal*, undated clipping circa November 1901, in thick clippings scrapbook circa 1901, Box 45, BICIA, BHL-UM.

7. Kryk, *Natural Enemies*, 83.

8. Yost summarized the differences in the various playing styles of the day as employed by powers East and West in his 1905 book *Football for Player and Spectator*, 53–73. That he employed a diverse playbook was evidenced in the dozens of plays he diagrammed in that book, as well as in many contemporaneous and reflective interviews given by Yost and by some of his players. For instance, Heston claimed at age seventy-eight that in his playing days Yost's playbook had fifty-two plays, unheard of at the turn of the century: George Leonard, "Willie Heston, Michigan's All-Time Grid Great, Re-lives His Career," *Nashville Banner*, March 23, 1957.

9. "Michigan's Coach and Captains: Fielding Harris Yost," *Michigan Alumnus*, November 1901, 56.

10. Hugh White, "Football: Review of Season," *Michiganensian*, 1902, 130.

11. *Michigan Daily*, September 24.

12. Yost, *Football for Player and Spectator*, 250.

13. "The Albion Game," *Michigan Alumnus*, October 1901, 24.

14. "Michigan Runs Up a Big Score," *Chicago Tribune*, September 29, 1901.

15. "Michigan's Backs Gain," *Chicago Tribune*, October 13, 1901.

16. "Eat 'Em Up, Big or Little," unidentified clipping, October 15, 1901, in Yost's 1901 clippings scrapbook, Box 45, BICIA, BHL-UM.

17. "Michigan Shows Class," *Chicago Tribune*, October 20, 1901.

18. "The Northwestern Game," *Michigan Alumnus*, November 1901, 79.

19. "Happenings on the Gridiron," *Detroit Free Press*, November 3, 1901.

20. "One Jump into Fame," unidentified Buffalo-area clipping, October 28, 1901, in Yost's 1901 clippings scrapbook, Box 45, BICIA, BHL-UM.

21. C. M. Frickert to Yost, 29 October 1901, "Papers 1901 October" folder, Box 1, BICIA, BHL-UM.

22. Lawton, *'Hurry Up' Yost*.

23. "Michigan, 128; Buffalo, 0," *Chicago Tribune*, October 27, 1901.

24. "Michigan, 128; Buffalo, Nothing," unidentified clipping, October 27, 1901, in Yost's 1901 clippings scrapbook, Box 45, BICIA, BHL-UM.

25. "Yost Sharpens His Knives," *Chicago Tribune*, November 2, 1901.

26. "Indians Fail to Score," *Chicago Tribune*, November 3, 1901.

27. Ibid.

28. "Indians Again Lose," *Chicago Record-Herald*, November 3, 1901.

29. Bill Cromartie, *The Big One: Michigan vs. Ohio State*, 2nd ed. (West Point, NY: Gridiron-Leisure Press, 1981), 17.

30. Stagg to W. S. Langton, 9 October 1901, Folder 3, Box 13, AAS, SCRC-UCL.

31. Bates to Baird, 13 November 1901, "Papers 1901 November" folder, Box 1, BICIA, BHL-UM.

32. Explanation of Stagg's Whoa-Back comes from an unidentified clipping, September 3, 1904, in Athletic Scrapbook No. 26, June–September 1904, Box 145, AAS, SCRC-UCL.

33. "Michigan Stops Stagg's Tricks," *Detroit Free Press*, November 17, 1901.

34. The *Chicago Tribune*'s staple day-after game "diagrams" of this era would be a fascinating graphical addition to the football-game coverage of any modern newspaper or website—a visual chronology of the action on a 110-yard "field," drive by drive, comprising hand-drawn or perhaps stencil-aided lines and circles, and partially typeset. The diagram for the 1901 Wolverines–Maroons clash is in the November 17, 1901, edition.

35. "Michigan, 22; Chicago, 0," *Chicago Tribune*, November 17, 1901.

36. "Michigan Beats Chicago, 22 to 0," *Chicago Record-Herald*, November 17, 1901.

37. "Michigan Stops Stagg's Tricks," *Detroit Free Press*, November 17, 1901.

38. "Michigan, 22; Chicago, 0," *Chicago Tribune*, November 17, 1901.

39. "Redden Disqualified," *Michigan Alumnus*, December 1901, 133; Albert H. Pattengill to Bates, 6 and 8 December 1901, "1900–1902" folder, Box 1, HMB, BHL-UM; "Redden's Reinstatement," *Michigan Alumnus*, January 1902, 178.

40. "Fine Row Raised to Advertise Games," *Chicago Inter Ocean*, November 22, 1901.

41. For other details of the Iowa–Michigan game in Chicago, and Stagg's displeasure over it, see "The Iowa Game," *Michigan Alumnus*, December 1901, 129–32; many Chicago daily clippings circa November 22–29, in Athletic Scrapbook No. 22 (November 1901–January 1902), Box 138, AAS, SCRC-UCL.

42. See myriad letters in an attached stack of official documents received and sent between Chicago and the combative parties, circa 1899, in Folder 1, Box 88, AAS, SCRC-UCL, the most important of which are C. R. Van Hise to Stagg, 29 November and 22 December 1899, and Stagg to Van Hise, 4 January 1900. See also Pattengill to Bates, 26 January 1902, "1900 to 1902" folder, Box 1, HMB, BHL-UM; "Notes," *Michigan Alumnus*, November 1902, 67; Yost to Stagg, 15 April 1903, Folder 28, Box 41, AAS, SCRC-UCL.

43. Baird to Bates, 23 January 1902, and Pattengill to Bates, 26 January 1902, "1900 to 1902" folder, Box 1, HMB, BHL-UM.

44. "Stagg Says Badgers Can Beat Michigan," *Chicago Record-Herald*, November 19, 1901.

45. Perry, *Wolverines*, 54–63; Behee, *Fielding Yost's Legacy*, 51–57; Birney H. Donnell, "Michigan Team Victorious over Men from Stanford," *Los Angeles Herald*, January 2, 1901, a clipping of which is in "Papers 1902 January & February" folder, Box 1, BICIA, BHL-UM; "The West on the Stanford Game," *Michigan Alumnus*, February 1902, 238–40; and a play-by-play of the game in a commemorative program published years later, bound in a special gift book given to Yost late in his career, titled a "Toast to Yost," Box 7, FHY, BHL-UM.

46. Perry, *Wolverines*, 62.

47. Wilson and Brondfield, *Big Ten*, 62.

48. "Caspar Whitney's Opinion," *Michigan Alumnus*, February 1902, 240.

49. Henry M. Bates, "Athletic Conference at Ann Arbor," *Michigan Alumnus*, January 1901, 144–49.

50. "Michigan Whips Iowa," *Chicago Inter Ocean*, November 29, 1901.

51. *Michigan Daily*, December 3, 1901; "Yost Comes Back—Rah!" *Michigan Alumnus* December 1901, 133; Yost's second contract with UM, 1902–1904, December 20, 1901, "Correspondence, December 1901" folder, Box 1, BICIA, BHL-UM.

8. 1902 OFF THE FIELD

1. "Stagg Will Change His Policy," *Chicago Inter Ocean*, November 26, 1902.

2. Ibid.; "Chicago Wants Prep Athletes," *Chicago Tribune*, November 26, 1902.

3. Lester, *Stagg's University*, 46–47.

4. Harper to Stagg, 22 July 1901, Folder 4, Box 9, AAS, SCRC-UCL.

5. Lester, *Stagg's University*, 46–47.

6. "'Prep' Boys in Meet," *Chicago Record-Herald*, March 6, 1902; "Entries for Dual Meet," *Chicago Tribune*, May 17, 1905; "Greatest Conference Meet," *Chicago Tribune*, June 4, 1905; "Coach Stagg Goes East," *Chicago Tribune*, June 12, 1905; Stagg to Harper, 11 September 1905, Folder 11, Box 9, AAS, SCRC-UCL; "Best Boy Talent in Stagg's Meet," *Chicago Tribune*, June 6, 1906; Lester, *Stagg's University*, 48.

7. "Hyde Park's Vacation Trip," *Chicago Tribune*, March 31, 1902. See also "Badgers Are After Hyde Park Athletes," *Chicago Record-Herald*, March 31, 1902.

8. "Baird Says It's Up to Stagg," *Chicago Record-Herald*, January 17, 1902; "Contract for Three Games," *Chicago Tribune*, February 2, 1902; "Michigan's Athletic Management," *Michigan Alumnus*, February 1902, 236–37; Pattengill

to Bates, 4, 6, 8, and 15 December 1901, 5, 9, 21, 23, 26 January 1902, "1900–02" folder, Box 1, HMB, BHL-UM; Baird to Bates, 23 January 1902, "1900–02" folder, Box 1, HMB, BHL-UM; Bates to Baird, 25 January 1902, "Papers 1902 January and February" folder, Box 1, BICIA, BHL-UM; Baird to Stagg, 28 January 1902, Folder 28, Box 41, AAS, SCRC-UCL; Contract, 1902–1904 UM–UC football games, 1 February 1902, "Papers 1902 January and February" folder, Box 1, BICIA, BHL-UM.

9. "Michigan's Athletic Management," *Michigan Alumnus*, February 1902, 235–37; "Many Students Opposed to Baird," *Chicago American*, January 17, 1902; James O. Murfin to Baird, 18 January 1902, "Correspondences 1902" folder, Box 1, CB, BHL-UM; Pattengill to Bates, 21 January 1902, "1900–02" folder, Box 1, HMB, BHL-UM.

10. Pattengill to Bates, 15 December 1901, "1900–02" folder, Box 1, HMB, BHL-UM.

11. "Stagg Concedes One Point," undated, unidentified clipping circa January 1902, Athletic Scrapbook No. 22, Box 138, AAS, SCRC-UCL; contract, UM–UW lease of Marshall Field, 3 March 1902, "Papers 1902 November–December" folder, Box 1, BICIA, BHL-UM.

12. "East vs. West," *Michigan Daily*, February 22, 1903; Baird, "Why It Is Difficult to Secure an Eastern Game," *The Inlander*, November 1904, 84; Yost to Baird, 21 and 26 February 1902, "Correspondence, 1902" folder, Box 1, CB, BHL-UM.

13. Yost to Baird, 14 March 1902, "Papers 1902 March–April–May" folder, Box 1, BICIA, BHL-UM.

14. Yost to Baird, 26 February 1902, "Correspondence 1902" folder, Box 1, CB, BHL-UM.

15. "The Illness of Shorts," *Michigan Alumnus*, May 1902, 373; "Shorts to Quit Athletics," *Chicago Record-Herald*, April 9, 1902.

16. "Walter Camp's All-Western Team," *Michigan Alumnus*, January 1902, 179.

17. Yost to Baird, 26 February 1902, "Correspondence 1902" folder, Box 1, CB, BHL-UM.

18. Harrison "Boss" Weeks mentioned in a letter to Baird, 9 July 1905, that he still owed Yost money, "Correspondence 1905" folder, Box 1, CB, BHL-UM.

19. Yost to Baird, 23 April 1902, "Correspondence 1902" folder, Box 1, CB, BHL-UM.

20. The January 31 and August 25 letters are in "Correspondence 1902" folder, Box 1, CB, BHL-UM. The others are in one of three folders—"Papers 1902 January–February," "Papers 1902 March–April–May," "Papers 1902 June–July"—in Box 1, BICIA, BHL-UM.

21. Weeks to Baird, 3 August 1902, "Papers 1902 August–September" folder, Box 1, BICIA, BHL-UM.

22. McDonald to Baird, 4 April 1902, "Papers 1902 March–April–May" folder, Box 1, BICIA, BHL-UM.

23. Associated Press obituary of Killilea, distributed 23 January 1929.

24. Killilea to Baird, 26 August 1902, "Correspondence 1902" folder, Box 1, CB, BHL-UM. See also Killilea to Baird, 9 September 1902, "Correspondence 1902" folder, Box 1, CB, BHL-UM.

25. McLean to Baird, 6 October 1902, "Correspondence 1902" folder, Box 1, CB, BHL-UM.

26. McLean to Baird, 3 September 1903, "Correspondence 1903 September-December" folder, Box 1, CB, BHL-UM.

27. Ira A. Campbell to Baird, 23 September 1903, "Correspondence, 1903 Sept-Dec" folder, Box 1, CB, BHL-UM; also Campbell to Baird, 30 January 1904, and Baird to Campbell, 14 October 1904, 5 and 19 December 1904, "Correspondence, 1904" folder, Box 1, CB, BHL-UM. Baird's quote is in the December 19 letter.

28. In addition to letters previously cited, Pattengill wrote many times to Bates circa 1900–1906 on athletic matters, which letters are in "1900–02" and "1903–6" folders, Box 1, HMB, BHL-UM.

29. Fuller to Baird, 23 January 1902, "Correspondence, 1902" folder, Box 1, CB, BHL-UM.

30. Fuller to Baird, 20 January 1902, "Correspondence, 1902" folder, Box 1, CB, BHL-UM.

31. Yost to Baird, 21 February 1902, "Correspondence, 1902" folder, Box 1, CB, BHL-UM.

32. Yost to Baird, 26 February 1902, "Correspondence, 1902" folder, Box 1, CB, BHL-UM.

33. Fuller to Baird, 3 March 1902, "Correspondence, 1902" folder, Box 1, CB, BHL-UM. See also Fuller to Baird, 27 and 30 July 1902, "Correspondence, 1902" folder, Box 1, CB, BHL-UM; and Yost to Baird, 26 and 30 August 1902, "Correspondence, 1902" folder, Box 1, CB, BHL-UM.

34. Yost to Baird, 23 April 1902, "Papers 1902 March–April–May" folder, Box 1, BICIA, BHL-UM; Yost to Baird, 15 July 1902, "Papers 1902 June–July" folder, Box 1, BICIA, BHL-UM; Yost to Baird, 26 August 1902, "Correspondence, 1902" folder, Box 1, CB, BHL-UM; Brush to Yost, 18 September 1902, "Papers 1902 August-September" folder, Box 1, BICIA, BHL-UM.

35. "To Join College Squads," *Chicago Tribune*, August 24, 1902; "Troublous Are Times in Many Fields of Sport," *Detroit Free Press*, August 31, 1902; "Stagg Sizes Up New Men," *Chicago Tribune*, September 10, 1902.

36. Yost to Baird, 30 August 1902, "Correspondence, 1902" folder, Box 1, CB, BHL-UM.

37. "Baird Lands Two Maroons," *Detroit Free Press*, September 18, 1902.

38. "Communication: Inducements to Young Athletes," *Michigan Alumnus*, October 1902, 23.

39. Niles to Baird, 25 September 1902, "Correspondence, 1902" folder, Box 1, CB, BHL-UM; "Baird Lands Two Maroons," *Detroit Free Press*, September 18, 1902; see also Phil Bartelme to Baird, 5, 9 (handwritten), 9 (typed), 10, and 15 September 1902, "Papers 1902 August-September" folder, Box 1, BICIA, BHL-UM.

40. Fielding Harris Yost, "Coach Yost Predicts Great Football Year," *Chicago American*, September 29, 1902.

9. 1902 ON THE FIELD

1. McLean to Baird, 6 October 1902, "Correspondence, 1902" folder, Box 1, CB, BHL-UM.

2. Yost to Baird, 30 August 1902, "Correspondence, 1902" folder, Box 1, CB, BHL-UM.

3. Fielding Harris Yost, "Coach Yost Predicts Great Football Year," *Chicago American*, September 29, 1902.

4. "The Case Game," *Michigan Alumnus*, November 1902, 63.

5. "Why Michigan Is Great," *Michigan Daily*, December 10, 1902.

6. "All Call for Speed," *Chicago Daily News*, October 15, 1902.

7. "Michigan Grid Immortal Recalls Wolverines Rise to Prominence," *St. Petersburg Times*, April 12, 1957.

8. "Michigan Wins 60 to 0," *Chicago Record-Herald*, October 12, 1902.

9. "Confidence in King's Coaching," *Chicago Tribune*, October 29, 1902.

10. "Game of Games at Hand," unidentified clipping, November 1, 1902, in Athletic Scrapbook No. 26, Box 140, AAS, SCRC-UCL.

11. Yost, *Football for Player and Spectator*, 251.

12. "Michigan Wins in Single Score," *Chicago Tribune*, November 2, 1902.

13. "Views of G. W. Woodruff," *Chicago Tribune*, November 2, 1902.

14. "Three Badly Hurt in Grandstand Wreck," *Detroit Free Press*, November 2, 1902; "Hurt in Crash," *Chicago Chronicle*, November 2, 1902.

15. Myriad letters explaining the UM/UW versus UC grandstand-collapse dispute, circa 1903–1905, fill up Folder 3, Box 88, AAS, SCRC-UCL.

16. "Raise from Stagg," *Chicago Record-Herald*, November 3, 1902.

17. "Yost's Men Make Record," *Chicago Tribune*, November 9, 1902.

18. "Maroon Hopes Rise," *Chicago Record-Herald*, November 14, 1902.

19. John Tinney McCutcheon, "The Chicago Football Team," cartoon, *Chicago Record-Herald*, November 13, 1902.

20. Pattengill to Bates, 6 November 1902, "1900–1902" folder, Box 1, HMB, BHL-UM.

21. "McGugin Is Said to Be Ineligible," *Chicago Tribune*, November 14, 1902; "Maroon Hopes Rise," *Chicago Record-Herald*, November 14, 1902.

22. "Maroon Hopes Rise," *Chicago Record-Herald*, November 14, 1902.

23. Pattengill to Bates, 14 November 1902, "1900–1902" folder, Box 1, HMB, BHL-UM.

24. "Statement of Michigan Case," *Chicago Tribune*, November 17, 1902.

25. "M'Gugin Declared Eligible," *Chicago Tribune*, November 15, 1902.

26. Pattengill to Bates, 21 January 1902, "1900–1902" folder, Box 1, HMB, BHL-UM.

27. Pattengill to Bates, 15 December 1901, "1900–1902" folder, Box 1, HMB, BHL-UM.

28. Pattengill to Bates, 21 January 1902, "1900–1902" folder, Box 1, HMB, BHL-UM.

29. Pattengill to Bates, 11 November 1902, "1900–1902" folder, Box 1, HMB, BHL-UM.

30. "Michigan Scores Brilliant Victory," *Chicago Record-Herald*, November 16.

31. Ibid.

32. Ibid.

33. Pattengill to Bates, 21 November 1902, "1900–1902" folder, Box 1, HMB, BHL-UM.

34. "Williams Makes Protest," *Minnesota Daily*, November 20, 1902.

35. "Are They Scared?," *Minnesota Daily*, November 22, 1902.

36. "Stagg and Dr. Williams," *Chicago Tribune*, November 29, 1902.

37. Pattengill to Bates, 21 November 1902, "1900–1902" folder, Box 1, HMB, BHL-UM.

38. "Palmer a Football Hero," *Michigan Daily*, December 17, 1902.

39. Palmer to Baird, 19 November 1902, "Correspondence, 1902" folder, Box 1, CB, BHL-UM. Includes attached telegram, Wm. Palmer to W. S. Palmer, 19 November 1902.

40. "Palmer a Football Hero," *Michigan Daily*, December 17, 1902.

41. *Michigan Daily*, December 3, 1902.

42. *Michigan Daily*, December 2, 1902.

43. "Michigan Wins Title," *Chicago Record-Herald*, November 28, 1902.

44. "The Minnesota Game," *Michigan Alumnus*, December 1902, 125.

45. *Michigan Daily*, December 3, 1902.

46. "Close of Football Year," *Chicago Tribune*, November 28, 1902.

47. *Michigan Daily*, December 2, 1902.

48. *Michigan Daily*, December 6, 1902.

49. *Michigan Daily* reported on *Daily Cardinal* analysis, January 22, 1903; "Curtis to Coach Badgers," *Chicago Daily News*, January 31, 1903.

10. 1903 OFF THE FIELD

1. *Chicago Daily News*, November 29, 1902.

2. "College Men Are Dined," *Chicago Record-Herald*, November 29, 1902.

3. "Coach Yost Leaves for Trip," *Chicago Record-Herald*, December 11, 1902; *Michigan Daily*, January 15, 1903; "Yost Wants to Quit Michigan," *Chicago Inter Ocean*, January 26, 1903.

4. Pattengill to Bates, 14 December 1902, "1900–1902" folder, Box 1, HMB, BHL-UM.

5. Pattengill to Bates, 27 January 1902, "1900–1902" folder, Box 1, HMB, BHL-UM.

6. Yost's second contract with UM for the 1902–1904 seasons, dated December 20, 1901, "Correspondence, December 1901" folder, Box 1, BICIA, BHL-UM.

7. "Curtis to Coach Badgers," *Chicago Daily News*, January 31, 1903.

8. "Yost Decides to Stay with Michigan Team," *Chicago Record-Herald*, January 27, 1903.

9. McGugin's contract with UM to be assistant football coach for 1903, 1 March 1903, "March–April" folder, Box 1, BICIA, BHL-UM; "McGugan to Assist Yost," *Chicago Record-Herald*, February 13, 1903.

10. Coach Yost Leaves for Trip," *Chicago Record-Herald*, December 11, 1902; *Michigan Daily*, January 15, 1903.

11. "Bear Reports from Michigan," *Chicago Tribune*, September 14, 1903; "The Outlook in Football," *Michigan Alumnus*, October 1903, 28; "Michigan's Amateurism Questioned," *Michigan Alumnus*, November 1903, 59.

12. *Kalamazoo Gazette-News*, excerpted in *Michigan Daily*, February 11, 1903.

13. *Detroit Tribune*, excerpted in *Michigan Daily*, February 13, 1903.

14. "Hyde Park Game Hangs in Balance," *Chicago Tribune*, November 30, 1902; "Stagg Will Coach Hyde Park Team," *Chicago American*, December 2, 1902; "Sectional Game of High Schools," *Chicago Tribune*, December 6, 1902; "Officials Praise Hyde Park," *Chicago Tribune*, December 7, 1902; *Michigan Daily*, December 7, 1902.

15. "Want Reforms in Athletics," *Chicago Tribune*, April 5, 1903.

16. "Stick Up for Yost," *Chicago Daily News*, April 6, 1903; "Discuss Athletic Reforms," *Chicago Tribune*, April 6, 1903.

17. "Defend Their Coach," *Chicago Record-Herald*, April 6, 1903.

18. Ibid.; "Are Wrought Up at Michigan," *Chicago Tribune*, April 7, 1903; *Michigan Daily*, April 7, 1903.

19. "Stagg Vexed at Stories," *Chicago Examiner*, April 11, 1903.

20. Yost to Stagg, 15 April 1903, and Stagg to Yost, 5 May 1903, Folder 28, Box 41, AAS, SCRC-UCL.

21. Background on Walter Eckersall from clippings in Folder 10, Box 14, AAS, SCRC-UCL: Edward Burns, "Eckersall . . . Football Immortal," *Chicago Tribune*, November 24, 1946; Merrill C. "Babe" Meigs, "The Greatest Football Player in the World: Walter Eckersall," *American Weekly*, October 26, 1947; Walter Eckersall, "My Twenty-Five Years in Football," *Liberty Magazine*, October 23, 1926. Also "Hyde Park Beat English High Men," *Chicago Record-Herald*, February 15, 1903; "Hyde Park Athlete Makes Fine Showing," *Chicago American*, February 18, 1903; Lester, *Stagg's University*, 55–57.

22. Meigs, "Greatest Football Player in the World"; "To Join College Squads," *Chicago Tribune*, August 24, 1902.

23. Meigs, "Greatest Football Player in the World."

24. Weeks to Baird, 24 July 1902, "Papers 1902 June–July" folder, Box 1, BICIA, BHL-UM.

25. "Old Captains Line Up," *Chicago Tribune*, December 18, 1895.

26. "Michigan Alumni at Smoker," *Chicago Tribune*, November 15, 1902.

27. *Detroit Tribune*, excerpted in *Michigan Daily*, February 13, 1903.

28. Lester, *Stagg's University*, 56.

29. Ibid.; "Eckersall Is Under the Ban," *Chicago Tribune*, August 27, 1903; "Trouble Between A.A.U. and the Colleges," *Chicago Tribune*, September 6, 1903; "Battle for Life Now on over Eckersall Dispute," *Chicago American*, October 21, 1903; Caspar Whitney, *Outing*, November 1903, 223–24.

30. "Eckersall Joins Stagg's Eleven," *Chicago Tribune*, September 15, 1903.

31. The after-the-fact flurry of signed affidavits and countercharges are in the *Chicago Tribune*, *Record-Herald*, *Examiner*, *American*, *Daily News*, and *Inter Ocean* from October 23 to 30, 1903, clippings of which are in Athletic Scrapbook No. 32, Box 43, AAS, SCRC-UCL. See also "Stagg Lands Most Lads," *Chicago Tribune*, September 6, 1903; "Stole Stagg's Hopes," *Detroit Free Press*, September 13, 1903; Bartelme to Baird, 19 September 1903, "Correspondence, 1903 Sept-Dec" folder, Box 1, CB, BHL-UM; "Recruiting College Athletes Is Reprehensible," *Chicago Tribune*, September 20, 1903; "Resent Talk of A. Stagg," *Detroit Free Press*, September 21, 1903; "Stagg Apologizes," *Detroit Free Press*, September 26, 1903; "Eckersall Exonerates McChesney," *Chicago Tribune*, September 27, 1903.

32. Lester, *Stagg's University*, 56, 234.

33. Bates to Baird, 11 September 1903, "Correspondence, 1903 Sept–Dec" folder, Box 1, CB, BHL-UM.

34. "Yost May Lose Star Men," *Chicago Tribune*, September 13, 1903; "Gregory and Heston Relent," *Chicago Tribune*, September 15, 1903.

35. "Stagg Lands Most Lads," *Chicago Tribune*, September 6, 1903.

36. "Jordan's Frenzied Athletics Received with Contempt," *Michigan Daily*, November 21, 1905.

37. "Stole Stagg's Hopes," *Detroit Free Press*, September 13, 1903.

38. Bates to Baird, 6 September 1903, "Correspondences, 1903 Sept–Dec" folder, Box 1, CB, BHL-UM.

39. "Yost's Men at Ann Arbor," *Chicago Tribune*, September 27, 1903; "The Outlook in Football," *Michigan Alumnus*, October 1903, 28–29.

40. "Koehler Brings Nebraska Guard," *Chicago Tribune*, September 16, 1903; "Teams Getting to Work," *Chicago Tribune*, September 21, 1903.

41. "Maroons May Get Star Football Man," *Chicago Record-Herald*, February 8, 1903.

11. 1903 ON THE FIELD

1. "Chicago Beats Lombard, 34 to 0," *Chicago Tribune*, September 20, 1903.

2. "Chicago Wins from Lawrence," *Chicago Tribune*, September 27, 1903.

3. "Maroons Win the First Real Game," *Chicago Tribune*, October 4, 1903.

4. "0 to 0 Score at Marshall Field," *Chicago Tribune*, October 18, 1903.

5. "Chicago Wins from Illinois," *Chicago Tribune*, October 25, 1903.

6. "Faith in Stagg Cheers Chicago," *Chicago Tribune*, October 30, 1903.

7. "Chicago Scores Great Victory," *Chicago Tribune*, November 1, 1903; "Those Chesty Badgers," *Minneapolis Journal*, November 3, 1903.

8. Lester, *Stagg's University*, 57.

9. Curtis G. Redden, "Football Season of 1903," *Michiganensian*, 1904, 138.

10. "East vs. West," *Michigan Daily*, February 22, 1903.

11. Kryk, *Natural Enemies*, 86.

12. After the author's discovery in 2010 of a *Michigan Daily* story dated October 24, 1903, that pointed out the scoring error, Michigan football's official online historical archive of past seasons added an explanatory asterisk. See the Bentley Historical Library's website, http://bentley.umich.edu/athdept/football/fbteam/1903fbt.htm.

13. Numerous letters between Williams and Baird in which they haggled over officials are in the September, October, and November 1903 folders, Box 1, BICIA, BHL-UM. In the second of two October folders is a handwritten copy of a telegram, Baird to Robert T. Barnard of University of Minnesota, 9 October 1903, in which Baird indicated a preference to employ "no one from Chicago coaching force."

14. "Views of Experts" (Captain Flynn), *Chicago Record-Herald*, November 28, 1902.

15. *Michigan Daily*, November 1, 1903.

16. "Big Crowd Watching Journal Bulletin," *Minneapolis Journal*, November 2, 1903.

17. In addition to usual game-chronology sources, see *Minneapolis Journal*, November 1–2, 1903.

18. Heston to Bennie Oosterbaan, 13 February 1961, "Heston, William" folder, Box 59, UMAD-IF, BHL-UM.

19. Ibid.

20. "No Doubt of Rough Usage," *Detroit Free Press*, November 3, 1903.

21. Les Etter, UM sports publicity director, "Mighty Willie Heston: Point-a-Minute Man," draft, circa 1948, "Heston, William" folder, Box 59, UMAD-IF, BHL-UM. Etter published this under the pseudonym Doc McGee, "Michigan's Marvel—Willie Heston," *1949 All-American Football Magazine*, 1st fall issue, 54–63.

22. Some game accounts gave Heston the credit for the score, or Tom Hammond, but Yost a day later insisted the scorer was Maddock: "Yost Says It Was Rough," *Minneapolis Journal*, November 2, 1903.

23. "Premature Celebration at Ann Arbor," *Chicago Tribune*, November 1, 1903.

24. Post-game reports said it was Norcross who fumbled the punt, but Yost said it was Graver: "Yost Says It Was Rough," *Minneapolis Journal*, November 2, 1903.

25. "Coaches Talk of Battle," *Chicago Tribune*, November 1, 1903.

26. Heston to Bennie Oosterbaan, 13 February 1961, "Heston, William" folder, Box 59, UMAD-IF, BHL-UM.

27. "Michigan Is Sore," *Minneapolis Journal*, November 2, 1903; "Threat to Drop Minnesota Game," *Chicago Tribune*, November 2, 1903.

28. "Yost Says It Was Rough," *Minneapolis Journal*, November 2, 1903.

29. "Minnesota Scribe's Counter-Charges," *Detroit Free Press*, November 5, 1903.

30. "Charges Are Denied at the University," *St. Paul Globe*, November 3, 1903.

31. Baird to Mr. E. J. Carpenter, 6 November 1903, "Papers 1903 November (1)" folder, Box 1, BICIA, BHL-UM.

32. "Threat to Drop Minnesota Game," *Chicago Tribune*, November 2, 1903.

33. Henry T. Clark Jr. to Baird, 5 November 1903, Baird to Clark, 11 November 1903, and Clark to Baird, 18 November 1903, "Papers 1903 November (1)" folder, Box 1, BICIA, BHL-UM.

34. "The Right Athletic Spirit," *Michigan Alumnus*, December 1903, 114–15.

35. Thomas T. Hoyne, "Indians' 'Yost-Machine' Shows Stagg's Weakness," *Chicago Examiner*, November 9, 1903.

36. "Penalty Costs Chicago Game," *Chicago Tribune*, November 15, 1903.

37. "Game as Viewed by Experts," *Chicago Tribune*, November 15, 1903.

38. Ibid.

39. "Sad News for Rival Elevens," *Chicago Tribune*, November 19, 1903.

40. Camp to Stagg, 20 November 1903, Folder 28, Box 41, AAS, SCRC-UCL.

41. Hale to Stagg, 12 and 23 November 1903, Folder 6, Box 46, AAS, SCRC-UCL.

42. "Alumni Coaches Help Chicagos," *Chicago Tribune*, November 24, 1903.

43. "Players Now Buck Padding," *Detroit Free Press*, October 23, 1903.

44. Stagg and Stout, *Touchdown!*, 214.

45. "Students Bitter in Defeat," *Chicago Record-Herald*, November 27, 1903.

46. "Comparison of the Players," *Chicago Tribune*, November 26, 1903.

47. "Michigan Victor in Final Contest," *Chicago Tribune*, November 27, 1903.

48. "Experts' Views of the Game," *Chicago Tribune*, November 27, 1903.

49. "Expert Opinion of Last Game," *Chicago Tribune*, November 27, 1903.

50. "Walter Camp on Western Football," *Michigan Alumnus,* January 1904, 186.

51. *Michigan Daily*, October 22, 1903.

52. Telegram, J. F. Seymour of Cal-Berkeley to Baird, 15 October 1903, "Papers 1903, October (1)" folder, Box 1, BICIA, BHL-UM; Joseph F. Seymour of Southern Cal, 9 November 1903, "Papers 1903, November (1)" folder, Box 1, BICIA, BHL-UM; Baird to Ezra W. Decoto, 20 November 1903, "Papers 1903, November (2)" folder, BICIA, BHL-UM; Decoto to Baird, 28 November 1903, "Papers 1903, November (2)" folder, BICIA, BHL-UM; Baird to Decoto, 4 December 1903, "Papers 1903, December" folder, Box 1, BICIA, BHL-UM.

53. "Michigan Victor in Final Contest," *Chicago Tribune*, November 27, 1903.

54. Fred Lowenthal, "Maroons, Man for Man, Better Than Wolverines," *Chicago American*, November 25, 1903.

55. Stagg and Stout, *Touchdown!*, 215.

56. "Coach Stagg in Danger," *Chicago Tribune*, December 4, 1903.

57. Ibid.; "Stagg Is Able to Be About," *Chicago Tribune*, December 14, 1903.

58. Stagg and Stout, *Touchdown!*, 214.

12. 1904 OFF THE FIELD

1. Stagg to H. P. Chandler, 7 January 1904, Folder 8, Box 9, AAS, SCRC-UCL.

2. Stagg and Stout, *Touchdown!*, 241.

3. "Chicago Player to Enter Yale," *Chicago Tribune*, January 10, 1903.

4. "Maxwell Plays with Swarthmore," *Chicago Tribune*, and "Robt. Maxwell Leaves Stagg to Join Swarthmore Team," *Chicago Examiner*, September 29, 1904.

5. "One More for Stagg," *Chicago Daily News*, August 16, 1904; "Another Recruit for Stagg," *Chicago Record-Herald*, August 17, 1904; "Scherer Will Go to Chicago," unidentified clipping from a Seattle-area newspaper, circa mid-September 1904, Athletic Scrapbook No. 36, Box 145, AAS, SCRC-UCL. Alfred Strauss was the other Washington Huskies player to transfer to UC.

6. Myriad newspaper reports circa September 1904 list backgrounds of Stagg's many new recruits, Athletic Scrapbook No. 36, Box 145, AAS, SCRC-UCL. Names of the other transfers are J. Fuller of Grinell, William Hewitt of Armour Institute, former Drake and Arkansas player Clyde H. Legate, and a man surnamed Turner from Bethany College.

7. "Stagg Gets New Center," *Chicago Tribune*, September 11, 1904; "Predicts Good Team," *Chicago Record-Herald*, September 12, 1904.

8. "Big Center Goes to Nebraska," *Chicago Chronicle*, September 16, 1904; "Borg Yields to Booth; Quits Maroon Camp," *Chicago Record-Herald*, September 16, 1904.

9. "Football," *Chicago Post*, September 16, 1904.

10. "Maroons May Get Star Center Rush of Coast," *Chicago American*, September 16, 1904; "Scherer Will Go to Chicago," unidentified clipping from a Seattle-area newspaper, circa mid-September 1904, Athletic Scrapbook No. 36, Box 145, AAS, SCRC-UCL.

11. Stagg to Lightbody, 28 July 1903, Folder 5, Box 13, AAS, SCRC-UCL.

12. All of the following Baird–Lightbody and Baird–Dvorak letters are in "Papers 1904, Sept–Oct" folder, Box 2, BICIA, BHL-UM: Baird to Lightbody, 6 August and 6 October 1904; Lightbody to Baird, 26 September 1904; Baird to Dvorak, 7, 14, 16, 23, and 26 September and 6 October 1904; and Dvorak to Baird, 15, 16, and 25 September and 4 and 25 October 1904. See also "Accused Coach Yost of Bribery," *Chicago American*, September 16, 1904; "Comstock Goes to Princeton," *Chicago Tribune*, September 11, 1904; and "Lightbody to Stay by Stagg," *Chicago Tribune*, September 18, 1904.

13. Stagg to Carl M. Bair, 16 August 1905, Folder 5, Box 13, AAS, SCRC-UCL.

14. Sources for ballparking the number and names of new players Stagg added in September 1904: alphabetical list of UC winners of major letters in athletics from 1892 to 1936, Folder 9, Box 16, AAS, SCRC-UCL; identifications underneath 1904 and 1905 team photographs, Photo Album No. 6, Box 310, AAS, SCRC-UCL; Stagg's chart and action plan for seventeen enrolled football players in summer 1905 with academic conditions, Folder 9, Box 30, AAS, SCRC-UCL; J. S. Patterson, "Stagg Secures Good Guard in Badenoch of Englewood," *Chicago Journal*, July 13, 1904; "Stagg Gains Another Star Prep Athlete," *Chicago Inter Ocean*, July 13, 1904; "Recruits for U. of C. Athletic Teams," *Chicago Tribune*, July 17, 1904; "Two More for Stagg's Squad," *Chicago Record-Herald*, August 12, 1904; "Loses 'Big' Maxwell," *Chicago Record-Herald*, September 2, 1904; "Call for Local Elevens," *Chicago Tribune*, September 4, 1904; "Western Elevens to Start Season," *Chicago Record-Herald*, September 4, 1904; "Stagg Gets New Center," *Chicago Tribune*, September 11, 1904; "Stagg Talks of Outlook," *Chicago Tribune*, September 12, 1904; "Score Eighteen on Schoolboys," "Tactics Weary Stagg," *Chicago Post*, September 27, 1904; *Chicago Tribune*, September 29, 1904.

15. Harper to Stagg, 9 February 1897, Folder 2, Box 9, AAS, SCRC-UCL.

16. Harper to Stagg, 1 February 1899, Folder 3, Box 9, AAS, SCRC-UCL.

17. Lists of UC athletes who were ineligible for university teams on account of scholarship, 1896-1901, Folder 3, Box 77, AAS, SCRC-UCL.

18. Lester, *Stagg's University*, 57–62.

19. For the original conference rules, see Wilson and Brondfield, *Big Ten*, 52.

20. "Why Do Not the Maroon Athletes Take Degrees?," *Chicago Chronicle*, September 27, 1904.

21. Lester, *Stagg's University*, 57.

22. Dvorak to Baird, 12 July 1904, and Baird to Dvorak, 13 July 1904, "Papers 1904, Sept-Oct" folder, Box 2, BICIA, BHL-UM.

23. Baird to Fitzpatrick, 18 July 1904, "Papers 1904, July–Aug" folder, Box 2, BICIA, BHL-UM.

24. "Cecil Gooding," *Michigan Alumnus*, February 1904, 234.

25. "Yost Has Six Veterans," *Chicago Tribune*, September 4, 1904; "First Line-up of Yost's Boys," *Detroit Free Press*, September 14, 1904; "Prospects in Football," *Michigan Alumnus*, October 1904, 30–31.

26. Baird to Fitzpatrick, 18 July 1904, "Papers 1904, July-Aug" folder, Box 2, BICIA, BHL-UM.

27. Baird to Evans Holbrook, 4 June 1904, "Papers 1904, June" folder, Box 2, BICIA, BHL-UM; Edward S. Jordan, "Buying Football Victories," *Collier's Weekly*, November 11, 1905.

28. "Michigan Loses Star 'Prep,'" *Chicago Record-Herald*, September 11, 1904.

29. G. Waddell, "Famous Has-Beens No. 10," *Los Angeles Times*, June 1, 1913; "Sporting," *Racine Daily Journal*, September 1, 1904, per http://en.wikipedia.org/wiki/Walter_Rheinschild#cite_ref-6.

30. Rose to Curtis Redden, 10 December 1903, Baird to Rose, 28 December 1903, "Correspondence 1903, Sept-Dec" folder, Box 1, CB, BHL-UM. Rose to Baird, 8 and 31 January 1904, Baird to Rose, 14 January 1904, "Correspondence 1904" folder, Box 1, CB, BHL-UM.

31. "Is Enticed by Michigan," *Urbana Daily Courier*, February 17, 1904; R.W. Wooley, editor, *Illustrated Sporting News*, to President, University of Michigan, 20 February 1904, "Papers 1904, February" folder, Box 2, BICIA, BHL-UM; Baird to Wooley, 23 February 1904, "Papers 1904, February" folder, Box 2, BICIA, BHL-UM.

32. Caspar Whitney, "Over-doses of Athletic Notoriety," *Outing*, November 1904, 239.

33. Hugh White to Baird, 17 September 1904, "Correspondence, 1904" folder, Box 1, CB, BHL-UM.

34. Baird to Henry J. Killilea, 30 March 1904, "Papers 1904, March (1)" folder, Box 2, BICIA, BHL-UM; Baird to Pattengill, 24 August 1904, "Papers 1904, July-Aug" folder, Box 2, BICIA, BHL-UM; H. W. Ford, "Coach Yost Hands a Few to Alonzo Stagg and Others," *Chicago Inter Ocean*, October 28, 1904; "The Suspension of Rose," *Michigan Alumnus*, February 1905, 228–29; Baird to Evans Holbrook, 13 March 1905, misfiled in "Papers 1905 May" folder, Box 2, BICIA, BHL-UM.

35. Unidentified clipping, circa early September 1904, Athletic Scrapbook No. 36, Box 145, AAS, SCRC-UCL.

36. The comprehensive *UM Catalogue of Graduates, Non-Graduates, Officers, and Members of the Faculties: 1837–1921* lists graduates and nongraduates alike.

37. Regent Henry W. Carey to Baird, 21 September 1903, "Papers 1903, September" folder, Box 1, BICIA, BHL-UM.

38. Carter to Baird, 8 August and 2 September 1904, "Correspondence, 1904" folder, Box 1, CB, BHL-UM.

39. V. H. Lane, "How Can Proper Attention Be Given to Athletics and a Proper Standard of Scholarship Maintained?," *Michigan Alumnus*, February 1905, 223.

40. Yost to Baird, 31 July 1901, and Yost to Baird, 27 July 1901, "Correspondence, 1901" folder, Box 1, CB, BHL-UM.

41. H. W. Ford, "Coach Yost Hands a Few to Alonzo Stagg and Others," *Chicago Inter Ocean*, October 28, 1904.

42. Baird to Dvorak, 13 July 1904, "Papers 1904, Sept–Oct" folder, Box 2, BICIA, BHL-UM.

43. Editorial, *Michigan Daily*, January 9, 1906.

44. Grid Iron, "Tactics Weary Stagg," *Chicago Evening Post*, September 27, 1904.

45. "Maxwell Not Treated Well by Stagg, Says His Mother," *Chicago Journal*, September 27, 1904.

13. 1904 ON THE FIELD

1. "'Big Nine' Rule Delays Yost," *Chicago Record-Herald*, September 4, 1904.

2. Ibid.

3. "Expect Swarm of Golphers," *Chicago Record-Herald*, September 4, 1904.

4. "Western Elevens to Start Seasons," *Chicago Record-Herald*, September 4, 1904.

5. "Many Vacancies at Madison," *Chicago Record-Herald*, September 4, 1904.

6. Baird to Pattengill, 3 September 1904, "Papers 1904, Sept–Oct" folder, Box 2, BICIA, BHL-UM.

7. "Predicts Good Team," *Chicago Record-Herald*, September 12, 1904.

8. "Michigan to Play Here," *New York Times*, December 18, 1903.

9. "Princeton against Michigan," *New York Times*, December 7, 1903.

10. "Princeton Not to Play Penn," *New York Times*, December 9, 1903.

11. Charles Baird, "Why It Is Difficult to Secure an Eastern Game," *The Inlander*, November 1904, 84.

12. C. G. Abbott to Baird, 29 November 1902, "Papers 1903 November (1)" folder, Box 1, BICIA, BHL-UM. This letter is misfiled by exactly a year.

13. Several letters from the attempts to schedule this game were excerpted in "The Columbia Game," *Michigan Alumnus*, November 1904, 84.

14. "Michigan Wants a Game," *New York Times*, May 18, 1904.

15. "Morley Says Game Is Sure," *Detroit Free Press*, September 11, 1904.

16. Baird to Mr. Marshall H. Uhl, 6 August 1904, "Papers 1904, July–Aug" folder, Box 2, BICIA, BHL-UM.

17. "Michigan–Columbia Game Assured," *New York Times*, August 27, 1904.

18. Baird to Carter, 2 September 1904, "Correspondence, 1904" folder, Box 1, CB, BHL-UM.

19. "Morley Says Game Is Sure," *Detroit Free Press*, September 11, 1904.

20. Baird to Carter, 2 September 1904, "Correspondence, 1904" folder, Box 1, CB, BHL-UM.

21. "Football Season Opens on Saturday," *New York Times*, September 12, 1904.

22. Baird to Hugh L. White, 19 September 1904, "Correspondence, 1904" folder, Box 1, CB, BHL-UM.

23. "The Columbia Game," *Michigan Alumnus*, November 1904, 84.

24. Morley to Baird, 7 October 1904, reprinted in "The Columbia Game," *Michigan Alumnus*, November 1904, 84.

25. Ibid.

26. "Columbia–Michigan Game Still Pending.," *New York Times*, October 13, 1904.

27. "Columbia Formally Calls Game Off," *Michigan Daily*, October 20, 1904.

28. "Football Season Opens on Saturday," *New York Times*, September 12, 1904.

29. Robert W. Maxwell, "Columbia Would Be Easy," *Chicago Record-Herald*, October 15, 1904.

30. "First of Season's Football Surprises," *New York Times*, October 16, 1904.

31. "Columbia Formally Calls Game Off," *Michigan Daily*, October 20, 1904.

32. *Michigan Daily*, October 23, 1904.

33. *UM Catalogue of Graduates, Non-Graduates, Officers, and Members of the Faculties: 1837–1921*, 569.

34. Grid Iron, "Tactics Weary Stagg," *Chicago Evening Post*, September 27, 1904.

35. Kryk, *Natural Enemies*, 68.

36. *Michigan Daily*, October 9, 1904.

37. USA Track & Field website, Archie Hahn historical profile, http://www.usatf.org/halloffame/tf/showBio.asp?HOFIDs=64.

38. "Michigan Grid Immortal Recalls Wolverines Rise to Prominence," *St. Petersburg Times*, April 12, 1957.

39. Etter, "Mighty Willie Heston."

40. Arch Ward, "Remember Him?," *Chicago Tribune*, December 28, 1936.

41. "Yost and Stagg Talk of Game," *Chicago Tribune*, November 1, 1904.

42. Account excerpted in "As Others See Us," *Michigan Alumnus*, December 1904, 134–35.

43. "Cogs in Yost's Great 'Machine' at University of Michigan," *Chicago Tribune*, October 30, 1904.

44. H. W. Ford, "Coach Yost Hands a Few to Alonzo Stagg and Others," *Chicago Inter Ocean*, October 28, 1904.

45. "Maroon Students Have Fun with Yost and Heston—Coach Sizes Up Chicago," unidentified clipping, November 6, 1904, Athletic Scrapbook No. 39, Box 146, AAS, SCRB-UCL.

46. "Chaff for Yost and Heston," *Chicago Tribune*, November 6, 1904.

47. The Bentley Historical Library website, "The Michigan Stadium Story; First U-M Football Film, Michigan vs. Chicago, 1904," http://bentley.umich.edu/athdept/stadium/stadtext/fbchi04.htm. The film has been digitized and posted at YouTube.com numerous times, although some are misidentified as the 1903 Michigan–Chicago game.

48. Thomas T. Hoyne, "Coach Yost Springs New and Effective Play on Badgers," *Chicago Journal*, October 31, 1904.

49. Second of two "Defense for Michigan plays—1904" cards, specifically the one with the diagrammed item that begins, "If the Michigan back field points at an angle . . . ," Folder 8, Box 30, AAS, SCRC-UCL.

50. Joe S. Jackson, "Michigan Line Twice Crossed," *Detroit Free Press*, November 13, 1904.

51. Harper to R. M. Strong, Hutchinson Commons, University of Chicago, 15 November 1904, Folder 9, Box 9, AAS, SCRC-UCL.

52. "Opinions on the Game," *Chicago Tribune*, November 13, 1904.

53. Ibid.

54. *Michigan Daily*, November 16, 1904.

55. *Michigan Daily*, November 18, 1904.

56. Kryk, *Natural Enemies*, 40.

57. Boda to Les Etter, 18 May 1963, "Heston, William" folder, Box 59, UMAD-IF, BHL-UM.

58. The author's annual touchdown totals for Heston: twenty in 1901, fifteen or sixteen in 1902, fourteen in 1903, twenty or twenty-one in 1904. Boda credited Heston for Michigan's touchdown in the 6–6 tie at Minnesota in 1903, but Yost is quoted in the November 3, 1903, edition of the *Minneapolis Journal*

correcting those reports (which Boda obviously had used) that credited Heston with Joe Maddock's score.

59. Scott E. Deitch, ed., *NCAA Football's Finest* (Indianapolis: NCAA, 2002), 40.

60. Deitch, *NCAA Football's Finest*, 72.

61. "Yost Criticises Yale Game," *Chicago Tribune*, November 20, 1904; "Michigan Could Beat Yale," *Chicago Tribune*, November 23, 1904; "Yost's Letter," *Michigan Daily*, November 29, 1904; F. H. Yost, "On the College Gridiron," *Chicago Tribune*, January 1, 1905.

62. Caspar Whitney, "1904 Ranking Football Teams," *Outing*, January 1905, 497.

63. Caspar Whitney, "How the Professional Coach Makes a Winning Team," *Outing*, September 1903, 747.

64. "Divided on One-Year Rule," *Detroit Free Press*, December 4, 1904.

65. "Hats Were off to Coach Yost," *Detroit Tribune*, December 16, 1904.

66. Stagg and Stout, *Touchdown!*, 241; "Stagg Yields to Doctor's Orders," *Chicago Tribune*, November 23, 1904.

67. "Coach Stagg's Unusual Burdens," *Chicago Tribune*, November 13, 1904.

68. "Hats Were off to Coach Yost," *Detroit Tribune*, December 16, 1904.

69. Yost to Stagg, 26 January 1904, Folder 28, Box 41, AAS, SCRC-UCL.

70. "Stagg's Health Causes a Slump," *Chicago Tribune*, November 11, 1904; unidentified newspaper clipping containing Harper statement of November 19, 1904, in Athletic Scrapbook No. 38 (October–November, 1904), Box 146, AAS, SCRC-UCL.

71. "University of Chicago's Great Athletic Instructor: A. Alonzo Stagg, Who Stands for Honesty, and Fairness in College Athletics," *Chicago Tribune*, November 20, 1904.

72. "Coach Stagg's Unusual Burdens," *Chicago Tribune*, November 13, 1904.

14. 1905 OFF THE FIELD

1. "Michigan Loses Star 'Prep,'" *Chicago Record-Herald*, September 11, 1904.

2. "Chance for Beneficial Alumni Influence," *Chicago Tribune*, September 25, 1904.

3. "Stagg Opposes Plan," *Chicago Chronicle*, November 22, 1904.

4. "Schoolboys Lining Up," *Chicago Tribune*, September 4, 1904.

5. Dr. William H. P. Faunce, "College Athletics and College Morals," *World To-Day*, October 1904, excerpted in "Condemns Athletic Evils," *Chicago Daily News*, September 22, 1904. See also "Head of Brown University Says College Athletics Breed Felons," *Chicago Record-Herald*, July 2, 1904.

6. William R. Harper, "Shall College Athletics Be Endowed?," *Harpers Weekly*, circa September 1904, excerpted in "Endowment of College Athletics, *Chicago Inter Ocean*, September 6, 1904, and entire clipping appears in Athletic Scrapbook No. 37, Box 145, AAS, SCRC-UCL.

7. "Plan New Rules for the Conference Athletes," *Chicago Journal*, November 21, 1904.

8. "Football Is Not for Freshmen," *Minneapolis Journal*, November 26, 1904; "Freshmen Barred from Athletics for a Semester," *Chicago Inter Ocean*, November 26, 1904; "Conference Puts Ban on Freshmen Football Players," *Chicago Examiner*, November 26, 1904.

9. "New Rules for College Sport," *Chicago Tribune*, November 26, 1904.

10. "Stagg Would Change Rule," *Chicago Record-Herald*, undated clipping but likely November 21–25, 1904, in Athletic Scrapbook No. 39, Box 146, AAS, SCRC-UCL.

11. "Freshmen Barred from Athletics for a Semester," *Chicago Inter Ocean*, November 26, 1904.

12. "The 'Freshman' Rule Again," *Michigan Alumnus*, February 1905, 280; "Transfer Power to Rule," *Chicago Tribune*, June 3, 1905; O'Loughlin, "College Amateur Standing Raised," *Minneapolis Journal*, June 3, 1905.

13. "Conference Rules Condemned," *Chicago Journal*, November 26, 1904.

14. "Promising End Joins Maroons," *Chicago Tribune*, September 26, 1905.

15. Alphabetical list of UC winners of major letters in athletics from 1892 to 1936, Folder 9, Box 16, AAS, SCRC-UCL; myriad Chicago newspaper reports circa 1904–1905 listing names and placement of Stagg's players.

16. Van Hise to Harper, 27 September 1904, Folder 9, Box 20, PHJB, SCRC-UCL; "Stagg Opposes Plan," *Chicago Chronicle*, November 22, 1904.

17. "Big Nine Makes Rules for 1905," *Minneapolis Journal*, November 25, 1904.

18. "Colleges in Tangle," *Chicago Record-Herald*, November 1, 1904; James E. Raycroft to Stagg, 12 January 1905, Baird to Raycroft, 14 January 1905, and Raycroft to Baird, 17 January 1905, Folder 3, Box 88, AAS, SCRC-UCL.

19. Correspondence concerning the one seriously injured spectator, circa 1903 and 1904: Stagg to Raycroft, 13 December 1904; Raycroft to Stagg, 28 January 1905; Raycroft to Judge Victor Lane of Michigan, 2 February 1905; UM Board in Control of Athletics to Edward F. Capps and Raycroft, 9 Febru-

ary 1905; and Raycroft to UM Board in Control, 18 February 1905, Folder 3, Box 88, AAS, SCRC-UCL.

20. UM Board in Control to Raycroft, 21 February 1905, Charles Van Hise of Wisconsin to Capps and Raycroft, 22 February 1905, Folder 3, Box 88, AAS, SCRC-UCL.

21. Contract, Yost with UM to coach football 1905–1909, 15 December 1904, "Papers 1904, November & December" folder, Box 2, BICIA, BHL-UM; "Yost for Next Five Years!," *Michigan Daily*, December 17, 1904.

22. "Football Coaching Costs Fortunes to American Colleges," *Chicago Record-Herald*, December 25, 1904.

23. Stagg and Stout, *Touchdown!*, 299.

24. Stagg to Harper, 6 July 1905, Folder 10, Box 9, AAS, SCRC-UCL.

25. Harper to Stagg, 19 July 1905, Folder 10, Box 9, AAS, SCRC-UCL.

26. Henry Beach Needham, "The College Athlete: How Commercialism Is Making Him a Professional," part 1, *McClure's*, June 1905; "The College Athlete: His Amateur Code, Its Evasion and Administration," part 2, *McClure's*, July 1905.

27. Bernstein, *Football*, 79.

28. Stagg's chart and action plan for seventeen enrolled football players in summer 1905 with academic conditions, Folder 9, Box 30, AAS, SCRC-UCL.

29. Lester, *Stagg's University*, 53.

30. Stagg to Harper, 11 September 1905, Folder 11, Box 9, AAS, SCRC-UCL.

31. Edward S. Jordan, "Buying Football Victories," *Collier's Weekly*, November 11, 18, and 25 and December 2, 1905.

32. Carl Bernstein and Bob Woodward, *All the President's Men* (New York: Simon & Schuster Paperbacks, 1974), 196.

33. Pattengill to Bates, 11 November 1902, "Correspondence, 1900–1902" folder, Box 1, HMB, BHL-UM.

34. "Coach Stagg Defends University of Chicago Athletics," *Chicago Record-Herald*, November 8, 1905.

35. Carl Bernstein and Bob Woodward, *All the President's Men*, 144.

36. "All Star Football Eleven of Chicago High Schools," *Chicago Tribune*, November 30, 1902.

37. Baird to Dvorak, 18 July 1904, "Papers 1904, September–October" folder, Box 2, BICIA, BHL-UM.

38. Steffen to Baird, 21 July 1904, "Correspondences, 1904" folder, Box 1, CB, BHL-UM.

39. "Supt. Cooley's Claim Is Illustrated," *Chicago Tribune*, September 18, 1904.

40. Jordan, "Buying Football Victories," *Collier's Weekly*, November 11, 1905.

41. "Coach Stagg Goes East," *Chicago Tribune*, June 12, 1905.

42. "Steffen Stars at the Midway," *Chicago Tribune*, October 6, 1905.

43. "Wisconsin Gets Walter Steffen," *Chicago Tribune*, October 9, 1905; "Expect Steffen to Return Today," *Chicago Tribune*, October 10, 1905; "Steffen Is Back in Midway Fold," *Chicago Tribune*, October 11, 1905.

44. Jordan, "Buying Football Victories," *Collier's Weekly*, November 11, 1905.

15. 1905 ON THE FIELD

1. Stagg and Stout, *Touchdown!*, 241–22; Henry C. Chandler to Stagg (in Mt. Clemens), 15 December 1904, Folder 9, Box 9, AAS, SCRC-UCL; "Stagg Back in Chicago," *Chicago Tribune*, February 9, 1905; "Stagg Puts Off Return," *Chicago Tribune*, March 31, 1905; Stagg (in Hot Springs) to Harper, 18 April 1905, Folder 10, Box 9, AAS, SCRC-UCL; "Coach Stagg Is Home from South," *Chicago Tribune*, April 22, 1905; "Greatest Conference Meet," *Chicago Tribune*, June 4, 1905.

2. "Stagg in Bad Shape: Is Threatened with the Loss of the Use of His Lower Limbs," *Minneapolis Journal*, April 6, 1905.

3. Jesse F. Matteson, "American Expert Says Wizard of Midway Has Proved His Superiority," *Chicago American*, December 3, 1905.

4. These notes are in Folder 9, Box 30, AAS, SCRC-UCL.

5. A small clippings scrapbook packed with nothing but rave reviews of Yost's 1905 book is in Box 45, BICIA, BHL-UM.

6. For example, "Nebraska Overwhelmed," *Michigan Daily*, October 22, 1905; "Substitutes Score Forty Points on Ohio State," *Michigan Daily*, November 12, 1905.

7. "Begin Work on Gridiron," *Chicago Tribune*, September 12, 1905.

8. "Michigan Talk Is Gloomy," *Chicago Tribune*, September 24, 1905.

9. Behee, *Fielding Yost's Legacy*, 27–33; Arthur Daley, "Sports of the Times: Unforgettable Dan McGugin," *New York Times*, May 8, 1956.

10. "One Maroon Place Open," *Chicago Tribune*, September 10, 1905.

11. "Stagg Closes the Gates," *Chicago Tribune*, September 14, 1905.

12. "Football Men at Work in Earnest," *Michigan Daily*, September 26, 1905; "Longman's Condition Is Serious," *Michigan Daily*, September 29, 1905; "Kalamazoo Eleven Fights Gamely, But Is Beaten 44–0," *Michigan Daily*, October 5, 1905; "Plucky Vanderbilt Holds Michigan to Eighteen Points,"

Michigan Daily, October 15, 1905; "Michigan Scores 70 Points on Albion," *Michigan Daily*, October 26, 1905.

13. "Michigan Wins, 33 to 0," *Chicago Tribune*, November 5, 1905.

14. Jesse F. Matteson, "Yost Must Lose One Game Is Opinion of Football Men; Perhaps Both," *Chicago American*, November 9, 1905.

15. Stagg to E. C. Patterson, 8 November 1905, Bolder 1, Box 17, AAS, SCRC-UCL.

16. "Badgers Score Great Victory over Gophers," *Chicago Inter Ocean*, November 5, 1905.

17. "Fear Wisconsin More Than Stagg," *Chicago Inter Ocean*, November 12, 1905.

18. "Meet on Even Terms," *Chicago Daily News*, November 14, 1905.

19. Matteson, "Yost Must Lose One Game Is Opinion of Football Men; Perhaps Both," *Chicago American*, November 9, 1905.

20. "Michigan, 12; Wisconsin, 0," *Michigan Daily*, November 19, 1905; "Michigan Beats Badgers, 12 to 0," *Chicago Tribune*, November 19, 1905; "Michigan 12; Wisconsin 0," *Michigan Alumnus*, December 1905, 130.

21. "College Football: Wisconsin Victory Celebration Turns Dangerous," *New York Times*, October 31, 1993.

22. "Opinions of Experts," *Chicago Tribune*, November 19, 1905.

23. "Michigan's Eleven the Greatest Ever," *Michigan Daily*, October 27, 1905.

24. "Michigan Outclasses Eastern Elevens," *Michigan Daily*, November 14, 1905.

25. "Stagg Loses Dan Boone," *Chicago Tribune*, November 12, 1905; "Stagg Is to Protest," *Chicago Daily News*, November 13, 1905.

26. "Boone Case Is Closed; No Protest on Dunlap," *Chicago Record-Herald*, November 15, 1905.

27. Bernstein, *Football*, 79–81.

28. "Union Football Player Dies after N.Y.U. Game," *New York Tribune*, November 26, 1905.

29. "Move to Oust Camp," *New York Tribune*, November 27, 1905; "Total Football Casualties of the Season Completed through Thanksgiving Day Games," *Chicago Tribune*, December 1, 1905 (which corrected its first, erroneous November 26 report).

30. Bernstein, *Football*, 81–82.

31. "Wheeler Attacks Camp," *New York Tribune*, November 26, 1905.

32. "Football Out at Columbia," *Chicago Tribune*, November 29, 1905; "Football Ousted by N.Y. University," *Chicago Tribune*, November 30, 1905.

33. "Halfback Hal Weeks Declared Ineligible," *Michigan Daily*, November 26, 1905; "Mass Meeting to Protest Rules," *Detroit Free Press*, January 23, 1906.

34. "Coach Stagg Loses Star," *Chicago Chronicle*, November 25, 1905.

35. "De Tray Is Declared Out of the Big Contest," *Chicago Examiner*, November 25, 1905.

36. "Say De Tray Will Play," unidentified clipping, November 30, 1905, Athletic Scrapbook No. 45, Box 149, AAS, SCRC-UCL.

37. "Opinions of the Game," *Chicago Tribune*, November 13, 1904.

38. "Stagg Has Hopes of Boone's Return," *Chicago Examiner*, November 27, 1905.

39. "Schulte Case Now," *Chicago Record-Herald*, November 28, 1905; "Claim Schulte Is Ineligible," *Chicago Tribune*, November 28, 1905.

40. "Illinois Is Against Boone," *Chicago Chronicle*, November 28, 1905; "Big Nine Vetoes Maroons' Appeal in Boone Case," *Chicago Inter Ocean*, November 29, 1905.

41. "Would Prefer Losing the Game to Winning with an Ineligible Player in the Lineup," *Chicago Journal*, November 29, 1905.

42. "Football Is Not for Freshmen," *Minneapolis Journal*, November 26, 1904.

43. "'Schulte Case' Now," *Chicago Record-Herald*, November 28, 1905.

44. G. W. Fuller to Baird, 31 August 1903, with enclosed Fuller to L. P. Hale, 28 August 1903, and Hale to Fuller, 31 August 1903, "Correspondence, 1903" folder, Box 1, CB, BHL-UM.

45. "Michigan Claims Player Has Proved Eligibility—Must Be Special Meeting, If He Is to Be Put under Ban," *Detroit Free Press*, November 28, 1905.

46. "Say Schulte Received Money," *Chicago Chronicle*, November 29, 1905.

47. Pattengill, "Professor Pattengill Gives Michigan's Side of the Schulte Case," *Chicago Record-Herald*, November 30, 1905.

48. Heckman to Harper, 23 November 1905, Folder 2, Box 10, PHJB, SCRC-UCL.

49. Newspapers and periodicals did not always agree on lengths of some games. The author has relied on consensus or, absent that, the *Michigan Alumnus*'s after-the-fact accounts in compiling these figures.

50. "Stagg Has Hopes of Boone's Return," *Chicago Examiner*, November 27, 1905.

51. "Football Climax Reached Today," *Chicago Tribune*, November 30, 1905.

52. Kryk, *Natural Enemies*, 81.

53. Bernstein, *Football*, 81.

54. Robert Leckie, *The Story of Football* (New York: Random House, 1974), 30.

55. In addition to the usual sources, and with exceptions noted, the author's account of this game relies particularly on the uncharacteristically detailed, exhaustive coverage provided on December 1, 1905, by the *Chicago Tribune* in these stories: "Chicago Is Victor; Leads the West," "Game of Defense; Equally Matched," "Maroons Wild with Joy," "All Join in a Celebration," "Umpire Talks of Curtis Case," "Michigan Men Go to Theater," "From Michigan, 'The Fallen,'" "Clark Heart Broken by Error," "Tag Ends of the Big Game," and a notebook of gossipy items without a headline, labelled in the Proquest searchable database of the *Tribune* as "Article 1—No Title."

56. "Score Shows Relative Merits," *Minneapolis Journal*, December 1, 1905.

57. Editorial, *Michigan Daily*, December 5, 1905.

58. Walter Camp, "The All-America Football Team," *Michigan Alumnus*, January 1905, 181–82; although not specifically bylined this year, the team captain in this era always wrote the football season summary for the Michigan student yearbook: "Football: The Season," *Michiganensian*, 1906, 168.

59. Lester, *Stagg's University*, 70.

60. Garrels's Olympic record can be found at Sports-Reference.com, http://www.sports-reference.com/olympics/athletes/ga/johnny-garrels-1.html; "Garrels in Hard Luck: Once Again Detroit Boy Knocked Out of a Record," *Detroit Free Press*, October 25, 1907; "Four Greatest American Athletes," *Boston Globe*, February 26, 1911.

61. "Say De Tray Will Play," unidentified clipping, November 30, 1905, Athletic Scrapbook No. 45, Box 149, AAS, SCRC-UCL.

62. Danzig, *Oh, How They Played the Game*, 142.

63. "Clark Is Heartbroken," *Detroit Free Press*, December 1, 1905.

64. *UM Catalogue of Graduates, Non-Graduates, Officers, and Members of the Faculties: 1837–1921*, 954; Wilson and Brondfield, *Big Ten*, 62.

65. "Suicide Story an Absurdity, Clark Says," *Minneapolis Journal*, December 1, 1905.

66. "Clark Much Alive," *Detroit Free Press*, December 2, 1905.

67. "'Rank Blunder' Lost Game, Declares Camp," *Minneapolis Journal*, December 1, 1905.

68. "Football: The Season," *Michiganensian*, 1906, 170.

69. Unidentified partial clipping, subheaded "Slips Quietly Away," "Clark, William Dennison" folder, Box 120, UMARNF, BHL-UM.

70. "Coach Stagg Is Ill in Chicago Hospital," *Chicago Examiner*, January 12, 1906.

71. "Yost's Reign of Terror Is Over and Stagg Is King Again," *Chicago Journal*, December 1, 1905.

16. FULLY DISMANTLED

1. Bernstein, *Football*, 81–83; Nelson, *Anatomy of a Game*, 96–108.

2. "Football Hit Hard by Western Colleges," *New York Times*, January 21, 1906; "Deals Football Knockout Blow," *Chicago Tribune*, January 21, 1906; "Mass Meeting to Protest Rules," *Detroit Free Press*, January 23, 1906.

3. "Conference Resolutions Cause Great Indignation," *Michigan Daily*, January 23, 1906.

4. "Mass Meeting to Protest Rules," *Detroit Free Press*, January 23, 1906.

5. "Michigan Students to Support Yost," *Detroit Free Press*, January 22, 1906.

6. Prof. A. H. Pattengill, "Professor Pattengill Tells of Conference," *Michigan Daily*, January 23, 1906; Behee, *Fielding Yost's Legacy*, 66.

7. "Deals Football Knockout Blow," *Chicago Tribune*, January 21, 1906.

8. Pattengill, "Professor Pattengill Tells of Conference," *Michigan Daily*, January 23, 1906; "Editorial Remarks," *Michigan Alumnus*, May 1903, 369.

9. "Put Up to Chicago," *Detroit Free Press*, February 11, 1906.

10. "Football Coach Necessary Evil," *Chicago Tribune*, March 10, 1906.

11. Ibid.

12. Wilson and Brondfield, *Big Ten*, 68, 74.

13. Lester, *Stagg's University*, 81–87.

14. Stagg to Hudson, 27 March 1906, Folder 10, Box 20, PHJB, SCRC-UCL.

15. Nelson, *Anatomy of a Game*, 123–25.

16. Yost to Baird, 29 June and 5 July 1906, "Correspondence, 1906" folder, Box 1, CB, BHL-UM.

17. Baird to Yost, 2 July 1906, "Correspondence, 1906" folder, Box 1, CB, BHL-UM; "Football Task at Michigan Not an Easy One for Yost," *Chicago Tribune*, September 23, 1906.

18. "Pennsylvania, 17; Michigan, 0," *Michigan Daily*, November 17, 1906; *Michigan Daily*, November 11, 18, and 20, 1906.

19. Behee, *Fielding Yost's Legacy*, 69–72; "College Reforms to Be Continued," *Chicago Tribune*, December 2, 1906; "'Big Nine' Keeps Athletic Lid On," *Chicago Tribune*, January 13, 1907; Wilson and Brondfield, *Big Ten*, 446; "Michigan to Go It Alone," *New York Times*, January 14, 1908.

20. "Presents Case of Michigan," *Chicago Tribune*, April 16, 1911.

21. Perry, *Wolverines*, 77–91; Behee, *Fielding Yost's Legacy*, 77–84.

22. Wilson and Brondfield, *Big Ten*, 76, 86; Lester, *Stagg's University*, 117.

23. Wilson and Brondfield, *Big Ten*, 446.

24. Lester, *Stagg's University*, 133–40.

25. Murray Sperber, *Shake Down the Thunder: The Creation of Notre Dame Football* (New York: Henry Holt and Company, 1993), 249.

26. *Annual Report, Board in Control of Athletics, University of Michigan*, 1 September 1928 to 31 August 1929, "Annual Report 1925-26–1930/31" folder, Box 16, BICIA, BHL-UM.

27. *The Handbook of the Intercollegiate Conference of Faculty Representatives, Revised 1941*, "Intercollegiate Conference and National Collegiate Athletic Association published materials" folder, Box 51, BICIA, BHL-UM.

28. *2012–13 NCAA Division I Manual* (Indianapolis: NCAA, 2012).

29. "Editorial Remarks," *Michigan Alumnus*, May 1903, 368.

17. FATES

1. "Positions," a typewritten list of sports jobs Stagg's athletes and subordinates landed, presumably at his referral, Folder 1, Box 14, AAS, SCRC-UCL.

2. "Michigan Players as Coaches," *Michigan Alumnus*, October 1903, 29; "Michigan Players as Coaches," *Michigan Alumnus*, January 1905, 178; *Michigan Daily*, September 23, 1902; Kryk, *Natural Enemies*, 48–62; Wikipedia on December 3, 2014, listed sixty-seven men (most with their own individual pages and citations) who either played or coached under Yost at his various stops and who themselves became college or pro head coaches: http://en.wikipedia.org/wiki/Fielding_H._Yost#Coaching_tree. The above *Alumnus* and *Michigan Daily* reports list others. Combining these sources, the thirty-four point-a-minute-era players or assistant coaches are as follows. Assistant coaches: Bennie Owen (Washburn College and Bethany College in Kansas, Oklahoma) and Leigh C. Turner (Purdue). Players: Neil Snow (University of Nashville), Tug Wilson (Wabash, Alma), Boss Weeks (Kansas), Al Herrnstein (Haskell, Purdue, Ohio State), Ev Sweeley (Morningside Academy in Iowa, Oregon Agricultural), W. C. "King" Cole (Marietta, Virginia, Nebraska), James Forrest (Ypsilanti Normal in Michigan), Paul Jones (Western Reserve in Ohio), James Maddock (Utah, Oregon), Dan McGugin (Vanderbilt), Bruce Shorts (Nevada, Oregon), Herb Graver (Marietta), Curtis Redden (Indiana Medics), Andrew Reid (Simpson College in Iowa, Monmouth College in Illinois), Willie Heston (Drake, North Carolina A&M), Roy Beechler (Mount Union in Ohio), John "Joe" Curtis (Tulane, Colorado School of Mines), James DePree (Tennessee), David Dunlap (Kenyon College in Ohio, North Dakota, Allegheny College of Pennsylvania), George "Dad" Gregory (Kenyon College in Ohio), Tom

Hammond (Ole Miss), Emory J. Hyde (Texas Christian), James Knight (Washington), Jesse R. Langley (Texas Christian), Frank "Shorty" Longman (Arkansas, Wooster in Ohio, Notre Dame), Jay Mack Love (Southwestern College in Kansas), Paul Magoffin (North Dakota Agricultural, George Washington University in Washington, DC), Walter Rheinschild (Washington State and three California colleges), Frederick Schule (Montana), Henry Schulte (Eastern Michigan, Missouri, Nebraska), Adolph "Germany" Schulz (Detroit), and Ted Stuart (Colorado School of Mines).

3. Gary King, "Bennie Owen: OU's Man for All Seasons," *Distinctly Oklahoma Magazine*, October 1, 2009, http://distinctlyoklahoma.com/sports/bennie-owen/; the National Football Foundation's online biography of Owen, http://www.footballfoundation.org/Programs/CollegeFootballHallofFame/SearchDetail.aspx?id=10070.

4. Vanderbilt University Athletics website, Hall of Fame biography of McGugin: http://www.vucommodores.com/ot/2008-hof-mcgugin.html; the National Football Foundation's online biography of McGugin, http://www.footballfoundation.org/Programs/CollegeFootballHallofFame/SearchDetail.aspx?id=10068.

5. Yost to McGugin, 26 September 1925, and McGugin to Yost, 29 September 1925, "1925 September" folder, Box 7, BICIA, BHL-UM; "Punt, Pass & Pray," *Columbus Citizen*, undated clipping circa 1931, outsized Yost scrapbook 1924–1928, FHY, BHL-UM.

6. Various versions of this speech were reported over the years. One account (Leckie, *Story of Football*, 34) even said McGugin gave his famous speech before the 1910 Yale game, not the 1922 Michigan game. The quotation used in the text is a meld of the most cited line about the respective Civil War grandfathers (Vanderbilt University Athletics website, history corner, http://www.vucommodores.com/ot/history-corner-083006.html) with a quote that better provides a flavor of the drama, and which cites McGugin's adopted southern drawl (Arthur Daley, "Sports of the Times: Unforgettable Dan McGugin," *New York Times*, May 8, 1956).

7. Kryk, *Natural Enemies*, 48–55.

8. Ohio State football early history website, Herrnstein bio: http://www.smashthroughtovictory.com/2013/09/albert-ernest-al-herrnstein-1906-1909.html.

9. Wikipedia, "Fred Norcross," http://en.wikipedia.org/wiki/Fred_Norcross.

10. Bruce Madej with Rob Toonkel, Mike Pearson, and Greg Kinney, *Michigan: Champions of the West* (Champaign, IL: Sports Publishing, 1997), 17; "Schulte to Coach Nebraska Eleven," *New York Times*, August 26, 1919.

11. "Schulte out of Game; Eligible Last Season," *Chicago Record-Herald*, March 13, 1906; "Schulte Barred," *Michigan Alumnus*, April 1906, 322.

12. "Says Curtis Didn't Mean to Hurt Him," *Chicago Journal*, December 6, 1905.

13. Stagg to Curtis, 11 November 1906, and Curtis to Stagg, 16 December 1906, Folder 28, Box 41, AAS, SCRC-UCL.

14. "Dr. Jordan Picks a New Victim," *New York Times*, December 31, 1907; "Coach Yost in Strong Denial" and "Jordan Makes Reply," *Chicago Tribune*, January 3, 1908; "Strikes Back at Jordan," *Chicago Tribune*, January 4, 1908.

15. Robin Lester, "Michigan–Chicago 1905: The First Greatest Game of the Century," *Journal of Sport History* 18, no. 2 (Summer 1991): 272–73; obituary clippings in "Clark, William Dennison" folder, Box 120, UMARNF, BHL-UM.

16. Leckie, *Story of Football*, 40; "$100,000 Changes Hands on a Game," *Minneapolis Journal*, December 1, 1905; Stephen R. Fox, *Big Leagues: Professional Baseball, Football, and Basketball in National Memory* (New York: Morrow, 1994), 243; Bob Carroll, Michael Gershman, David Neft, and John Thorn, eds., *Total Football: The Official Encyclopedia of the National Football League* (New York: HarperCollins, 1997), 8–9.

17. Madej et al., *Michigan: Champions of the West*, 19.

18. Danzig, *Oh, How They Played the Game*, 187.

19. Lester, *Stagg's University*, 58–63.

20. Sperber, *Shake Down the Thunder*, 89–90; "Heart Attack Kills Walter Eckersall," *Urbana Daily Courier*, March 25, 1930.

21. One was Grantland Rice's All-America team for college football's first fifty years: Jack Newcombe, ed., *The Fireside Book of Football* (New York: Simon and Schuster, 1964), 253–55.

22. UM Law website, Bates profile: http://www.law.umich.edu/historyandtraditions/faculty/Faculty_Lists/Alpha_Faculty/Pages/HenryMBates.aspx.

23. Madej et al., *Michigan: Champions of the West*, 8; Perry, *Wolverines*, 40; U.S. Track and Field and Cross Country Coaches Association, Fitzpatrick Hall of Fame bio: http://www.ustfccca.org/ustfccca-hall-of-fame/ustfccca-hall-of-fame-class-of-2011/keene-fitzpatrick-ustfccca-class-of-2011.

24. "Baird to Quit Michigan University," *Salt Lake City Evening Telegraph*, December 18, 1908; "Charles Baird Passes Away," *Michigan Alumnus*, December 16, 1944, 173.

25. UM website, "The Baird Carillon," http://www.umich.edu/~aamuhist/spimente/tasp/carillon.htm.

26. Stagg and Stout, *Touchdown!*, 215.

27. "Albert Henderson Pattengill," *Michigan Alumnus*, April 1906, 308–11; Behee, *Fielding Yost's Legacy*, 67–68.

28. Behee, *Fielding Yost's Legacy*, 31–46.

29. *NCAA Football Records: Official 2003* (Indianapolis: NCAA, 2003), 75.

30. Kryk, *Natural Enemies*, 52, 293.

31. Behee, *Fielding Yost's Legacy*, 109–10.

32. Sperber, *Shake Down the Thunder*, 209–11, 243–46, 249–50, 309–10, 420. See also Behee, *Fielding Yost's Legacy*, 85–89, 107–111; Kryk, *Natural Enemies*, 98–99.

33. One example, Stewart Mandel, "Finding Bowden's, Paterno's Place among All-Time Coaching Legends," SI.com, July 8, 2009.

34. Joe Williams, "Fears for Nassau," *Pittsburgh Press*, March 12, 1938.

35. Kryk, *Natural Enemies*, 80–113.

36. "Jordan's Frenzied Athletics Received with Contempt," *Michigan Daily*, November 21, 1905.

37. Lester, *Stagg's University*, 125–86.

38. Wilson and Brondfield, *Big Ten*, 449.

39. Wilson and Brondfield, *Big Ten*, 71; University of Chicago Library, Special Collections Research Center, Finding Aids, Guide to the Amos Alonzo Stagg Papers 1866–1964, "Biographical Note," http://www.lib.uchicago.edu/e/scrc/findingaids/view.php?eadid=ICU.SPCL.STAGG#idp20396304.

40. Arthur Daley, "Sports of the Times: Grand Old Man," *New York Times*, August 15, 1952; Newcombe, *Fireside Book of Football*, 244–45; Danzig, *Oh, How They Played the Game*, 55–57; Lester, *Stagg's University*, 102–4.

41. "University of Chicago's Great Athletic Instructor: A. Alonzo Stagg, Who Stands for Honesty and Fairness in College Athletics," *Chicago Tribune*, November 20, 1904.

42. Quoted in Considine, *Unreconstructed Amateur*, 15–16.

43. Quoted in ibid., 160.

44. Joanna Davenport, "Mr. Integrity—Amos Alonzo Stagg," *North American Society for Sport History: Proceedings and Newsletter*, 1988, 51–52.

45. The author listened live to this radio broadcast and transcribed the quote.

46. Stagg and Stout, *Touchdown!*, 58.

47. Erick Smith, "Big Ten Removing Joe Paterno's Name from Championship Trophy," *USA Today*, November 14, 2011, http://content.usatoday.com/communities/campusrivalry/post/2011/11/big-ten-championship-trophy-remove-joe-paterno-stagg/1#.VHZuWIvF-So.

ACKNOWLEDGMENTS

It took four years in the early 1990s to research and write my first college football history book, *Natural Enemies: The Notre Dame-Michigan Football Feud*. After that, my plan was to recharge for a couple of years then tackle another book subject. But jolting life and career changes tucked those thoughts high on the shelf, eventually out of mind.

A phone call around 2008 blew off the dust. Greg Dooley, proprietor of a wonderful Michigan football history blog, MVictors.com, found me at home. The foremost expert on the Michigan–Minnesota rivalry, Greg was searching for more details about the first time the Wolverines and Gophers played for the Little Brown Jug in 1909. He knew from *Natural Enemies* that I was intimately familiar with that season, as two integral storylines in 1909 impacted the Michigan–Notre Dame rivalry. Greg and I hit it off straightaway. I hauled out my old *Natural Enemies* research files in banker boxes and found a few helpful clippings for Greg.

The dust has remained off. I owe it to Greg, these six years later, for reawakening my passion for college football history. Eventually, I decided to get cracking on book number two. I brainstormed project ideas in 2009 until deciding on Fielding H. Yost's point-a-minute teams of 1901–1905. The introduction of this book explains why it morphed into the book you hold in your hands. Greg and I are now good friends. He was the first to read the completed draft manuscript in July 2013.

Greg's enthusiasm for this project, as well as for UM football history in general, has been a constant inspiration.

My friend Murray Sperber, the preeminent college sports historian of our time, offered useful advice early on as to how I might shape the material I was uncovering. Murray critiqued an early draft chapter and, being a good Canadian, checked me hard into the boards upon discovering that my writing style, after twenty years at the *Sun*, had become more than a little too tabby for this kind of project. He was right.

Another best-selling author friend, John U. Bacon, read other sample chapters and generously offered his insights, praise, constructive criticisms, and publishing advice. Thanks, "Bacs."

John W. Wright, a brilliant, bighearted New Yorker whose agency represented *Natural Enemies*, for a year helped me to settle on a better, more clearly expressed focus for this book. Invaluable advice, John.

Besides Greg Dooley, others in the UM sports writing fraternity and blogosphere have solicited and supported my freelance work for several years now, which has afforded me a greater profile in that community. Thanks especially to Brian Cook, Seth Fisher, and John Borton.

Some Michigan fans who learned about this project a few years ago inspired me with regular encouragement. That helped to motivate me during tough times to keep pushing the project forward, to keep trying to get this book into print. Thanks, folks.

My best friend, Steve "Dr. Sap" Sapardanis, has since the early '80s on Borrelli Drive in Windsor, Ontario, been my pitch-perfect sounding board for any Michigan football story or project idea. Our mutual close friend, Jeff Teague, now does likewise for us both.

In 2012, after I'd spent more than a decade as an editor elsewhere in the *Sun* newsroom, I jumped back into sports journalism as our chain's national NFL columnist. To become the first Canada-based sports journalist writing year-round about American football was my outlandish career goal when I left Windsor at age twenty-one in 1986. Thank goodness the boss who gave me that awesome job, *Sun* sports editor Bill Pierce, is as patient a man as he is a well-read football expert. Bill's understanding as I scrambled to wrap up this project in autumn 2014 meant the world.

Thanks to my mother, Patricia Kryk, and to our dear family friend Ruthann Lumb for their online ancestry assistance in my quest to unearth new, useful information about the pasts of Yost and Amos Alonzo Stagg and their families.

My brother Jason Kryk expertly edited and prepared many of the archival photographs —especially newspaper cartoons and photos from yellowed clippings—that appear in this book. It was our father, Lewis Kryk, who inspired Jason to love and master the art of photography to the extent he has. It is not boasting when I say these family members are the most talented photographers I have known.

Thanks to the archivists and reference assistants in the Special Collections Research Center in the Regenstein Library at the University of Chicago, who aided me greatly prior to, during, and many times after my two agenda-packed research visits there in 2010 and 2011. A special shout-out to Maggie Grossman.

In researching two books and a couple of small writing projects, I figure I have spent three months of my life at the University of Michigan's Bentley Historical Library. Since my first visit there twenty-four years ago, the Bentley's archivists and reference staff have been as accommodating and helpful as any visiting researcher could hope to encounter. My thanks to Karen L. Jania, head of the Access and Reference Services division, and her kind staff.

Greg Kinney, athletics archivist at the Bentley, works with the UM athletic department to both preserve and facilitate access to the historical records of Wolverine athletics. Greg was immensely helpful to me, again, by suggesting photographs, by spotting mistakes of a factual and (praise him) even grammatical nature upon reading the manuscript, and in sharing his knowledge of the point-a-minute teams, Yost, his players, and that entire era of UM sports.

Brian Williams, UM Bicentennial archivist at the Bentley now and a longtime UM athletics archivist as well, helped me more than anybody. He at least twice spared me 550-mile round-trips from Toronto to Ann Arbor by volunteering to look up information in various collections for me, which surely took him many hours to do. Brian's unflagging generosity, friendship, deep knowledge of the subject matter, and keen interest in helping me locate and turn over as many of this story's stones as possible made this book so much better. It was Brian, for instance, who discovered the backstory to the Oberlin–Michigan feud, which opens the book.

Thanks to my acquisitions editor at Rowman & Littlefield, Christen Karniski, for her enthusiasm in and backing of this project, to production editor Andrew Yoder for his patience and accommodations, and to copyeditor Andrew White for saving my butt countless times.

Lastly, thanks to my wife, Melinda, my grown sons, Russell and Carson, and my girls, Abigail and Olivia, for their love, interest, support, sacrifices, and understanding as I devoted so much of my spare time in recent years to completing this book.

SELECTED BIBLIOGRAPHY

AMOS ALONZO STAGG AND UNIVERSITY OF CHICAGO FOOTBALL

Biographical and Geneological History of the City of Newark and Essex County, New Jersey: Illustrated. New York: Lewis, 1898.

Burns, Edward. "Eckersall . . . Football Immortal." *Chicago Tribune*, November 24, 1946.

Chicago Tribune, Chicago Record-Herald, Chicago Inter Ocean, Chicago Daily News, Chicago Journal, Chicago Chronicle, Chicago Evening Post, Chicago American, articles on Stagg and University of Chicago football, circa 1892–1906.

Considine, Bob. *The Unreconstructed Amateur: A Pictorial Biography of Amos Alonzo Stagg.* San Francisco: Amos Alonzo Stagg Foundation, 1962.

Eckersall, Walter. "My Twenty-Five Years in Football." *Liberty Magazine*, October 23, 1926.

Lester, Robin. *Stagg's University: The Rise, Decline, and Fall of Big-Time Football at Chicago.* Urbana: University of Illinois Press, 1995.

Meigs, Merrill C. "Babe." "The Greatest Football Player in the World: Walter Eckersall." *American Weekly*, October 26, 1947.

Stagg, Amos Alonzo (as told to Wesley Wynans Stout). *Touchdown!* New York: Longmans, Green and Co., 1972.

"University of Chicago's Great Athletic Instructor: A. Alonzo Stagg, Who Stands for Honesty and Fairness in College Athletics." *Chicago Tribune*, November 20, 1904.

Wilson, Kenneth (Tug), and Jerry Brondfield. *The Big Ten.* Englewood Cliffs, NJ: Prentice-Hall, 1967.

FIELDING H. YOST AND MICHIGAN FOOTBALL

Behee, John. *Fielding Yost's Legacy to the University of Michigan.* Ann Arbor, MI: Lithocrafters, 1971.

Cohen, Richard M., Jordan A. Deutsch, and David S. Neft. *The University of Michigan Football Scrapbook.* Indianapolis: Bobbs-Merrill, 1978.

Detroit Free Press, Detroit Journal, Detroit News, articles on Yost and University of Michigan football, circa 1901–1906.

Green, Jerry. *University of Michigan Football Vault: The History of the Wolverines*. Atlanta: Whitman, 2008.

Kryk, John. *Natural Enemies: Major College Football's Oldest, Fiercest Rivalry, Michigan vs. Notre Dame*. Updated edition. Lanham, MD: Taylor Trade, 2007.

Lawton. J. Fred. *"Hurry Up" Yost in Story and Song*. Draft manuscript, "Yost, Fielding H. (1)" folder, Box 2, JFL, BHL-UM.

Madej, Bruce, Rob Toonkel, Mike Pearson, and Greg Kinney. *Michigan: Champions of the West*. Champaign, IL: Sports Publishing, 1997.

Michigan Alumnus, articles on University of Michigan football, circa 1895–1906.

Michigaensian, articles on Yost and University of Michigan football, circa 1902–1906.

Michigan Daily, articles on University of Michigan football, circa 1894–1906.

Perry, Will. *The Wolverines: A Story of Michigan Football*. Huntsville, AL: Strode Publishers, 1974.

Sperber, Murray. *Shake Down the Thunder: The Creation of Notre Dame Football*. New York: Henry Holt and Company, 1993.

University of Michigan Catalogue of Graduates, Non-Graduates, Officers, and Members of the Faculties: 1837–1921. Ann Arbor: University of Michigan, 1923.

Wilson, Kenneth (Tug), and Jerry Brondfield. *The Big Ten*. Englewood Cliffs, NJ: Prentice-Hall, 1967.

Yost, Fielding H. *Football for Player and Spectator*. Reprint edition. Ann Arbor: Sarah Jennings Press, 1992. Original published Ann Arbor, MI: University Publishing Company, 1905.

EARLY COLLEGE FOOTBALL HISTORY, ON THE FIELD

Danzig, Allison. *Oh, How They Played the Game: The Early Days of Football and the Heroes Who Made It Great*. New York: Macmillan, 1971.

Kryk, John. *Natural Enemies: Major College Football's Oldest, Fiercest Rivalry, Michigan vs. Notre Dame*. Updated edition. Lanham, MD: Taylor Trade, 2007.

Leckie, Robert. *The Story of Football*. New York: Random House, 1974.

Nelson, David M. *Anatomy of a Game: Football, the Rules, and the Men Who Made the Game*. 2nd edition. Newark, DE: University of Delaware Press, 1994.

Newcombe, Jack, ed. *The Fireside Book of Football*. New York: Simon and Schuster, 1964.

Wilson, Kenneth (Tug), and Jerry Brondfield. *The Big Ten*. Englewood Cliffs, NJ: Prentice-Hall, 1967.

Yost, Fielding H. *Football for Player and Spectator*. Reprint edition. Ann Arbor: Sarah Jennings Press, 1992. Original published Ann Arbor, MI: University Publishing Company, 1905.

EARLY COLLEGE FOOTBALL HISTORY, OFF THE FIELD

Behee, John. *Fielding Yost's Legacy to the University of Michigan*. Ann Arbor, MI: Lithocrafters, 1971.

Bernstein, Mark F. *Football: The Ivy League Origins of an American Obsession*. Philadelphia: University of Pennsylvania Press, 2001.

Jordan, Edward S. "Buying Football Victories." *Collier's Weekly*, November 11, 18, 25, and December 2, 1905.

Kryk, John. *Natural Enemies: Major College Football's Oldest, Fiercest Rivalry, Michigan vs. Notre Dame*. Updated edition. Lanham, MD: Taylor Trade, 2007.

Lester, Robin. *Stagg's University: The Rise, Decline, and Fall of Big-Time Football at Chicago*. Urbana: University of Illinois Press, 1995.

Needham, Henry Beach. "The College Athlete: How Commercicalism Is Making Him a
    Professional." Part 1, *McClure's*, June 1905. "The College Athlete: His Amateur Code, Its
    Evasion and Administration." Part 2, *McClure's*, July 1905.
Smith, Ronald A. *Pay for Play: A History of Big-Time College Athletic Reform.* Urbana:
    University of Illinois Press, 2011.
Stagg, Amos Alonzo (as told to Wesley Wynans Stout). *Touchdown!* New York: Longmans,
    Green and Co., 1972.
Wilson, Kenneth (Tug), and Jerry Brondfield. *The Big Ten.* Englewood Cliffs, NJ: Prentice-
    Hall, 1967.

INDEX

ABOUT THE AUTHOR

John Kryk is the national NFL columnist for the *Toronto Sun* and Postmedia, Canada's largest newspaper chain. In his varied twenty-nine-year journalism career, Kryk has written or edited for almost every section of the newspaper. At the *Sun*, he rose to become associate sports editor, entertainment editor, and deputy managing editor, and at Sun Media, national entertainment editor.

Kryk has won awards for spot news reporting, sports photography, and section editing. He even helped to redesign the *Toronto Sun* in 2005. Kryk's postuniversity alma mater in his hometown of Windsor, Ontario—St. Clair College—honored him in 2010 with an Alumnus of Distinction award for his journalistic successes. The Province of Ontario followed that with a Premier's Award nomination in 2011.

This is Kryk's second book. His first was *Natural Enemies*, a history of the Notre Dame–Michigan football feud that has been published three times (1994, 2004, 2007). He has written numerous freelance news stories and historical features on college football in general, Michigan football, Notre Dame football, Nebraska football, the NFL, and the NHL—for magazines, websites, game programs, even page-a-day calendars.

Kryk lives in Newmarket, Ontario. He is married and is the proud father of two grown sons and two young daughters.